Praise for *Your Money or Your Life*

"This is a wonderful book. It really can change your life."
—Oprah Winfrey

"One of the ten best business books of the year . . . The seminal guide to the new morality of personal money management."
—*Los Angeles Times*

"Shows us an astonishingly simple method to measure our personal economic values. We learn that spending less doesn't have to be limiting, but can actually be liberating."
—Amy Dacyczyn, *The Tightwad Gazette*

"If you want to know how to make the maximum contribution you possibly can to the world—and to your own happiness—follow the steps in this book."
—Donella H. Meadows, author of *The Limits to Growth* and *Beyond the Limits,* adjunct professor of environmental studies, Dartmouth College

"A cornucopia of insight—financial, practical, emotional and spiritual—that is delivered with a generous measure of good humor. Energized with the personal stories of real people, their book brings alive an inspiring path for living with integrity and compassion."
—Duane Elgin, author of *Voluntary Simplicity* and *Awakening Earth*

"We live on such a beautiful planet, naturally rich in possibilities for enjoyment and love, that it is a shame so many people are wasting their lives and the life of the planet on consuming more than they need. Follow the steps in this book for your own sake and for the Earth."
—Robert Muller, chancellor, University for Peace, and retired assistant secretary-general of the United Nations

"An extraordinary antidote to the fog that permeates our society."
—Michael Toms, Co-founder and host, "New Dimensions" National Public Radio interview series

"Their program is practical and efficient—it has been tried and found successful by many people; and it is spiritual and ecological—it is grounded in ancient wisdom concerning the meaning of life, and is drawn by a vision of the future as a time of peace and true prosperity for humanity."

—Brian Swimme, author of *The Universe Is a Green Dragon*

"The investment of life energy (time) you make in reading this book will return to you a thousand-fold before you even hit the final page."

—Andy and Kate Lipkis, authors of *The Simple Act of Planting a Tree*

"This book, at once wise and practical, shines a light into the inner recesses of our discontent and points us step by step toward a more fulfilling and sustainable alternative."

—Paul L. Wachtel, author of *The Poverty of Affluence* and Distinguished Professor of Psychology at the City University of New York

"Dominguez and Robin's call . . . is more than hand wringing. They draw on their considerable experience to show us how we can step off the more-is-better treadmill."

—Lester Brown, Director of WorldWatch Institute

"Required reading for everyone seeking a new attitude toward money and its role in one's life. Full of uncommon good sense and warmth."

—Jacob Needleman, author of *Money and the Meaning of Life*

"This unique book will grow and grow on you. . . . Madison Avenue will not like what authors Dominguez and Robin show can be the road toward achieving the enjoyable freedoms of frugality."

—Ralph Nader

"This is one of those rare books that can *really* change your life! The authors live their own advice, and it works."

—Ernest Callenbach, author of *Ecotopia* and *Ecotopia Emerging*

PENGUIN BOOKS

YOUR MONEY OR YOUR LIFE

Joe Dominguez was a successful financial analyst on Wall Street before retiring at the age of thirty-one. He and Vicki Robin are founders of the New Road Map Foundation, an all-volunteer, nonprofit organization that promotes a humane, sustainable future for our world. They live in Seattle.

JOE DOMINGUEZ
AND VICKI ROBIN

YOUR MONEY OR YOUR LIFE

Transforming Your Relationship with Money and Achieving Financial Independence

PENGUIN BOOKS

PENGUIN BOOKS
Published by the Penguin Group
Penguin Books USA Inc., 375 Hudson Street,
New York, New York 10014, U.S.A.
Penguin Books Ltd, 27 Wrights Lane, London W8 5TZ, England
Penguin Books Australia Ltd, Ringwood, Victoria, Australia
Penguin Books Canada Ltd, 10 Alcorn Avenue,
Toronto, Ontario, Canada M4V 3B2
Penguin Books (N.Z.) Ltd, 182–190 Wairau Road,
Auckland 10, New Zealand

Penguin Books Ltd, Registered Offices: Harmondsworth, Middlesex, England

First published in the United States of America by Viking Penguin,
a division of Penguin Books USA Inc., 1992
Published in Penguin Books 1993

10 9 8

PUBLISHER'S NOTE
This publication is designed to provide accurate and authoritative information in regard to the subject matter covered. It is sold with the understanding that the publisher is not engaged in rendering accounting or other professional service. If expert assistance is required, the service of a competent professional person should be sought.

Portions of this work first appeared in Mr. Dominguez's audio tape course and workbook entitled *Transforming Your Relationship with Money and Achieving Financial Independence.*

"Purpose in Life" test reprinted by permission of Psychometric Affiliates, Box 807, Murfreesboro, TN 37133.

THE LIBRARY OF CONGRESS HAS CATALOGUED THE HARDCOVER AS FOLLOWS:
Dominguez, Joseph R.
Your money or your life: transforming your relationship with money and achieving financial independence/Joseph R. Dominguez and Vicki Robin.
p. cm.
Includes bibliographical references.
ISBN 0-670-84331-8 (hc.)
ISBN 0 14 01.6715 3 (pbk.)
1. Finance, Personal. I. Robin, Vicki. II. Title.
HG179.D624 1992
332.024'01—dc20 92-3027

This book is printed on acid-free 40% post-consumer-waste recycled paper, using a soy-based ink.

Printed in the United States of America
Set in Meridien
Designed by Victoria Hartman

We dedicate this book to all of the people who are actively engaged in leaving our planet in better shape than they found it.

ACKNOWLEDGMENTS

Our grateful acknowledgment goes to Monica Wood, the godmother of this program from the very beginning.

We wish to acknowledge especially the pioneers who had the vision and diligence to make this program work for them in the 1980s, when so many others were going in the opposite direction. Their contribution to this book—through their letters, their self-revealing stories, and often their hands-on assistance—has been an exemplary expression of the spirit of service: Lu Bauer and Steve Brandon, Marilynn Bradley, Tom Clayton, Anita Cleary, Amy and Jim Dacyczyn, Ken Freistat, Wanda Fullner, Diane Grosch, Paula Hendrick, Lynn Kidder, Kees and Helen Kolff, Terry Krueger, Evy McDonald, Karen McQuillan, Carl Merner, Marcia Meyer, June and Mike Milich, Gordon Mitchell, Tim Moore, Sally Morris, Chris Northrup, Lani O'Callaghan, Ted and Martha Pasternak, Roger and Carrie Lynn Ringer, Hilda Thompson, Rhoda Walter, Steve West, Jason and Nedra Weston, Dwight Wilson, Lucy Woods and Penny Yunuba—truly to name just a few.

Special thanks go to the over 30,000 people who bought our tape course, "Transforming Your Relationship with Money and Achieving Financial Independence," for their willingness to take an honest and courageous look at money in their lives and for their persistent encouragement that we make this material available to a wider audience through this book.

Our New Road Map Foundation Board of Advisers deserves a big thank-you: Herbert Benson, Ernest Callenbach, Joyce and Rosh

Doan, Duane Elgin, Robert and Diane Gilman, John Graham and Ann Medlock, Dorothie Hellman, Dorothea and Jim Jewell, Sister Miriam MacGillis, Ann Niehaus, Roger Pritchard, Ivan Scheier, Bernie and Bobbie Siegel, Brian Swimme, Michael and Justine Toms and Paul Wachtel. They have helped us shape our message to be relevant to the general public. A special thank-you needs to go to our adviser, Robert Muller, who inspired our work by saying, "The single most important contribution any of us can make to the planet is a return to frugality." As a former Assistant Secretary-General of the United Nations and Chancellor Emeritus of the University for Peace, he should know.

Nea Carroll, Jack Parsons, Bob Schutz, Carolyn Vesper, Mary Vogel, and others critically read various versions of this book and gave us valuable input. Margaret Moore volunteered for some of the housekeeping chores of getting a manuscript ready for publication.

Beth Vesel, our agent, deserves high praise for convincing us that people do still read and that the material in our tape course should also be available as a book. Without her persistence, creative partnership and skillful negotiating, this book would not have happened. Thanks also to the whole team at Viking, who have dedicated themselves to making this book readable, relevant and successful. Mindy Werner, our editor, took special care in making sure we spoke to the broadest audience possible.

Finally, we want to thank the many other authors, lecturers, teachers and activists who are encouraging all of us to rethink and restructure our personal and collective relationship with money—for the sake of the earth.

WARNING TO READER:

You have seen them advertised—usually on the backs of matchbooks or equally incendiary publications, or on late-late-late TV:

"Lose 180 pounds in 1 Week While Eating All You Can"

"Make a Million **$$$** a Month While You Sleep ZZZ"

Well, the program contained in this book DARES TO BE DIFFERENT!!

It asks you to DO something.

It asks you to actually **apply** the 9 steps it describes. YES. You need to **put** them into effect. REALLY. You have to do them, every one. As directed.

ONLY BY ACTUALLY, REALLY, HONESTLY DOING THE STEPS WILL THE PROGRAM WORK.

Then, and only then, will the results described in the personal stories begin to make sense.

So don't **WASTE** your precious energy saying to yourself, "That's impossible" or "Nobody can do that in **this** economy" or "No way could **I** save money like that," or . . .

Instead, **SAVE** your energy—DO THE STEPS YOURSELF. After a few months, reread this book.

SEE?

CONTENTS

PROLOGUE

WHY READ THIS BOOK?

Ask yourself these questions:

- Do you have enough money?
- Are you spending enough time with your family and friends?
- Do you come home from your job full of life?
- Do you have time to participate in things you believe are worthwhile?
- If you were laid off from your job, would you see it as an opportunity?
- Are you satisfied with the contribution you have made to the world?
- Are you at peace with money?
- Does your job reflect your values?
- Do you have enough savings to see you through six months of normal living expenses?
- Is your life whole? Do all the pieces—your job, your expenditures, your relationships, your values—fit together?

If you answered "no" to even one of these questions, this book is for you.

MANAGING YOUR LIFE AS AN INTEGRATED WHOLE

Many books on money are available today. Books on the philosophy of money. Books on the psychology of money. Books on home accounting and budgeting. Books on how to earn money. Books on how to save money. Books on how to invest the money you've earned and saved. Books on how your spending affects the environment. Books on how to get rich. Books on how to file for bankruptcy. Books on how to retire.

What these books have in common is that they assume that your financial life functions separately from the rest of your life. This book is about putting it all back together. It is about integration, a "whole systems" approach to life. It will take you back to basics—the basics of making your spending (and hopefully your saving) of money into a clear mirror of your life values and purpose. It is about the most basic of freedoms—the freedom to think for yourself.

The purpose of this book is to transform your relationship with money. That relationship encompasses more than just your earning, spending, debts and savings; it also includes the time these functions take in your life. In addition, your relationship with money is reflected in the sense of satisfaction and fulfillment that you get from your connection to your family, your community and the planet.

To transform something is to change in a fundamental way its nature or function. Once you have changed the nature and function of your interaction with money, through following the steps in this book, your relationship with money will be transformed—you will reach new levels of comfort, competence and consciousness around money. And that's only the beginning of what's possible—once you start following this new road map for money.

THE OLD ROAD MAP

Imagine trying to find your way around a strange city—but where your road map shows a zoo you find a shopping mall, and where it indicates a route to the beach you find that it dead-ends at a train station. After a few such experiences, you may question the usefulness of the map—and then examine it and to your dismay discover that it was drawn in *1890*. If you want to get to where you want to go, you'd better get a new road map!

Now, just as you can't navigate well with such an outdated map, neither can you successfully find your way through today's money maze with a financial road map charted during the latter part of the nineteenth century as the Industrial Revolution was gaining momentum.

The Industrial Revolution was successful to the degree that it provided the material goods that were seen as necessary to American society. Transportation—first railroads, then personal automobiles and ultimately airplanes—was vital to the population's westward expansion. Mechanized agriculture was crucial to feed the ever-greater numbers of people, cheap energy and labor-saving devices to free up human energy, mass communication so that we could stay in touch with one another across the vast continent.

Like all revolutions, this one promised a better life for all Americans. And it delivered—but only as long as people really needed more material possessions. The landmarks of the old road map were clear: "nine to five till you're sixty-five"; "owe your soul to the company store"; trust in the company to take care of you in your old age; the United States is the world's greatest economic power and can do no wrong; we must push for a higher "standard of living" regardless of moral, ethical, emotional, cultural, spiritual, marital, environmental and political consequences.

At some point in the last forty years, though, conditions began to change. For many people, material possessions went from fulfilling needs to enhancing comfort to facilitating luxury—and even beyond to excess. We went from individual national economies to an increasingly global economy. Unlike in the past, problems began to emerge that could not be solved by providing more material goods. Not only that, but these problems were not restricted to Western industrialized nations but became global in nature.

The planet itself began showing signs of nearing its capacity to handle the results of our economic growth and consumerism—water shortages, topsoil loss, global warming, ozone holes, species extinction, natural resource degradation and depletion, air pollution and trash buildup are all signs that our survival is in question. By 1989 these problems had become so pervasive and serious that an entire issue of *Time* magazine, "The Planet of the Year," was devoted to depicting the gravity of our situation. In addition, we've seen that our dependence on oil can lead to international conflict.

Even though we "won" the Industrial Revolution, the spoils of war are looking more and more spoiled. This is especially true for us as individuals. The old road map for money has us trapped in the very vehicle that was supposed to liberate us from toil. There is an abundance of evidence that this old road map is no longer guiding us to the American Dream:

- Personal bankruptcies have been climbing steeply since the 1950s.
- The number of individuals spending more than they earn has increased greatly among those whose income is in the lower 40th percentile.
- The number of American children living below the poverty line has increased from 14.9 percent in 1970 to 19 percent in 1990.
- 31 percent of those surveyed worry that they don't spend enough time with their families and friends, and 38 percent say they are cutting back on sleep to make more time (to earn more money).
- "90 percent of all divorces are caused by money," according to financial planner and psychologist Victoria Felton-Collins.
- The divorce rate is 34 percent higher than in 1970.
- The life savings of the average fifty-year-old is $2,300.
- The average North American works 20 percent more today than in 1973 and has 32 percent less free time per week.
- 48 percent of 4,126 male executives saw their lives as "empty and meaningless" despite years of professional striving.

The Not-So-Merry Money-Go-Round

Once upon a time "earning a living" was the means to an end. The means was "earning"; the end was "living."

Over time our relationship with money—earning it, spending it, investing it, owing it, protecting it, worrying about it—has taken over the major part of our lives.

Most of us spend much more than 40 hours out of the week's total of 168 hours earning money. We must take time to dress for our jobs, commute to our jobs, think about our jobs at work and at home, "decompress" from our jobs. We must spend our evenings and weekends in mindless "escape entertainment" in order to "recreate" from our jobs. We must occasionally "vacate" our jobs, or spend time at the doctor's office to repair our job-stressed health. We need to plan our "careers," attend job seminars or union meetings, lobby or picket for our jobs.

We must spend money to maintain our jobs—job costuming, commuting costs, food bought expensively at the workplace. We must spend so that our neighborhood, house, car, life-style and even life mate reflect our "position" in the work world.

With all that time and money spent on and around our jobs, is it any wonder that we have come to take our identities from them? When asked, "What do you do?" we don't say, "I *do* plumbing." We say, "I *am* a plumber."

When we are not taking our identity from our jobs, we are identified as "consumers." According to the dictionary, to consume is to "destroy, squander, use up." We consider shopping to be recreation, so we "shop till we drop." We want a good future for our kids, so we work harder or become a two-income family and relegate raising the kids to day-care centers or nannies. We buy them the newest toy to prove our love. We earn for their college educations but relinquish the opportunity to spend time with them during their formative years. We bemoan the influences of "bad company," but we ourselves have never been in their company long enough to influence them. We are spending so much of our precious time earning in order to spend that we don't have the time to examine our priorities.

Our old financial map, instead of making us more independent, fulfilled individuals, has led us into a web of financial dependencies. From birth to death we have become financially dependent—on our parents for our first financial sustenance, on "the economy" in order to get a good job after graduation, on "the job" for our survival, on "unemployment" handouts to tide us over between jobs, on our corporate pension to pay our way in old age, on Social Security to supplement our corporate pension (or supplant it if the corporation or its insurer goes bankrupt) and on Medicare or Medicaid if we get sick before we die. The old road map has hit the end of the road. The material progress that was supposed to free us has left us more enslaved.

Conditions have changed, but we are still operating financially by the rules established during the Industrial Revolution—rules based on creating more material possessions. But our high standard of living has not led to a high quality of life—for us or for the planet. Remember that the old road map had nothing wrong with it—it was wonderfully useful in 1890 and for many years afterward—but the territory has changed. New tools for navigation are needed. What we need now is a new financial road map that is based on current global conditions and offers us a way out.

CREATING A NEW ROAD MAP

How do you find a new road map for money? It requires thinking in new ways, managing your life as an integrated whole and identifying old assumptions.

Thinking in New Ways: The Ham-and-Cheese Stories

For all our brainpower, we humans are creatures of habit, often unwilling to let go of old patterns of behavior. The following story illustrates this:

> One day a young girl watched her mother prepare a ham for baking.
>
> At one point the daughter asked, "Mom, why did you cut off both ends of the ham?"
>
> "Well, because my mother always did," said the mother.
>
> "But why?"
>
> "I don't know—let's go ask Grandma."
>
> So they went to Grandma's and asked her, "Grandma, when you prepared the ham for baking, you always cut off both ends—why did you do that?"
>
> "My mother always did it," said Grandma.
>
> "But why?"
>
> "I don't know—let's go ask Great-grandma." So off they went to Great-grandma's.
>
> "Great-grandma, when you prepared the ham for baking, you always cut off both ends—why did you do that?"
>
> "Well," Great-grandma said, "the pan was too small."

Just as we can get caught in outmoded patterns passed down through generations, we can also get trapped by our own obsolete certainties and by the unconscious and invisible boxes that limit our ability to think in new ways, as illustrated by the following story:

> Once upon a time there was a rat. He was an ordinary rat, not particularly intelligent—but he had an appetite, and a nose, for cheese.
>
> One day the air was pungent with the odor of good cheese. He sat up on his hind legs, nose twitching. "Where is that cheese?" he asked himself.
>
> In front of him were four tunnels. Down he scurried into the closest tunnel. No cheese. Down into the second tunnel. No cheese. Into tunnel number three he scampered. Still no cheese. One tunnel left. Down tunnel number four. There it was—a big succulent hunk of cheese! And it tasted just as good as it smelled.
>
> The next day, there was that smell again. Down tunnel number four he ran. Cheese! And the next day, and the next day, and the next. He was a very contented rat, for he knew where to find the cheese.
>
> One day he smelled cheese, but no cheese could be found in the rat's favorite tunnel. He raced out, checked again. Yup, tunnel number four. Back in he ran. Still no cheese. Back out and back in again for one more try. *No cheese!*
>
> But wait one minute. He could still smell that cheese. Maybe it was in tunnel number three? He checked. No cheese. Tunnel number two? No cheese. Tunnel number one? Cheese! And with a sense of satisfaction he ate his cheese.

In some ways we humans are like that rat. We smell the cheese, we set our sights and our sniffers for the goal, and after some searching we find the tunnel where the cheese is. And it usually tastes pretty good. But what happens on the day the cheese isn't there anymore? We head down the tunnel again, looking and sniffing. No cheese. We try again. And again.

At this point the rat starts trying out the other tunnels. But what do we humans do? We keep going down tunnel number four, and again down tunnel number four, and again down tunnel number four.

What, then, is the difference between rats and humans? Rats are

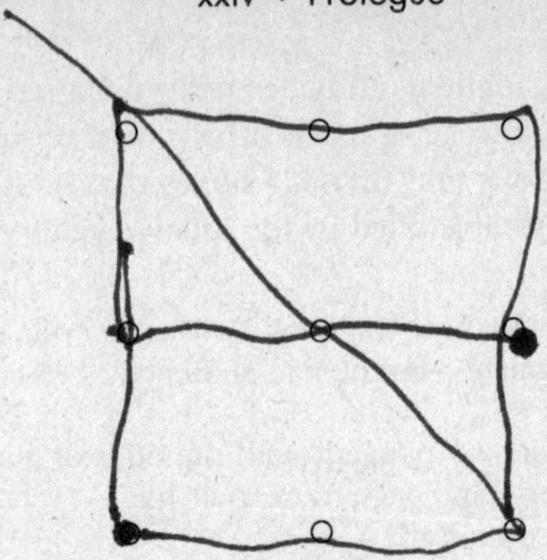

FIGURE P-1

The Nine Circles Puzzle

interested only in cheese. Humans are more interested in looking good, being right, keeping up appearances, keeping up with the Joneses, tradition, self-esteem, doing it the way it's always been done. "I've got to prove myself," "Everyone has one," "The government will fix it."

As a matter of fact, after a certain point we may not even be concerned that the cheese isn't there anymore. Whether through habit (the ham) or stubbornness (the cheese), we often won't give up our old ways of thinking, even if it kills us . . . which it just might.

To see whether or not there is cheese at the end of your tunnel you have to begin to think outside your boxes. Here's a puzzle for you (Figure P-1). Connect these nine circles with three straight lines without lifting your pen or pencil from the paper.

You can't solve the puzzle by staying inside your customary frame of reference. This book is about learning how to think in new ways, how to find a new tunnel to go down, how to look beyond what you "know" to be true and discover your new road map for money.

Financially Independent Thinking

One of the keys to creating your new road map is what we call "FI thinking." This is the process of examining those basic assumptions that you have unconsciously adopted, of evaluating your old road map. FI thinking is noticing that you no longer need to cut off the ends of the ham, that tunnel number four no longer has cheese and that "More Is Better" is no longer the name of the road to happiness. FI thinking is waking up from the American Dream.

FI thinking is about cartography—making your own map, one that accurately depicts the terrain of your life as it actually is today. This map will allow you to choose your own path through the territory of your earning and spending—and to integrate that path with the rest of your life.

FI thinking is essential for anyone who wants a clear, relaxed relationship with money. Until you can *think* independently, you can't *be* independent. Until you can deliberately and dispassionately question your own inner road map for money, you will be stuck in classic financial dead ends, such as:

- Spending more than you earn.
- Buying high and selling low.
- Not liking your job, but not having a way out.
- Needing two paychecks to make ends meet.
- Just when you get ends to meet, seeing someone (your boss, the government) move the other end.
- Being so confused by money that you leave it to the experts, who in turn feed on your ignorance.

The Results of FI Thinking

FI thinking is about applying consciousness to the flow of money in your life. Just reading this book will initiate FI thinking in your life, but there is more. Actually doing the simple steps outlined here will transform your relationship with money. You will go from FI thinking to FI living.

FI thinking will lead naturally to Financial Intelligence, Financial Integrity and Financial Independence.

Financial Intelligence

Financial Intelligence is being able to step back from your assumptions and your emotions about money and observe them objectively. Does money really buy happiness? Does everyone really "gotta make a living"? Is money really something to fear or covet, to love or hate? If I sell the majority of my time for money, will I really be secure?

In order to gain Financial Intelligence you first need to know how much money you already have earned, what you have to show for it, how much is coming into your life and how much is going out.

But that isn't enough. You also need to know what money really is and what you are trading for the money in your life.

One tangible outcome of Financial Intelligence is getting out of debt and having at least six months of basic living expenses in the bank. If you follow the program presented in this book, it will lead inexorably to Financial Intelligence.

Financial Integrity

The dictionary defines integrity as "1: an unimpaired condition: SOUNDNESS 2: adherence to a code of esp. moral or artistic values: INCORRUPTIBILITY 3: the quality or state of being complete or undivided: COMPLETENESS."

Financial Integrity is achieved by learning the true impact of your earning and spending, both on your immediate family and on the planet. It is knowing what is enough money and material goods to keep you at the peak of fulfillment—and what is just excess and clutter. It is having all aspects of your financial life in alignment with your values. If you follow the program presented in this book, it will lead inexorably to Financial Integrity.

Financial Independence

Financial Independence is the by-product of diligently following *all* the steps of the program outlined in this book. It is defined as having an income sufficient for your basic needs and comforts from a source other than paid employment.

While Financial Independence may not be one of your current goals, it is, eventually, in everybody's future. Think about it. Financial Independence is the totally natural, and inescapable, by-product of life. After a certain point you will no longer need to earn a living. The only choice in the matter is when and how that point is reached. In some cases that point is reached while you are still alive. It is then called retirement. In many industries today there is a trend toward early retirement; the practice often prevents the laying off of a larger number of younger workers.

One purpose of this book is to teach the tools that allow you to become financially independent much sooner than traditional retirement and without dependence on traditional retirement sources of income such as pensions and Social Security. As you go through this book you will also discover that Financial Independence encompasses a lot more than having a secure income. It is also independence from crippling financial beliefs, from crippling debt, and from a crippling inability to manage modern "conveniences"—from repairing your car to fixing your central heating. Financial Independence is *anything* that frees you from a dependence on money to handle your life.

What Is an "FIer"?

"FIer" is our shorthand for a person who embodies FI thinking, who is gaining Financial Intelligence, learning Financial Integrity and moving naturally toward Financial Independence. Anyone who applies FI thinking to his or her life through following the steps of this program, we call an FIer.

HOW THIS BOOK CAME ABOUT

This book is not based on theory, good ideas or a new philosophy. It is the result of fifty years of combined experience (thirty years for Joe Dominguez, twenty years for Vicki Robin) in living all the principles presented here. This book didn't just happen, it evolved.

In 1969, at the age of thirty-one, Joe retired from his career on Wall Street—never again to accept money for any of his work. Throughout his life Joe was accustomed to thinking in new ways, and FI thinking was a natural extension of that.

In his ten years as a technical analyst and institutional investment adviser, he had been pursuing a secret agenda: to learn enough about money to develop a program that would allow him to retire with an income adequate to maintain his chosen life-style for the rest of his life—all from a modest salary, without speculation or big "killings."

The program he ended up with (after much trial and error and repeated testing and modification) had nothing to do with risky investment strategies or new, complex analytical methods. Rather, it was about applying common sense, following basic business practices, reexamining outmoded assumptions and diligently following nine simple steps.

To his surprise, Joe found that what he had thought of as a purely personal project was of interest to others—and worked just as well for them as it had for him, regardless of what kind of job they had. Vicki was one of his earliest "students." They met in 1969, several months after she had left a budding career in film and theater in New York, intent on finding out what else life might have to offer. Having graduated at the top of her high-school class and with honors from Brown University, Vicki was no stranger to success. She just wondered whether success had to mean the kind of stress and egocentricity she'd seen in the professional world. Her open mind and substantial savings allowed her to recognize the value of Joe's new road map for money and apply it to her own life. She had to adjust her life-style to live within her new means, but the changes only increased her sense of self-reliance and freedom.

In the twenty years that followed, many friends and volunteers working with Joe and Vicki on various service projects would elicit from them the details of the program, apply them and discover that all aspects of their financial lives were clearing up—from earning to spending to paying off debts to having time for their families to meeting once-dreaded tax deadlines to building up savings to affording better housing to overcoming "poverty consciousness," job insecurity, fear of lack . . . and on and on—without even having early retirement as a goal.

During those years neither Joe nor Vicki had any intention of producing financial seminars. They were enjoying life as full-time volunteers on a wide range of projects, from helping establish a center for young people with drug problems to working with other charitable and community service projects. The seminar overtook them while they were doing other things. Initially it was informal one-on-one sharing between Joe and his friends; as these friends applied the steps and saw that they worked, they enthusiastically spread the word. And Joe began giving evening seminars called "Transforming Your Relationship with Money and Achieving Financial Independence." The demand increased, and the course became a daylong seminar with capacity crowds. In less than two years these seminars were held in over forty North American cities. And the demand continued to grow, still by word of mouth.

In 1984 Vicki founded the New Road Map Foundation, a nonprofit charitable and educational foundation. Its primary purpose was to answer this demand by publishing an eight-hour audiocassette-and-workbook compilation of the best of Joe's seminars. In keeping with Joe's policy, the price was kept low ($60) and the net proceeds have been distributed to other nonprofit organizations working for a better world.

During the past several years, Vicki's passion to communicate the principles of this new financial road map has led her to lecture widely. She, like Joe, has never taken any money for this work. In addition, the New Road Map Foundation pays no salaries, royalties, honorariums or personal expenses.

By 1991 over 30,000 people had taken "Transforming Your Relationship with Money and Achieving Financial Independence." The course had reached every state, every province of Canada and twenty foreign countries, and it had attracted the attention of the national media, with radio interviews and feature articles appearing in various magazines and countless newspapers. And virtually all of this from word of mouth and "word of letter." No paid advertising, no late-night television hucksterism.

Throughout the years, feedback from individuals continued to underscore the idea that this course was not simply about retiring early but about thinking in new ways.

WHAT YOU CAN EXPECT FROM THIS BOOK

The chapters that follow are constructed to aid you in learning FI thinking by helping you to identify your old road map about money and to develop your own new road map.

Exploring the concepts in this book and *diligently applying* the nine steps *will* transform your relationship with money and lead you to FI —Financial Intelligence, Financial Integrity and even Financial Independence. In this book you will also read the stories of individuals—from cooks to counselors, mathophobes to managers, trainers to truck drivers—whose lives have become fuller and more satisfying through their application of what they learned from following the nine steps presented here.

Through the hundreds of letters we've received we know some of the ways people's lives have been enriched by following this program:

- They finally understand the basics of money.
- They reconnect with old dreams and find ways to realize them.
- With a great sense of freedom and relief, they learn how to distinguish between the essentials and the excess in all areas of their lives and how to unburden themselves.
- They find that their relationships with their mates and children improve.
- Their new financial integrity resolves many inner conflicts between their values and their life-styles.
- Money ceases to be an issue in their lives, and they finally have the intellectual and emotional space to take on issues of greater importance.
- At a tangible level, they retire their debts, increase their savings and are able to live happily within their means.
- They increase the amount of their "free time" by reducing expenses and the amount of time on the job.
- They stop buying their way out of problems and instead use such challenges as opportunities to learn new skills.
- Overall, they heal the split between their money and their life—and life becomes one integrated whole.

Each person who follows this program will gain something unique that adds to his or her life. How long will it take? It depends on you—and the road map you create.

GETTING ON THE ROAD

So you want to create your own financial road map? All you need is a notebook, a pen and a willingness to think in new ways.

The nine-circle puzzle is a fine exercise in thinking outside your ordinary mental boxes and in discarding assumptions. Most people who can't immediately solve it have assumed that they're not allowed to go outside the imaginary box defined by the nine circles. There is nothing in the rules that says you can't extend your lines out to the edges of the paper—or even beyond. Another common assumption is that those round things are dots instead of good-sized circles, which have a top, center and bottom. Enough hints? If you haven't yet discovered the solution, keep working with the steps in the book and it will present itself.

To create your own financial road map you don't need to know a lot of math—anyone can do the arithmetic required here. You can start wherever you are financially ($50,000 in debt or with substantial savings) and wherever you are psychologically (from a money-phobe to a money-lover).

It will take commitment to do the steps of this program, but every step you take will generate a reward. The rewards will not all be achieved by the time you finish reading this book. At first, some of the steps may look as if they would be time-consuming to put into practice consistently—however, people who have been doing the steps for some months report that they are actually *spending less time on their money matters than before the course.* The fact that their checkbooks always balance, that they don't ever have to rush to the bank to cover overdrafts, that they spend no time on unrealistic budgets, that they have no more arguments with their spouses over money, that they don't have to spend hours wondering "where it all went" and that the automatic record-keeping makes income-tax time a breeze are just a few of the ways that applying the steps consistently produces savings of your most precious resource—your time.

THE BIGGER MAP

Remember that our current financial road map was developed for the American community during the Industrial Revolution. Much has changed in the last 100 years—but there have been too few cartographers.

Today we must expand our financial road map beyond our own family, beyond even our own American community, and include all the world's peoples. Further, considering the major environmental problems we are facing worldwide, we must expand to include the natural world. Simply said, *The Planet* is now our community.

The new set of needs of this global community requires that individuals reexamine and realign their thinking and their choices about their personal financial lives.

The Industrial Revolution has been won! Have you adjusted to the "peacetime economy"? Does your road map reflect a life that has reached the peak of fulfillment?

If this book assists you in developing such a life, we have done our job.

From our experience over the years of presenting this program, we know that it can be done and that *you* can do it. Those participants who have achieved Financial Independence have discovered the exciting fulfillment that comes from contributing their time, talent and love to the welfare of our planet and its inhabitants. It is the authors' fervent hope that this book will increase your freedom to contribute to your world.

YOUR MONEY OR YOUR LIFE

1

THE MONEY TRAP: THE OLD ROAD MAP FOR MONEY

MONEY: THE TENDER TRAP?

"Your money or your life."

If someone thrust a gun in your ribs and said that sentence, what would you do? Most of us would turn over our wallets. The threat works because we value our lives more than we value our money. Or do we?

Chris Northrup *was a woman trying to make it in a male-dominated profession—medicine. Like so many other minorities cutting through centuries of custom and prejudice, she felt compelled to outdo her peers on every level. She kept long hours, served on boards, spoke at conferences and even tried to play Supermom and raise two children without skipping a beat. Her job, which in many ways she loved, was consuming her life to the tune of eighty hours a week.*

During ***Gordon Mitchell****'s first seven years out of college he'd been a national organizer with a militant black organization. He had no income, but his needs were taken care of by the organization. His compatriots were his family and his mission was his life. There were flaws, however, in this "perfect" marriage of work and wages. Gordon became disillusioned with the disparity between what the organization preached and what the leaders practiced, and he left. He joined the nine-to-five world and became a "successful" financial planner in Michigan. And, like many other people whose* *lives are consumed by their jobs, his marriage ended in divorce and he acquired debts of $120,000. He found himself dreaming of the old days when he had lived simply and had had an exciting mission. Would he ever get back to that?*

Penny Yunuba *worked seventy hours a week as a successful saleswoman, but that wasn't* It. *She reports, ''After reading books like* The Poverty of Affluence [*by Paul Wachtel*] *I realized that my feeling that 'something was missing' wasn't something only I experienced. I began to talk with others and found they often felt similarly let down. Having gotten the prize of a comfortable home with all the trimmings, there was a sense of 'Is this all?' Do I have to work and work and then retire—worn out—to be put out to pasture? To do nothing then but to try to spend money I saved up and to waste my time till my life is over?''*

Carl Merner*'s love was music, but his life was working in data processing for Snohomish County, Washington—and he'd all but given up the hope that love and life could go together. Unsure of what it meant to be a man, he'd assumed all the trappings of adulthood and waited for the day when they'd catapult him into manhood. He'd graduated from college and gotten a wife, a skill, a job, a car, a house, a mortgage and a lawn to mow. Instead of feeling like a man, however, he felt increasingly trapped.*

Diane Grosch *just plain hated her job as a computer programmer. She did the bare minimum she had to do in order to keep her job—but did it so well that she couldn't be fired. She accumulated all the symbols of success—a Mazda RX-7, a house in the country—but they barely balanced the boredom of her job. She went on to travel and participate in a variety of workshops, but none of these pleasures countered the doldrums of the work week. She finally decided that this must be as good as it gets—with her job biting the center out of her life.*

Even though many of us like our jobs, very few of us can say with honesty that our work lives are perfect. The perfect work life would offer enough challenge to be interesting. Enough ease to be enjoyable. Enough camaraderie to be nourishing. Enough solitude to be productive. Enough hours at work to get the job done. Enough leisure to feel refreshed. Enough service to feel needed. Enough silliness to have fun. And enough money to pay the bills . . . and then some. Most of us have let that fantasy go along with *Father Knows Best* and *Leave It to Beaver*. Even the best of jobs have trade-offs. Midlife comes and we discover we've been living our parents' agenda. Or worse, we've been filling teeth for twenty years because some seventeen-year-old (was that really me?) decided that being a dentist would be the best of all possible worlds. We've joined the "real world," the world of compromise. For all the hype about "going for the gold," we're so weary at the end of the day that going for the sofa is as good as it gets.

Yet most of us still cling to the notion that there is a way to live life that makes more sense, that brings more fulfillment and has more meaning. The people you'll be hearing about in this book have found that *there is another way*. There is a way to live an authentic, productive, meaningful life—and have all the material comforts you want or need. There is a way to balance your inner and outer lives, to have your job self be on good terms with your family self and your deeper self. There is a way to go about the task of making a living so that you end up more alive. There is a way to approach life so that when asked, "Your money or your life?" you say, "I'll take both, thank you."

We Aren't Making a Living, We're Making a Dying

For so many working people, however, from people who love their work to those who barely tolerate their jobs, there seems to be no real choice between their money and their lives. What they do for money dominates their waking hours, and life is what can be fit into the scant remaining time.

Consider the average American worker. The alarm rings at 6:45 and our working man or woman is up and running. Shower. Dress in the professional uniform—suits or dresses for some, coveralls for others, whites for the medical professionals, jeans and flannel shirts for construction workers. Breakfast, if there's time. Grab commuter mug and briefcase (or lunch box) and hop in the car for the daily punishment called rush hour. On the job from nine to five. Deal with the boss. Deal with the coworker sent by the devil to rub you the wrong way. Deal with suppliers. Deal with clients/customers/patients. Act busy. Hide mistakes. Smile when handed impossible deadlines. Give a sigh of relief when the ax known as "restructuring" or "downsizing"—or just plain getting laid off—falls on other heads. Shoulder the added workload. Watch the clock. Argue with your conscience but agree with the boss. Smile again. Five o'clock. Back in the car and onto the freeway for the evening commute. Home. Act human with mates, kids or roommates. Eat. Watch TV. Bed. Eight hours of blessed oblivion.

And they call this making a *living*? Think about it. How many people have you seen who are more alive at the end of the work day than they were at the beginning? Do we come home from our "making a living" activity with more life? Do we bound through the door, refreshed and energized, ready for a great evening with the family? Where's all the life we supposedly made at work? For many of us, isn't the truth of it closer to "making a dying"? Aren't we killing ourselves—our health, our relationships, our sense of joy and wonder—for our jobs? We are sacrificing our lives for money—but it's happening so slowly that we barely notice. Graying temples and thickening middles along with dubious signs of progress like a corner office, a private secretary or tenure are the only landmarks of the passage of time. Eventually we may have all the comforts and even luxuries we could ever want, but inertia itself keeps us locked into the nine-to-five pattern. After all, if we didn't work, what would we do with our time? The dreams we had of finding meaning and fulfillment through our jobs have faded into the reality of professional politics, burnout, boredom and intense competition.

Even those of us who *like* our jobs and feel we're making a contribution can recognize that there is a larger arena we could enjoy, one that is beyond the world of nine-to-five: the fulfillment that would come from doing work we love with no limitations or restraints—and no fear of getting fired and joining the ranks of the unemployed. How many times do we think or say, "I would do it this way if I could, but the board members/Zilch Foundation want it done *their* way"? How much have we had to compromise our dreams in order to keep our funding or our job?

We Think We Are Our Jobs

Even if we were financially able to turn our back on jobs that limit our joy and insult our values, however, we are all too often psychologically unable to free ourselves. We have come to take our identity and our self-worth from our jobs.

Our jobs have replaced family, neighborhood, civic affairs, church and even mates as our primary allegiance, our primary source of love and site of self-expression. Reflect on that for yourself. Think about how you feel when you respond to that getting-to-know-you question, "What do you do?" with "I am a ______." Do you feel pride? Do you feel shame? Do you want to say, "I'm *only* a ______," if you aren't meeting your own expectations for yourself? Do you feel superior? Inferior? Defensive? Do you tell the truth? Do you give an exotic title to a mundane occupation to increase your status?

Have we come to measure our worth as human beings by the size of our paychecks? Would teachers have more status than doctors if they made more money? How is it that an M.B.A. became the ticket to success with the opposite sex in the 1980s, while in earlier decades M.B.A.'s were considered boring—at best? When swapping tales at high-school reunions, how do we secretly assess the success of our peers? Do we ask whether our classmates are fulfilled, living true to their values, or do we ask them where they work, what their positions are, where they live, what they drive and where they are sending their kids to college? These are the recognized symbols of success.

Along with racism and sexism, our society has a form of caste system based on what you do for money. We call that jobism, and it pervades our interactions with one another on the job, in social settings and even at home. Why else would we consider housewives second-class citizens?

The High Cost of Making a Dying

Psychotherapist Douglas LaBier documents this "social dis-ease" in his book *Modern Madness.* The steady stream of "successful" professionals who showed up in his office with exhausted bodies and empty souls alerted him to the mental and physical health hazards of our regard for materialism. LaBier found that focusing on money/position/success at the expense of personal fulfillment and meaning had led 60 percent of his sample of several hundred to suffer from depression, anxiety and other job-related disorders, including the ubiquitous "stress."

Even though the official work week has been pegged at forty hours for nearly half a century, many professionals believe they must work overtime and weekends to keep up. A Harris Poll of 1,255 adults conducted in November 1990 showed that 54 percent of Americans believe they have less free time than five years ago. Opinion Research Corporation showed dramatic drops in job satisfaction among all age groups, in every occupation, in every social class, in every part of the country, despite the simultaneous increase of commitment to career in the mid-twenties to mid-forties age range. We are working more, but enjoying life less (and possibly enjoying less life as well). We have developed a national dis-ease based on how we earn money.

What Do We Have to Show for It?

Even if we aren't any happier, you'd think that we'd at least have the traditional symbol of success: money in the bank. Not so. Our savings rate has actually gone down. The savings rate (savings as a percent of disposable income) was 4.5 percent in 1990 (and was as low as 4.1 percent in 1988), whereas in 1973 Americans saved an average of 8.6 percent. The Japanese, by the way, save over 15 percent of their disposable income.

Not only are we saving less, but our level of debt has gone up—way up. Consumer debt exceeded $735 billion in 1990 (that's 42 percent more than in 1985 and 146 percent more than in 1980). That's $3,000 for every man, woman and child in the country. Every eight seconds a baby is welcomed into our society with a big "Howdy, you owe us $3,000"—and that figure doesn't even count the newcomer's share of the *national* debt. You'd cry too.

Debt is one of our main shackles. Our levels of debt and our lack of savings make the nine-to-five routine mandatory. Between our mortgages, car financing and credit card debts, we can't afford to quit. More and more Americans are ending up living in their cars or on the streets. And we're not talking just about poor people or the mentally ill. White-collar workers are the fastest-growing category of the jobless. Layoffs are happening at an increasing rate in all sectors, from the timber industry in the Pacific Northwest to the financial industry on Wall Street.

We Make a Dying at Work so We Can Live It Up on the Weekend

Consider now the average American consumer, spending his or her hard-earned money. Saturday. Take your clothes to the cleaners, your shoes to get reheeled and your car to the service station to have the tires rotated and the funny noise checked out. Go to the grocery store to buy a week's worth of food for the family and grumble at the check-out that you remember when four sacks of groceries used to cost $50 instead of $150. (Sure, you could cut costs by clipping coupons and shopping sales, but who has time?) Go to the mall to buy the book everyone in your support group is reading. Emerge with two books, a suit (half-price on sale) with shoes to match, and a new "personal manager" loose-leaf notebook with a zipper and calculator—all paid for with a credit card. Home. Yard work. Oops . . . a trip to the nursery for pruning shears. Come home with two flats of primroses and a lawn ornament . . . and, oh yes, the pruning shears. Fiddle with the toaster that's burning every slice, even on the lightest setting. Fail to get it apart to find the problem, and fail to find the warranty. Go to the local hardware store to buy a new one. Come out with shelves and brackets for the den, color samples for painting the kitchen . . . and, oh yes, the toaster. Dinner out with your mate, leaving the kids with a sitter. Sunday morning. Pancakes for the whole family. Oops . . . no flour. To the grocery store for flour. Come home with frozen strawberries and blueberries for the pancakes, maple syrup, Sumatra coffee . . . and, oh yes, the flour. Take the family for a drive in the country. Buy gas. Drive for two hours. Stop at a cute restaurant, paying for dinner with the credit card. Spend the evening reading magazines, allowing the ads to float you on fantasies of the *really* good life available if you'd only buy a Porsche or a European vacation or a new computer or . . .

The bottom line is that we think we work to pay the bills—but we spend more than we make on more than we need, which sends us back to work to get the money to spend to get more stuff to . . .

What About Happiness?

If the daily grind were making us happy, the irritations and inconveniences would be a small price to pay. If we could believe that our jobs were actually making the world a better place, we would sacrifice sleep and social lives without feeling deprived. If the extra toys we buy with our toil were providing anything more than momentary pleasure and a chance to one-up others, we'd spend those hours on the job gladly. But it is becoming increasingly clear that, beyond a certain minimum of comfort, money is not buying us the happiness we seek.

Participants in our seminars, whatever the size of their incomes, always said they needed "more" to be happy. We included this exercise in our seminars: We asked people to rate themselve on a happiness scale of 1 (miserable) to 5 (joyous), with 3 being "can't complain," and we correlated their figures with their incomes. In a sample of over 1,000 people, from both the United States and Canada, the average happiness score was consistently between 2.6 and 2.8 (not even a 3!), *whether the person's income was under $1,000 a month or over $4,000 a month.* (See Figure 1-1.)

The results astounded us. They told us that not only are most people habitually unhappy, but they can be unhappy no matter how much money they make. Even people who are doing well financially are not necessarily fulfilled. On those same worksheets we asked our seminar participants, "How much money would it take to make you happy?" Can you guess the results? It was always "more than I have now" by 50 to 100 percent.

These findings are confirmed by numerous other studies on happiness. In one classic study, Roy Kaplan of the Florida Institute of Technology tracked 1,000 lottery winners over a span of ten years. Very few felt any greater happiness—or had any idea of what to do with the money. A surprising number were *less* happy six months later, having left jobs that had been a source of self-esteem and gained money they felt they didn't deserve. Many turned to drugs and suffered feelings of isolation.

So here we are, the most affluent society that has had the privilege to walk the face of the earth, and we're stuck with our noses to the grindstone, our lives in a perpetual loop between home and job and our hearts yearning for something that's just over the horizon.

FIGURE 1-1

Life Rating Scale

Select the list that most closely applies to your life right now

1	2	3	4	5
Uncomfortable	Dissatisfied	Content	Happy	Joyous
Tired	Seeking	Doing OK	Growing	Enthusiastic
Incomplete	Not enough	Average	Satisfied	Fulfilled
Frustrated	Relationships could be better	Acceptable	Productive	Overflowing
Fearful	Coping	Sometimes happy, sometimes blue	Relaxed	Ecstatic
Frequently lonely	Getting better	Stable	Free of tension	Powerful
Angry	Not very productive	Normal	Efficient	Making a difference
Need love	Need reassurance	Few risks	Time available	
Insecure		Fitting in	Fun	
			Secure	

Quality of Life Correlated to Income Level

Monthly income:	$0–1000	$1001–2000	$2001–3000	$3001–4000	Over $4000
Average of quality-of-life rating for all participants in that income range:	2.81	2.77	2.84	2.86	2.63

PROSPERITY AND THE PLANET

If this were just a private hell it would be tragedy enough. But it's not. Our affluent life-styles are having an increasingly devastating effect on our planet.

We are depleting the earth's resources, clogging its arteries (rivers and roads), and polluting the air, water and soil. Distinguished members of the United Nations World Commission on Environment and Development, after three years of study and public hearings around the world, agreed: one of the primary engines driving global environmental problems is North American patterns of excess consumption. Couple this consumption with the understandable envy and yearning growing in the "have-nots" to acquire the same luxuries that we enjoy, and you have a scenario for disaster. And this disaster isn't in the future. It has already begun.

We can all recite the tragic indicators of this looming disaster—from the greenhouse effect to the hole in the ozone layer. They are front-page news, making reluctant and frightened ecologists of us all. And these conditions are made worse by an advertising industry that creates demand for products we don't need that are using up raw materials we may soon run out of.

As economic commentator Lester Thurow, speaking on National Public Radio, put it, it's as if we borrowed up to our eyeballs for the greatest New Year's Eve party ever. During the party everyone was happy. But come January 2, there was no more fun and only bills to pay. The 1980s have been our blow-off bash, and it looks like "January 2" will be the reality for the next generation. This is particularly serious because in the last decade the United States has gone from being the world's largest creditor nation to the world's largest debtor nation. U.S. businesses, houses, land and government bonds are increasingly owned by foreign investors. We've mortgaged the farm, and the rent collector may come knocking any decade now.

Concurrently, the last decade has seen an increasing gulf between the rich and poor, both within the United States and around the world. Millions are homeless for want of affordable housing, while others have many thousands to spend on luxury homes. Historically such disequilibrium is the forerunner of dramatic and even violent change.

Financially, socially, politically and spiritually we've rung up some serious debts in our post–World War II spending spree. One way or another, we will pay up—with interest.

The Biggest Loser in the Money Game

The pity is, many of us are not even aware of this debt because our primary benefactors don't have a voice and we didn't even know we were borrowing from them. We haven't just borrowed from "the bank." We've borrowed from future generations, and from our very generous Mother Earth.

On our shrinking planet, nature is like the village commons where we all graze our sheep. If we respect each other and respect the commons, all our sheep get fed and the commons and the community thrive. But if some folks start looking out only for themselves, they may start grazing extra sheep. Suddenly, goodwill is gone, we're all grazing extra sheep and the commons is destroyed.

Competing nations have depleted our planet's common resources. Everything we eat, wear, drive, buy and throw away comes from the earth. Many of these products are fabricated from nonrenewable resources. Once we throw them away, those pieces of the earth will not be available to support meaningful life for perhaps thousands of millennia. It's a one-way trip from the earth to the factory to the store to our house to the dump. We have ignored the fact that we enjoy our current level of affluence by the good (and free) graces of nature—soil, water and air that cost nothing yet are being taxed to the limit. We now face the grim possibility that the earth may one day no longer support life—or at least life as we know it and want it to be. As civilized and advanced as we may have become, we still depend on breathable air, potable water and fertile soil for our daily existence. But we have done massive, perhaps irreparable, damage to our earth.

But Why?

How is it that we've backed ourselves into this corner? And why do we stay here?

For one thing, many of us don't even recognize that we're in a corner, while others think that just around this very corner, happiness is waiting. In their book *New World, New Mind,* Robert Ornstein and Paul Ehrlich point out that our minds were designed to respond well to short-term threats—tigers and fires and the whites of our enemy's eyes. In today's world, however, the environmental threats are building up so slowly that our minds can't register the danger. We must, Ornstein and Ehrlich contend, learn to react to the distant early warnings of sophisticated environmental measurements with the same vigor with which we used to climb trees to escape the jaws of a tiger.

We also put up with this "making a dying" existence because we think we have no choice. "Another day, another dollar." "Everybody's gotta make a living." The "nine to five till you're sixty-five" pattern, so recent in human history but so pervasive today, seems like the only choice for someone who is neither a sports or entertainment superstar nor an eccentric. After all, there are bills to pay and an identity to maintain, and besides, what would I do with my life if I didn't have a job?

Is More Better?

And many of us are out there "making a dying" because we've bought the pervasive American myth that more is better. Even though Buckminster Fuller likened the earth to a spaceship, we cling to the silver-screen images of the Frontier, where "there's always more where that came from."

We build our working lives on this myth of more. Our expectation is to make more money as the years go on. We will get more responsibility and more perks as we move up in our field. Eventually, we hope, we will have more possessions, more prestige and more respect from our community. We become habituated to expecting ever more of ourselves and ever more from the world, but rather than satisfaction, our experience is that the more we have, the more we want—and the less content we are with the status quo.

More is better; this is the motto that drives us. It's the motto that leads us to trade in our car every three years, buy new clothes for every event and every season, get a bigger and better house every time we can afford it and upgrade everything from our stereo systems to our lawn mowers simply because some new automatic widget has been introduced. Paul Wachtel, author of *The Poverty of Affluence*, calls into question our reliance on "more is better" as the solution to all our yearnings. He shows how our frantic pursuit of more ends up working against the very ends it's designed to serve, security and fulfillment:

> In 1958, when economist John Kenneth Galbraith appropriately described the United States as "The Affluent Society," 9.5

> percent of U.S. households had air conditioning, about 4 percent had dishwashers, and fewer than 15 percent had more than one car. By 1980, when Ronald Reagan's successful bid to replace Jimmy Carter was based on the widespread sense that people were suffering economically, the percentage of homes with air conditioning had quintupled, the percentage with dishwashers had increased more than 700 percent and the percentage with two or more cars had about tripled. Yet, despite the astounding economic growth—despite owning more of the gadgets, machines and appliances thought to constitute "the good life"—Americans felt significantly less well-off than they had twenty-two years before, polls showed.

If you live for having it all, what you have is never enough. In an environment of more is better, "enough" is like the horizon, always receding. You lose the ability to identify that point of sufficiency at which you can choose to stop. This is precisely the psychological cul-de-sac Paul Wachtel describes, the invisible Catch-22 of the American myth of more. If more is better, then what I have is *not* enough. Even when I do get the "more" I was convinced would make life "better," however, I am still operating out of the belief that more is better—so the "more" I now have *still* isn't enough. But hope springs eternal. If I could only get more, then . . . and on and on we go. We get deeper in debt and often deeper in despair. The "more" that was supposed to make life "better" can *never* be enough.

The Limits to Growth

Our economy's version of "more is better" is "growth is good."

Modern economics worships growth. Growth will solve poverty, the theory goes. Growth will increase our standard of living. Growth will reduce unemployment. Growth will keep us apace with inflation. Growth will relieve the boredom of the rich and the misery of the poor. Growth will bolster the GNP, boost the Dow and beat the Japanese. A rising tide lifts all boats.

What we overlook is that the fuel for economic growth comes from nature, and even under the best of circumstances, nature is not infinitely abundant. Resources can and do run out.

There *are* limits in nature. At a physical level, nothing grows forever. Every plant and every animal reaches an optimal size and then begins mature function, participating in life—leafing, fruiting, responding to stimuli and providing nourishment and competition for other forms of life around it. We also know that every population of plants or animals reaches a maximum number, based on the finite resources of energy, food, water, soil and air, and then begins to stabilize or decrease in size. There *always* comes a point where the individual or the specific population either collapses or dies due to lack of resources, or stabilizes at a level that the environment can handle.

By ignoring this fundamental reality of the natural world, we as individuals, and our economy, have moved dangerously close to the limit of Mother Nature's capacity to handle our demands on her. While we've heard much debate on how to calculate the number of human beings that can be supported by the earth's ecosystem (the earth's carrying capacity), one scientist, Peter Vitousek, calculates that humans *now* appropriate 40 percent of what nature has to offer—even though we are but one species among as yet uncounted millions. Continued growth, either in population or in consumption, could spell disaster—and our human numbers and our expectations for a higher standard of living are still heading up.

Even though we clearly need to confront our personal and collective addiction to growth, we are exhibiting the classic resistance to change called denial. We don't have to change because we're sure that technology will save us. After all, we say, look at the past. Science and technology have eliminated deadly diseases from smallpox to diphtheria. Surely we'll develop the technology to purify our water, genetically engineer seeds that can grow after global warming, clean up pollution and find the key to unlimited cheap energy. And if technology doesn't save us, surely the government will. Look at our social progress as a species. If we lobby for appropriations, the government will develop a program. There are experts who know what's going on and are handling it for us. Anyway, we conclude, it's not *my* problem. It's a Third World problem. If only "they" would stop having so many babies and burning their forests we'd survive. It's they who need to change. In any event, it would be silly to change because the reports are probably wrong. Scientists and politicians and the media have lied to us before. This environmental problem is a fabrication of some smart lawyers and Nervous Nellie alarmists. And anyway, what can "I" do? After all, I'm in debt so I *can't* stop commuting forty miles a day to the nuclear widget factory, even if the continuance of life on earth depended on it, which it doesn't . . . does it?

As people and as a planet we suffer from *upward mobility* and *downward nobility*. We need at least to pause and wonder if it's all worth it, if we're getting the fulfillment we're seeking. And if not, why do we persist, like addicts, in habits that are killing us?

The Creation of Consumers

Perhaps we cling to our affluence—even though it isn't working for us or the planet—because of the very nature of our relationship with money. As we shall see, money has become the movie screen on which our lives play out. We project onto money the capacity to fulfill our fantasies, allay our fears, soothe our pain and send us soaring to the heights. In fact, we moderns meet most of our needs, wants and desires through money. We *buy* everything from hope to happiness. We no longer live life. We consume it.

Americans used to be "citizens." Now we are "consumers"—which means (according to the dictionary definition of "consume") people who "use up, waste, destroy and squander." Consumerism, however, is just a twentieth-century invention of our industrial society, created at a time when encouraging people to buy more goods was seen as necessary for continued economic growth.

By the early 1920s a curious wrinkle had emerged in the U.S. economy. The astounding capacity of machinery to fill human needs had been so successful that economic activity was slowing down. Instinctively knowing they had enough, workers were asking for a shorter workweek and more leisure to enjoy the fruits of their labors. Two sectors of American society were alarmed at this trend. The moralists who had internalized the Protestant work ethic believed that "idle hands would do the work of the devil." Leisure is debasing, they thought, leading at least to sloth if not to the rest of the seven deadly sins. The other sector to sound the alarm was the industrialists. Reduced demand for factory output threatened to halt economic growth. Workers did not seem as instinctively eager to buy new goods and services (like cars, chemicals, appliances and entertainment) as they did the old ones (like food, clothing and shelter).

The alternative to growth, however, was seen not as maturity but as the precursor to the stagnation of civilization and the death of productivity. New markets were needed for the expanding cornucopia of goods that machines could turn out with such speed and precision—and for the continued profit of the industrialists. And here's the stroke of genius: these new markets would consist of the same populace, but the people would be educated to want not only old and necessary items but new things that they didn't need. Enter the concept of "standard of living." A new art, science and industry was born to convince Americans that they were working to elevate their standard of living rather than to satisfy basic economic needs. In 1929 the Herbert Hoover Committee on Recent Economic Changes published a progress report on this new (and very welcome) strategy:

> The survey has proved conclusively what has long been held theoretically to be true, that wants are almost insatiable; that one want satisfied makes way for another. The conclusion is that economically we have a boundless field before us; that there are new wants which will make way endlessly for newer wants, as fast as they are satisfied. . . . Our situation is fortunate, our momentum is remarkable.

Instead of leisure being relaxed activity, it was transformed into an opportunity for increased consumption—even consumption of leisure itself (as in travel and vacations). Henry Ford concurred:

> Where people work less they buy more . . . business is the exchange of goods. Goods are bought only as they meet needs. Needs are filled only as they are felt. They make themselves felt largely in the leisure hours.

The Hoover Committee agreed. Leisure was not, in fact, a reason for not working. It was a reason for working *more*. Somehow the consumer solution satisfied both the industrial hedonists hell-bent on achieving a material paradise and the puritans who feared that unoccupied leisure would lead to sin. In fact, the new consumerism promoted all the deadly sins (lust, covetousness, gluttony, pride, envy) *except* perhaps anger and sloth.

Only mildly subdued by the Depression, consumerism returned with added vigor in the post–World War II era. Victor Lebow, a U.S. retailing analyst of the early postwar era, proclaimed:

> Our enormously productive economy . . . demands that we make consumption our way of life, that we convert the buying and use of goods into rituals, that we seek our spiritual satisfaction, our ego satisfaction, in consumption. . . . We need things consumed, burned up, worn out, replaced, and discarded at an ever increasing rate.

And thus the rat race was born, leading to our excruciating balancing act between working more to buy luxuries and having enough leisure to enjoy them. In our initial enthusiasm for our new status as consumers, we learned to assert our rights, standing up to unscrupulous business. "Rights," however, have since taken on a different hue.

The Right to Buy

We have come to believe, deeply, that it is our *right* to consume. If we have the money, we can buy whatever we want, whether or not we need it, use it or even enjoy it. After all, it's a free country. And if we don't have the money . . . heck, what are credit cards for? Born to shop. Whoever dies with the most toys wins. Life, liberty and the pursuit of material possessions.

Beyond the constitutional rights of free speech, assembly, due process, and so on, there is the right to have anything you want, as long as you are willing to pay for it (or at least promise to pay for it . . . on time). Environmentalists who question the right to buy a new gas-guzzler or social activists who question the cost to society of one person's owning a forty-five-room house while others sleep on the street are maligned as interfering with the rights of free individuals. Now, we aren't questioning the right to own private property. We are simply highlighting how profoundly we have taken our right to consume to heart, and perhaps placed it above other rights, privileges and duties of a free society.

In the coming years, our right to consume what we want, when we want, how we want and where we want may be called increasingly into question as we struggle with the issues of the global marketplace, human rights, free trade, environmental damage and dwindling resources. Wouldn't it be easier to wage our personal battles with our urge to splurge *before* the public battles begin? We can learn *now* the joys of having less rather than have our pet purchases snatched away by tough regulations and public outrage. It's so much easier to be good by choice than by coercion.

To Buy Is Right

Having challenged and confronted this sacred cow called the right to consume, we can look at another kind of "right."

We have absorbed the notion that it is *right* to buy—that consuming is what keeps America strong. "Penny Pinching by Consumers May Tarnish Economy," a recent newspaper headline admonished. If we don't consume, we're told, masses of people will be thrown out of work. Families will lose their homes. Unemployment will rise. Factories will shut down. Whole towns will lose their economic base. We *have* to buy widgets to keep America strong.

Part of why our "consumers" have less money to spend is that saving has clearly become un-American. Even the language of modern economics promotes consumption. What else would we do with "disposable" income besides dispose of it—we certainly wouldn't want to keep it around where it would just rot!

So if consuming is the way to keep the economy strong and savers are people willing to put their fellow citizens out of work, a day at the mall can be considered downright patriotic. The only down side is that our rising expectations have outstripped our incomes, leaving the average consumer-patriot increasingly in debt. This puts us in a bind: the only way for us to exercise our economic patriotism is to go deeper into debt. If you've felt confused about your urge to splurge, perhaps this is part of the reason. You, and every one of your fellow citizens, is in a no-win situation. You're wrong if you buy and wrong if you don't.

All of this is exacerbated by advertising. By the time an average teenager receives his or her high-school diploma, he's been exposed to well over 100,000 ads—a rate of 3 to 4 hours of ads per week. And Alan Durning indicates that "the typical American is exposed to 50 to

100 advertisements each morning" before 9 A.M. The advertising industry now spends nearly $500 per year on each U.S. citizen.

Marketing theory says that people are driven by fear, by the promise of exclusivity, by guilt and by greed—with the need for approval being the up-and-coming motivation of the nineties. Advertising technology, armed with market research and sophisticated psychology, aims to throw us off balance emotionally—and then promises to resolve our discomfort with a product. Fifty to 100 times before 9 A.M. Every day.

If We're a Cancer, What's the Cure?

At the same time, between the ads, our televisions, radios and newspapers are reporting the bad news about the environment. Product packaging is clogging the landfills. Product manufacturing is polluting the groundwater, deforesting the Amazon, fouling the rivers, lowering the water table, depleting the ozone layer and changing the weather. If I wear synthetic fabrics I'm depleting our limited supply of fossil fuel, but if I wear cotton grown in Arizona I'm condoning deep water wells that are making the soil too salty to grow anything. If I wear nothing, I'm putting people out of work. It's damned if we do and damned if we don't—and even damned if we dam, as the Pacific Northwest is learning, since its hydroelectric power dams are preventing salmon from swimming upstream to spawn.

It seems there is no way consumers can be "right." Everything we do exacts a cost from the environment. Even the new fad of "green consuming"—buying products that are less environmentally damaging—is only *less* stressful to the earth and by no means benign.

As consumers, we are becoming like a cancer on the earth, consuming our host. Paul Ehrlich, who besides cowriting *New World, New Mind* has written *The Population Bomb* and many other books, claims that in the United States an individual does 100 times more damage to the planet's environment, thanks to our extravagant use of resources, than an individual in a less developed country. We even use twice the energy per capita that Europeans do—for no greater standard of living.

Clearly we don't think about this as we're driving to work in the morning. We don't ponder, "To consume or not to consume, that is the question." But the notion that it's right to consume bumps daily into the admonition that we're deep in debt personally and playing Russian roulette with the environment besides.

But what can we do? How in the midst of our busy lives can we become aware of, much less do something about, acid rain, deforestation, species extinction, the hole in the ozone layer, global warming and exponential population growth? "What can one person do?" we ask, and then change stations on the radio. And so we continue, making a stab at changing one week, bingeing the next and depending on denial to shield us from the tough choices ahead.

If we continue to rely on making small changes, however, we will merely slow our headlong rush toward a diminished and impoverished future. What's needed isn't change, it is transformation. Transformation doesn't just move the pieces around, it changes the game board. Transformation doesn't just try a new set of solutions to intractable problems, it asks a new set of questions that allows us to see the problems themselves in a new light.

In 1981 Jonas Salk published *World Population and Human Values: A New Reality*, which presented the hopes and perils of this transformation from a growth-oriented world to a more sustainable, values-oriented world.

> As population growth slows and as we approach a plateau in world population size, our greatest challenges lie in the human and social realm. Human and social challenges—improving quality of life, feeding billions of people, avoiding the disastrous depletion of resources, creating societies that meet the material and cultural needs of the individual—challenges that now seem insurmountable, may in time be no more insoluble than previously "impossible" challenges—development of heavier-than-air flight, modern agriculture, electronics, space travel.
>
> . . . We will, in the process of responding to the forces and limits of nature, learn whether we have the capacity to meet this challenge. If we do, then we will emerge from the present period not merely as survivors, but as human beings in a new reality.

The shift from an ethic of growth to an ethic of sustainability will certainly require each one of us to transform our relationship with money and the material world. Transforming our relationship with money and reevaluating our earning and spending activity could put us *and* the planet back on track. We need to learn from our past, determine our present reality and create a new, reality-based relationship with money, discarding assumptions and myths that don't work. We need a new road map for money and materialism—one that is truly in tune with the times.

THE BEGINNING OF A NEW ROAD MAP FOR MONEY

What makes consuming so all-consuming? While advertising and industry may have conspired to sell us on materialism, the fact is, we bought it. What is it in us that was so easily distracted from life's deeper pleasures?

Psychologists call money the "last taboo." It is easier to tell our therapist about our sex life than it is to tell our accountant about our finances. Money—not necessarily how much we have, but how we feel about it—governs our lives as much or more than any other factor. More marriages are wrecked by money than any other factor. Why?

Patterns of Belief

To begin to understand this, we need to understand a bit about the human mind. Numerous sources, from modern brain researchers to ancient Eastern philosophers, seem to agree on the basic notion that the mind is a pattern-making and pattern-repeating device. Scientists say that we are the only species that doesn't have a fixed behavioral response for every stimulus. We create our patterns of response. Some come from personal experience, primarily in the first five years of life. Some patterns are genetic. Some are cultural. Some seem to be universal. All of them are there, presumably, to increase our chances of survival. Once a pattern is recorded, once it's been tested and deemed useful for survival, it becomes very hard to change. We salivate to the smell of sautéing onions, step on the brakes at the sight of a red light and pump adrenaline when someone yells, "Fire!" Clearly we couldn't survive if we didn't have these huge libraries of interpretations coupled with behaviors. But here's the rub: not all (or even a majority) of these patterns have anything to do with objective reality—yet they persist, governing our behavior. They are so tenacious, in fact, that we will often ignore or deny reality itself in favor of one of our interpretations. The snakes on a child's bedroom floor that are banished if Mother leaves the door ajar are an obvious example of an absurd but convincing interpretation of reality. We usually call such obviously erroneous notions superstitions. But which of our many beliefs are superstitions, and which are fact?

Does walking under a ladder or breaking a mirror really bring bad luck? Most of us are beyond such primitive superstitions. But what about other, less suspect beliefs? How do we catch a cold? By going outdoors with a wet head? By being exposed to germs? The former we recognize as an old wives' tale, but the latter? After all, there are people who don't get the cold going around the office. Did the germs skip them? Could the germ theory be just a modern superstition? The earth has always been round, but it wasn't round in human consciousness until the fifteenth century. To us the notion of a flat earth is quaint. Which of our beliefs will look quaint to future generations?

What Do Our Actions Say?

As with the flat earth and the snakes in the bedroom, there are many realities that our financial beliefs and our financial behavior do not take into account. Although we are largely unconscious of our financial belief system, our blindness condemns us to prisons of our own making.

While we might vigorously maintain that we know that "money can't buy happiness" and "the best things in life are free," honesty requires that we look deeper. Our behavior tells a different story.

What do we do when we are depressed, when we are lonely, when we feel unloved? More often than not we buy something to make us feel better. A new outfit. A drink (or two). A new car. An ice cream cone. A ticket to Hawaii. A goldfish. A ticket to the movies. A bag of Oreos (or two).

When we want to celebrate good fortune, we buy something. A round of drinks. A catered wedding. A bouquet of roses. A diamond ring.

When we are bored, we buy something. A magazine. A cruise. A board game. A bet on the horses.

When we think there must be more to life, we buy something.

A workshop. A self-help book. A therapist. A house in the country. A condo in the city.

None of this is wrong. It's just what we do. We have learned to seek external solutions to signals from the mind, heart or soul that something is out of balance. We try to satisfy essentially psychological and spiritual needs with consumption at a physical level. How did this happen?

Here's an illustration.

The Fulfillment Curve

The Fulfillment Curve (see Figure 1-2) shows the relationship between the experience of fulfillment and the amount of money we spend (usually to acquire more possessions). In the beginning of our lives, more possessions did indeed mean more fulfillment. Basic needs were met. We were fed. We were warm. We were sheltered. Most of us don't remember the fear of hunger and cold that was remedied by just a blanket and a breast—but we all went through it. When we were uncomfortable, when we cried, something came from the outside to take care of us. It seemed like magic. Our needs were filled. We survived. Our minds recorded each such incident and *remembered:* look outside yourself and you will be fulfilled.

We then went from bare necessities (food, clothing, shelter) to some amenities (toys, a wardrobe, a bicycle), and the positive relationship between money and fulfillment became even more deeply embedded. Remember your excitement when you got your Captain Midnight Decoder Ring or baseball mitt or Barbie Doll? For some of us, school supplies were sheer delight. If our parents were being responsible, they soon taught us, "Those things cost money, dear. Money that we go out and earn for you—because we love you." We got an allowance to learn the value of money. We could select and purchase happiness ourselves! And so it went, year after year. There was the prom tux and corsage. The tennis racket.

Eventually we slipped beyond amenities to outright luxuries—and hardly registered the change. A car, for example, is a luxury that 92 percent of the world's population never enjoys. For us, however, our first car is the beginning of a lifelong love affair with the automobile. Then there's the luxury of our first trip away from home. For many of us, there was going away to college. Our first apartment. Notice that

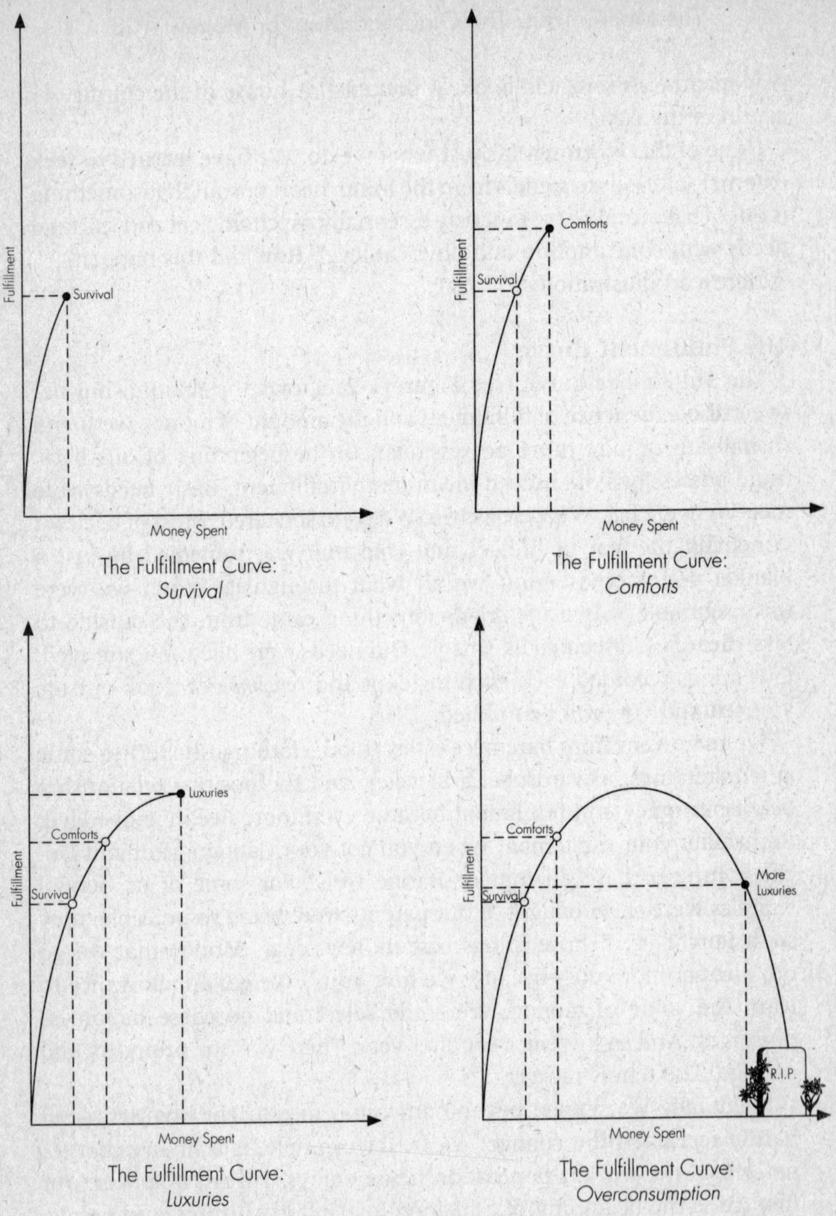

FIGURE 1-2

Evolution of the Fulfillment Curve

while each one was still a thrill, it cost more per thrill and the "high" wore off more quickly.

But by now we *believed* that money equals fulfillment, so we barely noticed that the curve had started to level out. On we went into life. House. Job. Family responsibilities. More money brought more worry. More time and energy commitments as we rose up the corporate ladder. More time away from the family. More to lose if we were robbed, so more worry about being robbed. More taxes and more tax accountants' fees. More demands from community charities. Therapists' bills. Remodeling bills. Just-keeping-the-kids-happy bills.

Until one day we found ourselves sitting, unfulfilled, in our 4,000-square-foot home on 2.5 wooded acres with a hot tub in the back yard and Nautilus equipment in the basement, yearning for the life we had as poor college students who could find joy in a walk in the park. We hit a fulfillment ceiling and never recognized that the formula of money = fulfillment not only had stopped working but had started to work against us. No matter how much we bought, the Fulfillment Curve kept heading down.

Enough—The Peak of the Curve

There's a very interesting place on this graph—it's the peak. Part of the secret to life, it would seem, comes from identifying for yourself that point of maximum fulfillment. There is a name for this peak of the Fulfillment Curve, and it provides the basis for transforming your relationship with money. It's a word we use every day, yet we are practically incapable of recognizing it when it's staring us in the face. The word is **"enough"**. At the peak of the Fulfillment Curve we have enough (see Figure 1-3). Enough for our survival. Enough comforts. And even enough little "luxuries." We have everything we need; there's nothing extra to weigh us down, distract or distress us, nothing we've bought on time, have never used and are slaving to pay off. Enough is a fearless place. A trusting place. An honest and self-observant place. It's appreciating and fully enjoying what money brings into your life and yet never purchasing anything that isn't needed and wanted.

Once you have discovered what is enough for you, your Fulfillment Curve can reverse direction and head straight up. Stay tuned.

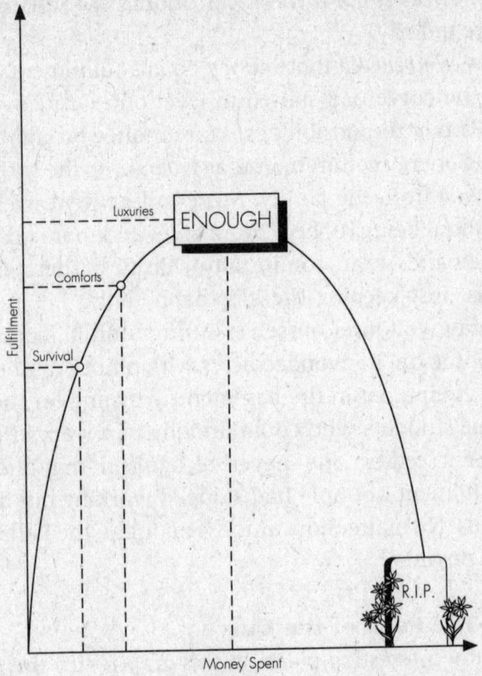

FIGURE 1-3

The Fulfillment Curve: *Enough*

Clutter—A Fate Worse Than Dearth

So what's all that stuff beyond enough—beyond the peak, where the Fulfillment Curve begins to go down? Clutter, that's what! Clutter is anything that is excess—*for you*. It's whatever you have that doesn't serve you, yet takes up space in your world. To let go of clutter, then, is not deprivation, it's lightening up and opening up space for something new to happen. As self-evident as these ideas may be, many people experience a subtle (or not so subtle) resistance to letting them in. This is why downscaling, frugality and thrift sound like deprivation, lack and need. On the contrary! Enough is a wide and stable plateau. It is a place of alertness, creativity and freedom. From this place, being suffocated under a mountain of clutter that must be stored, cleaned, moved, gotten rid of and paid for on time is a fate worse than dearth.

We just received a letter from a single mother who is following the FI program. She had been on the brink of building a hot tub when she got one of our occasional newsletters. Like a cartoon character, she stopped midstride and asked, "Do I really *want* a hot tub?" After all, she reasoned, I can soak in a hot *bath*tub. The hot tub will be just one more thing to clean, maintain, buy chemicals for and fix. Thinking further, she recognized that she could move her washing machine up from the cellar, where she has to lift a heavy hatch to even get to it, and put it in the hot-tub space. That way she could do her laundry without straining her back (saving money on chiropractor bills), eliminate the expenses of building and maintaining the hot tub, save the time she would have spent being hot-tub social secretary for her friends—and still enjoy hot baths. A win on all counts! She experienced what most people experience when they resist being lured down the slippery slope of clutter: relief.

Stations of the Crass

What creates clutter? The Fulfillment Curve strongly suggests that most clutter enters our lives through the "more is better" door. It comes from the disease of materialism, of looking for inner fulfillment in outer possessions. It comes from the early programming that discomfort can be alleviated by something external—a baby bottle, a blanket, a bicycle, a B.A., a BMW or, eventually, another kind of bottle.

It also comes from unconscious habit. Take gazingus pins. A gazingus pin is any item that you just can't pass by without buying. Everybody has them. They run the gamut from pocket calculators and tiny screwdrivers to pens and chocolate kisses. So there you are in the mall, a shopping robot on your weekly tour of the stations of the crass. You come to the gazingus-pin section and your mind starts cranking out gazingus-pin thoughts: Oh, there's a pink one . . . I don't have a pink one . . . Oh, that one runs on solar cells . . . That would be handy . . . My, a waterproof one . . . If I don't use it I can always give it away . . . Before you know it, an alien arm (attached to your body) has reached out and picked up the gazingus pin, and off you go to the checkout, still functioning like a wind-up zombie. You arrive home with your purchase, put it in the gazingus-pin drawer (along with the five or ten others) and forget about gazingus pins until your next trip to the mall, at which point you come to the gazingus-pin section and . . .

Faces and Functions of Clutter

Just because something is out of sight doesn't mean it isn't clutter. Our various gazingus-pin drawers—including our attics, basements, garages, closets and storage sheds—are havens of clutter, filled with projects and products we'll probably never use. Unfinished projects sap you of vitality. Clothing discarded after a few wearings leaves a vague feeling of dissatisfaction and superficiality.

One friend had a garage filled with electronic parts and other valuable doohickeys collected over many years, most of which he knew he'd never use. But if he cleaned out his garage, he'd have to admit his house was too big for him and his wife now that the kids were grown. If he did that, he'd have to move. If he did that, he'd have to admit that his marriage had died many years earlier, but that he was too scared to leave. It was easier to ignore the garage and hang on to the clutter.

Once you catch on to what clutter is, you'll find it everywhere. Isn't meaningless activity a form of clutter? How many of the power lunches, cocktail parties, social events and long evenings glued to the television have been clutter—activities that add nothing positive to your life? What about disorganized days, full of busyness with no sense of accomplishment? And what about items on your To Do list of tasks that never get done? Stumbling over them, week in, week out, on your list is like the frustration of navigating the perennial newspapers and kids' toys that litter some people's living rooms.

There is also sound clutter. Is it any wonder that clutter and clatter are only one letter apart? For many of us there are the noises of city life and of our workplaces that we filter out daily. For denizens of urban canyons the silence of the desert can be deafening. While not everyone is cut out to be a desert-dweller, it's a sad commentary on modern life to realize what a luxury it is to have control over our aural environment, enjoying only the sounds of nature and good conversation. Instead, there's the cacophony of cars and buses, television and radio, microwaves and dishwashers, and trivial chatter. All of it is clutter—elements in your environment that don't serve you yet take up space.

There are cluttered motives, such as when we are of many minds about everything from public policy to personal decisions. Unplanned errands are often clutter—running to the store twice a day for items forgotten on your weekly shopping. Hobbies are clutter-intensive when the ratio of what you have to what you use climbs—like the photography buffs with suitcases full of lenses and filters who get their best shots with a pocket automatic.

As your awareness of clutter deepens, you'll be inspired to spring-clean your whole life. As you follow the nine steps outlined in this book, you will develop your own personal definition of clutter and will slowly, painlessly, even joyfully, rid yourself of it. The first step will be to examine the past so you can understand and take responsibility for the present.

Step 1: Making Peace with the Past

Are you ready to survey your own relationship with money and the things that money can buy? The purpose of this exercise is to increase your awareness, not your arrogance or your shame. It serves to locate you in time and space, to review—without blame—your earning and spending activity in the past.

To get the most out of this program, we suggest that you make notes of your answers to questions posed in the text and of your calculations for each of the nine steps. You may want to write in this book. Or write in a spiral notebook. Whatever system you devise, we recommend that you do it in such a way that you can easily review your answers later. This program initiates a *process* of awareness and change that will continue for many years. Reviewing your notes every six months or year will add great depth and insight to your journey toward transforming your relationship with money.

There are two parts to this step:

A. Find out how much money you have earned in your lifetime—the sum total of your *gross* income, from the first penny you ever earned to your most recent paycheck.

B. Find out your net worth by creating a personal balance sheet of assets and liabilities.

A. HOW MUCH HAVE YOU EARNED IN YOUR LIFE?

Initially this task may seem impossible. "I haven't kept track!" you may protest. A little bit of archaeology pays off. First, dig out your copies of old income-tax returns. Adjust the figures to reflect any cheating you did—tips you didn't report, jobs that paid you under the table, informal consulting, gambling winnings, gifts from relatives that went unreported, any money you've stolen, cash prizes you've won, rent collected from the extra room in your house or the extra house you never use, and all other unreported income. Go down memory lane to those summer jobs you had during high school and college, and all the twists and turns of your own financial meandering through adulthood. Spend a few days with whatever financial records you may have stashed away: check stubs, bankbooks, paycheck stubs, old abandoned account books. If you have a résumé, use it as an outline for a year-by-year job history. Tell the truth about those three years you glossed over as "further career training": what odd jobs did you have and how much did you earn picking apples, house-sitting, watering the neighbors' plants and animals or making wreaths for Christmas?

For those of you who've been salaried employees your entire working lives, the Social Security Administration has also kept a record. Contact your local or state office or the national one and apply for a Statement of Earnings form. But if no records exist anywhere, even in the computers at Social Security, estimate as best you can. The object is to get as accurate and honest a figure as possible for the total amount of money that has entered your life.

The Value of Step 1

This step is useful in several ways:

1. It clears the fog shrouding your past relationship with money. Most people have no idea how much money has entered their lives, and therefore no idea how much money *could* enter their lives.

2. It eradicates such myths and false self-concepts as "I can't earn

very much money" and even "I don't have to worry, I can always earn lots of money" (often said by individuals being supported by someone else). If you are one of the many who grossly underestimate how much money has entered their lives, this step can be amazingly powerful. You are worth more than you thought.

3. It gets you to ground zero, enabling you to begin the financial program with a clear head and confidence in your wage-earning ability.

4. It allows you to see and let go of any skeletons from the past you may have in your closets—any secrets or lies that may be distorting your current relationship with money.

The power of this step can be seen in this story about a divorcée in her mid-thirties who had attended one of our seminars. She had been a suburban housewife most of her adult life, afflicted with the mental malady that often accompanies this profession: she had an image of herself as dependent, unworldly and (if the truth be known) superfluous. She "knew" this step didn't apply to her: after all, she had made no financial contribution to her marriage and was, to that day, ashamed of accepting the divorce settlement money—money she felt she hadn't earned. But, faithful to the warnings about every step being essential, she sent away for her Statement of Earnings—and learned that she had earned over $15,000 from assorted odd jobs during those years of her marriage when she was contributing "nothing." In the mirror of that statement, she saw herself for the first time as a competent wage-earner. Merely doing this step gave her the confidence to apply for and land a job at twice the salary she had previously assumed she was worth.

Useful Attitudes

No shame, no blame. This step may bring feelings of self-criticism—even shame—to the surface. Here's a way to work those through gently, a valuable exercise that people use to help them thoroughly "change their minds" and learn to think in new ways. Some people call it by its Sanskrit name, mantra, but it's really any simple word or phrase that embodies a particular attitude or attribute you want to focus on. Counting to ten is a sort of mantra for people who are quick to anger. Very often parents and other people who deal on a regular basis with irrational behavior will repeat "Patience, patience, patience" before responding to the latest crisis. A mantra is like a rudder, something that allows you to steer your mind away from danger and toward a clear, open horizon. A useful mantra for following this financial program is "No shame, no blame."

In choosing to change unwanted behavior, there is a difference between "recrimination" and "discrimination." Recrimination is about shame and blame, good and evil, while discrimination sorts out the true from the false. Sinking into blame and shame slows your progress toward financial freedom. Recrimination immobilizes, demoralizes and distracts you. Discrimination, however, simply shines a bright light on potential pitfalls so that you can skirt them.

You may stumble repeatedly over the desire to blame yourself (or other people) based on what you learn by following this program. At those times, remember discrimination and remember the mantra: No shame, no blame. As a case in point, your lifetime earnings represent just *a* number, not *your* number. That figure is neither too much nor too little. It does not prove your worth or your unworthiness; it is justification neither for despair because none of the money is left nor for gloating because your friend earned so much less.

Impeccability. This step is one of the foundation stones of this program. It will influence the efficacy of the following eight steps. Since accuracy and accountability are called for in every step of the program, starting out impeccably sets a good example for you to live up to. Not only that, but doing this step impeccably may even get you a better job with better pay. So check again. Have you *really* done this step with integrity? Have you really searched your files and your memory banks for *all* your income? Look at your reasons for doing a less-than-impeccable job on this step. Have you used similar reasons to step back from other challenges? People who do a half-hearted job often get a life to match!

CHECKLIST

1. Statement of earnings from Social Security
2. Income-tax returns
3. Checkbook records
4. Old and current bankbooks

5. Gifts
6. Winnings
7. Loans
8. Capital gains
9. Illegal sources
10. Contract labor not reported to the IRS (tips, baby-sitting, errands)

B. WHAT HAVE YOU GOT TO SHOW FOR IT?

For the years you have been working for wages, a certain amount of money (which you just calculated) has entered your life. The amount that is left in your life now is your *net worth*.

Be Prepared. You will be calculating your net worth (your total assets minus your total liabilities), perhaps for the first time in your life. Brace yourself. You may discover that you are deeply in debt, and until this moment you have been unaware of the awful extent of it. Now is the time to face that truth. It's like getting on the bathroom scale after the holidays: there's a little sting, and then the chance to make some changes. On the other hand, you may make the delightful discovery that you are in a position to be financially independent *now*. Many people have made that discovery, simply from doing this step.

There is an implied challenge in the phrasing of this step: "What have you got to show for it?" Say it out loud. Use different intonations. It usually comes out sounding a bit critical—snotty, even. Your commitment to Financial Integrity is stronger than your faintheartedness, however. So on with it: What do you have to show for all those dollars that have entered your life? Let's find out.

***Creating a Personal Balance Sheet* simply means going through your material universe and listing everything you own (*assets*) and everything you owe (*liabilities*).**

Liquid Assets

Cash, or anything that can easily be converted to cash, belongs in this category. Include the following:

- Cash on hand—include the piggybank, the change on your dresser, the emergency money hidden in the glove compartment.
- Savings accounts. Look for old bankbooks that you may have forgotten about, and that account that you opened with the minimum $100 to get the Free Bonus Digital Doohickey.
- Checking accounts.
- Savings certificates or certificates of deposit.
- U.S. savings bonds (including that one that you got as a graduation gift and have since forgotten).
- Stocks. List at current market value.
- Bonds. List at current market value.
- Mutual funds. List at current market value.
- Money market funds. List at current market value.
- Brokerage account credit balance.
- Life insurance cash value.

Fixed Assets

In listing these, start with the obvious: the market value of your major possessions—e.g., your house, your car (or cars). Contact a realtor for the current market value of your house. Consult the "blue book" (available at a bank or at your library) for the going price on the make, model and year of your car.

Go through your attic, basement, garage and storage shed. Itemize everything, without subjective evaluations like "That's worthless." Have fortitude. This process alone has stopped several inveterate pack rats, tinkerers and collectors with garages full of real treasures.

Go through every room of your house and inventory *everything*. Look up at those decorative light fixtures. Look down at that rug. How about the nice walnut shelves you put in a few years ago, and those Indian artifacts? Confront your clutter squarely. Be thorough, but not irrational—that is, not every knife, spoon, and fork has to be listed individually, but do list separately that expensive rosewood-handled carving set with the mahogany case. And the two sets of dishes that are still in their packing crates.

Give an approximate cash value to everything you own. That means *current* cash value, what you could get for each item at a swap meet, consignment shop or garage sale. For help in pricing your possessions, look through your newspaper's "For Sale" classifieds and your local "penny-saver" weekly. Spend a Saturday strolling through a swap meet, jotting down prices of items similar to those you own. Get your more valuable personal or household items appraised.

Don't ignore anything. One person's useless junk is another's precious antique. Just because you don't value an item doesn't mean it has no value.

Don't overlook debts owed to you, at least those you can reasonably expect to collect. Include security deposits on utilities, phone, house or apartment rental.

Any material that can be converted into cash should be listed.

You are playing the role of appraiser for your own estate. Let it be an enjoyable exercise. You needn't sell any of it if you don't choose to, so don't let sentimentality deter you from your inventory. In fact, don't allow *any* emotions to waylay you. Don't let grief dissuade you from assigning a cash value to the power tools your husband left behind. Don't let embarrassment about your compulsive spending discourage you from pricing the twenty pairs of shoes sitting in your closet unworn. Don't let guilt keep you from cataloging all the exercise paraphernalia you bought and have never used. Instead, rejoice! You are finally discovering the *real* value of that stationary bicycle and rebounder: not the pounds you'll lose but the price they'll command at a garage sale.

While some people can knock this exercise off in a day or two, one woman took three months to do her inventory. She went through every box, looked at every photo and opened every drawer and cupboard, not only listing the items, but recalling how and why each had come into her life. The process led her into a deep experience of gratitude for what she already had. So much dissatisfaction comes from focusing on what we *don't* have that the simple exercise of acknowledging and valuing what we *do* have can transform our outlook. Indeed, some people would say that, once we're above the survival level, the difference between prosperity and poverty lies simply in our degree of gratitude.

Liabilities

This category includes all your debts, whether payable in money, goods or services—everything you owe, from loans to bills outstanding.

If you list as an asset the current market value of your house, include as a liability the balance owed on it. Do the same with the balance on your car payments.

Don't forget to include bank loans or loans from friends, credit card debts, educational loans and unpaid medical and dental bills.

Net Worth

Add the figures for liquid assets and fixed assets, and subtract from that the figure for liabilities. In the most simplified, concrete, material sense, this is your current net worth. That is what you currently have to show for your total lifetime income; the rest is memories and illusions, as far as the reality of balance sheets is concerned.

We do not include your nonmaterial assets: your education, the skills you have acquired, the goodwill you've bought by treating everyone to a free round of drinks, the tax-deductible receipt from United Way, the well-adjusted personality that cost you eight years of therapy to get, the increased business that comes your way because you belong to the "right" club. Valuable as these may be, they are all intangibles, and as such are impossible to evaluate in the crisp, numeric, objective ways that we are learning to apply to our personal finances.

After completing this evaluation of net worth, some people come to the sober realization that they actually have a negative net worth; some are surprised at how little they have to show for their lifetime earnings; and others are amazed at the quantity and value of the possessions on which they have spent their lifetime earnings.

Whatever you find, it's important to remember that *net* worth does not equal *self* worth.

WHY DO A BALANCE SHEET?

1. While it may not initially appear so, this point in the program is very encouraging. So far your financial life has had very little direction or consciousness. Financially speaking, you have been like someone driving around without any destination—burning gas, spinning your wheels and getting nowhere. You may have many happy memories and other intangibles, but only a few real souvenirs that could be

converted into cash. With the full power and clear direction that taking the reins of your financial affairs will give you, you will have the ability to be far more effective in the world.

2. You now have an overview of your financial status and can objectively choose whether or not to convert some of your fixed assets into cash, thus increasing your savings—or getting a bit further out of debt.

One person, upon completing this step, realized that she could liquidate her excess possessions, invest the proceeds and have enough interest income to immediately be financially independent in comfort and style. While she didn't choose to do that right away, the awareness itself allowed her to take more risks in the direction of her real love, art—and she is still doing the other steps and getting tremendous value.

Another individual realized that he had many possessions that he wasn't using and no longer wanted, but had been hanging on to because he "just might need them someday." His creative solution was to sell these belongings and set aside the proceeds to be used to replace any of them he might find himself in need of in the future. Meanwhile, his money was earning interest, his life became simpler, and someone who really needed those items was getting use out of them.

And remember, **No shame, no blame.** In creating your balance sheet, many feelings associated with your material universe may arise: sadness, grief, nostalgia, hope, guilt, shame, embarrassment, anger. A dispassionate and compassionate attitude can go a long way toward making this step truly enlightening—i.e., able to lighten the physical and emotional loads you've been toting around for so many years.

CHECKLIST FOR CREATING YOUR BALANCE SHEET

Assets, Liquid
Cash on hand
Savings accounts
Checking accounts
Savings certificates or certificates of deposit
U.S. savings bonds
Stocks

Bonds
Mutual funds
Money market funds
Brokerage account credit balance
Life insurance cash value

Assets, Fixed
House
Vacation home
Car(s)
Furniture
Antiques
Art
Clothes
Stereo equipment
TV(s)
Wedding dress
Shoes/handbags
Lamps
Jewelry
Debts owed you
Security deposits
Office: typewriter(s), computer(s)
Sports equipment
Bicycle/motorcycle
Silverware
Bathroom: scales, towels
Kitchen: refrigerator, stove, microwave
Power tools

Liabilities
Bank loans
School loans
Credit card debts
Loans from friends
Unpaid bills: medical, dental
Balance on house

Balance on car
Other time payments

With the completion of this step you have entered the here and now. You have examined and come to terms with your past relationship with money, and you have seen how much money you have been able to earn and what you currently have to show for it in measurable terms. You are now ready to look at the present.

SUMMARY OF STEP 1

A. Find out how much money you have earned in your lifetime.
B. Create a balance sheet of your assets and liabilities. What do you have to show for the money you've earned?

2

MONEY AIN'T WHAT IT USED TO BE—AND NEVER WAS

It wasn't too difficult for **Jason and Nedra Weston** *to do Step 1. Jason, a twenty-two-year-old idealist, had been "allergic" to money for many years. He grew his hair long, rented a small room in a house in a rural area and considered deep conversation the best entertainment money could buy. Even though (or because?) he had "avoided" money, he had accumulated a $5,000 debt that he planned to pay off "someday." When he met Nedra in 1983, he was attracted to the thoughtful and dedicated person inside her, not to her life-style. It was only after falling in love that he discovered she was $15,000 in debt. Like so many young people, Nedra had equated being on her own with accumulating possessions, furnishing an apartment and going into debt. Debt was a way of life for young urban professionals and Nedra was in no rush to pay it off. Paying the interest was less of a burden than paying the debt, especially since she had other things she wanted to do with her time. So she worked intermittently as an administrative assistant to cover immediate expenses and gave her all to personal growth and volunteering for organizations she believed in. There was plenty of time to pay the debt—later. When Jason and Nedra moved in together, most of her furniture and possessions went into storage. Even then, Nedra wasn't quite ready to kiss her acquisitiveness good-bye. She was as leery of Jason's austerity as he was of her penchant for shopping. Then they came to our financial seminar, and Nedra saw the disparity between her desire to make a difference in the world and her desire to ignore the implications of her mounting debt. How could she be free to do the things that mattered to her if she was locked into servicing her debt? She made a commitment to examine and question her attachment to "having* *nice things." Jason, in turn, agreed not to push her, to let her discover what was right for her rather than pressure her to comply with his value system. They decided to get married, and Jason said "I do" not only to his beloved, but to tripling his debt. Doing Step 1 forced them to face the fact that they had a net worth of* minus *$20,000—and a new way of life was born for both of them.*

If you've done Step 1 for yourself, you too know how much you are worth.

Or do you? Like the Westons, you have a dollar figure (we hope a positive one), but what, if anything, does that mean? Our task now is to unravel the mystery of money. What *is* money, anyway? This is an important task because we can't have an effective working relationship with anything (or anyone) when we don't know what (or who) it is —or worse, when we identify it as something it is not. Without a universally and consistently true definition of money, our handling of this substance is anywhere from inept to insane, and almost always incapable of getting us what we think we want.

Before you rush ahead like an eager student to "find out the right answer" (i.e., *our* answer), take a moment now and write down the most accurate definition of money you know. What is a universally and consistently true definition of money?

Done? Then join us for a journey into the depths of money, as we seek that absolute truth.

CONTEMPLATING MONEY

Normally, when we talk about money, we are really talking about what to do about it. How to get it, spend it, invest it, save it, pay (or avoid paying) our taxes with it, and ensure that we'll have plenty of it in our old age. Hate it or love it, rail against it or lust for it, accuse it of evil or praise it for all the good it can do, money itself is a fact of life. Yet most of us understand it far less than we do those other "facts of life." And almost none of us has stood in its presence the way we might with a redwood, a Rembrandt or a starry desert night. We may worship it, pay homage to it or sacrifice our lives for it—but we don't contemplate it.

What *is* money? What are we contemplating when we contemplate money?

Money as an object of contemplation is like a koan—that unanswerable sort of question meditated on in Zen Buddhism. What is the sound of one hand clapping? What is the reality of money? You can even imagine silent monks gliding through manicured gardens, whittling away at their rational minds with such an inscrutable question. "What *is* money?" is the perfect koan for soul-sick M.B.A.'s who turn to religion when the market lets them down.

Our first impulse might be to get some dollar bills or coins out of our wallet and place them on a small altar. We could then sit down in front of it, straighten our spines, relax our shoulders, steady our breath and . . . contemplate "money." But what is there in front of us isn't money; it's just the physical form of our nation's currency, and it has no intrinsic value. You can't eat it, you can't wear it and in many parts of the world you can't even buy anything with it. These pieces of paper and metal can't be what money *is*.

What, then, *is* money?

To answer this question we have to widen our horizons. We must observe not only the material level of money but, going beyond "stuff," the nonmaterial aspects as well.

THE FOUR PERSPECTIVES OF MONEY

Let's illustrate this broader perspective by taking a little trip to see the landscape of money from ever-higher perspectives. We'll use the image of a city as a metaphor for this—while this image will be most vivid for city dwellers, most of us have some acquaintance with metropolitan areas. We'll start out at the street level of Major Metropolis, U.S.A., travel in an elevator to the observation deck of a downtown office building, the Tower of Baubles, hop onto a news and traffic helicopter to get a more comprehensive view and then catch an airplane for an even broader vista.

1. The Street-Level Perspective of Money—
The Practical, Physical Realm

We start out at ground level. What we see is the normal chaos of city life: people walking in all directions, some purposeful, some ambling, looking in shop windows. Cars, trucks and buses honk and belch and screech up and down the street. Couriers whiz by on bicycles and mopeds. Vendors push carts. A few street people hold out cups or hats. The sounds are so numerous and varied that they seem to disappear into one background roar. Simply crossing the street is perilously close to risking your life. Actually finding where you fit into the dissonance of this one city street would be a challenge.

This represents the everyday, "pedestrian" perspective of money. It has to do not only with the physical pieces of paper and metal but also with all of our financial transactions from cradle to grave. Our first allowance. Our efforts to get a job. Our efforts to get a better job. Indeed, this realm encompasses all of our paid employment. In addition, this is where we learn money management. How and where to bank. The difference between a checking account and a savings account. The difference between a CD and a money market account. How to get a loan. What a mortgage is. How to comparison-shop for price and quality. How to balance a checking account. IRA's. IRS. Which insurance to buy—health, life, homeowner, disability, automotive, jewelry? What deductibles and riders and premiums are. Then there's investing. Knowing the differences among and advantages of municipal bonds, zero coupon bonds, Fannie Maes, Sallie Maes and Freddie Macs. Buying and selling stocks, and futures, and options, and junk bonds. And we mustn't forget that all-American rite of passage—the credit card, ticket to the American Dream. Which often leads to that all-too-common midlife crisis, filing for bankruptcy. Chapter 11. Then there's tax planning and retirement planning. Income averaging. Keogh plans. Trust funds. Charitable donations. Wills. Burial insurance.

From the simplest information to the most sophisticated formulas, this street-level perspective represents the whole range of financial transactions we encounter during our lives. Most books about money educate us on how to navigate this street level more skillfully and more profitably. It is here that we dance to the beat of the "more is better" mambo, rarely, if ever, listening to that different drummer.

More, Better and Different

Notice, too, that this level is where most of our financial woes seem to exist—and where we look for the solution. If we are dissatisfied with our clothes or car or house, we shop for new ones. If we're short on cash, we know we need to beg, borrow, steal or earn more. That's obvious. Or is it? As a friend once said, "Every time I get ends to meet, someone moves the other end." He, and most of the rest of us, keep doing "more, better or different" within the same limited field of options and opportunities, without ever questioning whether or not the game is worth playing at all or whether there might be a better game to play.

For example, the majority of individual investors probably have no business being in the stock market. They base their decisions on hunches, whims, what they should have done last week, what their broker tells them and their own uneducated assessment of the future. In other words, they rush in where angels, and professionals, fear to tread. When they lose money on a stock, however, do they step back and reassess their motives and qualifications for being in the market? No. They decide they should buy more stock, a better stock or a different stock so that they can recoup their losses.

How do "more, better and different" work in *your* life? Have you ever noticed that for every so-called solution, another problem appears? Trying to solve our financial problems solely at this physical level is like manipulating the pieces on a game board without getting a bird's-eye view of the game itself.

Not that this level isn't important. It's part of the fabric and folk knowledge of our culture, and every high-school student should graduate with the knowledge of at least the fundamentals.

Unfortunately, neither ***Jason*** *nor* ***Nedra*** *(nor most other people) had that education. Nedra didn't understand the implications of buying "on time." She believed she could afford the "low monthly payments" and never assessed the long-term cost of her apartment full of furniture and her closets full of clothes. The notion of investing savings was way beyond her reach—she never accumulated enough savings to invest. The extent of her fiscal responsibility was paying her bills and balancing her checkbook. Jason was equally undereducated about money, but his ignorance showed up in different ways. Ever since leaving home after graduation from high school he'd sidestepped money* *fairly adroitly. He lived with a group devoted to growth and honesty and traded chores for room and board. For the minimal cash flow he needed to exist in twentieth-century North America he took on odd jobs—as an aide for the handicapped, or a driver for a courier service. With regard to money, Jason and Nedra were functionally illiterate—and not very different from many of their peers.*

Clearly there must be more to money than what we've explored up to now. Even with "financial literacy" some people thrive while others perish. Our investigation of money can't stop here. So let's go inside the steel-and-glass forty-story office building, the Tower of Baubles, and take the elevator up to the observation deck, where our perspective increases, our horizons widen and another aspect of money comes into view.

2. The Neighborhood Perspective of Money—
The Emotional/Psychological Realm

From the observation deck, we can look down on all the confusion of the street and see how it fits into the neighborhood. We see an orderly pattern in the bustle of people. We see them leaving one building and walking three blocks to another building. They have origins and destinations. We see kids playing on side streets, with their mothers watching from the steps of a housing project. We see people shopping for groceries and stopping to talk with one another. The apparently random activity of the street level becomes coherent as we begin to see how the actions of people and vehicles relate to one another. This neighborhood perspective could represent the first "nonmaterial" level of money, the emotional and mental glue that holds together daily interactions with money. This is the level of our personal thoughts and feelings about money—our money style or personality. Are you impulsive? Cautious? Competitive? Generous? A show-off? A miser? A sexist ("My husband/wife takes care of all that")? A worrier? An ostrich? A snob? Hopelessly helpless? At this level we come to see how our own attitudes about money were shaped by the psychological environment we grew up in.

Did your family consider itself rich, poor or just average? Did you grow up in a family where money was discussed openly? Or was it considered impolite to talk about money? Did you have an allowance? Did you have to earn it by doing chores? Did it set you apart from your peers because you had less or more money than others? Who handled the money in your family? How did they feel about it? Did you grow up believing your family had enough money to buy you anything you really wanted and needed? If your parents said no to one of your desires, was it because of money? In your family did you associate money with rewards? With arguments? With never seeing your father? What were the messages your parents gave you about money? The vast majority of divorces are over money, as you can well imagine once you understand how each of us is brought up in a different financial environment. Just answering these questions could be life-changing. Take a moment to reflect on them. Or take an evening with your mate and share your answers. Mine them for all they are worth.

There are books and even therapists to help us understand our particular money personality and to correct the dysfunctional patterns of our money behavior. We can readily see that understanding this first nonmaterial aspect of money could help us make better choices back at the street level of money. Knowing your financial psychology is another level of sophistication about money.

This second perspective of money also encompasses what money means to us, our money mythology. We should be aware as we explore these deeper myths that our rational minds may deny what our behavior reveals. We may say we're not superstitious, but we still walk around ladders. We may say that money is simply bits of paper and metal that we manage either well or poorly, but our actions speak louder than words. We each live in an intricate web of beliefs about these bits of paper and metal.

What are some of *your* personal myths about money?

Money as Security

Is money security for you? Seeing money as security—a buffer between our fragile, vulnerable selves and the cold, cruel and often unpredictable world—is one of the most common perceptions. Indeed, for many people security is having money in the bank and a tenured position so that they can always get more. The hoarding behavior of people who equate money with security runs the gamut from penny-pinching (denying themselves not only luxuries but even downright necessities of life) to addictive interest in bargains (buy now, buy more, buy two) to compulsive saving (the pathological extreme of which involves stashing away sheaves of dollar bills in mattresses and cardboard boxes). For many people, financial security means emotional security. We see people using money to defend against unpleasant emotional states like fear, worry, anxiety and loneliness through buying companions, bodyguards, accountants, friends, memberships in the right organizations and, when all else fails, therapists to clean up the mess.

Actually, the belief that money is security is one of the more rational insanities you can have. If you live in this culture, it is appropriate to give credence to this belief to the extent that we can feed, clothe and shelter ourselves adequately. But if you were a courier walking through downtown Chicago at night with a briefcase filled with money handcuffed to your wrist, would you feel secure? If money were truly security, you would. So the myth that money is security is just that—a myth.

Money as Power

What about power? Is money power to you? Do you act as though the road to power were paved with money? Do you believe in the "power of the purse strings"? It would seem that a person in the position of giving or withholding money can command compliance and loyalty (or at least the appearance of it) from those dependent on him or her—family, employees, favorite charities. Do you believe that without a costly college education (or without an exorbitantly expensive Ivy League college education) you are doomed to failure?

Money seems to bestow a power to do what you want to do and go where you want to go, when you want to. Money also gives the power *not* to do something you don't care to do—you can pay someone else to do it.

But if money is power, how do you account for the power of someone like Gandhi? The kind of power that freed India from the British had nothing to do with money, but with what Gandhi labeled *satyagraha*, or "soul force." Money had no potency when faced with the indomitable will of Gandhi and his followers, people who lived a life of what we would call poverty and yet experienced irrepressible joy and exerted tremendous influence.

While in our culture there is some validity to the notion that money is powerful, if we act from this myth we miss the many opportunities to exercise "soul power"—and are vastly weaker for the error.

Money as Social Acceptance

Some of us operate from the myth that money is social acceptance. The urge to be part of a group is a deep one. To be excluded is experienced, on an unconscious level, as a threat to survival. The desire to keep up with the Joneses may not be grounded solely in ostentation and competition, but also in a profound desire for acceptance by others. Our advertising industry capitalizes on our epidemic low self-esteem by promoting products to make us more tolerable to our fellow humans: we can smell better from head (shampoo) to toe (foot powder), have slimmer bodies and the right car, and learn how to dance—for money. Even friendship seems to cost money. Do you need to spend money to enjoy the company of your group of friends?

Let's look at another form of social acceptance: dating and mating. Historically and cross-culturally we know that money (or cows or goats or plots of land) almost always figured in the marriage contract. But what about our liberated society? Does money play a part in romance? Do we, on some level, still hold some belief that money represents success with the opposite sex?

As with the other misconceptions about money, operating from the myth that money equals acceptance seems to have some merit. After all, enjoying the company of other people while dining, seeing a movie or sunning on a beach is a pleasure you wouldn't want to eliminate simply because it costs money. It becomes dangerous only when we lose sight of the fact that companionship, friendship and intimacy are all available free of charge to people who sincerely extend their love to others. It's when we equate money with social acceptance that the distortions begin. It's like going to a fine restaurant which serves many delicious entrees and eating the menu rather than the meal. There's no joy in that, just as there is no joy in spending money to gain acceptance but never experiencing true intimacy.

Money as Evil

Perhaps you live in a world where money is seen as bringing sorrow and pain. In your personal mythology, is money evil? What does your behavior say? Does it say that money is dirty, dehumanizing or a tool of repression? Do you keep a mental catalog of the sins money has committed?

The notion that money is evil probably stems from the Biblical admonition that "the love of money is the root of all evil." It is our attachment to things over people that pushes us into wrong action. A moment of reflection should be enough for us to see that money doesn't hurt people—people hurt people. Money isn't evil—people sometimes choose to do evil things with money. Money isn't dirty—people do dirt to each other, and sometimes do it using money. Money is morally neutral. It is our addiction to what money can buy that leads us into deeds harmful to life.

Nedra*'s and* ***Jason****'s very different money personalities were a setup for either conflict or growth. Nedra grew up in a working-class family in Southern California. Her father died when she was young, so her mother worked to support the children. That left Nedra at home to do much of the mothering. After just two years at a Baptist college she dropped out, determined to live a worldly life with plenty of the material satisfactions she hadn't had growing up. One of Nedra's myths was that money meant happiness and "the good life." Jason's parents, on the other hand, were "alternative" from the word go and emphatically not into materialism. He grew up traveling in a school bus and marching for peace, and he went to sleep at night to the sound of his parents and their friends discussing politics into the wee hours. Jason examined his parents' values, found them sound and chose to continue living by them. Jason's money mythology included the belief that "money just wasn't important." And so Jason and Nedra, two young adults from two very different backgrounds, entered their marriage trying to blend two opposing economic points of view. The task, as daunting as it might seem, was no tougher than what most young married couples face.*

What About You?

Take a few minutes now to do a bit of brainstorming and see where *you* stand with money. What is your money personality? What are your thoughts about money? Your personal belief systems? What are your money quirks and myths? How have your relationships with others been influenced by your economic pride and prejudice? How does money relate to your personal sense of worth? As far as money goes, do you feel "one up" or "one down" as compared with those around you? What does money mean to you? Take a look at your behavior around money. Is it ever irrational? What does that tell you? This is the time to take a deeper look into what you have learned about money and how you relate to it—really. What is *your* money personality?

There is great value in healing the wounds that our money psychology and mythology may have inflicted on us and on others. It's clear that understanding this neighborhood perspective of money illuminates and informs our interactions with the physical reality of money. But it's equally clear that our internal money map is not the territory. There's more to do on this journey of discovering the truth about money. We still don't have a universally and consistently true definition of money.

3. The Citywide Perspective of Money—The Cultural Realm

From the observation deck we take off in the news and traffic helicopter to get an even more comprehensive view of the city. From here the people and cars at the street level fuse into a flow of motion. Neither the individuals nor their relationships to one another capture our attention. What takes our breath away is being able to see the whole city in one scan of the horizon. We pick out landmarks that identify the various neighborhoods, but rather than seeing each district as an island, we have an instant understanding that what binds the city together is more important than what separates its inhabitants in ethnic or economic enclaves. We are all part of this larger metropolitan entity. This citywide perspective of money encompasses the assumptions we all share about money, our cultural understanding about money. We live and die by the assumption that money is worth something. Money, the economists tell us, is a "store of value" and a "means of exchange."

Even though we refer to it as the almighty dollar, there's nothing sacred about money. Money is a human social invention, a mere 4,000 years old. In families, we (normally) don't charge for our household tasks of sweeping, dusting, cooking, child care and gardening. Nor do we pay for each meal we eat. It was once like that in clans and tribes as well. Eventually, however, transactions became too complex for straight barter. So, "on the eighth day" humans created money as an IOU for goods or services received. Money gets its value at the moment of trade. Money is simply a token, an essentially valueless marker for something that *theoretically,* at one time, had value to someone. But there are still plenty of people on earth who never touch the stuff. And despite our arrogance about the almighty dollar, it isn't honored everywhere in the world. Money is a "store of value" and a "means of exchange" only within the confines of cultural agreement. Yes, at a practical level in North America at the end of the twentieth century, most often money *is* a means of exchange. But we are trying to penetrate the deepest reality of money. We want to arrive at essence, not at K Mart.

This citywide perspective of money surveys not only the history of money and the principles of economics but the sociology and anthropology of money as well. Here we come to understand that our definition of money has been conditioned by many cultural forces—and this insight allows us even greater distance from it. For example, as North Americans we share some common assumptions about money and work—assumptions that an Italian or a native of the Amazon rain forest might well not share.

As we said in Chapter 1, one of our pervasive assumptions is that growth is good. Our economy depends on growth to survive—and we, as Americans, have absorbed that growth ethic into our own aspirations for our lives. If we have one car, we need two. If we have one pair of pants, we need two; if we have two, we need three. We ignore intellectual, emotional and spiritual growth, having gotten stuck trying to continue to grow physically by adding more and more possessions.

Fears That Rear Their Ugly Heads

It is at this level that we find a number of economic bogeymen: inflation, cost of living, recession and depression. If the Gross National Product is growing at a rate of 1 percent or below, we're said to be in a recession—and (whether or not our income is affected) we all feel the pinch. We take these economic indicators personally. If the economists tell us the cost of living is up, we automatically feel poorer, even though what's now included in the Consumer Price Index was a luxury item just twenty years ago, something we all did without and never missed—like staying in hotels or traveling by airplane. Likewise, we believe in inflation as tenaciously as children believe in invisible playmates. But we, the authors, haven't suffered from inflation for twenty years. By intelligent shopping (as discussed in Chapter 6) you can be exposed repeatedly to the fire of the marketplace and not get burned. While the price of housing in some parts of the United States may have gone up, many other prices have gone down, and 1950s luxury products are now available to 1990 consumers at discount department stores.

These specters—inflation, cost of living, recession and depression—frighten us into adherence to the economic recipe for well-being, "growth is good," and its corollary, the American myth of "more is better." And, like any religion based on fear, this economic creed keeps us bound by our own ignorance, depending on the priests at the Federal Reserve to preserve our safe passage from cradle to grave with our cost-of-living-adjusted incomes just narrowly outpacing the specter of inflation. As many of us discovered at the beginning of the 1990s, however, Our Lady of Perpetual Growth hasn't brought us the security and happiness we trusted would be ours for believing in her. Meanwhile, living in this never-never land of eternal immaturity has kept us from devoting that same energy to growth at other levels.

These "more is better, growth is good" cultural assumptions also breed in us subtle economic prejudices. We judge our own and others' importance by material yardsticks—the size of our paychecks, the size of our houses, the size of our portfolios. We "size" each other up—and feel one up or one down on the basis of these barely conscious assessments. From the citywide perspective, this informal caste system becomes quite apparent—in others and in ourselves.

*However different **Jason** and **Nedra** were psychologically, they were both children of "more is better" America. They just responded differently to the message. Nedra complied and Jason rebelled. But neither one of them was freely choosing a mature relationship with money and the material world. In a sense, Jason's "money isn't important" attitude was just as limiting as Nedra's search for happiness in tangible possessions. Because he refused to* *participate in the standard cultural job-and-money game, his choices in life were severely limited. He found that he spent more time in making do and making trades than he would have in working at a steady job. If asked, neither one of them would have acknowledged that they were living out their cultural programming. Neither one had taken Economics 101. Neither one even knew the classic definition of money as a "store of value." In this unconsciousness, too, they were typical. Who of us grows up with a clear cultural understanding of money?*

The broader economic and cultural understanding we gain from the helicopter sheds much light on our money psychology as well as on that activity so ironically called "making a living." We can see much better the reasons behind some of the strategies for making money in our particular cultural environment and the reason that some of our money madness appears to be sane—because that's what everyone thinks. This is the level we learn about at Harvard Business School or on Wall Street. While education on this level is illuminating, this perspective still doesn't give us a universally and consistently true definition of money, one that we can count on to apply in any situation. Understanding the many faces of money doesn't necessarily lead to truth.

4. The Jet Plane Perspective of Money—Personal Responsibility and Transformation

Now it's time to step back—to let go of all you *think* you know about money. Empty your mind. Like classic monks, we've exhausted our learned "truths" about money and are called to reach into an inner reservoir of Truth. Here is where we will discover the doorway to another realm of money. Our helicopter drops us at the airport and we take off in a jet to get an even higher perspective on money. With a roar we taxi down the runway and lift gracefully off the ground. Quickly we achieve an altitude from which we see the whole region. Here we recognize that the city itself is not the total world. Beyond the city limits, the agricultural and natural world rolls on to the horizon. From here we can see that all of our money beliefs and behaviors come from having chosen to live in this particular city. Beyond the borders of the city, other choices are available. You are not a prisoner of Major Metropolis, U.S.A., destined to spend your life making money in the marketplaces it offers. Even if you were born here, you have stayed by choice. This is where personal responsibility begins.

The definition of money we discover in this realm of personal responsibility cuts through the entangling web of thoughts, feelings, attitudes and beliefs. It is a qualitatively different definition, one that is universally and consistently true, and it returns to us the power we have unconsciously given over to money.

All our false notions about money thus far have one common flaw —they identify money as something external to ourselves. It is something we all too often don't have, which we struggle to get, and on which we pin our hopes of power, happiness, security, acceptance, success, fulfillment, achievement and personal worth. Money is the master and we the slaves. Money is the victor and we the vanquished.

What, then, is the way out? What is the one consistently true statement we can make about money that will allow us to be clear, masterful and powerful in our relationship with it?

Money is something we choose to trade our life energy for.

We will repeat this because you may have missed its full significance: **Money is something we choose to trade our life energy for.**

Our life energy is our allotment of time here on earth, the hours of precious life available to us. When we go to our jobs we are trading our life energy for money. This truth, while simple, is profound. Less obvious but equally true, when we go to the welfare office, we are trading our life energy for money. When we go to Reno, we are trading our life energy for money (we hope). Even windfalls like inheritances must in some way be "earned" to actually belong to the heir—life energy must be exchanged. Time is spent with lawyers, accountants, trustees, brokers and investment counselors to handle the money. Or time is spent in therapy working out the relationship with the deceased or the guilt at receiving all that money. Or time is spent investigating worthy causes to fund. All this is life energy traded for money.

This definition of money gives us significant information. Our life energy is more *real* in our actual experience than money. You could even say money *equals* our life energy. So, while money has no intrinsic reality, our life energy does—at least to us. It's tangible, and it's finite.

Life energy is all we have. It is precious because it is limited and irretrievable and because our choices about how we use it express the meaning and purpose of our time here on earth.

*When **Jason** and **Nedra** took our seminar in the early 1980s, the awareness that money = life energy transformed each of their relationships with money. For Nedra the formula cut through her denial about her debt. She saw, with considerable clarity and remorse, that the life energy coming in from her salary and the life energy she was spending to maintain her life-style would never add up to paying off her debt. It was no longer possible for her to use her credit card to plug the leaks in her financial ship. The load was too heavy, and using credit to pay for debt was like ripping planks off the side of the hull. She acknowledged that she was sinking. For Jason the formula made him see clearly that for all his best intentions to "make the world a better place," his stubborn financial ignorance made his efforts ineffectual. To be truly effective in his desire to make a difference in the world, he needed to master money. Wherever he went in the world to march or picket or build or heal, he must support himself or be a burden to others. While money and religion seem to be poles apart, for both Jason and Nedra the insight that money = life energy was an enlightening experience.*

Your Life Energy

What does "money = life energy" mean to you? After all, money is something you consider valuable enough to spend easily a quarter of your allotted time on earth getting, spending, worrying about, fantasizing about or in some other way reacting to. Yes, there are many social conventions regarding money that are worth learning and abiding by, but ultimately *you* are the one who determines what money is worth *to you*. It is *your* life energy. You "pay" for money with your time. You choose how to spend it.

If you are forty years old, you can expect to have approximately 329,601 hours (thirty-seven years) of life energy left before you die. (See Figure 2-1 for life expectancy at various ages.) Assuming about half of your time is spent on necessary body maintenance—sleeping, eating, eliminating, washing and exercising—you have 164,800 hours of life energy remaining for such discretionary uses as:

- your relationship to yourself
- your relationship to others
- your creative expression
- your contribution to your community
- your contribution to the world
- achieving inner peace and . . .
- holding down a job

Now that you know that money is something you trade life energy for, you have the opportunity to set new priorities for your use of that valuable commodity. After all, is there any "thing" more vital to you than your life energy?

A FIRST LOOK AT "FINANCIAL INDEPENDENCE"

As we said in the prologue, one purpose of this book is to increase your Financial Independence. By following the steps you will move

FIGURE 2-1

Age and Average Remaining Life Expectancy

Age	Average Remaining Life Expectancy: Years	Average Remaining Life Expectancy: Hours
20	56.3	493,526
25	51.6	452,326
30	46.9	411,125
35	42.2	369,925
40	37.6	329,601
45	33.0	289,278
50	28.6	250,708
55	24.4	213,890
60	20.5	179,703
65	16.9	148,145
70	13.6	119,218
75	10.7	93,796

Data taken from U.S. National Center for Health Statistics, *Vital Statistics of the United States*, annual. As printed in U.S. Bureau of the Census, *Statistical Abstract of the United States: 1991* (111th edition), Washington, D.C., 1991, p. 74.

inexorably toward Financial Integrity and Financial Intelligence and will one day (we hope before you die) arrive at Financial Independence. In showing you how this is possible, however, we must first show you what Financial Independence isn't.

Let's begin by exploring what images the phrase "Financial Independence" conjures up for you. Making a killing? Inheriting a fortune? Winning the lottery? Cruises, tropical islands, world travel? Jewels, Porsches, designer clothes? Most of us picture Financial Independence as an unreachable fantasy of inexhaustible riches.

This idea that Financial Independence means wealth comes out of the first, street-level perspective of money. This is Financial Independence at a material level. While it simply requires that we be rich, there's a hidden Catch-22. What is "rich"? Rich exists only in comparison to something or someone else. Rich is a helluva lot more than I have now. Rich is way more than most other people have. But we know the fallacy of the myth of more. More is like a mirage. We can never reach it because it isn't real. John Stuart Mill once said, "Men do not desire to be rich, only to be richer than other men." In other words, as soon as rich becomes available to the likes of us, it will no longer be rich.

It is at the jet plane perspective of money, in the realm of personal responsibility, where we find our first definition of true Financial Independence.

Our definition of Financial Independence cuts through the Gordian knot of not knowing what rich is. Financial Independence has nothing to do with rich. Financial Independence is the experience of having *enough*—and then some. Enough, you will remember, is found at the peak of the Fulfillment Curve. It is quantifiable, and you will define it *for yourself* as you work with the steps of this program. The old notion of Financial Independence as being rich forever is not achievable. Enough is. Enough for you may be different from enough for your neighbor—but it will be a figure that is real for you and within your reach.

Financial and Psychological Freedom

Your first step toward the experience of having **enough—and then some**—is extricating yourself from identification with the pedestrian level (the material reality of money), the neighborhood perspective (the psychological reality of money) and the citywide perspective (the cultural agreements about money). When you have done that, you have achieved Financial Independence, no matter how much money you have. And until you *can* do that, you will never be financially independent, no matter how much money you have.

Financial Independence is an experience of freedom at a psychological level. You are free from the slavery to unconsciously held assumptions about money, and free of the guilt, resentment, envy, frustration and despair you may have felt about money issues. You may have these feelings, but you have them the way you have an article of clothing—you can try it on, but you are free at any time to take it off. You are no longer compelled by the parental and social messages you received as a child—messages about how we *should* relate to money in order to be successful, respected, virtuous, secure and happy. You are free of the confusions you had about money. You are no longer intimidated by balancing your checkbook or by deciphering your broker's babble about no-load mutual funds and annuities. You never buy things you don't want or need and are immune to the seductiveness of malls, markets and the media. Your emotional fortunes are no longer tied to your economic fortunes; your moods don't swing with the Dow Jones Band. The broken record in your mind stops, the one that calculates hours till quitting time, days till payday, paydays till you have a down payment for a motorcycle, costs for the next home improvement project and years till retirement. The silence, at first, is thundering. Days and even weeks can go by without your thinking about money, without your mentally reaching for your wallet to handle life's challenges and opportunities.

When you are financially independent, the way money functions in your life is determined by you, not by your circumstances. In this way money isn't something that happens to you, it's something you include in your life in a purposeful way. From this point of view, the normal drama of "nine to five till you're sixty-five," of making a dying, of getting ahead, of being rich and famous—all these brass rings we automatically reach for—can be seen as just one series of choices among many. Financial Independence is being free of the fog, fear and fanaticism so many of us feel about money.

If this sounds like peace of mind, it is. Fiscal bliss. And if this sounds as unattainable as being rich, it isn't. It's been the experience of thousands of people who have followed the approach to money described in this book, who have done the practical steps and made the simple observations recommended.

Step 2: Being in the Present—Tracking Your Life Energy

How does this great truth—**money = life energy**—manifest itself in your life? When you thought money was just something to deal with, or that it was security, power or a tool of the devil, or that it was first prize in the All-American Carnival, you could rationalize your behavior in terms of should's and ought's. But now you know that money = life energy, *your* life energy, and you have a rising interest in knowing just how much of the stuff is actually passing through your hands. Step 2 on the road to financial freedom is where you satisfy this curiosity.

There are two parts to Step 2:

A. Establish the actual costs in time and money required to maintain your Job, and compute your *real* hourly wage.

B. Keep track of every cent that comes into or goes out of your life.

A. HOW MUCH ARE YOU TRADING YOUR LIFE ENERGY FOR?

We have established that money is simply something you trade life energy for. Now let's look at how much life energy (in hours) you are currently trading for how much money (in dollars)—i.e., how much money are you making for the amount of time you work?

Most people look at this life-energy/earnings ratio in an unrealistic and inadequate way: "I earn $440 a week, I work 40 hours a week, so I trade one hour of my life energy for $11."

It's not likely to be that simple.

Think of all the ways you use your life energy that are directly related to your money-earning employment. Think of all the monetary expenses that are directly associated with the job. In other words, if you didn't need that money-earning Job, what time expenditures and monetary expenses would disappear from your life?

Be Prepared . . . Some people resent their work—the hours of drudgery, the boredom, the office politics, the time away from what they really want to be doing, the personality conflicts with their boss or coworkers—and many feel powerless to change their circumstances. One response to those feelings of resentment and powerlessness is to spend money. "It was such a tough day that I deserve a little fun. Let's go out to dinner/dancing/a movie/the mall." So be prepared to discover how much you indulge yourself with "I hate my job" as the underlying reason.

Be prepared, too, to discover how much you spend on expensive alternatives to cooking, cleaning, repairs and other things that you would do yourself if you didn't have to work.

Be prepared to discover the many costs of career ambition, all the things you "must" have in order to continue up the ranks. The right car. The right clothes. The right vacation spots. The right house in the right neighborhood in the right city. The right private schools for your kids. Even the right therapist.

Using the following discussion as a stimulus, discover for yourself the *real* trade-offs in time and energy associated with keeping your nine-to-five Job. Not all of the categories will necessarily apply to you, and you may think of other categories relevant to you that are not mentioned here.

In the examples below we will assign *arbitrary* numeric values to these time and money trade-offs simply to generate a hypothetical tabulation. Any resemblance to your situation is purely accidental. At the end of the discussion we will tabulate these calculations and come up with an *actual* exchange rate of life energy for money—remembering that this "actual" hourly rate is still arbitrary, based on our hypothetical figures. (When you do your own calculations you will be using your actual figures and will figure out your own personal hourly wage.)

Commuting

Getting to and from work incurs an expenditure of time or money, or both, whether you drive, walk or take public transportation. For our purposes here, let's assume you commute by car. Don't forget to include parking fees and tolls for bridges or turnpikes, as well as wear and tear on your car. Let's say that you commute 1½ hours a day or 7½ hours a week at a cost, in gas and maintenance, of $50 a week. (If you use mass transit your figures will be somewhat different.)

7½ hours/week—$50/week

Costuming

Are the clothes you wear at work the same ones you wear on your days off or on vacations—or do you need a special wardrobe to be appropriately attired for your Job? This includes not just the obvious costumes like nurses' uniforms, construction workers' steel-toed boots and chefs' aprons, but also the tailored suits and the high-heeled shoes, the pantyhose and neckties that are the norm in offices. Look at those clothes. Would you wear a noose around your neck or walk around on three-inch heels every day if it weren't expected for the Job? Consider, too, the time and money spent on personal grooming, from aftershave to exotic cosmetics.

Quantify all your costuming activities, from shopping to putting on mascara, shaving, and tying your tie. Let's say you spend 1½ hours a week on this at an average cost of $15 a week (i.e., annual clothing expense divided by 52 weeks, plus cost of cosmetics).

1½ hours/week—$15/week

Meals

Extra costs, in time and money, for meals affected by your Job take many forms—for example, money for morning coffee and doughnuts, time spent in line in the employees' cafeteria, expensive convenience foods that you buy because you are too tired to cook dinner, unreimbursed restaurant expenses, weight-reduction programs that you enroll in because you ignored decent nutrition thanks to your busy Job.

Let's say you attend Weight Watchers 1 hour a week and spend 50 minutes each day at lunch for 4 hours a week, totaling 5 hours a week. Your lunches at the local deli cost about $15 a week more than if you made lunch at home, and the espresso breaks you treat yourself to as a reward for working come to $5 a week. Total spent: $20.

5 hours/week—$20/week

Daily Decompression

Do you come home from your Job zestful and full of life, joyously launching into personal or planetary projects, or into intimate sharing with your family or other loved ones? Or are you tired and drained, taciturnly lurching into the soft chair in front of the television set, beer or martini in hand, because "It's been such a day"? If it takes a while for you to "decompress" from the pressures of the Job, that "while" is a Job-related expense. A wild guess would put this at 5 hours a week and $20 a week in recreational substances.

5 hours/week—$20/week

Escape Entertainment

Notice that common phrase "escape entertainment." Escape from what? What is the prison or restrictive circumstance from which you must flee? If your experience of life were consistently fulfilling and exciting, from what would you escape? Would those hours in front of the television or movie screen be necessary? Take a look at scenarios like "It's been such a heavy week at work, let's have a night on the town to blow it off!" or "Let's get away from it all this weekend and go to Vegas!" Would these be necessary? What are the costs in life energy and money? How much of your weekend entertainment do you consider your just reward for sticking it out at a boring Job? Let's assign this whole area 5 hours a week and $20 a week.

5 hours/week—$20/week

Vacations and Expensive Playthings

If what you did *every day* were truly satisfying, providing you with a sense of accomplishment and inner fulfillment, of real contribution to the lives of those around you and to the global family, would you want to "vacate"? Would you need that trip to Hawaii? How about the vacation home, boat or recreational vehicle that you use only a few weeks each year just to "get away"? What proportion of the time and money involved in such pursuits is due to the Job? Consider the dues for the country club or your professional organization: would you belong if it weren't for your Job? String this all out, divide by 52, and you might have 5 hours a week and $20 a week.

5 hours/week—$20/week

Job-Related Illness

What percentage of illness is Job-related—induced by stress, by physical work conditions, by the desire to have a "legitimate" reason to take time off from work, or by conflict with employers or fellow employees? More and more medical evidence indicates that a good percentage of illness is psychosomatic. Stated simply, happy, fulfilled people are healthier. In our own experience over the years we have seen considerably less illness and illness-caused absenteeism in volunteers than in paid employees.

For this category a more subjective "inner sensing" is the only way to evaluate what percentage of medical costs (time and money) is attributable to your Job. Let's imagine that in the course of a year you'll be out of commission due to Job-related illness for a week, at an out-of-pocket cost of $15 a week for exotic remedies not covered by insurance.

1 hour/week—$15/week

Other Job-Related Expenses

Examine your balance sheet of assets and liabilities (Step 1). Are items listed there that you wouldn't have bought had they not been directly related to your Job? Look at what you pay "servants": would you need a housekeeper, gardener, handyman or mechanic if you didn't have a Job? Day-care expenses for single parents or two-income families take a big chunk out of your salary and wouldn't be necessary if you didn't have a Job. Do a time log for a typical week. How many hours accounted for are strictly Job-related? Things like reading the classified ads looking for another Job or social evenings to "network" for business. Are the hours of taking your frustrations about work out on your mate a Job-related activity? As you progress through the other steps in this program, make special note of such hidden Job-related expenses.

FIGURE 2–2

Life Energy vs. Earnings: What Is Your *Real* Hourly Wage?

	Hours/Week	Dollars/Week	Dollars/Hour
Basic Job (before adjustments)	40	440	11
Adjustments			
Commuting	+7½	−50	
Costuming	+1½	−15	
Meals	+5	−20	
Decompression	+5	−20	
Escape entertainment	+5	−20	
Vacation	+5	−20	
Job-related illness	+1	−15	
Time and money spent on maintaining Job (total adjustments)	+30	−160	
Job, with adjustments (actual total)	70	280	4

Every dollar spent represents 15 minutes of life energy.

Don't overlook Job-enhancement expenses, such as educational programs, books, tools and conferences. Remember, your situation is unique, but the basic ideas will apply. Discover your own categories of Job-related time and money expenses.

Your *Real* Hourly Wage

Now compile these figures and create a table, *adding* the approximate extra Job-related hours to your normal "work week" and *subtracting* the Job-related expenses from your usual pay. On longer-term items like vacations or illness, simply prorate over 50 weeks (1 year minus 2 weeks for your vacation). A $1,000 vacation that you wouldn't have taken if you enjoyed your Job would be computed as $1,000 divided by 50 weeks equals $20 a week . . . and so on.

The specific entries will be approximations, of course, but with diligence you can come up with fairly accurate figures.

Figure 2-2 illustrates this process of calculating your real hourly wage—as well as a corollary figure: the number of minutes of your life that every dollar you spend represents. Remember, the numbers are arbitrary, chosen solely for their "round number" value. Your figures will probably be considerably different from these, as might your categories.

The Bottom Line: Figure 2-2 clearly shows that you are actually selling an hour of your life energy for $4, not the apparent $11. Your *real* hourly wage is $4. A good question to ask at this point is: Are you willing to accept a Job that pays this hourly wage? (You should make this calculation every time you change your Job—or change your Job-related habits.)

The corollary figure is also interesting. In this example, every dollar you spend represents 15 minutes of your life. Think of that figure next time you're shelling out your money for yet another gazingus pin. Ask: Is this item worth 120 minutes of my life energy?

Notice that our calculations have ignored such intangibles as time spent on planning strategies for moving up the corporate ladder, time handling deteriorating family life due to Job demands, and time and expenses incurred in maintaining a life-style in line with the Job.

When ***Larry Graham*** *did the first part of Step 2, his life turned upside down. He had been working as a project manager in the construction industry for some ten years. "I was unhappy with what I did for a living," he wrote, "but income equaled expenses, so I went on with the attitude of 'Well, that's life in the big city.' " Then Larry did Step 2 and calculated his* ***real*** *hourly wage. "After I analyzed our spending patterns, it became clear that nearly half of what I made was spent on the job; that is, spent on gas, oil, repairs, lunches, a little here, a little there, and most of it unrecoverable. In short, I could stay home, work part-time where I live and actually save money by making half of what I formerly made." It was then, when he realized he could give up this job and pursue his real desires and goals, that everything changed. Affairs in his financial life that he'd procrastinated about handling for years got handled—everything from paying off credit cards to eliminating restaurant lunches to being able to have money discussions with his wife without the old arguments. As he rearranged his financial world, he and his wife recognized that they could survive quite well on her paycheck from a job she loved (teaching the educationally handicapped), and he could go back to school to train for the career he'd always wanted as a counselor and therapist. "We're actually feeling less stress because we're focused on healing our crazy relationship with money, not just [focused on] the bucks."*

Why Do This Step?

Why is this exercise essential to a transformed relationship with money?

1. This exercise puts paid employment into real perspective and points out how much you are actually getting paid, which is the bottom line.

2. It allows you to assess current and future employment realistically, in terms of actual earnings. It is useful to apply the information gathered in this step to prospective Jobs: a Job that requires a longer commute or has more costuming expectations might be less remunerative in reality than one with a lower salary. Compare Job offers from the *true* perspective of how much you are really selling your life energy for.

3. Knowing the financial bottom line for your Job will help to clarify further your motives for working and for selecting one Job over another. Larry Graham's story is not an anomaly. Many, many people spend all of their income and then some on maintaining their Job—and consider themselves fortunate. Another "FIer" said that doing this step increased his consciousness of unnecessary Job-related expenses to such an extent that his net earnings per hour doubled. Once he recognized how many of his expenses were due to his Job he was able to reduce or even eliminate many of them. For example, he began bringing his own lunch instead of sending out to the deli, switched from driving to using mass transit (doubling the benefit of this choice by using the time for decompression on the way home), reevaluated the supposed need for so many changes of stylish clothes, and began taking a daily walk with his wife (thus improving their relationship as well as their health). Someone else used the results of this step as a criterion for accepting or rejecting Jobs. When she could figure out just what hourly wage she'd be getting, she could see very clearly whether or not the Job was worth it to her. Indeed, there are some Jobs that she might have applied for previously that she now doesn't even consider.

Is it coincidence that "Job" is also the name of the Old Testament character who was plagued by difficulties? "The trials of Job" takes on a whole new meaning; many of us have certainly pondered Job's question "Why me, Lord?" as we've bucked rush hour traffic or endured excruciating tedium.

No Shame, No Blame

And remember . . . this is where your feelings about your work/job/identity will most strongly bubble to the surface. Compassionate self-awareness is the key. Just notice each feeling as it presents itself, without criticizing it—and without criticizing your job, your boss, yourself or this book as good or bad. So what if you've been paying to work? So what if you've been blowing every paycheck on "rewarding" yourself for surviving another week? So what if you've been leading a fast-track life-style on a $4-an-hour paycheck? That's all in the past. It's what you needed to do before you knew that money = your life energy.

CHECKLIST: LIFE ENERGY VS. SALARY

	Time *hrs/week more*	*Money* *$/week less*
Commuting:		
wear and tear for commute miles		
gas and oil		
public transportation		
parking fees		
tolls		
tires		
walking or bicycling		
Costuming:		
clothes bought for work		
makeup bought for work		
impressive briefcase		
shoes bought for work		
shaving for work		
Meals:		
coffee breaks		
lunches		
entertaining for work		
food rewards for unpleasant Job		
convenience food		

CHECKLIST: LIFE ENERGY VS. SALARY (cont.)

	Time hrs/week more	*Money $/week less*
Daily decompression:		
time till kids can yell again		
additional time till civil		
recreational substances		
time till able to work productively		
Escape entertainment:		
movies		
bars		
HBO		
weekend retreats		
Vacations, expensive playthings:		
vacation to ______		
exercise equipment		
sports equipment		
boat		
summer home		
country club dues		
Job-related illness:		
colds, flu, etc.		
hospitalizations		
Other job-related expenses:		
hired help to:		
clean house		
mow lawn		
fix car		
wash and iron clothes		
babysit		
day care for kids		
educational programs		
color consultant		
magazines (trade)		
conferences		
tutors for kids		
special telecommunications systems to keep yourself current		

B. KEEP TRACK OF EVERY CENT THAT COMES INTO OR GOES OUT OF YOUR LIFE

So far we have established that money equals life energy, and we have learned to compute just how many hours of life energy we exchange for each dollar. Now we need to become conscious of the movement of that form of life energy called money in every moment of our lives—we need to keep track of our income and expenses by keeping a Daily Money Log. The second part of Step 2 is simple, but not necessarily easy. From now on, keep track of every cent that comes into or goes out of your life.

Many people intentionally remain aloof from money. Their mythology puts "money" and "love-truth-beauty-spirituality" in two separate boxes. There are a number of variations of this dichotomy. There are the grass-roots activist organizations that can't balance their books—or even keep them. There are people who can't say no when a friend asks for a loan but who would never dream of writing up an IOU for the transaction (because after all, we *are* friends!). Then there are people who attend workshops, support groups and conferences about "personal and planetary growth," paying for everything by check or credit card and keeping no records to verify the expenses—they let their bank handle such details. There are churches going bankrupt because they can't approach the congregation with their nitty-gritty financial needs. There are even couples who won't discuss their shared finances because . . . well, they love each other. All of these situations stem from the same root thought: money is money and love is love and never the twain shall meet. Look at your own attitudes. Do you excuse financial unconsciousness with "spiritual" precepts?

A Spiritual Discipline

Religions, ancient and modern, and the personal growth workshops of the human potential movement all have techniques for training the mind to be here now, "in the moment." These practices take many forms and include such seemingly diverse techniques as counting breaths, keeping the attention on each incoming and outgoing breath; repeating a phrase over and over in order to focus the wandering mind;

concentrating on an object without entertaining past memories or future fantasies about it—just being with the object, right now; practicing various martial arts (such as aikido or karate); developing an inner, objective "witness" to simply observe what you are doing now.

To this list we add another discipline designed to sharpen awareness—one that is indispensable to the financial program and perhaps more easily accepted by our grounded, materialistic Western mentality than some of the more "esoteric" practices. Instead of watching your breath, you watch your money. This practice is simple: **Keep track of every cent that comes into or goes out of your life.**

The rules for this highly developed tool of transformation technology are: **Keep track of every cent that comes into or goes out of your life.**

The methodology for this marvel of monetary metaphysics is: **Keep track of every cent that comes into or goes out of your life.**

Followers of this teaching can be found everywhere and are identified by their unfailing habit of reaching into pocket or purse for a small notebook and pen whenever money is about to enter or leave their presence.

There are no specifications for this Daily Money Log. There is no official notebook to buy ("only $49.95 with indices, quick-reference charts and a solar calculator"). This Daily Money Log is one place in the financial program where you can be creative and do things your own way. For many people, a pocket-sized memo book is the perfect constant companion in which to note every cent that enters or leaves their lives, along with the occasion of its entering or leaving. After years of refining her system, one individual has found that a three-by-five-inch index card and small pen tucked right in her wallet keep her honest about writing down every time she spends or receives money. Another, more enamored of time than money, logs his expenses and income in a special section of his appointment book. Someone else, who in the past had been very absentminded about money, likes the heft and significance of carrying her whole account book with her and logging each item by category, with space for daily, weekly and monthly running tallies.

Whatever system you choose, *do* it (the program works only if you do it!)—and be accurate. Let it become a habit to write down any and all movements of money, the exact amount and the reason for the exchange. *Every* time you spend or receive money, make it second nature to note it instantly. This practice is so valuable that you may find yourself continuing to do it long after your financial goals are met—for the authors, it has become a lifelong habit.

Figure 2-3 is a fictional example of two days' entries. Note the degree of detail given for each expenditure. Notice how expenditures at work are specifically labeled as such. Observe the differentiation of the expenditures at the Circle K between snacks ("chips, dip, soda") and the "3-pack blank cassettes." Similar differentiations of spending categories are made in Saturday's Safeway and K Mart shoppings. The subcategories or "breakouts" within the total are rounded approximations (though you are certainly encouraged to be close in your approximations, it would be time-consuming to calculate the exact cost of toilet paper, wine, etc.), but the total must be accurate to the penny.

Every Cent? . . . But Why?

Remember that the purpose of this procedure is simply to **keep track of every cent that comes into or goes out of your life.**

"Why," you may ask, "do I need to go to such great lengths?"

Because it's the best way to become conscious of how money actually comes and goes in your life as opposed to how you *think* it comes and goes. Up to now most of us have had a rather cavalier attitude toward our small, daily monetary transactions. In practice we often reverse the old adage of "penny wise, pound foolish." We might search our souls and discuss with our mate the advisability of spending $40 for a new four-color left-handed veeblefitzer, yet over the course of a month an even larger amount has unconsciously gone out of our universe in small "insignificant" purchases (the "nickel and diming yourself to death" syndrome).

"But must I keep track of every *cent*?" you may ask.

Yes, every cent!

Why every cent, rather than just rounding off to the nearest dollar, or using approximate figures? Because this helps to establish important lifelong habits. After all, how big is a "Finagler's Constant"? What's the definition of a "Fudge Factor"? How close is "close enough"?

FIGURE 2-3

Sample Daily Money Log

Friday, August 24		In	Out
Bridge toll to work			1.00
Coffee and Danish at work			1.50
[Found in rest room]		.25	
Lunch at work			4.63
Tip for lunch			1.00
[Repaid by Jack for Monday's lunch]		5.00	
Coffee break (work)			1.00
Office contribution (Di's shower)			5.00
Coke from machine at work			.75
Candy bar from machine at work			.50
Gas: 10 gal at $1.28/gal			12.80
Circle K: chips, dip, soda			3.65
Circle K: 3-pack blank cassettes			5.89
[Paycheck, net for week] (see stub for deduction)		285.40	
Saturday, August 25			
Safeway shopping			68.14
	Breakout: approx.		
motor oil	4.00		
cassettes, 3-pack	2.50		
magazines	3.00		
household	12.00		
toiletries	8.50		
wine	6.00		
approx. subtotal	36.00		
groceries	32.14		
TOTAL	68.14		
K Mart shopping			46.84
	Breakout: approx.		
household	8.00		
shirt, for work	14.00		
candies	3.00		
photos	10.80		
hardware	4.00		
auto accessories	7.04		
TOTAL	46.84		
Lunch, Burger King			3.60
Dinner with friend, China Star			16.20
Tip for dinner			3.00
Movies with friend			12.00

Human nature being what it is, if you start cheating, even "just a little bit," that little bit tends to get bigger and soon you'll find yourself thinking, "Well, I don't have to write *everything* down, just the major expenses"; and then, "Well, I've done this for a month now, so I think I'll start rounding it off to the nearest thousand." (It's like dieting: if you break your diet on Tuesday morning by having a buttered English muffin instead of dry toast, the tendency is to cheat even more, and by evening you're gobbling down a carton of ice cream and a pound cake.) If you want this to be a worthwhile undertaking, it's worth your while to do it right.

Since money has a direct correlation to your life energy, why not respect that precious commodity, your life energy, enough to become conscious of how it is spent?

This is the step that somehow makes the biggest impact on people. Often an enthusiastic seminar participant will come up to us and say, "Your seminar was the greatest thing that ever happened to me financially. Ever since I came to it I've kept track of every penny!"

To which we reply, "Wonderful! And have you done the other steps?"

"No, they don't apply to me—but I've been faithful about doing your program and keeping track of every cent."

While this is an important step, it is not the only one; it is just one piece of the entire machinery that makes this program work. The sole guaranteed result of doing *only* this step is that you will have a collection of small notebooks with records of every penny you've spent from the day you began.

You may have some initial resistance to doing this impeccably, but ultimately this step must be embraced, regardless of feelings, for it is a vital section of the royal road to money mastery:

Keep track of every cent that comes into or goes out of your life.

Useful Attitudes

No leeway. Either you are for Financial Integrity 100 percent or you are not. A telescope with only *one* lens just a *wee* bit out of alignment still doesn't allow you to see the stars. The same holds true for a human life. A little bit of fudging cuts down the amount of light that can shine through. This is where you get to be ruthless, tough-minded and absolute.

Your commitment to clearing up your relationship with money is really tested here. In most of us there is a penchant for giving ourselves leeway and latitude, and the temptation to "forget" to keep track of every cent may be great. One of the keys to your success in this program (and in life) is a shift in attitude from one of laxity and leeway to one of accuracy, precision and impeccability. (By the way, such integrity might work miracles in other aspects of your life. People have lost weight, kept their desks cleared and patched up broken relationships —all through doing this step. Integrity is integrity is integrity.)

No judgment—lots of discernment. Judgment (blaming ourselves and others) is labeling things in terms of good and bad. Judgment is what got Adam and Eve kicked out of the Garden of Eden: they ate of the tree of the *knowledge* of good and evil—i.e., they started judging everything, beginning with their bodies, and made themselves ashamed. On the road to transforming your relationship with money and achieving Financial Independence, you will find that judgment and blame do not serve. *Discernment,* on the other hand, is an essential skill. Discernment is sorting out the true from the false, separating the wheat from the chaff. Just in the process of writing down every cent that comes into or goes out of your life, you will begin to discern which expenses are fitting and fulfilling and which are unnecessary, extravagant or even downright embarrassing. Discernment has to do with that higher faculty that we all have—the one that knows the truth, that sees what is needed and wanted by life, that recognizes as real our desire to make a difference before we die. This faculty will be increasingly on duty as you work with the financial program. Aligning your spending with this faculty is the key to Financial Integrity. Through writing down every cent that comes into and goes out of your life, you are awakening this faculty and inviting it increasingly to direct your life.

SUMMARY OF STEP 2

1. **Establish (accurately and honestly) how much money you are trading your life energy for, and discover your *real* hourly wage.**
2. **Learn about your money behavior by keeping track of every cent that comes into and goes out of your life.**

3

WHERE IS IT ALL GOING?

Congratulations! You've made it into the present. Knowing how much money has come into and gone out of your life—today, last week, last month and since your first allowance—is a monumental feat, a giant step toward Financial Intelligence. In terms of where this program will take you, however, you've just begun. The insights you've had, as vivid as they may have been, are just a taste of what's in store.

To do Steps 1 and 2 you only needed to take the word of some apparent experts (the authors and all the others who have successfully used this program) that this kind of obsessive counting is necessary to break the hold that money has over your life. You've only needed to name and number such tangible items as your income, expenses, bank balances and possessions. With Step 3, however, more of *you* will be needed to make it work. Here you'll begin the process of evaluating the information you've collected. To use a dieting analogy, Steps 1 and 2 were counting calories. Step 3 is getting on the scale.

BUDGETS, LIKE DIETS, DON'T WORK

Budgets! Did they say budgets? We all know about budgets, don't we? You go to the stationery store and buy a standard budget book (writing down how much it cost, of course). Then you try very hard to make your life conform to the standard categories. Do the shots for the dog I got last week at the vet's go under Medical? And what about his food? Is that Groceries? Is the loan to Sally an Expense? And gas for my motorcycle to ride around the racetrack . . . is that Transportation? Having done your best at assigning your whole range of eccentricities to the ten standard categories (how can Miscellaneous be more than Housing?), you progress to the spending plan. How much should I budget for each category for the coming month? You put down your best guess, given that the categories don't quite fit, and lurch on into the next month. This ritual usually gets repeated for two more months, at which point you conclude that you either have to adopt a much more restricted and boring life or quit this farce. Quitting seems a lot easier. Many of us have repeated this ritual of fiscal repentance several times in our lives, to no avail. **Don't worry. Relax. This program is *not* about budgeting!**

Let's go to the dieting analogy again to highlight the essential difference between this financial program and your standard budgets.

None of us was born knowing what a calorie is. There is a time when we ate Oreos and ice cream and gobs of mayonnaise just because we liked them. Usually, calories (and the first diet) come on the scene around puberty, since puberty is when we become painfully aware that we are not a perfect 10 (size, that is). From that day on, the way our clothes fit is the bottom line. If the red pants fit, we are good. If not, we are useless, ugly, undisciplined and unworthy—with no chance of parole. And banished to the next diet. But diets don't work. They don't work because they deal with the symptoms and not the cause. The cause of fat is not really the calories in the food, it's the desires in our mind. While a dieter may claim he is starving, the truth is he is withdrawing from the fix that he uses to relieve boredom, get back at his mother, structure time, quell restlessness, feel included, boost self-esteem, overcome loneliness and generally cure what ails him.

What does all this have to do with money? A lot. Just as overeaters abhor getting on the scale, overspenders dread tax time—and, indeed, any time they're asked to tally up expenses—because that means it will be Budget Time. For dieters, there is the initial disbelief (like stepping off and on the scale to make sure the needle is returning to zero). Then there are the excuses ("I'm retaining water," or "What do you expect after Thanksgiving?" or "It's winter, all animals put on weight in the winter"). Then there will be self-recrimination ("Ugly, undisciplined, useless, unworthy"). And then, head hung low and tail between legs, they submit themselves to the penance of The Diet. Facing reality (the scale) means punishment.

And that's how unconscious spenders feel. They refuse to open anything that looks like a bill, charge their whole array of credit cards to the limit, write postdated checks hoping the paycheck arrives at the bank before the rubber one gets cashed, borrow from friends, take out debt-consolidating loans, rob Peter but fail to pay Paul, and on and on until, after months (or even years) of denial and rationalization, they gird their loins and take their pitifully disorganized and incomplete records to the financial planner (or, if frugal, to the free consumer credit counseling service) to confess their sins and submit to a redemption budget. No more fun. No more movies. No more spontaneous weekends in Las Vegas. No more pretty clothes or trips to the tanning salon. Just desperate promises not to use any credit cards ("But please don't make me cut them up!"), and bread and water and nose to the grindstone.

While these examples may be extreme, they hold a kernel of truth about patterns of unconscious spending. Are any of them similar to things you might have felt or done? The focus of your addiction may not be money or food, but millions of us are substance abusers of one kind or another. The only difference is that some addicts go to jail, some to bankruptcy court, some to Weight Watchers and some to the top of the Social Register.

Does it seem odd to think of money as a socially acceptable addiction? Surely, since everyone wants money, and wants it in abundance, it can't be an addiction. But what else would you call a substance or activity that we reach for compulsively even though it doesn't bring fulfillment? What else would you call something that we are convinced we could not live without? Indeed, the very thought of not having it overwhelms us with fear. What else would you call a need that is intense, chronic and seen as essential to our sense of wholeness? What else would you call something that goes beyond a rational concern, that fills our daydreams and our night dreams as well? What else would you call something that becomes more important to us than our relationships with family and friends, the acquiring of which becomes an end in itself? What else would you call something that we hoard, building up unreasonably large supplies in order to feel secure? An addiction is a need that's gotten out of control, that's become a cancer, migrating into healthy tissue and eventually consuming its host.

Not long ago a friend told us about a wealthy friend of hers, long tormented by insecurity, who had recently committed suicide. To honor our friend's long-standing relationship with the deceased, the family invited her to select a keepsake from among the woman's possessions. It was a bittersweet task, but perhaps the most disturbing aspect was opening a drawer that contained thirty-eight white sweaters, each folded neatly. What did this collection of nearly identical sweaters say? To our friend, they told a tale of a desperately unhappy woman whose addictive substance was clothes—and particularly white sweaters. Every time that increasing sense of something missing would overtake her, out she'd go to buy an item to "cheer her up." Perhaps some moments of pleasure came from purchasing each white sweater, a happiness that probably dissipated soon after the sweater had disappeared into the white-sweater drawer. As one wise person said, you can never get enough of what you don't really want.

Greed is another component of our irrational and addictive relationship with money. "Greed," said Gordon Gekko, the wheeler-dealer in the movie *Wall Street,* "is good." It is, indeed, a socially acceptable and even encouraged motivation. Along with its dark cousin, fear, it runs the casino called Wall Street and gets reported on in the most respectable journals and newspapers in the world. Greed is also what possesses so many of us as we shoot right past the peak of the Fulfillment Curve and accumulate clutter (hoarding). Our society, with its skewed distribution of wealth, rewards greed over need—so much so that it seems slightly un-American to suggest that the poor deserve at least a small piece of the action. "Let 'em work for it like I do," say those whose stash is safe and sufficient. In fact, greed is so much a part of our nature that we don't even recognize it as a signpost of addiction.

JUST SAY "YES" TO BEING CONSCIOUS

None of this is meant to make you squirm. In fact, squirming is a sign of guilt, and guilt will most likely lead you back into cold-turkey strategies like diets or budgets. In contrast, recognizing and telling the truth about our irrationality around money and our addictive behavior are simply the first step toward sanity. And here is where this program is different from the tens or hundreds of other recipes for fiscal health. This program is based on consciousness, fulfillment and choice, not on budgeting or deprivation.

To return to the diet analogy, a book called *Diets Don't Work* by Bob Schwartz offers four rules for getting off the diet-go-round:

1. Eat when you're hungry.
2. Eat exactly what your body wants.
3. Eat each bite consciously.
4. Stop when your body has had enough.

Very simple. All you have to do is be conscious. No counting calories or sticking to high-cost liquid diets. No deprivation. No measured portions of food. Those all deal with the symptoms, and you become a compulsive dieter instead of a compulsive eater. Being conscious means you become aware of what you are thinking and feeling when you are eating. You learn to eat when your body is hungry—not because you are bored, at the dinner table, alone in the kitchen, between tasks, wanting a treat for a job well done, blue with depression, green with envy or red with fury. You eat what your body tells you it needs. You stop when you have had enough. And you pay attention. Simple—but not always easy. It takes discovering and exercising some mental muscles that may have atrophied from misuse. You have to identify what "hungry" is, what "full" is, what you truly want as opposed to what you crave out of feeling perpetually deprived, and what you are actually eating while you are eating it. The two important aspects of being conscious, as opposed to dieting, are:

1. You need to identify and follow internal signals, not external admonishments or habitual desires.
2. You need to change your patterns of eating over the long term, not what you eat over the short term.

This financial program points you in the same direction. This is not about following our (or anyone else's) budgets, with standardized categories and a suggested percentage of income that should go toward each category. This is not about swearing at the beginning of each month that you'll do better. This is *not* about guilt. It's about identifying, for yourself, what you need as opposed to what you want, what purchases or types of purchases actually bring you fullfillment, what represents "enough" to you and what you actually spend money on. This program is based on *your* reality, not a set of external norms. Consequently, the success of this program rests on *your* honesty and integrity. Step 3 is where you begin to exercise these muscles. If you're out of shape you may feel some pain, but *in reality* there is nothing painful about doing this step. In fact, it's fun!

NO SHAME, NO BLAME

Remember the mantra: No shame, no blame. What you are confronting is just the truth about the choices you've been making in your life. No shame, no blame. How fortunate to be able to do this yourself, instead of being audited by the IRS. How lucky you are to be doing this now and not in your last hours on earth. No shame, no blame. Remember to use the mantra at those moments when you want to hide under the bed, go on a spending spree till you've forgotten what was bothering you or decide that this program doesn't work and give up. No shame, no blame.

Anita Cleary *needed something like that mantra to help her survey her closet with this new spotlight of consciousness. No doubt about what her addiction was: clothes and costume jewelry. She had been a "shopaholic." Any time she was out in her car she had a compulsion to stop at the mall—just to see what was on sale. Somehow this ritual of shopping and spending helped her feel OK about herself. But there it all was—the result of years of addiction—sitting in her closet. It would be nice if she had had a conversion experience right then, but she didn't. She continued to shop until the balance tipped and it no longer felt good to her to have so much and not wear it. As an interim measure, she justified her excess by giving it away as presents. It was fun to place things she'd never worn with just the right friend or relative. Slowly the desire to shop weakened. Then one day she found herself at one* *of her favorite department stores, surveying the new colors in sweaters. Consciousness struck. "Is this going to be what I do with my life? Is this what it's all going to be about? What am I doing?* I have enough already!" *She left the store empty-handed, puzzled by what that revelation was really about. Sometime after that experience, Anita discovered that she had lost her desire to shop.*

If Anita had been working with the standard budget and spending plan strategy, she might not have recognized her shopping as an addiction. She would have remained a "social shopper," like the many social drinkers who deny that they are alcoholics. By steadily applying consciousness and compassion to her shopping habit, she was able, eventually, to have the profound insight that she already had enough. She is now so allergic to shopping that she's lost a few old friends whose central social ritual is browsing through the mall. But she's gained a lot more.

So, having set the context, let's get on with Step 3, creating your Monthly Tabulation.

Step 3: Monthly Tabulation

After a month of keeping track of your money (Step 2), you will have a wealth of specific information on the flow of money in your life—down to the penny. In this step you will establish spending categories that reflect the uniqueness of *your* life (as opposed to the oversimplified budget-book categories like Food, Shelter, Clothing, Transportation and Health).

While you still might choose to have such basic categories, within each major category you will find and separate out numerous important subcategories that will give you a vastly more accurate picture of your spending. The fun—and challenge—of this step will come in discovering your own unique spending categories and subcategories. These subcategories will be like a dictionary of your unique spending habits. They will be perhaps your most accurate description to date of your life-style, including all your peculiarities and peccadilloes.

This detailed portrait of your life is your true bottom line. Forget the mythology of your life. Forget the story you tell yourself and others. Forget your résumé and the list of associations you belong to. When you do Step 3 you will have a clear, tangible mirror of your actual life—your income and expenses over time. In this mirror you will see exactly what you are getting for the time you invest in making money.

ESTABLISHING CATEGORIES

In establishing your categories you will want to be accurate and precise, without becoming overly fussy.

Food

Unless you are *very* different from other humans, you will have a broad category called Food. As you look at your food expenses for the month, however, you may observe that there are actually several different types of food buying that you can usefully track. There is the food you eat at home with your family. There is also the food you eat at home when you are entertaining. So you might have two categories, At Home, Family and At Home, Entertaining. But don't get fanatic. Don't hover over your dinner guests, recording in your little notebook how much and what they eat. "Would you like seconds, Mr. Snodgrass?" could take on a whole new meaning. It is sufficient to estimate, within the *exact total* of your grocery bill, what proportion went to guests. For example, if four guests are invited and you normally shop for just two people, approximately two-thirds of that grocery bill should be attributed to At Home, Entertaining. The totals are accurate to the penny, but the breakouts from the totals are estimates.

You might also want to see what snacking is costing you. What do those coffee breaks actually cost a month? What about TV food—the chips and popcorn and candies and soft drinks that so often go hand in hand (or hand in mouth) with TV watching? Are you spending extra on groceries for the finest organic food and then undermining your scruples with junk food between meals?

Another subcategory that might be instructive is lunches at work, whether they are power lunches with clients or just a daily pastrami on rye from the corner deli. All such spending patterns will show up if you establish categories that reflect your actual behavior rather than just writing everything in the budget-book column called Food. This precision is not for the purpose of a more exact confession to your financial adviser. It's so that when you throw your hands up in disgust, crying, "Where does it all go? I hardly buy anything!" (dieter's translation: "How can I have gained five pounds? I eat like a bird!") you can answer yourself in a firm and steady tone, "It goes to the candy machine on the third floor of my office building."

Clothing

When it comes to clothing, you may find that you aren't getting enough information about your unique spending patterns by simply having one category called Clothing. You may need to distinguish between utility and vanity (the need never to appear in the office in the same outfit twice in a row, for example, or one-upmanship in elegant attire at social gatherings). In other words, be specific. Make appropriate distinctions. To get an accurate map of your spending patterns, you may need several subcategories. There is the clothing you wear in your everyday home life, the clothing you believe is appropriate attire for the workplace, and whatever specialized apparel you think you need for recreational activities. One doctor, who followed this program to get a handle on where a consistently unaccounted-for 20 percent of his income disappeared, discovered that he had a real penchant for buying shoes. He had golf shoes, tennis shoes, running shoes, boating shoes, walking shoes, hiking shoes and climbing shoes, as well as cross-country-ski shoes, downhill-ski boots and after-ski boots. Just having a category for shoes helped him find some of that missing income—and face the fact that he rarely wore anything but comfortable around-the-house shoes. He wasn't alone in his shoe fetish. A typical man in the United States, on average, owns 2.5 pairs of sneakers, a typical woman, 2.6. Reebok estimates that by the mid-1990s, its customers will own six to seven pairs. Even more amazing is that 80 percent of the athletic shoes in this country are never used for the activity for which they've been designed.

This isn't just accounting—this is a process of self-discovery. It may even be the only process of self-discovery that promises to leave you in better shape financially than when you embarked on it.

What are some other ways of categorizing clothing? It is often used as a means of self-expression, as an attempt to make up for a poor self-image or to sell yourself. Having a "color analysis" is a great way to double your clothing expenses. Then there is the endless (and perversely contradictory) advice in women's magazines on how to dress to get a job (one wardrobe) or get a man (yet another wardrobe). Clothing is also used as a tranquilizer or stimulant: "I'm so depressed, I think I'll go cheer myself up by buying a new outfit." A friend of ours calls it "retail therapy." The following item appeared in a Madrid newspaper:

> Nine women are being treated for a curious problem caused by modern social habits. The malady, which experts have named "Fashion Syndrome," is characterized by the uncontrolled buying of clothing, jewelry and cosmetics in quantities and costs disproportionate to need or means. The disorder was first identified by an American psychiatrist in 1984. Other doctors around the world have also become interested in the problem. Fashion Syndrome is usually accompanied by other disorders such as depression and bulimia [bingeing and purging]. The women exhibit low self-esteem, feelings of guilt and a distorted image of their bodies.

Now, if *you* suffered from "Fashion Syndrome," wouldn't you rather discover it through a simple accounting exercise instead of through other more painful or humiliating situations?

Transportation

By using appropriate subcategories for Transportation, you may gain insights that save you hundreds of dollars a year. Doing your tallies is a great opportunity to reflect on why you own a car at all instead of relying on public transportation. Convenience, status, necessity, fitting in, a sense of freedom . . . ? It is also a good time to review your insurance: what portion of your insurance is necessary and how much is habit, convention and buying into your agent's scare tactics? And what category would your second car go under: Transportation, Hobby, or Ostentation? What about your motor home—is it transportation, housing or a dead loss because it sits in the driveway fifty-one weeks a year?

Refining Your Categories

What makes this sort of ruthless honesty bearable is that you can confront your peccadilloes, your indiscretions, in the privacy of your own account book, rather than when you "get caught." So don't skimp on being truthful if you find yourself face-to-face with some of your faults and frailties while innocently doing your Monthly Tabulation. What better way to face the music? If you remember that doing this exercise will lead not to the punishment of a budget but rather to the freedom of self-acceptance, you will press on regardless. For example, into what category do you put the part of the food money that you use to play the horses or buy lottery tickets? Yet another moment of truth may come as you vacillate over where to record liquor. Is it food? Is it entertainment? Or is it a drug?

It is also important to distinguish between job-related expenses and other expenses. For example, under Transportation you would list separately the cost of commuting and other work-related transportation expenses (nonreimbursed). If the same vehicle is used for both commuting and pleasure, then split costs according to mileage in each category. Similarly, if you use your telephone for work-related as well as personal calls, those costs should be listed separately.

Within your medical category you may find several subcategories: sickness; wellness (i.e., what you purchase to keep yourself vital and alive, like vitamins, membership in a health club, annual checkup); health insurance; prescription drugs; nonprescription drugs; etc. You can see why this process has allowed people to transform more than just their relationship with money.

A further refinement will come as you decide how you want to account for large, "unusual" expenses like annual insurance premiums, capital expenses like a new refrigerator, the money you put into IRA's or a balloon payment on your house. As far as we are concerned, there is no "right" way to do this. For us, after a year of hearing ourselves make the same excuse every month about all the extraordinary expenses ("This was an unusual month because the ______ needed to be paid"), we realized that every month is an unusual month and that these extraordinary expenses are a continuing part of life.

You may perfect your categories over time. The exercise should be easy and a lot of fun. It will draw on a blend of honesty and creativity, stimulate your imagination and challenge your morality—all at the same time. It's better than most card, TV and board games all rolled into one.

Remember, you are also recording all the money that flows *into* your life as well and may want to establish subcategories for income also. It is important to distinguish between wages/salaries/tips and interest/dividend income. Where will you record the pennies you find on the sidewalk, the quarters you retrieve from public phones and your gambling winnings? If you are a free-lancer, you will need to decide how and when to record irregular payment for your work.

After you have examined the month's itemized entries in your Daily Money Log and created categories that accurately depict your spending patterns, devise a form of recording expenses under each category in a way that works for you. Figure 3-1 will give you an idea of how such a tabulation might be set up. You will notice that there are four blank lines at the bottom of the tabulation. We will talk later about what these boxes are for, but for now just draw them in.

TOTALING IT ALL UP

A word of warning. The computer addicts among you will want to find or write a program that can "assist" in this accounting task. Beware. The Monthly Tabulation is a fairly simple task and usually does not require sophisticated software. Both of the authors achieved Financial Independence without computers. So please make sure that your love affair with the computer isn't robbing you of hours while returning to you minutes. While we haven't done a survey, we would bet that there is no correlation between sophistication of accounting and actually doing the steps of this program. There may even be an inverse relationship.

At the end of the month you will transfer each entry from your Daily Money Log into the appropriate column on your Monthly Tabulation. Add up your income columns to get your total monthly income. Add up the expenditures in each column and enter the total of each subcategory at the bottom of that column. Then add the totals for all expenditure categories—this sum is your total monthly expenses.

	FOOD			SHELTER			UTILITIES			CLOTHING		
	At Home	Outside	Entertaining	Principal	Interest	Hotels	Electricity	Phone	Gas	Necessary	Work	Special
Total Dollars												

HEALTH			RECREATION				TRANSPORTATION				OTHER	INCOME			
Prescription Drugs	Nonprescription Drugs	Doctor	Drugs	Shows	Hobbies	Booze	Gas/Oil	Maintenance	Public Transportation	Tolls/Parking		Paycheck	Bonuses/Tips	Interest	Loans

(A) Total Income for Month ____________

(B) Total Spent This Month ____________

Total Saved This Month ____________

(A – B)

FIGURE 3-1

Sample Monthly Tabulation Form—with Income and Expenses

THE BALANCING ACT

Next count the cash in your wallet and piggybank and accurately balance your check registers and your savings account passbooks. Now you have enough information to see how closely you have kept track of the money flowing into and out of your life over the past month. If you have kept accurate records (and haven't physically lost any money), the money you actually have at the end of the month (in cash and bank accounts) will be equal to the money you had at the beginning of the month *plus* your total monthly income *minus* your total monthly expenses. If you haven't kept accurate records (or have physically lost some money), you will have lost or gained cash that you can't account for. The difference between your total monthly income and total monthly expenses (plus or minus your monthly error) is the money you have saved this month. When your monthly error is consistently zero, you will know you have mastered Step 2 (keeping track of every penny). Congratulations! You have achieved a minor miracle.

Figure 3-2 shows a sample set of monthly figures, but please use it only as a model. The fun and empowerment come from creating a balancing system that works for your particular situation.

MAKING MONEY REAL

Now comes one of the magic keys to this program. What you have in front of you, as accurate and balanced as it may be, does not yet have the power to transform your relationship with money. It is simply the by-product of a month of successfully tracking little pieces of paper and bits of metal. You may have had emotional reactions to this accounting, but they will be forgotten as soon as you embark on your next trip to the gazingus-pin store. The fact that you may spend, let's say, 88 pieces of paper on magazines does not have any direct relevance to your experience of life. However, remembering that money is something you trade your life energy for, you can now translate that $88 into something that *is* real for you—your life energy. Use the formula that follows on page 92.

FIGURE 3-2

Sample End-of-Month Balancing

Part I

Equation:
\$ at START of month + \$ IN during month − \$ OUT during month = \$ at END of month

\$ at START:	Cash on hand	68.75	
	+ Checking account balance	+255.73	
	+ Savings account balance	+963.07	
		1287.55	
+ \$ IN:	+ Total monthly income (from Monthly Tabulation)	+1348.17	
		2635.72	
− \$ OUT:	− Total monthly expenses (from Monthly Tabulation)	−982.46	
= \$ at END:	= \$ You should have at end of month	1653.26	(A)

Part II

ACTUAL \$ AT END OF MONTH:	Cash on hand	94.88	
	+ Checking account balance	+369.21	
	+ Savings account balance	+1188.07	
	= \$ You actually have at end of month	1652.16	(B)

Part III

MONTHLY ERROR:	\$ You should have (A)	1653.26	(A)
	− \$ You actually have (B)	−1652.16	(B)
	= \$ Lost or improperly recorded	1.10	

Part IV

SAVINGS:	Total monthly income	1348.17
	− Total monthly expenses	−982.46
	± Monthly error	−1.10
	= \$ Saved this month	364.61

$$\frac{\text{Dollars spent on magazines}}{\textit{Real}\text{ hourly wage}} = \text{Hours of life energy}$$

In Chapter 2 we did a sample calculation that showed how a theoretical $11-an-hour salary could end up being, in reality, $4 an hour. Obviously your real hourly wage will end up being a different figure, but for the sake of this example, let's use $4 an hour. So, in the case of this magazine habit, you can divide that $88 by your real hourly wage ($4) and find out that you spent 22 hours of your life for this particular pleasure:

$$\frac{\$88}{\$4/\text{hour}} = 22 \text{ hours of life energy}$$

Now you can measure your growing pile of all the wonderful (yet unread) magazines in your bathroom against something real—22 unredeemable hours on your one-way journey from cradle to grave. Those magazines drain your energy three times over: once in earning the money to buy them, again in staying up late to read them and finally in feeling guilty when you haven't finished them by the time the next issue arrives (to say nothing of having to store or dispose of them). Could those 22 hours have been better spent? Is it still true that you have no time to spend with your family? What does this do to habitual procrastination? You've been wanting to catch up on your sleep—did you just find a way to do that? Or were those magazines worth every hour spent to acquire them? Did they give you 22 hours of pleasure, and then some? Don't answer these questions yet. Just notice that translating dollars into hours of your life reveals the real trade-offs you are making for your style of living. In Chapter 4 we'll analyze these findings further.

Let's look at another example: your rent or mortgage payment. Let's say you pay $1,000 a month for the privilege of living in your house or apartment. To some of you that figure may seem outrageously high, to others outrageously low. Remember, we're not suggesting that this is an appropriate housing cost, just offering an example. Applying the awareness that your real hourly wage is $4, divide that $1,000 by 4.

Here's reality. It costs you 250 hours a month to put this particular roof over your head. If you're putting in the standard 40 hours a week you'll soon realize that your housing costs you more hours than you put in at your job. Every working hour is going to pay for a house that you get to enjoy perhaps two or three hours a day. Is it worth it? Notice that we're not talking about the housing market in your town or city. We're not talking about what everybody knows you can or should do about housing. We're simply noticing that it is costing you 250 hours a month to live where you do. Just awareness. No shame, no blame —and no excuses either.

Now take the total of each column and convert the dollars spent in each subcategory into hours of life energy spent (you may round off to the nearest half hour). Your Monthly Tabulation form will now look something like the one in Figure 3-3.

SOME PICTURES WORTH A THOUSAND WORDS

Let's look at some real-life examples of how some FIers put this step to work for themselves.

Take a look at how **Rosemary Irwin** *set up her categories in Figure 3-4. Don't you feel as if you know a little about her unique personality just from looking at her tabulation for January 1991? She obviously puts a high value on beauty, since she has two categories that refer to it (Beauty and Aesthetics). She obviously takes care of her body and is willing to spend money on maintaining her health. It is telling that she has ''wellness'' categories like Health Products and Health Services, rather than ''sickness'' categories like Drugs and Doctors. The Donations category says that she contributes to causes enough to have a separate category, rather than lumping donations under Miscellaneous. The Personal Growth category is one you wouldn't find in a standard budget book.*

The very process of creating this form provided Rosemary with valuable information about her priorities and gave her a tangible way to track how much of her life energy she was devoting to the things that mattered to her. The monthly ritual of filling in the numbers has the quality of an exciting game. How did she do in each category? Is it up or down from last month?

	FOOD			SHELTER			UTILITIES			CLOTHING		
	At Home	Outside	Entertaining	Principal	Interest	Hotels	Electricity	Phone	Gas	Necessary	Work	Special
Total Dollars												
Total Hours of Life Energy												

HEALTH			RECREATION				TRANSPORTATION				OTHER	INCOME			
Prescription Drugs	Nonprescription Drugs	Doctor	Drugs	Shows	Hobbies	Booze	Gas/Oil	Maintenance	Public Transportation	Tolls/Parking		Paycheck	Bonuses/Tips	Interest	Loans

(A) Total Income for Month ________________

(B) Total Spent This Month ________________

Total Saved This Month ________________

(A – B)

FIGURE 3-3

Sample Monthly Tabulation Form—with Hours of Life Energy

Month: January Year: 1991 Actual Hourly Wage: $6.75

Expenses	Total Dollars	Hours of Life Energy	Income	
Rent	200.00	30	Salary	1345.16
Natural gas			Mileage reimbursement	23.87
Electricity	14.00	2	Other	15.00
Combined utilities				
Phone	3.72	.6		
Household	18.96	2.8		
Groceries	55.00	8		
Treats	2.22	.3		
Eating out	3.89	.6		
Alcohol	4.24	.6		
Gasoline/oil	24.44	3.6		
Car repair/maintenance				
Car insurance/registration	160.30	24		
Parking	.25			
Bus/ferry				
Health insurance	36.06	5		
Health products				
Health services	5.00	.7		
Hygiene				
Beauty	8.50	1.3		
Clothing, necessary	6.93	1		
Clothing, unnecessary	16.42	2.4		
Entertainment				
Aesthetics				
Gifts/cards	12.00	1.8		
Books/magazines	16.20	2.4		
Personal growth				
Postage	2.03	.3		
Office supplies				
Photocopy				
Donations				
Bank charges				
Miscellaneous	.40			
Loan payments	50.32	7		
TOTAL	640.88		TOTAL	1384.03

FIGURE 3-4

Rosemary's Monthly Tabulation with Hours of Life Energy

FIGURE 3–5

Steve and Lu's Calculation of *Real* Hourly Wage

Life Energy vs. Earnings

	Hours/week	Dollars/week	Dollars/hour
Lu's basic job, after taxes (before adjustments)	50	750	15
Lu's adjustments (list):	Add hours	Subtract costs	
Commuting	3	7	
At-work food	5	15	
Getting ready	½	2	
Entertainment and eating out	7	30	
Vacation	12	25	
Lu's total adjustments	+27½ hours	−79	
Job with adjustments: Lu	77½ hours	671	
Steve	67½	250	
Total	145	921	6.35

How does it compare to last year's average for the same category? Are trends up or down?

Now let's look at how one couple has gone about creating categories and a Monthly Tabulation form for tracking them.

Lu Bauer *and* ***Steve Brandon*** *live in rural Maine. Professionally they are at opposite ends of the spectrum—he drives a truck and she's an accountant. Personally, though, they are best buddies and are enjoying the awareness and communication that come from combining their incomes and expenses. When they computed their real hourly wage, they combined their totals to come out with a single figure for the two of them: $6.35 an hour. As you can see in Figure 3-5, Lu's total adjusted hours were 77½ and Steve's were 67½, or 145 hours combined. Lu's total income was $671 and Steve's was $250, making a grand total of $921. Dividing combined income by combined hours is how they established that figure of $6.35 per hour, which meant that every dollar spent represented nearly 9½ minutes of life energy. Now*

STEVE BRANDON AND LU BAUER—RECEIPTS AND DISBURSEMENTS 1990

For the month of August 90

RECEIPTS

	Steve	Lu	Total
Steve's business income			
Steve's net paycheck	684.64		684.64
Lu's business draw		2075.31	2075.31
Disability income			
Gifts received	150.00		150.00
Tax refunds			
Interest income (MSFCU)		.52	.52
Dividends (Calvert)			
Money found			
Miscellaneous receipts			
______________			
______________			
______________			
Total receipts for the month	834.64	2075.83	2910.47

DISBURSEMENTS

	Steve	Lu	Total	FI Life Units *(hours)*
Steve's business expenses				
Dues and subscriptions				
Laundry	15.60		15.60	2.5
Ads and promotion	17.00		17.00	2.7
Education				
Telephone				
Total business expenses	(32.60)		(32.60)	(5.2)
Autos—Steve		265.35	265.35	41.8
Auto excise tax—Steve				
Bank service charges		2.65	2.65	0.4
Charitable contributions	10.00	2.00	12.00	1.9
Contribs.—nondeductible		35.00	35.00	5.5
Clothing				
Medical/health/counseling		140.00	140.00	22.0
Dues and publications	29.97	41.40	71.37	11.2
Film and processing				
Garden supplies				
Gifts to be given	34.00	170.00	204.00	32.1
Groceries/food at home	55.96	63.91	119.87	18.9
Household—miscellaneous	42.96	79.99	122.95	19.4
House repairs				
House building materials		264.58	264.58	41.7
House building labor				
House mortgage payment		817.97	817.97	128.8

	Steve	Lu	Total	FI Life Units (hours)
Insurance:				
Homeowners'		1.00	1.00	0.2
Health		171.26	171.26	27.0
Total insurance		172.26	172.26	27.2
Junk food and lunches		30.08	30.08	4.7
Meals out		168.79	168.79	26.6
Music and home entertainment	42.50	93.39	135.89	21.4
Movies, concerts, etc.		16.00	16.00	2.5
Misc. itemized deductions				
Misc. expenses		(1.02)	(1.02)	(0.2)
Pet expenses:				
Birdseed				
Bonneau				
Darby	38.44		38.44	6.1
Annie	11.25		11.25	1.8
Other				
Total pet expenses	49.69		49.69	7.9
Postage				
Student loan payment—Steve	81.29		81.29	12.8
Travel, tolls and parking		1.75	1.75	0.3
Utilities:				
Electric		10.78	10.78	1.7
Gas—propane	22.40		22.40	3.5
Firewood				
Heating oil				
Telephone—total		87.29	87.29	13.7
Trash collection		21.00	21.00	3.3
Total utilities	22.40	119.07	141.47	22.2
Voided checks				
Unidentified cash				
TOTAL DISBURSEMENTS	401.37	2483.17	2884.54	454.3

Note: Circled numbers are totals of subcategories; numbers in parentheses represent income.

FIGURE 3-6

Steve and Lu's Monthly Tabulation with Hours of Life Energy

let's look at Figure 3-6, their tabulation for August 1990. You'll notice that their incomes don't tally directly with their previous computation, which is understandable since both of them work variable hours according to the season and other factors. However, on average that figure of $6.35 an hour is still accurate. Now look at their categories. The number of subcategories under Pets pegs them as animal lovers. And what does that "other" under Pets mean? Stray cats? House guests? The cow when she isn't producing any milk? They seem to be generous types as well, with two categories for Contributions. Those house expenses tell us that they might be building or remodeling their house as a continuing project, and they probably are do-it-yourself types, judging from the low cost of labor that August. The mortgage payment of $818 includes $200 extra toward the principal. They are saving a lot of mortgage interest by paying off their mortgage as quickly as possible. In addition, Steve reports that the tabulation itself saved him money in a very unusual way. One month (not this particular month), looking at the Junk Food and Lunches category, Steve discovered that he was a "cookie junkie." He had spent twice as much on cookies as on music, one of his greatest loves. "If it hadn't been for the tabulation," he claims, "I would have gone into therapy for ten months for behavior modification to handle my weight. Instead I got all the awareness I needed from my Monthly Tabulation."

Combining their income and expenses works for Lu and Steve. Other couples have found that separating out their income and expenses was the only way to get an accurate reflection of their unique patterns.

You'd think that because **Lynn and Carl Merner** *shared the same passion (music) and the same profession (computer programming), it would be natural for them to track their income and expenses together. But while they were outwardly a matched pair, their personalities and styles were at opposite ends of the spectrum. Carl was near the rational, conservative and deliberate end. Lynn was more toward the emotional, experimental and disorganized end. Their gazingus pins were different. Their shopping habits were different. Their hobbies (besides music) were different. Doing their Monthly Tabulations together wasn't giving either one of them much good information. Not only that, but soon after starting on the program Lynn left her programming job and started teaching piano full-time out of their home. Her hours and pay became irregular, so they decided that she would offset her smaller contribution to the* *household kitty by doing the housekeeping chores. This nonmonetary arrangement didn't show up to their satisfaction on the Monthly Tabulations. The more they struggled to make it work, the more tension arose. In order to maintain a friendly marriage and stay on the program, they decided to separate their finances. To Carl it was sensible. To Lynn it was threatening—but she agreed to give it a try. To her amazement Lynn found that having her own accounts gave her a wonderful feeling of autonomy. She discovered that she'd become dependent in many subtle ways during the years of her marriage, and she reconnected with the strength and independence she'd felt when she was single.*

Let's look now at how another FIer did her balance sheet.

Diane Grosch *applied her computer programmer's logical mind to the task of setting up a balance sheet for herself. Her Monthly Tabulation categories are enough like Rosemary's that we don't need to reproduce them, but her balance sheet has a precision and elegance that are instructive (see Figure 3-7). Setting up this form for herself made the end-of-the-month balancing process easy and accurate. Her capital is the combination of what she has in savings, a money market account and bonds. This is all money that is earning interest, which she likes to keep separate from the money in her checking account.*

The point of these stories is not to provide you with a standard to follow but to inspire you to create a Monthly Tabulation form that works for *you*. Remember, this is not a budget book or a spending plan. This is not trying to fit your round (or octagonal) peg into society's square hole. Creating *your* form will be a process of self-discovery. You aren't learning "the right way," you are creating your own way. There is no right way to do it *other than to do it*, as the next story reminds us.

What is notable about **Leslie Nelson***'s experience with the Monthly Tabulation is not her form, but the impact that doing the tabulation has had on her life. Leslie is a waitress and activist from Santa Fe, New Mexico. By nature she is much more interested in politics than in paychecks. Tracking did not come instinctively to her, which is perhaps why this step has been so important for her. Before doing the FI program she was "in debt and totally*

August 1990

	Ending	Beginning	Difference
Capital: Savings	5.64	5.61	.03
CBA	1538.84	3695.19	− 2156.35
Bonds	70,000.00	65,000.00	5,000.00
Checking account	1341.61	435.03	906.58
Cash on hand	69.44	94.24	− 24.80
Rolled coins	—	—	—
		Total difference	= 3725.46
		Total expenses	+ 537.38
		Total income	− 4272.40
		Amount out of balance	= − 9.56

FIGURE 3-7

Diane's Balance Sheet

unconscious about money." Doing her tabulations has provided an anchor for her life. When she lets it slide, she finds herself slipping once again toward debt. The fact that she has her tabulation form set up so that she can record her expenses daily makes her that much more impeccable about writing everything down. This diligence has paid off. Over the course of about five years she has accumulated $20,000 in savings—and that is inviolate, even when she gets off track and finds herself tempted to splurge. Not only that, but it has transformed tax time from a nightmare to a dream.

This step is crucial to the whole rest of the program, which is why those people who proudly report that they are on the program because they're keeping track of every penny are so off base. This step provides insight and empowerment and will be worth every minute you invest in setting it up to work for you.

The following is an example of some possible ways of breaking down the large categories into smaller subcategories that reflect the personal quality of your life. *This is an example, just for the purpose of illustration.* If you merely adapt it for yourself, you will be missing an important part of this step—discovering and refining your own personal spending patterns. This program is designed so that *you* become *conscious.*

CHECKLIST

1. Food
   A. At home, basic meals
   B. At home, snacks and goodies
   C. At home, entertaining friends
   D. At work, basic meals
   E. At work, snacks and coffee breaks
   F. Outside, restaurants, for enjoyment
   G. Outside, fast food, convenience while shopping, etc.
   H. Health foods, special diet, current fad, etc.
   I. Junk foods, current addictions
   J. Special treats: Baskin-Robbins, smoked baby clams, etc.
   K. Vegetable garden supplies: seeds, fertilizer, etc.

2. Shelter
   A. Mortgage payment (principal—see category 11 for interest) or rent
   B. Motel, hotel
   C. Vacation rental
   D. Home repairs
   E. Remodeling
   F. Property taxes

3. Utilities
   A. Electric bill
   B. Heating fuel
   C. Firewood
   D. Propane or natural gas
   E. Charcoal for barbecues
   F. Water bill
   G. Phone bill
   H. Garbage pickup and/or dump fees
   I. Sewer bill

4. Household maintenance
   A. Cleaning materials
   B. Laundry and dry cleaning
   C. Hardware and repairs
   D. Bathroom supplies
   E. Kitchen supplies (nonfood)
   F. Special services: plumber, maid, lawn mowing, etc.
   G. Tools bought for household projects, even if projects weren't done
   H. Yard and garden expenses

5. Clothing and ornamentation (jewelry and accessories)
   A. Everyday necessities, clothing to keep the body covered and protected
   B. Clothing for work
   C. Clothing for fashion display
   D. Recreational clothing: jogging suit, tennis outfit, golf shoes, hiking boots, bicycling gear, bathing suits, leathers, riding jodhpurs, workout tights and leotards, square-dancing dress, etc.
   E. Compulsive clothes-buying
   F. Psychological and emotional clothing

6. Transportation
   A. Commuting to and from work
   B. Automobile: gas

C. Automobile: oil
D. Automobile: regular maintenance
E. Automobile: repairs
F. Automobile: insurance, inspection, registration, driver's license
G. Public transportation, local
H. Airplane, train, long-distance bus
I. Car rental
J. Bicycle repair and maintenance
K. Car payments
L. Tolls and parking fees

7. Communication
A. Telephone: base rate, long-distance charges, cost of cellular phone (all divided into work-related and social)
B. Postage, stationery, overnight mail, courier service
C. Photocopies, printing
D. Telegram, mailgram
E. Fax
F. Modem
G. Electronic-mail service
H. 900 number charges (or is this recreation?)

8. Health
A. Doctor bills
B. Dental bills
C. Health insurance
D. Other health practitioners: chiropractor, acupuncturist, etc.
E. Prescription drugs
F. Vitamins and supplements
G. Medically recommended diets
H. Gymnasium or health salon
I. Orthotics, prosthetics, physical aids: eyeglasses, arch supports, braces

9. Recreation and leisure time
A. Alcohol: at home, at bar
B. Tobacco

C. Nonprescription "recreational" drugs
D. Sporting events
E. Theater, concerts, museums
F. Movies
G. Audiotapes, records, CD's
H. Videotapes
I. Electronic equipment: VCR's, radios, televisions, cassette recorders (Walkman, boom box, stereo sound system, etc.)
J. Weekends, vacation, resorts, retreats
K. Educational—workshops, classes, lectures
L. Books, magazines, newspapers
M. Hobbies, crafts, art supplies
N. Toys
O. Home computer equipment and supplies
P. Sports and camping equipment
Q. Sports fees (lift tickets, skating rink admission, etc.)

10. Gifts and donations
A. Personal gifts
B. Church
C. Charitable organizations (United Way, Salvation Army, etc.)
D. Office collections
E. Activist (equal rights, antinuclear, etc.)
F. Political contributions
G. Panhandlers, street people

11. Interest and bank charges (the cost of making and spending money)
A. Interest on mortgage(s)
B. Annual cost of credit cards
C. Interest on credit cards
D. Car payment interest
E. Installment-buying charges and interest
F. Bank loan interest and charges
G. Excess cost of buying gasoline on credit cards vs. cash
H. Checking account charges

I. Late payment charge
J. State and federal income tax

12. Losses
A. Money actually lost
B. Money stolen
C. Money lost in vending machines and telephones
D. Money lent (when repaid, treat as income)
E. Gambling losses, betting pools, etc.
F. Lottery tickets
G. Shortfalls in monthly accounting

13. Gazingus pins
For a partial listing of potential "gazingus pins" consult your favorite mail-order catalog. Every item on every page is potentially one of yours—from art supplies to zoom lenses to zithers.

14. Other expenditures

15. Income
A. Wages, salary, tips: net ("take-home")
B. Money found
C. Loans repaid to you
D. Inheritances, gifts
E. Interest on savings accounts
F. Interest on investments
G. Dividends
H. Income tax refunds
I. Bonuses
J. Mail-in rebates (when received)
K. Refunds
L. Proceeds from garage sales
M. Proceeds from sale of arts, crafts
N. Cash prizes
O. Gambling winnings

16. Savings—capital

A. Bank savings accounts

B. Piggybank, cookie jar, government bonds, certificates of deposit, etc.

C. Nonspeculative, insured investments—government bonds, certificates of deposit, etc.

D. Other investments and speculations

By the way, it took a lot longer to read this section than it will take you to do your Monthly Tabulation once it has been set up.

SUMMARY OF STEP 3

1. **Discern your unique spending and income categories and subcategories from the month's worth of entries in your Daily Money Log.**
2. **Set up your Monthly Tabulation.**
3. **Enter all money transactions in the appropriate category.**
4. **Total money spent in each subcategory.**
5. **Add up total monthly income and total monthly expenses. Total your cash on hand and balance all bank accounts. Apply equation (total monthly income minus total monthly expenses plus or minus monthly error) to see how accurate you've been. The money you actually have at the end of the month should equal what you had at the beginning *plus* your monthly income *minus* your monthly expenses.**
6. **Convert the "dollars" spent in each subcategory into "hours of life energy," using the real hourly wage that you computed in Step 2.**

4

HOW MUCH IS ENOUGH? THE NATURE OF FULFILLMENT

What is fulfillment? Whether in the sense of accomplishing a goal or enjoying a moment of real contentment, fulfillment is that experience of deep satisfaction when you can say, Aaahh . . . that was a delicious meal, a job well done or a purchase worth the money. To find fulfillment, though, you need to know what you are looking for. It's fairly easy to know what fulfillment is in terms of food or other temporary pleasures. But to have fulfillment in the larger sense, to have a fulfilled life, you need to have a sense of purpose, a dream of what a good life might be.

For many of us, however, "growing up" has meant outgrowing our dreams. The aspiration to write a great book has shrunk to writing advertising copy. The dream of being an inspiring preacher has evolved into being an administrator and a mediator between the factions in the congregation. Instead of really knowing who their patients are, how their patients live or the challenges in their lives, doctors today are plagued with back-to-back fifteen-minute patient visits and malpractice suits. The dream of traveling around the world becomes two weeks a year of hitting the tourist traps. Living a fulfilling and meaningful life seems almost impossible, given the requirements of simply meeting day-to-day needs and problems. Yet, at one time or another practically every one of us has had a dream of what we wanted our lives to be.

Wherever you are, take a few moments now to reflect upon your dreams. So many of us have spent so many hours, days and years of our lives devoted to someone else's agenda that it may be hard to get in touch with our dreams. So many of us have whittled away at our uniqueness so that we could be square pegs in square holes that it seems slightly self-indulgent to wonder what kind of hole we would be inclined to carve for ourselves. Indulge yourself now. Stare out a window. Shut your eyes. And envision what would be a truly fulfilling life for you. To help you get started on this journey, ask yourself the following questions:

- What did you want to be when you grew up?
- What have you always wanted to do that you haven't yet done?
- What have you done in your life that you are really proud of?
- If you knew you were going to die within a year, how would you spend that year?
- What brings you the most fulfillment—and how is that related to money?
- If you didn't have to work for a living, what would you do with your time?

You may want to write your answers down. These questions help you focus on what you truly value, what makes your life worth living. In this next step, you'll be finding out how well your spending is aligned with those values.

EVERYBODY'S GOT A DREAM

Some people have fairly conventional dreams, the kinds many Americans would cherish.

***Amy and Jim Dacyczyn**, for example, had a simple dream. They wanted to raise a family in a big farmhouse in a rural area. When they got married they had, between the two of them, logged more than twenty years in the workaday world—Jim as a career Navy man and Amy as a graphic artist—yet they had only $1,500 in savings to show for it. Their first child, according to Amy, was born "nine months and fifteen minutes after we were married." They recognized that they valued family and community above the fast lane of life in which they had both been living and decided to raise their children* *and realize their dream on only one income—Jim's salary from the Navy. To realize their dream they called upon all the frugality training they'd gotten from their thrifty parents and devised scads of new strategies for saving money. Neither had any sense of deprivation. They thrived on this challenge to their creativity, and their relationship thrived on their shared purpose. In seven years they had four children and saved $49,000 (all from Jim's income, which was under $30,000 a year; Amy stayed home with the kids)—enough to make a down payment on a rural farmhouse in Maine, pay off all debts and buy a new car, furniture and appliances. Two years after that, Amy decided to put her graphic skills to work and create a forum where frugal ideas could be exchanged. In June 1990 she published the premier issue of* The Tightwad Gazette, *an eight-page newsletter full of practical tips about living the good life on a shoestring. A year later they had twins—and they are* still *able to live within their means. Their story is testimony to the fact that simple dreams, like having a house in the country and staying home to raise a family, are truly within reach.*

Other people have more unconventional dreams:

Wes Lambert*'s passion is nature—both being in it and preserving it. For him the FI program is a way to do what he's always wanted to do: contribute to humanity's understanding of and respect for the natural world—full-time. He's aligning as many parts of his life as possible with this dream. His paid employment is as a chemist measuring air quality. He's moved within walking distance of work so he won't contribute as much to the air pollution he's measuring. On vacations he kayaks through unspoiled wilderness areas, and on weekends he teaches kayaking to help others experience nature safely and respectfully. And with his ''disposable income'' he builds up his savings and supports major conservation organizations. The compass of his life is the natural world, and every aspect of his life points in that direction.*

And some people look forward to fulfilling a number of dreams.

Kees *(pronounced ''Case'')* ***and Helen Kolff*** *are a case in point. Kees is a physician and the medical director of a clinic that provides medical care to minorities and migrant workers. Helen is a former teacher who now participates in the programs of a number of nonprofit organizations as well as* *holding down the fort for her family. Their lives reflect the dreams they had when they met in college. While they've loved their twenty-four years of marriage and raising two children, they are looking forward to an "empty nest" so that they too can fly the coop. The financial program has given them a way to retire from their paid employment at the same time they retire from being full-time parents, and they're already exploring projects they might volunteer on together—perhaps in a Third World country.*

Step 4 of this financial program allows you to evaluate your priorities and rebalance your accounts. It allows you to take your dreams out of hock and reincorporate them into your everyday, making-a-dying life. Eventually, you'll find you are finally making a living!

Step 4: Three Questions That Will Transform Your Life

In this step you evaluate your spending by asking three questions about the total spent in each of your subcategories:

1. Did I receive fulfillment, satisfaction and value in proportion to life energy spent?
2. Is this expenditure of life energy in alignment with my values and life purpose?
3. How might this expenditure change if I didn't have to work for a living?

To do this step, go back to your Monthly Tabulation form and notice the three blank rows along the bottom. This is where you will write the answers to our three questions (see Figure 4-1). You have already converted "dollars" to "hours of life energy"; now you can take a look at how you want to spend that precious commodity. These three questions, applied to each spending subcategory on your Monthly Tabulation, will give you a basis for evaluating the way you spend your money.

QUESTION 1: DID I RECEIVE FULFILLMENT, SATISFACTION AND VALUE IN PROPORTION TO LIFE ENERGY SPENT?

This question provides a way to evaluate your expenditures. Take a look at each subcategory with this question in mind. If you received so much fulfillment from this expense of life energy that you'd even like to increase spending in this subcategory, place a + (or an up arrow) in the first box. If you received little or no fulfillment from it, put a – (or a down arrow) in that box. If the expense feels OK just as it is, mark the box with a 0.

This simple exercise will show you where your spending is automatic, perhaps even addictive. You might even find your "shopping weaknesses," your gazingus pins. At first you might angrily defend one or another of your gazingus-pin habits. "I *like* having lots of shoes. Every pair has a function. Anyway, it's my money." But no one is trying to take your gazingus pins away from you. In fact, no one is even listening, since the honesty this exercise requires emerges most readily in solitude. Over time, seeing the number of hours of *your* life you spent in order to reward yourself with yet another gazingus pin might make it less of a treasure and more of a booby prize.

***Evy McDonald**, an intensive-care nurse, talks about her pet purchase: "I discovered that every month I bought at least one new pair of shoes, wore them a few times and then placed them in the back of my closet with the other forty-plus pairs—making room for my next new shoes. I calculated that in one month I spent ten hard hours at work to pay for* one pair of shoes. *A large minus sign went in the box under my category for shoes. No amount of rationalization could keep me from seeing the simple truth: I did not get value from having so many pairs of shoes."*

On the other hand, you might find you've been too much of a penny-pincher in categories where you get a lot of fulfillment. Make sure you note these areas of supreme satisfaction and put your + (or up arrow) in the columns where you are actually *under*spending.

	FOOD			CLOTHING		
	At Home	Outside	Entertaining	Necessary	Work	Special
	35.47 20.10 5.17 3.23 7.82	22.30 3.48 .55 2.90 .35 .40 10.11 13.84 .40 .75 .50 .80 1.08 4.00	5.63	2.15 10.00	5.98 35.00 55.00	25.00 36.52
Dollars	71.79	61.46	5.63	12.15	95.98	61.52
Hours of Life Energy	18	15	1½	3	24	15
Fulfillment	0	–	+	0	0	–
Alignment	0	–	+	0	0	–
After FI	0	–	+	0	–	0

HEALTH			RECREATION			
Prescription Drugs	Nonprescription Drugs	Doctor	Drugs	Shows	Hobbies	Booze
8.17	5.42	55.00	50.00	4.50	1.98	3.98
10.82	3.20	18.00		4.50	3.10	6.65
4.63				10.00	25.00	1.75
						2.00
						5.60
						4.55
						6.50
23.62	8.62	73.00	50.00	19.00	30.08	31.03
6	2	18	12½	5	7½	8
0	0	0	0	0	+	–
0	0	0	–	0	0	–
–	0	–	–	0	0	–

Key: Fulfillment = Did I get fulfillment from this expenditure of life energy?
Alignment = Was this expenditure of life energy in alignment with my stated life purpose?
After FI = How much might I spend in this category if I didn't have to work for a living?
\+ = increase for more fulfillment
– = decrease for more fulfillment
0 = OK as is

FIGURE 4-1

Typical Monthly Tabulation—with the Three Questions

The trick to doing this evaluation is to do it objectively, without rationalizing to yourself why the expenditure was so high or so low and without condemning yourself by agonizing about how *you* could have spent *that much* in *that category.* The key phrase to remember is "No shame, no blame."

Couples have also found this step a valuable way to discuss differences in their spending habits with equanimity and objectivity.

Ted and Martha Pasternak *discovered that this question provided a gentle way to evaluate each other's spending patterns without getting defensive or adversarial. Rather than directly challenging one of Ted's purchases, Martha can just calmly ask whether he really got fulfillment, satisfaction and value in proportion to the amount of life energy spent. They find that they are able to observe—and even comment on—each other's gazingus pins with a lot more compassion. For Martha it's books. For Ted it's phones (he has one in every room—and some don't always work). Being able to discuss financial choices without subtle bickering has been invaluable for them and has actually helped their marriage.*

Developing an Internal Yardstick for Fulfillment

Answering this question helps you develop an **internal yardstick for fulfillment** and in the process kick any unhealthy shopping habits. You may discover that you've been measuring your fulfillment, or lack of it, by what those around you have or by what advertising says you should want. Being fulfilled is having just enough. Think about it. Whether it's food or money or things, if you don't know, from an internal standard, what is enough, then you will pass directly from "not enough" to "too much," with "enough" being like a little whistle-stop town. You blink and you've missed it. You will rarely have an experience of fulfillment. By diligently working with this question you will begin to identify, for yourself, an internal yardstick that you can use to measure how much is enough.

The primary tool for developing this internal yardstick is awareness. The affluence that surrounds us has been called the American Dream, and with good reason: we've been asleep. We wake up by questioning the dream. **Asking yourself, month in, month out, whether you actually got fulfillment in proportion to life energy spent in**

each subcategory awakens that natural sense of knowing when enough is enough.

You come to differentiate between a passing fancy and real fulfillment, that point of perfect balance where desires disappear because they have been completely met. Any less would be not enough. Any more would be too much. A fulfilling meal is one where all the flavors, smells and textures blend perfectly and your appetite is satisfied without even a trace of the discomfort of having overeaten. In the same way, a fulfilling car is one that meets your transportation needs perfectly, that you will enjoy owning for many thousands of miles, that doesn't insult your wallet or your values and that, with good maintenance, will be both reliable and a pleasure to drive. Your internal yardstick would dismiss any superficial desires to impress others, to relieve the boredom of driving a two-year-old car, to own a Mercedes because you want the status symbol or to have a blue convertible that matches your eyes. Those are all external yardsticks. If an experience or a purchase is truly fulfilling, the desire disappears for a long time. You are satisfied, contented, at peace.

Having an internal yardstick for fulfillment is actually one part of what we call Financial Integrity. You learn to make your financial choices independently of what advertising and industry have decided would be good for their business. You are free of the humiliation of being manipulated into spending your life energy on things that don't bring you fulfillment. Marcia Meyer, whose story we'll be hearing in Chapter 7, reported that before doing this evaluation she used to feel powerless over the money in her wallet. "I'd walk into a store and my money would fly out of my wallet. Not literally, but that's how it felt. I couldn't stop it." It is a form of Financial Independence to be able to "just say no" to unconscious spending.

To Recap

When evaluating your subcategories place a 0 in the box if the expenditure feels fine just as it is, a + (or an up arrow) if you got so much satisfaction that you might even like to increase that expenditure or a – (or a down arrow) if the amount of money spent was not fulfilling. This question is an opportunity to look at the degree of satisfaction in your life by examining something as simple and tangible as the way you use your life energy. No shame, no blame. It's simply the facts.

QUESTION 2: IS THIS EXPENDITURE OF LIFE ENERGY IN ALIGNMENT WITH MY VALUES AND LIFE PURPOSE?

This question is illuminating. It gives you a concrete way of looking at whether or not you're practicing what you preach. As you did with the first question, ask of each spending subcategory, "Was this expenditure of life energy in alignment with my values and my life purpose?" If your answer is a strong "Yes," put a + (or an up arrow) in the second box, under that column. If it's a "No," just put the − (or a down arrow). If it's fine as it is, put a 0. Take as long as you need to think it through.

People like Amy and Jim Dacyczyn had a clear set of values and a strong sense of purpose when they undertook their tightwad campaign. So did Wes Lambert and Kees and Helen Kolff. Measuring their financial choices against these two factors helped them to align their finances with their dreams. On the other hand, many people living otherwise well-off lives are suffering from a poverty of ideals. Many heirs and heiresses are among the lost and confused—all dressed up financially and nowhere to go. And lots of ordinary people who've achieved the American Dream are also wondering whether there isn't more to life than . . . this.

What about you? Are your values and life purpose clear, or are they out of focus, buried under the weight of a life-style that doesn't seem to fit?

Values

Let's talk about values first. What *are* values, anyway? Our values are those principles and qualities that matter to us, that are really important to our sense of well-being. On one level, values are the ideas and beliefs on which we base our decisions. They are like an invisible

DNA, made up of our sense of right and wrong, that structures our choices. When we choose to provide food, shelter and clothing for our children, we are making that choice on the basis of values. Whether we spend our day off walking in the park or going back to the office, our choice is based on values. How we spend our "free" time and "disposable" income reflects our values.

So our values are our beliefs. But since how we act reveals our real motivations, our values are also behaviors. (Parents try to sidestep this fact with the phrase "Do as I say, not as I do!") This book deals with one of the chief social manifestations of our values—how we handle money in our lives.

You learn quite a lot about the values you are living when you look at your Monthly Tabulations. What values do the $100 (or 25 hours of life energy, at the $4 per hour we calculated in our example in Chapter 2) spent on eating out reveal? They could indicate any number of things: that you value convenience, that you like good food or that you want social time with friends. What about the 12 hours donated to a charity? The 30 hours for the phone bill?

You may find that you are comfortable with many of these expenditures. And some you may question. Twenty-five hours of life energy spent on eating out may seem fine—until you realize upon reflection that you devoted only eight hours this month to one of your children. For many people, the values expressed in their expenditures are not the values they really want to be living. Your totals in some of your categories may reveal that habit, peer pressure or even boredom has gotten the best of you.

Go back to the questions at the beginning of the chapter. If you didn't have to work for a living, what would you do with your time? What have you done with your life that you are really proud of? How would you spend the next year if you knew it was the last year of your life? Your answers to these questions will tell you a lot about what you truly value.

Your Monthly Tabulations are like a mirror. As you ask the question, "Is this expenditure in alignment with my values?" month in and month out, you will find that you are looking deeply into yourself. Simply as a result of asking and answering this question you will make changes, large and small, that bring you closer to Financial Integrity, where all aspects of your financial life are in harmony with your true values. The process of coming into integrity is like that telescope we talked about in Chapter 2. The multiple lenses of the telescope allow you, the viewer, to extend and expand your vision—but only if each lens is clear and polished, and only if all the lenses are aligned and properly oriented one to the other. If any aspect of ourselves is out of alignment with the whole of our being, we will not be able to see very far; in fact, our vision will be completely obstructed by that one lens that is out of line.

In 1985 **Tom Clayton** *had the makings of a very nice life. All the pieces were there to add up to success: a terrific wife, two kids, two cars, a lovely house and plenty of tangible and intangible benefits from his job as a school administrator. He had respect, a good income and security. He was successful—but he wasn't happy. In fact, he was mad. He was angry and frustrated with the system that had led him to believe that if he had the right stuff (i.e., house, cars, job, etc.), he'd feel fulfilled. He didn't. Looking for a way out, he attended one of our FI seminars. On that day he realized something he knew but didn't* know—*that happiness doesn't come from externals. It comes only from integrating your values with your relationship with money. Nothing was wrong with his life, but the pieces didn't add up to something he was internally proud of. His life was good, but it wasn't real. When he looked at his values, he realized that his overarching desire was to contribute something toward solving some of the world's problems instead of just being one of the decent yet sleeping millions who consider minding their own business their highest good. But how could he* live *his values? His job, while good, did nothing to express his concern for the world. He took a risk, and a cut in pay, by leaving the school system to develop a private counseling practice and to work in a clinic in conjunction with a doctor. His new career slowly came into focus. Eventually he went into partnership with an associate, holding training sessions and seminars as Wellness Unlimited. Tom and his partner help people get in touch with their values and worth, and with their responsibility to themselves and the larger community. Tom has pieced together his skills, values and concerns into a life that fits for him. His insides match his outsides, and he's finally happy.*

What Is Purpose?

The second part of this question calls on you to evaluate your expenditures in light of your "life purpose." You must have an understanding of what it means to have purpose in living. For some people, like Amy and Jim Dacyczyn, doing work they enjoy or raising a loving family defines their purpose. For others the sense of purpose may be elusive, not quite in focus. Some individuals spend years looking for their purpose, while others, like Wes Lambert, seem to have it identified from the moment of birth. What is this thing called purpose in life?

In one view purpose is discovered in the answer you give when someone asks, "Why are you doing what you are doing?" The act may be obvious, like eating lunch, but the motivation could be anything from hunger to a desire for social acceptance to a need to load up on carbohydrates for physical endurance on a ski trip.

Purpose is also the meaning you ascribe to actions. There is a story about three stonecutters, each chipping away at a large block. A passerby approaches the first stonecutter and asks, "Excuse me, what are you doing?" The stonecutter replies rather gruffly, "Can't you see? I'm chipping away at this big hunk of stone." Approaching the second craftsman, our curious person asks the same question. This stonecutter looks up with a mixture of pride and resignation and says, "Why, I'm earning a living to take care of my wife and children." Moving to the third worker, our questioner asks, "And what are *you* doing?" The third stonecutter looks up, his face shining, and says with reverence, "I'm building a cathedral!"

The meaning we give to an action comes from within us. Like the first stonecutter, we have the choice of denying that our actions have any meaning beyond the physical reality of what we are doing. Like the second, we can absorb the meanings that our culture ascribes to our actions. Supporting a family is a culturally accepted purpose. So are getting an education, getting married and having children, creating a successful business, discovering the cure for a disease, winning honors . . . the list goes on. The third stonecutter's answer points to another level of meaning—living our highest ideals, dedicating ourselves to something that seems noble and worthy of our steadfast devotion.

There is also a sense in which "purpose" is generic. Beyond "my" purpose, many believe there is "the" purpose. Religions teach that there is a core of goodness within each of us, an ability to know right from wrong and a desire to "do the right thing." While every culture may have a different definition of the good, the true and the beautiful, all cultures honor the individuals who embody those ideals.

Finally, purpose is also our mission, that passionate commitment that keeps fueling our actions. A mission statement, whether it's for a corporation or an individual, usually has a tangible clause ("Our mission is to manufacture widgets") and an intangible clause ("Following the highest standards of precision and integrity"). People often have a sense of mission about making their community or the world a better place—perhaps helping solve problems of hunger, homelessness, abusive family relationships, global warming. Sometimes a person's mission is to embody certain qualities, such as love, peace or nonviolence. In this sense, purpose is about our extension of ourselves out into the world.

How Do We Find Our Mission?

Joanna Macy, an educator, ecologist and author, has suggested three directions in which to look for your own mission:

1. *Work with your passion,* on projects you care deeply about. What was your dream before you stopped dreaming? What's the work you would do even if you weren't paid to do it? You're not looking for those superficial preferences depicted on bumper stickers, like "I'd rather be surfing." You're looking for something you love more than your own comfort and convenience.

2. *Work with your pain,* with people whose pain touches your heart. Have you "been there so you know how it feels"—in grief, sorrow, despair, hunger, terror? Can you offer others the wisdom and compassion you gained from this experience? Is there an aspect of suffering in the world that calls you to action? If you are in such pain that you've lost touch with your ability to help others, then now is the perfect time to extend your hand to others in pain. It's healing.

3. *Work with what is at hand,* with the opportunities that arise daily for responding to the simple needs of others. Finding your purpose has often been equated with discovering the perfect job or service project that will galvanize you to be as saintly as Mother Teresa. This suggestion to work with what's at hand is a reminder that in an interconnected

world, all acts of service contribute to the good of the whole. If you remember that there is no single act of greatness, just a series of small acts done with great passion or great love, then doing what you see needs to be done—taking dinner to a sick neighbor, helping a child learn to read, writing a letter to the editor of your newspaper, being an advocate for the homeless in your city—you will discover a life filled with the experience of having a purpose worth living for.

Passion, pain, what's at hand—these are doorways into finding a purpose beyond material acquisition.

Measuring Our Movement Toward Purpose

Once again, go back to the questions at the beginning of this chapter. What have you always wanted to do that you haven't done yet? What brings you the most fulfillment? Your musings in response to these questions will also provide clues to your purpose.

Take a few minutes right now to write down your purpose in life. It may have nothing to do with how you now spend your time. It may or may not seem significant to others. It may not even be very clear for you yet. Just do the best you can. Use this stated purpose to measure your actions. If over time you see your purpose changing, that's fine; simply write what life purpose now means to you and use this new statement of purpose as your measuring stick.

However you define your purpose, you'll need a way to *measure* your results, some feedback to tell you if you are on track. Often we measure how we are doing in fulfilling our purpose by material success, or by professional or community recognition.

There is another, more accurate, measure of whether you are living your purpose—one that goes beyond material success and beyond rewards and recognition. It is your answer to the question "Is this expenditure of life energy in alignment with my values?" Asking this question faithfully—every month, for every category—will nudge you toward clarifying your values, living in alignment with your stated purpose and defining further your true purpose in life.

George Bernard Shaw, so the story goes, once said to a society matron, "Madam, I'll wager you would go to bed with me for five pounds." She was instantly indignant. How could he think such a thing? He paused as if thinking and asked, "What if I offered you one hundred thousand pounds?" She hesitated—and her silence gave her away. "So," Shaw said, "we aren't arguing about the act, but merely about the price." Money is an extremely compelling measure for all of us—even those dedicated to lofty ends.

Another way to measure your movement toward your purpose is through the Purpose-in-Life Test, based on the work of Viktor Frankl. Having survived the Nazi death camps, Frankl observed that there was a factor beyond intellect or psychology that allowed some people to retain their humanity in inhumane circumstances. This factor, he concluded, was "meaning" (or purpose)—a capacity to find, through deep dialogue with one's conscience, a positive significance in the events of one's life. The will to have meaning and purpose in life, he said, is superior to the will to have power or the will to find pleasure. Indeed, these latter drives take over when the will to find meaning has been thwarted. Frankl also observed that "being human means relating and being directed to something or someone other than oneself." Going through the questionnaire in Figure 4-2, which is based on Frankl's profound work, will assist you in your own movement toward meaning in your life.

To tally your score, add the numbers circled. If you were below 92 you probably lack meaning and purpose in life; if you were in the 92-to-112 range your sense of purpose is indecisive or hazy; and if your score was greater than 112 you have a clear purpose. How did you do? Remember that asking the question "Is this expenditure in alignment with my purpose?" will help you in defining and putting together the building blocks to your sense of purpose.

Take time to make some notes. And perhaps read Frankl's moving book, *Man's Search for Meaning*.

Returning to Integrity

Back to the second question in Step 4: "Is this expenditure of life energy in alignment with my values and life purpose?" Now that you've taken a deeper look at values and purpose, ask this question again. Ask without criticism or self-condemnation, but honestly and dispassionately. Look at the way you previously rated your expenditures. Do you still agree? Change your answers if your evaluation of a particular category is now different.

FIGURE 4-2

Purpose-in-Life Test

For each of the following statements, circle the number that would be most nearly true for you. Note that the numbers always extend from one extreme feeling to its opposite kind of feeling. "Neutral" implies no judgment either way; try to use this rating as little as possible.

1. I am usually:	1.	1 completely bored	2	3	4 (neutral)	5	6	7 exuberant, enthusiastic
2. Life to me seems:	2.	7 always exciting	6	5	4 (neutral)	3	2	1 completely routine
3. In life I have:	3.	1 no goals or aims at all	2	3	4 (neutral)	5	6	7 very clear goals and aims
4. My personal existence is:	4.	1 utterly meaningless, without purpose	2	3	4 (neutral)	5	6	7 very purposeful and meaningful
5. Every day is:	5.	7 constantly new	6	5	4 (neutral)	3	2	1 exactly the same
6. If I could choose, I would:	6.	1 prefer never to have been born	2	3	4 (neutral)	5	6	7 like nine more lives just like this one
7. After retiring, I would:	7.	7 do some of the exciting things I have always wanted to do	6	5	4 (neutral)	3	2	1 loaf completely the rest of my life
8. In achieving life goals I have:	8.	1 made no progress whatever	2	3	4 (neutral)	5	6	7 progressed to complete fulfillment
9. My life is:	9.	1 empty, filled only with despair	2	3	4 (neutral)	5	6	7 running over with exciting good things
10. If I should die today, I would feel that my life has been:	10.	7 very worthwhile	6	5	4 (neutral)	3	2	1 completely worthless
11. In thinking of my life, I:	11.	1 often wonder why I exist	2	3	4 (neutral)	5	6	7 always see a reason for my being here
12. As I view the world in relation to my life, the world:	12.	1 completely confuses me	2	3	4 (neutral)	5	6	7 fits meaningfully with my life
13. I am a:	13.	1 very irresponsible person	2	3	4 (neutral)	5	6	7 very responsible person
14. Concerning man's freedom to make his own choices, I believe man is:	14.	7 absolutely free to make all life choices	6	5	4 (neutral)	3	2	1 completely bound by limitations of heredity and environment

15. With regard to death, I am:	15.	7	6	5	4	3	2	1
		prepared and unafraid			(neutral)			unprepared and frightened
16. With regard to suicide, I have:	16.	1	2	3	4	5	6	7
		thought of it seriously as a way out			(neutral)			never given it a second thought
17. I regard my ability to find meaning, purpose, or mission in life as:	17.	7	6	5	4	3	2	1
		very great			(neutral)			practically none
18. My life is:	18.	7	6	5	4	3	2	1
		in my hands and I am in control of it			(neutral)			out of my hands and controlled by external factors
19. Facing my daily tasks is:	19.	7	6	5	4	3	2	1
		a source of pleasure and satisfaction			(neutral)			a painful and boring experience
20. I have discovered:	20.	1	2	3	4	5	6	7
		no mission or purpose in life			(neutral)			clear-cut goals and a satisfying life purpose

You now have a black-and-white map of your spending patterns and their relationship to your defined values and purpose. You may see gaps between your statement of purpose and your expression of it—gaps that you were unaware of before. To return to integrity (alignment of values and actions), you can either adjust your spending or adjust your purpose. Indeed, this question is your primary tool for achieving FI in the sense of Financial Integrity. Charles Givens makes this same point in his book *Financial Self-Defense*:

> When your actions are out of alignment with your values, you can experience fear, guilt, frustration and emotional imbalance. Fortunately, you can get rid of those negative, unwanted feelings. You can either:
>
> **1.** Change your actions to align with your values, or
> **2.** Change your values to align with your actions.

QUESTION 3: HOW MIGHT THIS EXPENDITURE CHANGE IF I DIDN'T HAVE TO WORK FOR A LIVING?

Use this question to evaluate how much your job costs you and to begin to focus more clearly on your life apart from work. Ask yourself, "Which expenses would decrease and which expenses would disappear if I didn't go to work every day?" In the third row under your expense categories mark a – (or down arrow) if you think this expense would decrease, a + (or up arrow) if it would increase or a 0 if it would probably remain unchanged. If you can come up with an estimated dollar figure, write it in a separate line on the Monthly Tabulation.

This question opens the possibility of a life-style in which you don't have to report to a job week in, week out. What would your life be like if you didn't work for money forty or more hours a week? What expenses would disappear? If you didn't have to work for money, would you buy more clothes? Fewer clothes? Burn more gas? Less gas? Sell your car entirely? Move to a cheaper house farther from a center of commerce? Would you have higher or lower medical bills (insurance might go up, but illnesses down)? Would you still take weekend breaks in hotels? Would your travel expenses go up or down?

As you ask yourself this question over time, you may find yourself coming to a startling conclusion. If you weren't trying to fit your round peg into a square hole all the time, life could be a whole lot cheaper! Because your days are consumed by your job, you need money to handle every other aspect of your life—from day care to home repair, from entertainment to being listened to with compassion.

Here's a riddle: Who is more financially independent—someone who can fix a toaster, or someone who must pay another person to fix it?

In many ways we have actually become more financially dependent. How many times have you been stymied by a modern convenience that won't work? When you try to get it repaired locally, you're told to send it back to the factory. Postage alone is more than it would cost to replace it. You'd fix it yourself, but how? Isn't needing money to make it through life actually a form of dependence? If that is so, then asking the question "What would this expenditure look like if I had the time and skills to maintain my possessions myself?" will lead you toward less dependence on money to fill your needs.

ASSESSING THE THREE QUESTIONS

Now take a look at your tabulation sheet. Find all of your – marks (or down arrows). Note which subcategories didn't meet your criterion for Question 1—you did not receive fulfillment in proportion to the amount of life energy spent. Which ones didn't measure up on Question 2—this expenditure was not in alignment with your values and life purpose? And which ones are expenses that would change significantly if you didn't have to "make a dying"? Now look at your list. Do you see any patterns? What have you learned about yourself? Don't punish yourself and don't resolve to "do better next month." (Remember, this is not a budget!) Simply use this information and any insights you've gained to assist in clarifying your values and purpose. Remember: No shame, no blame.

Let's go back to the monthly tabulations we looked at in Chapter 3 and see how Rosemary and Lu and Steve did these evaluations.

Rosemary's is fairly straightforward. While she didn't choose to estimate how much she would be spending in each category if she stopped working for a living, the categories she thinks would go down provide some food for thought. Lu and Steve's chart is particularly interesting because they came up with some novel adaptations and interpretations.

The first thing you'll notice is that Lu and Steve added a fourth question: "Is this level of expenditure helpful to the planet?" What would change in your own spending patterns if you were to ask yourself this question?

The other twist you'll notice is that their figure for charitable contributions post-FI (when they are financially self-sufficient and no longer working for pay) is the same as their post-FI income. Lu and Steve recognize that once they are free of paid employment they will

Month: January Year: 1991 Actual Hourly Wage: $6.75

Expenses	Total Dollars	Hours of Life Energy	Fulfillment	Alignment	After FI
Rent	200.00	30	0	0	0
Natural gas					
Electricity	14.00	2	0	0	0
Combined utilities					
Phone	3.72	.6	0	0	0
Household	18.96	2.8	0	0	0
Groceries	55.00	8	0	0	0
Treats	2.22	.3	0	0	0
Eating out	3.89	.6	0	0	0
Alcohol	4.24	.6	0	0	0
Gasoline/oil	24.44	3.6	–	–	–
Car repair/maintenance					
Car insurance/registration	160.30	24	0	–	0
Parking	.25		0	0	0
Bus/ferry					
Health insurance	36.06	5	0	0	0
Health products					
Health services	5.00	.7	0	0	0
Hygiene					
Beauty	8.50	1.3	0	0	0
Clothing, necessary	6.93	1	0	0	0
Clothing, unnecessary	16.42	2.4	–	–	–
Entertainment					
Aesthetics					
Gifts/cards	12.00	1.8	0	0	0
Books/magazines	16.20	2.4	–	–	–
Personal growth					
Postage	2.03	.3	0	0	0
Office supplies					
Photocopy					
Donations					
Bank charges					
Miscellaneous	.40		0	0	0
Loan payments	50.32	7	–	–	–
TOTAL	640.88				

FIGURE 4-3

Rosemary's Monthly Tabulation of Expenses—with the Three Questions

STEVE BRANDON AND LU BAUER—RECEIPTS AND DISBURSEMENTS 1990

For the month of August 90

FI Question 1: Are you receiving value commensurate with the life energy units this expenditure costs?

FI Question 2: Is this level of expenditure in keeping with your life purpose?

FI Question 4: Is this level of expenditure helpful to the planet?

Steve and Lu dollars per hr: $6.35

	Steve	Lu	Total	FI Question 3		FI Life Units (hours)	FI Questions Steve 1	Steve 2	Steve 4	Lu 1	Lu 2	Lu 4
					Total/FI							
RECEIPTS												
Steve's business income												
Steve's net paycheck	684.64		684.64		1505							
Lu's business draw		2075.31	2075.31									
Disability income												
Gifts received	150.00		150.00									
Tax refunds												
Interest income (MSFCU)		.52	.52									
Dividends (Calvert)												
Money found												
Miscellaneous receipts												
______												
______												
______												
Total receipts for the month	834.64	2075.83	2910.47		1505							
DISBURSEMENTS												
Steve's business expenses												
Dues and subscriptions												
Laundry	15.60		15.60	–	0	2.5	–	0	–	0	0	0
Ads and promotion	17.00		17.00	–	0	2.7	–	0	–	0	0	0
Education												
Telephone												
Total business expenses	32.60		32.60		0	5.2						
Autos—Steve		265.35	265.35	0	265	41.8	0	0	0	0	0	0
Auto excise tax—Steve												
Bank service charges		2.65	2.65	0	2	0.4	+	0	0	+	0	0
Charitable contributions	10.00	2.00	12.00	+	1505	1.9	–	0	+	–	–	+
Contribs.—nondeductible		35.00	35.00	–	0	5.5	–	–	–	–	–	–
Clothing												
Medical/health/counseling		140.00	140.00	–	130	22.0	–	–	–	–	–	–
Dues and publications	29.97	41.40	71.37	0	71	11.2	0	0	0	–	–	0
Film and processing												
Garden supplies												
Gifts to be given	34.00	170.00	204.00	–	50	32.1	–	–	–	0	–	–
Groceries/food at home	55.96	63.91	119.87	0	120	18.9	0	0	0	0	0	0
Household—miscellaneous	42.96	79.99	122.95	0	123	19.4	0	0	0	0	0	0
House repairs				+	100							
House building materials		264.58	264.58	–		41.7	0	0	–	0	0	0
House building labor												
House mortgage payment		817.97	817.97	–	0	128.8	0	0	0	0	0	0

Insurance:												
Homeowners'		1.00	1.00	+	22	0.2	0	0	0	0	0	0
Health		171.26	171.26	–	0	27.0	0	0	0	–	–	–
Total insurance		(172.26)	(172.26)	–	(22)	(27.2)						
Junk food and lunches		30.08	30.08	–	0	4.7	–	–	0	0	0	0
Meals out		168.79	168.79	–	60	26.6	–	–	0	–	–	–
Music and home entertainment	42.50	93.39	135.89	–	15	21.4	+	+	+	0	0	0
Movies, concerts, etc.		16.00	16.00	0	16	2.5	0	0	0	0	0	0
Misc. itemized deductions												
Misc. expenses		(1.02)	(1.02)			(0.2)						
Pet expenses:												
Birdseed												
Bonneau												
Darby	38.44		38.44	0	38	6.1	0	0	0	0	0	0
Annie	11.25		11.25	0	11	1.8	0	0	0	0	0	0
Other												
Total pet expenses	(49.69)		(49.69)	0	(50)	(7.9)						
Postage												
Student loan payment—Steve	81.29		81.29	–	0	12.8	0	0	0	0	0	0
Travel, tolls and parking		1.75	1.75	0	2	0.3	0	0	0	0	0	0
Utilities:												
Electric		10.78	10.78	0	10	1.7	0	0	0	0	0	0
Gas—propane	22.40		22.40	0	22	3.5	0	0	0	0	0	0
Firewood												
Heating oil												
Telephone—total		87.29	87.29	–	40	13.7	–	–	0	0	–	0
Trash collection		21.00	21.00	–	7	3.3	0	0	0	0	0	0
Total utilities	(22.40)	(119.07)	(141.47)		(79)	(22.2)						
Voided checks												
Unidentified cash												
TOTAL DISBURSEMENTS	401.37	2483.17	2884.54	–	2610	454.3						

Note: Circled numbers are totals of subcategories; numbers in parentheses represent income; FI Question 3 = How might this expenditure be different after FI?; Total/FI = projected income and expenses after FI.

FIGURE 4-4

Steve and Lu's Monthly Tabulation—with the Three Questions

be able to volunteer full-time to causes they care about. Instead of giving token donations each month, they will be able to give themselves. Their lives will be their charitable contribution.

Now take a look at how Kees and Helen Kolff have estimated what their expenses will be once their kids have graduated from high school, leaving them free to do community service projects together. In Figure 4-5 they compare their 1990 average monthly expenses in each category with their projected expenses in 1994. They arrived at these figures after several years of tracking expenses and asking the three questions. The 1994 estimates are *not* a budget. They are experientially derived from months of tracking and evaluating the real cost of a fulfilling life.

You don't have to know precisely what you would do if you didn't have a job. You don't even have to want to do anything other than your job. You just need to ask the question of each expense category: How would expenditures in this category change if I didn't have to work for a living? Remember: No shame, no blame. You aren't violating your commitment to your profession by asking that question. Nor are you expressing disloyalty to your boss or dissatisfaction with your job by considering how you might spend your money if you were doing something else. If you love your job, the simple monthly exercise of asking this question will only increase your job satisfaction because you will increase your certainty that you are there by choice.

IMPLICATIONS OF THIS STEP

Step 4 is the heart of this program. Don't worry if your life purpose or your internal yardstick is not crystal-clear. For some individuals this program has been the process by which they defined their values and purpose. The very process of asking and answering the three questions month in and month out will clarify and deepen your understanding of fulfillment and purpose. Just ask the questions and mark your responses at the bottom of each expense column, using your intuition as much as your intellect.

The nine steps of this program are easy. You don't have to understand them, you just have to do them. In fact, the people who get into the most trouble making this program work are those who believe they

	Average Cost/Month—Actual and Projections	
	Actual 1990	Projection 1994
Food	510	300
Restaurant	32	10
Cat	5	5
Electricity	33	30
Gas	35	40
Other utilities (sewer, water, etc.)	33	30
Kitchen/toiletries	32	20
Home maintenance	89	100
Garden/flowers	18	10
Clothes	59	50
Car: gas/repair	167 (77 + 90)	150
Phone	47	50
Office/printing/postage	42	20
Sports	51	40
Entertainment	33	20
Travel	51	100
Education/books	117	50
Gifts	187	50
Donations	131	30
Allowance	150	0
Medical/dental	68	25
Dental insurance		50
Misc. (photo)	(10)	100
Mortgage	349.07	350
Car insurance	144.17	150
House insurance	28.50	40
Jewel insurance	6.17	0
Life insurance	122.25	0
Health insurance	110.26	180
Property tax	195.85	300
TOTAL EXPENSES	2,856/mo (× 12 = 34,272/yr)	2,300/mo

Income tax not included.

FIGURE 4-5

Kees and Helen's Tabulation of Average Monthly Expenses

can skip steps that they think don't apply to them. If we could make this program any shorter, with fewer steps, we would. The fact is, this is the shortcut. We are practical people. We haven't included any window-dressing or arcane wisdom in here just for the fun of it. Every step of the program is essential. The steps work synergistically, building upon and enhancing one another. So just relax and do the steps.

Over time, amazing changes will occur—not only in your relationship with money but in your relationship with life itself. Here are a few reminders about working with Step 4 to maximize your benefits.

Information and Awareness, Not Shame or Blame

This is simply an information-gathering process. It is the first step toward reprogramming yourself. Any unconscious, addictive patterns of spending will be exposed and identified when you bring them into the light of honest evaluation and clear, numeric expression. The point is not to drive yourself to change through guilt or self-criticism. The point is to adjust your spending until you have 0's or +'s in all your columns.

Valuing Yourself

A shift will take place in the realm of values as your handling of money increasingly comes into alignment with what really matters to you. In the 1980s (as in many other eras) we managed to convince ourselves that buying things for ourselves was an expression of self-esteem. "I deserve the best," we learned to think. "No more second-class citizenship for me. If I want it, I can have it—and if I don't have the money I'll just put it on my credit card." Then along comes this process of rethinking your relationship with money and with the world, and everything turns upside down. "Spending money on myself in ways that might bring superficial happiness but don't contribute to lasting fulfillment," you think, "is actually *not* valuing myself. It's frittering away *my* precious, one-way life energy. Who did I think was going to pay off the Visa card, anyway?" True Financial Intelligence is understanding that if *you* buy now, *you* will pay later—with interest. Financial Intelligence is knowing that if *you* spend *your* life energy on stuff that brings only passing fulfillment and doesn't support your values, *you* end up with *less life*.

This step is not about budgeting, not about self-condemnation and not about depriving yourself. It is about honoring and valuing that limited resource called your life energy. It's about using this high self-esteem to bring about greater fulfillment, greater satisfaction and a greater sense of wholeness, alignment and integrity. You do this by becoming conscious of your unexamined and unrewarding spending patterns—painlessly.

Integrity and Synergy

This step helps you align values and behavior by adjusting one or the other. Financial Independence is built on Financial Integrity, and Financial Integrity is built on alignment of vision and values with action.

As shocking as it may be to see your unconscious spending patterns materialize as neatly totaled columns of dollars and cents, this exacting honesty is essential. People pay thousands of dollars for therapy, workshops and seminars in order to confront their self-defeating patterns of thinking and acting. This step allows you to accomplish that same goal, at no cost and in the privacy of your own home. When you can go through this entire process of tabulation and evaluation with a totally peaceful mind and heart, you will have earned your black belt in Financial Integrity.

Integrity is naturally fulfilling. Alignment of vision, values and action—whether we are talking about one person, a team of people, or a whole society—fosters a process known as synergy. Synergy is that state of functioning in which the whole is greater than the sum of its parts. With synergy, more energy comes out of a system than has seemingly been fed in. Synergy is potent.

Because we so often work at cross-purposes, within ourselves and within our organizations, synergy feels like magic, grace, a miracle. It's not. Synergy occurs within an individual when all aspects of his or her nature are aligned and focused in the same direction. If you're a tiger at work but a mouse at home, something within you is not aligned. Your energy will be tied up in a juggling act in which you keep dropping the balls. But if happiness, clarity and peace characterize all aspects of your life, and what you do is in alignment with your purpose, then you are a potent and fulfilled individual. And that's made possible by taking a few minutes each month to ask these three questions of each of your spending subcategories. You will discover what is enough at the material level, and you will have an abundance of the joy that comes from living a life that matters.

Getting to Enough

In Chapter 1 we talked about the Fulfillment Curve and that interesting place at the peak of the Fulfillment Curve called "enough." You have enough for your survival, enough for your comforts and even some special luxuries, with no excess to burden you unnecessarily. Enough is a powerful and free place. A confident and flexible place. And it's a place that you will define for yourself numerically as you follow this program. Asking the three questions, month in and month out, is the primary tool for defining, experientially, how much is enough *for you.*

Our own experience and that of seminar participants is that "enough" has four components, four common qualities:

1. **Accountability**, knowing how much money is flowing into and out of your life, is basic Financial Intelligence. Clearly, if you never know how much you have or where it's all going, you can never have enough.

No matter how much money she made, every month ***Marilynn Bradley****, a cook and caterer, was anxious that her money would run out before her next paycheck. While she always had enough, she never had enough* in her experience, *because she didn't know where she stood. It wasn't until she started meticulously keeping track of her money that the fears went away.*

Rich and poor alike benefit from accountability. Some people on government entitlement programs, from welfare to disability to Social Security, have enough, and others don't. *The Wall Street Journal* told the story of a mother on a $500-a-month welfare income who managed to save $3,000 over four years through care, thrift and prudence. The explanation was simple. She was saving for her daughter's college education, so she made every penny count. At the same time, an advocate for a homeless family in Los Angeles told the story of wangling $800 out of the system so parents and kids alike could get decent clothes and nourishing food. Instead, the father went out and bought an $800 stereo system. He figured everyone had been through such a bad time they deserved something nice. Many people go bankrupt and end up on the street in part because they haven't learned basic principles of money management—especially accountability.

2. **An internal yardstick for fulfillment**. As we pointed out earlier, you can never have enough if you are measuring by what others have or think.

3. **A purpose in life** higher than satisfying your own wants and desires, because you can never have enough if every desire becomes a need that must be filled. Desire begets desire. That's what the astute potato-chip company told us when it said, "Bet you can't eat just one." If you base your sense of having enough on your wants and desires it will be, at best, an ephemeral experience.

What is a purpose higher than getting what we want? The opposite of getting is giving—and therein lies a secret to fulfillment. Beyond the point of enough, we achieve happiness by exercising our capacity to give. If you have a purpose for your life that is higher than getting more and getting ahead, your energies will be focused on fulfilling that purpose—whether it is loving your family, serving on the school board or working for peace. When you are no longer defining your worth in dollars and cents you can get off the futile and endless money-go-round where your life was about trying to get ahead of the person in front of you.

4. **Responsibility**, a sense of how your life fits with your community and with the needs of the world. If we don't give a hoot about anyone but ourselves, we can never have enough until we have it all. Within the word "responsibility" is the key to why it's an essential part of having enough. Break it down and you see it contains "response" and "able." If you are going through life robotically, following patterns laid down by genetics, parents or society, you can *react* but not *respond*. To respond you must be conscious that you have a choice, that you can select your response. If you are responsible, you can choose when to stop. If you are not "response-able," you stop only when an external barrier is put up—be it the size of your stomach, the size of your credit limit or the limit of the law. With "response-ability" we can choose our limits and maintain a sense of balance, both within ourselves and with our neighbors. Initially, responsibility is about identifying when

you have enough and stopping there—for your own well-being. Ultimately responsibility is about everyone in the world having enough, and finding ways for all of us to get there—for the well-being of the earth. We become response-able to life itself.

MEANWHILE, BACK ON THE PLANET: THE SPACESHIP VIEW OF MONEY

Let's set aside our exploration of values and purpose for a moment and go on an imaginary journey in a spaceship so that we can look back and see the whole planet. What do we see? We see a small blue planet suspended in a vast darkness. We see one world with no national boundaries—one interconnected life-support system.

From our spaceship we can learn about the biggest possible view of money and economics, one that encompasses the other four perspectives on money we talked about in Chapter 2. As you remember, the first level of money was what we saw from the street—the nuts and bolts of financial transactions and money management. At the next level, where we had a view of the neighborhood, we encountered our thoughts and feelings about money. On the third level we explored our cultural agreements about money, and finally we understood the jet-plane perspective of Financial Independence, where we choose for ourselves the role of money in our lives.

The spaceship perspective on money and economics illuminates how "money" acts at a global level. Not money in the sense of the GNP and debt load of each country. Not global economics in the sense of multinational corporations or the billions of dollars that slosh around among drug and arms dealers and terrorists of every stripe. It's global economics in the sense of understanding that everything we eat, wear, live in and are comes out of the earth and the earth's billions of years of relationship with the sun.

From our spaceship we see that all of our economic activity is merely adding our will, ingenuity, greed and genius to what has been given to us for free by eons of generative interaction between the sun and the elements on the earth—our natural bank account. All of our manufacturing relies on chemical and biological processes that precede human intelligence. The quarter we put into a pay phone came from the earth. The clothes we buy, wear and then pass along to a thrift store came from the earth. The gas to run our car comes from a limited supply of stored sunlight (fossil fuels) in the earth. The toaster that breaks and must be replaced because we can't repair it comes from the earth. This book and the eyes you use to read it are part of the earth. And we should not kid ourselves that all these things will eventually decompose in landfills and nourish life again in any meaningful time period. For most of our modern products, it's a one-way ticket—out of the living earth and into a sealed tomb of landfills.

An awareness of the vigor and the fragility of nature can be awesome—and awful. Contemplating creation can inspire wonder at the goodness and perfection of life. That we exist at all is a miracle. In fact, this spaceship perspective also embraces that sense of wonder at the oneness of all life. The fact that we are literally made of the body of the earth means that all of life is one creation, unfolding everywhere all at once. We belong. We are one human family, part of the family of life. What binds us together is stronger and more fundamental than what keeps us apart. In some strange way, life is living us as surely as we are living life.

This awareness of nature can also inspire an awful feeling of how careless we've become with what's been given to us. Our very lives depend on access to clean air, clean water and fertile land, all of which are being used up and destroyed at frightening rates. Our true wealth has been compromised by what we call economic activity—converting natural resources into products to be sold—with its by-products of pollution and destruction. What if the ship sinks on our watch? Or becomes so waterlogged and depleted that future generations must spend all their energy merely surviving?

Sustainability

The search for a point of view that acknowledges our dependence on the natural world for all our activity, economic and otherwise, leads us to the concept of sustainability. How can we and others of our generation meet our needs without compromising the ability of future generations to meet theirs? Sustainability recognizes that "economics" and "ecology" have the same root, "eco," which means "house." It is a true "home economics" with which we can implement our realization that our home is our resource base, its resources are finite and our need for a clean, fertile planet is absolute.

From individual consumers to large corporations, we are reassessing our financial choices in terms of principles of sustainability—not just in order to jump on the environmental bandwagon, but because it makes good economic sense. As you progress through this program, you may well find yourself making more sustainable choices naturally. You may notice that buying one good coat and keeping it for ten years makes better economic sense than buying ten trendy coats, one for each fashion year. You may notice that buying food with less packaging actually lowers your grocery bill. You may even wake up one morning and discover that you've stopped wanting a luxury car.

Buckminster Fuller made this provocative statement: "I learned very early and painfully that you have to decide at the outset whether you are trying to make money or make sense—I feel that they are mutually exclusive." And there's more that you will discover as you look at money from a planetary perspective.

For example, at the Global Tomorrow Coalition conference in Los Angeles in November 1989, a passionate young man from the Philippines, Maximo Kalaw, described a comprehensive self-help program he'd helped develop to lift the indigenous peoples of his country out of poverty and despair. Like many others, he cited Western consumerism as one of the most destructive forces on the planet. He was asked what reforms he would need to see happening in North America to believe that we had indeed changed and would be fair and equitable partners in a sane, sustainable development process. He did not mention carpooling, recycling or even reduced consumer spending. He cited two things:

1. Beginning to work once again in community to solve our problems.
2. Reconnecting with our spirituality.

Many Americans wouldn't appreciate this observation. We usually think of ourselves as good, community-minded, religious people. Why would someone from the developing world find those very qualities lacking? Have we really gained the world and lost our soul?

The American Dream led us to believe that we might enjoy an ever-higher standard of living without giving up anything we already had. We were all on an escalator rising into the great cornucopia of unlimited abundance. Indeed, the promise was that we would need to work less and less and still have more and more. Already it is estimated that, thanks to burning fossil fuels, the average American lives a life-style that is equivalent to the work produced by approximately 200 slaves. This is El Dorado. The Fountain of Youth. The yearnings of all humanity, realized in our very lives. Yet, as everyone from academician Paul Wachtel to pollsters Roper and Harris has amply demonstrated, we aren't any happier. What gives? Or perhaps we should ask, what (or who) doesn't give anymore?

Reconnecting with Community

We need to recognize that we have actually traded something more than time for the money we have. In its cover story on April 8, 1991, *Time* magazine reported on the growing desire among successful professionals to return to "the simple life." A survey of 500 adults, done by *Time* in conjunction with CNN, uncovered a distinct "back to basics" trend:

- 69 percent said they'd like to "slow down and live a more relaxed life," while only 19 percent wanted to "live a more exciting, faster-paced life."
- 61 percent agreed that "earning a living today requires so much effort that it's difficult to find time to enjoy life."
- A stunning 89 percent said they thought it was more important to them now to spend time with their families, and 56 percent wanted to find time for personal interests and hobbies.
- Only 7 percent thought shopping for status symbols was worth the time and money, and a mere 13 percent wanted to keep up with fashions and trends.

Fortune magazine heralded this return to frugality in its August 14, 1989, article "Is Greed Dead?" by Ronald Henkoff. Drawing on a survey done by Research & Forecasts for Chivas Regal, the article reported that 75 percent of working Americans between the ages of 25 and 49 would like "to see our country return to a simpler lifestyle, with less emphasis on material success." Only 10 percent of those polled thought that "earning a lot of money" was an indicator of success, while 62 percent said a "happy family life" was the most important status symbol.

It would seem that the primary "thing" many people have sacrificed in "going for the gold" is their relationships with other people. Whether you think of that as a happy marriage, time with the children, neighborliness, a close circle of friends, shopkeepers who know you, civic involvement, community spirit, or just living in a place where you can walk to work and the beat cop is your friend, it's disappearing across the country. The web of human connection, which is filled with opportunities for synergy, has been replaced by an affluence that measures success by the amount of house, yard, and acreage you can put between yourself and another human being.

Lewis Thomas, author of *The Lives of a Cell*, tells us about the fate of the Iks, a tribe of former hunters and gatherers in Uganda who were displaced from their normal terrain by a national park and forced to become farmers on poor hillside soil. The complete dismantling of their traditional culture coupled with the meagerness of their new existence stripped them of their experience of community. They became stingy and sullen, heartened only by stealing one another's food or defecating on one another's doorsteps, repelling one another through every means available. Is this, Thomas asks, what's left of being human when our sense of community collapses, when we cease recognizing others as part of ourselves? And isn't this, he further asks, how many groups, from clubs to cities to nations, behave in relation to one another—with that same quality of "greed, rapacity, heartlessness, and irresponsibility?"

The hallmark of and key to community is a foundation of cooperation. Indeed, each one of us cooperates within many communities (where everyone is an "us") and competes with many other entities (where everyone is a "them"). It all has to do with where we place our boundaries—and how well and compassionately we honor others' boundaries.

Ultimately the whole planet can be seen as a community of communities—ever-extending circles of "us," filled with ever-expanding opportunities for synergistic co-creation. Roger Ringer, who lives in rural Kansas, wrote in a letter to us:

> What is good for an individual household is also good for the Planet if it's done with vision and purpose. Self-interest can be our ally in helping each other to get off the treadmill. But the consumer culture has become adept at blurring the distinction between self-interest and selfishness, so most of us find it easy to slide into quagmires of debt, spending and consuming when all we really want is a reasonable level of comfort and security.

Reconnecting with Our Spirituality

As Maximo Kalaw, the young man from the Philippines, indicated, widening our sense of identity to encompass this larger community of communities is only half of the journey to a sustainable future. We also need to deepen our identity by reconnecting with our spirituality. If problems are really opportunities to grow, then the problems we face as a species constitute a call to a new understanding of what it means to be human. This kind of understanding won't come from technology, science or government establishments. It will come from deep within each one of us. Both within and outside the structures of traditional religions, Americans have been struggling to reconnect with this deeper aspect of life. What would be a compassionate way to relate with those billions of fellow humans—people who may live halfway around the planet, yet who enter our homes nightly via TV? What respect and protection do I owe to other species? What do my values say about war, about how my consumption might affect our biosphere, about homelessness and hunger amid plenty? We have the awesome task of living in this global community of communities and participating as "global citizens." The enormity of this task is sending us back to our roots, both within our religious traditions and within ourselves. The new road map for money is part of this new road map for the human family—coexisting with all of life on our shared home, the earth.

Having Enough

Global citizens living sustainably in a global community of communities—what kind of world would that be? Let's try to imagine for a moment such a world, a world in which everyone had enough—enough for his or her survival, enough for comforts and even enough extra for those special times that represent real pleasure.

We began this chapter talking about our personal dreams and about aligning our earning and spending with our values and our sense of purpose. The dream of "everyone having enough" has been with us as a species for thousands of years, yet has never been fulfilled.

Following the steps of this program, doing your tracking and Monthly Tabulation and asking yourself the three questions will become so simple, so much second nature, that you might wonder what would happen if everyone who's living on "more than enough" did it. The dream of a sustainable world might begin to seem quite possible if what wasn't needed, the clutter of life, faded away. Does this sound like an impossible dream? Perhaps . . . but if you agree with Viktor Frankl that we each possess a will to have meaning, then possibilities abound.

The Japanese have a wonderful saying: "The gods only laugh when people ask them for money."

And the Tao Te Ching, the ancient Chinese book of wisdom, puts it this way: "He who knows he has enough is rich."

SUMMARY OF STEP 4

1. **Of each spending subcategory in your Monthly Tabulation ask Question 1: "Did I receive fulfillment, satisfaction and value in proportion to life energy spent?" Mark your answer with a + (or an up arrow), a – (or a down arrow), or a 0.**
2. **Of each spending subcategory in your Monthly Tabulation ask Question 2: "Is this expenditure of life energy in alignment with my values and life purpose?" Mark your answer with a + (or an up arrow), a – (or a down arrow), or a 0.**
3. **Of each spending subcategory in your Monthly Tabulation ask Question 3: "How might this expenditure change if I didn't have to work for a living?" Mark your answer**

with a + (or an up arrow), a − (or a down arrow), or a 0 and write the estimated change on the Monthly Tabulation.

4. **Review and make a list of all subcategories with the − symbol (or down arrow).**

5

SEEING PROGRESS

Step 5: Making Life Energy Visible

In Step 5 you make visible the results of the previous steps, plotting them on a graph that gives you a clear, simple picture of your current relationship with money (life energy) as well as the *trend* of your financial situation, and the transformation in your relationship with money.

MAKING YOUR WALL CHART

Step 5 entails setting up a graph of your income and your expenses, one that is large enough to accommodate three to five years of data. This graph will be simple to create, simple to maintain and simple to interpret. All the information you need is already on your Monthly Tabulation. You don't need a computer program to do Step 5. You just need to do it!

From a business supply store or college bookstore get a large sheet of graph paper (an 18-by-22-inch sheet with 10 squares to the centimeter or a 24-by-36-inch sheet with 10 squares to the inch will do nicely). If you can't find one, never fear. You can use any large piece of paper and rule it yourself (see Figure 5-1). The left-hand, vertical axis represents money. On it you will chart both your income and your

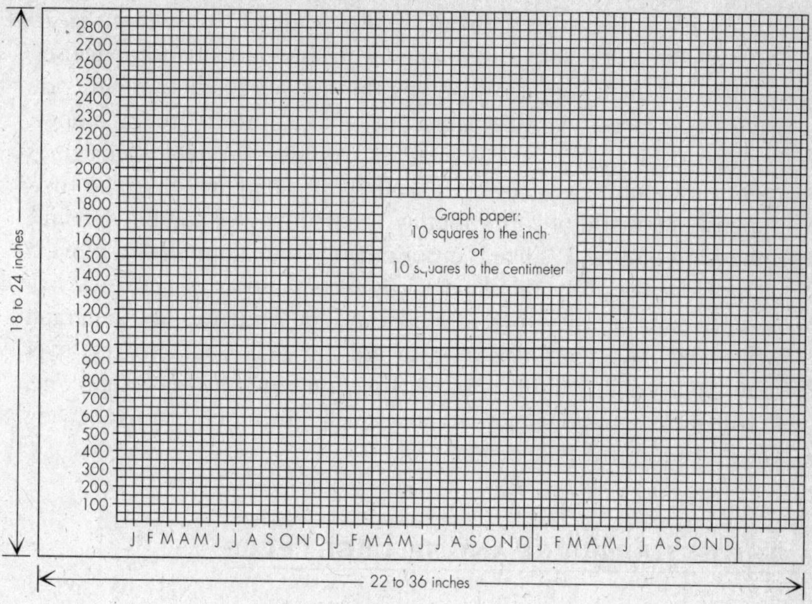

FIGURE 5-1

Suggested Size and Layout of Wall Chart

expenses. Mark it in increments of dollars. Start with 0 at the bottom, leaving plenty of room on the upper part of the chart. As outrageous as this may sound at the moment, you should probably allow enough space at the top for your income to double. More than one FIer has sheepishly shown us a chart with extra graph paper taped at the top to account for a level of earnings he or she never thought possible. Set up your scale so that the larger of the two figures (income or expenses) for this month falls about halfway up the scale. The lower horizontal scale represents time in increments of months. Allow five to seven years on this axis. That's enough to see large-scale trends—and maybe enough to see you through to Financial Independence!

At the end of each month you will plot the figures for your total monthly income and total monthly expenses. It is useful to use one color for your income and another for your expenses. Connect each point with a line to the previous month's entry. You will be creating two different colored lines, one for income and one for expenses.

That's all there is to it. When you do this step the first month, you have a snapshot—a very revealing one—of your habits around money. But the real learning, and the real fun, come as you plot your figures month by month, year by year. Your Wall Chart will take the two-dimensional world of your Monthly Tabulations and add the dynamic dimension of time. It's like transforming a photo album into a moving picture: the Monthly Tabulations are like snapshots of particular *moments* in your journey toward Financial Independence, but the graph will make vivid your *movement* toward the goal, your progress over time. Your graph will be a "moving picture" in more ways than one. It will show you your motion, and it will also move you—renewing your commitment to keep going.

THE INITIAL PURGE AND SPLURGE CYCLE

In the first month of recording your figures you might confront one of our national foibles. Your income entry may well be lower than your expenses entry. You may have spent more than you earned. (It is, after all, the American way.) Seeing this reality might come as a bit of a shock. Chances are you'll want things to change—and change now. Accustomed to budgets, diets and New Year's resolutions, you swear on a stack of bank statements and credit cards that next month will be better.

This is when people often go on a "wallet fast" with the kind of zeal characteristic of first-time dieters. They scrimp. They save. They deprive themselves and their families, putting everyone on beans, rice and oatmeal rations. They concentrate daily on that expenses line, determined to cut it in half in one short month. Amazingly enough, many do. Entering the expense figure the second month, they proudly note a steep decline.

This kind of austerity, however, isn't sustainable. By the third month expenses often rebound with a vengeance, making up for the second-month deprivation.

Now what? In the old way of thinking, you might be tempted to take up the burden of budgeting again . . . or to quit. But take heart. There is a better way, and it works.

Diane Grosch, *the computer programmer we met in Chapter 1 who hated her job but couldn't find a way out, had no trouble setting up her Wall Chart. Numbers and tracking were her business. While she had acquired many trophies to prove her success—from a pricey sports car to mementos collected on travels to exotic destinations—her Wall Chart looked no different from those of many other American Dreamers. Her expenses were higher than her income.*

"What I saw truly shocked me. I had no idea I spent more than I earned. But there it was: income $2,280 for that month and expenses $2,470."

She felt challenged. If the odds were against spending less than you earn, she wanted to beat the odds. She decided to experiment on ways to lower her expenses. Rather than going out to lunch with her coworkers or even ordering less expensive meals, she chose to eat lunch at work. For a month she bought no new clothes or dinners out—after all, you can take anything for a month. Lo and behold, by month two her expenses had dropped way below her income. She'd proved she could do it.

"I was elated! The next month I paid less attention, returning to my old shopping habits and wiping out much of the financial gain of the previous month. My Wall Chart looked bad.*"*

And she realized that instead of trying to change the chart, she would need to change herself. Yet, through the years, she'd spent thousands of dollars on seminars that were designed to change everything from her self-esteem to her effectiveness on the job, but the change never lasted. So what was different this time? A major component was the Wall Chart. The Wall Chart seemed to be a challenge to the way she was living her whole life. It drew a picture of her spending habits, graphically showing her why there was not enough money at the end of the month. She decided to follow the steps and see where they led. She'd beaten plenty of other odds. She would beat these too. (See Figure 5-2.)

How did this change in spending happen? Diane explains that as she followed the steps of the program and noted her successes, her self-esteem rose. She saw that she could do it—and her dissatisfaction turned into a drive to do the best job she could. This spirit transformed

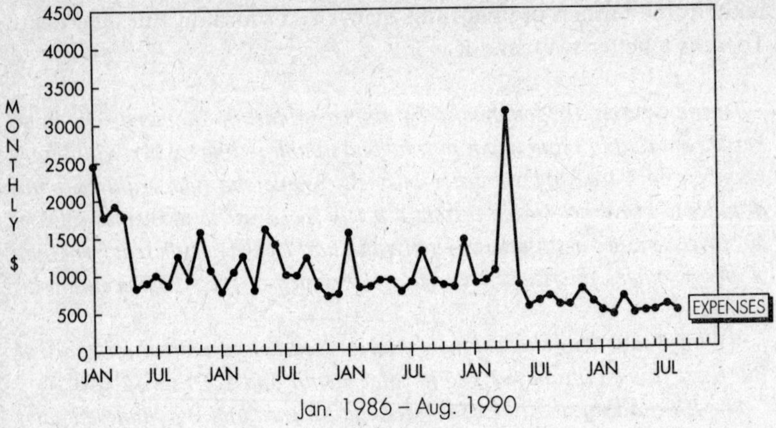

FIGURE 5-2

Diane's Wall Chart—with Expenses

her experience of working—surprising her as much as it surprised her supervisors.

"Within four months I was debt-free and my expenses were down to $850. I had cut my grocery bill from $186 a month to $105 without even trying. Perhaps part of it was that I was happier on my job so I needed fewer treats. My restaurant bill dropped to $40 a month from $120, just by eating out only when I really *wanted to. I moved to a house for less rent that was closer to work, so my gas bill was 60 percent lower. My medical costs were also cut in half, most likely for the same reason my food bill went down. I was enjoying my job more and had no need to get sick. None of this felt like deprivation. I wasn't* struggling *to spend less. It didn't even feel like I was* doing *anything in particular. It all happened gradually. At the same time, I* loved *putting my figures on the Wall Chart each month and seeing the changes. What a thrill!"*

The Wall Chart reminds us that transforming our relationship with money takes time and patience. Impatience, denial and greed are actually part of what is being transformed. It takes time to reflect on our lives and see if we still want to go where we're headed. Insight can happen in a minute, but growth happens over time. Reading this book may take only a few days, but transforming your relationship with money will happen over time. Remember the lottery winners. Even if you should win the lottery, your *relationship* with money would not be transformed, and your life would not all of a sudden be filled with more joy or peace of mind. By *observing* your reactions to your Wall Chart instead of getting upset about it, you will be clearing away the attitudes and beliefs that got you where you are today.

There are two keys to making this process work for you:

1. Start.
2. Keep going.

We often hear that the journey of a thousand miles begins with a single step. What we don't hear as often is that you arrive at your destination by hundreds of thousands of additional small steps forward. Keep taking those steps. They are important to the continuing growth of your awareness and strengthening of your integrity—day by day. Eventually you'll begin to experience the magic of this process. Without even trying you'll find your expense line heading down. How?

HOW THE THREE QUESTIONS CAN SAVE YOU MONEY

Remember those three questions in Step 4? You will be finding out the profound effect these questions have on your consciousness about money—and consequently on your Wall Chart.

Automatic Lowering of Expenses

Question 1 is: **"Did I receive fulfillment, satisfaction and value in proportion to life energy spent?"** Asking this question every month about each of your spending categories increases your consciousness about your choices and thus results in an automatic reduction in your total monthly expenses, giving you the pleasure of seeing the expenses line on your chart go down. As we saw in Chapter 4, greater consciousness about which expenditures actually bring us happiness and which do not activates our "survival mechanism." In fact, you are reprogramming yourself. Each of your – marks is an affront to your survival instinct, that automatic movement toward pleasure and away from pain. This powerful mechanism becomes an ally as you become aware that some expenditures that you thought brought pleasure, or that you simply incurred out of habit, are actually not fulfilling or pleasurable at all.

Remember our gazingus pins? You will soon know what yours are. Those blinding moments of awareness as you catch yourself about to spend your life energy on yet another gazingus pin will all add up to lower expenses. Let's see how this works.

In the past, when you tried to change your habits and thus increase your experience of satisfaction, you didn't have an accurate overview of your spending patterns. Rather than identifying gazingus-pin buying as a source of dissatisfaction, you continued to think it was the one thing to hang on to. Sometimes you might have tried to give up gazingus pins as a painful penance for your spendthrift ways . . . only to find yourself once again at the gazingus-pin counter thinking, "Just this once. Just this once." But now you have identified those dead ends and are looking down from above the money maze. You have seen the light: "I am not getting fulfillment, in reality, from this expenditure of life energy." You will feel as if you are waking up from a dream, realizing, with great relief, that it wasn't real. As a matter of fact, that's just what is happening.

This kind of reprogramming is amazingly powerful. It will click in, strongly, next time you are about to robotically buy something. There you are, mechanically reaching out to pick up yet another gazingus pin, and all of a sudden a "red alert" goes off in your brain: "Wait! Do I really want another gazingus pin? *No!* It will just go in my gazingus-pin drawer along with the twenty others. There's five hours of my life in each of those gazingus pins—and I don't even use them." Shrinking back from your gazingus-pin addiction, you cry, "No!" (After a while you'll learn to be cool during this process.) That little moment of awareness makes a big difference. Now that the link between spending money and getting fulfillment is in place, a gazingus pin no longer automatically means satisfaction—quite the opposite. Now you can be in line with yourself—you're neither fighting yourself nor trying to buy happiness and satisfaction. On the contrary, you're now getting fulfillment from other uses of your life energy; you are valuing your life energy and thus yourself. From this perspective, it is easy to change direction.

Ivy Underwood *had grown up poor, the daughter of Mexican-American parents. There was never enough money, but rather than acknowledge and talk about the pain of poverty, her parents gave her platitudes. "We are blessed," her Catholic father would say, "because only the poor can enter the kingdom of heaven." Religion and poverty and frustration at counting pennies got all tangled up, leaving Ivy confused and resentful. She resolved that when she grew up she'd have enough money so that she'd never have to worry about balancing her checkbook and would be able to buy whatever she wanted.*

Ivy easily identified her "gazingus pin": it was clothes. In doing her inventory in Step 1 she breezed through her home, satisfied with her simplicity, until she came to her closet. Where did all these clothes come from? Of course, they came from a variety of stores—most of them expensive department stores. But why? Her determination to never again be poor had turned into the need to always be perfectly dressed. She could measure her distance from poverty by the number of daily compliments on her attire.

Yes, as a career professional she did need to look her best. But for Ivy that had been translated into several new outfits every month. If she even wore last month's blouse with this month's new suit she felt shabby.

In doing her Monthly Tabulations she quickly saw that she did not *get fulfillment commensurate with the hours of life energy she put into keeping several department stores in the black. With no struggle, no denial or deprivation, she stopped buying clothes she didn't need. To her amazement, the number of compliments she received per day didn't decrease at all.*

All was well for many months. Then one day, depressed over something, she found herself back at the clothing racks. She was looking for a pair of shorts and had a blinding moment of awakening. "What am I doing here? I don't even need *shorts!" She walked out of the store empty-handed and with a stronger sense of her own power and integrity.*

Gordon Mitchell, *the black activist turned financial planner whom we met in Chapter 1, found that his unconscious spending categories were far more devastating than Ivy's "gazingus pin" of clothing. You would have to* *call them mega-gazingus pins—or simply major spending blind spots. The FI course for him was more like cataract surgery than simply getting a new pair of glasses.*

When he asked himself the questions about fulfillment and alignment, he realized how bored and tired he'd been for the past eight years. He also saw clearly what had gotten him into trouble. First of all, to play the role of financial planner he had assumed he needed an expensive office. But when he looked at the amount of life energy his office was costing him—$2,600 per month—he questioned whether he was really getting value. In fact, he wasn't. He did most of his business on the phone, through the mail or in clients' homes. Nobody ever saw him in his office. So he moved his office to his home. Total current office cost: $500 per month.

The second biggest blind spot for Gordon had been his kids. They lived with their mother, but he provided well for their support. That was no problem. The problem was that he gave his kids extra money every time they asked because he felt guilty about not being with them. He has nine children, so that added up. No matter how much he gave, they always wanted more. Having had his street smarts sharpened by this process of honest evaluation, Gordon recognized that his kids had become addicted, and he was the enabler. He decided to change, and even though the children are now going through a form of withdrawal, Gordon is satisfied with his choice to stop paying guilt money for being an absent father. With a few other minor adjustments, asking the three questions cut 50 percent off Gordon's expenses—and he is a lot happier for it.

Not everyone has the amount of "padding" that Gordon did, but after looking at hundreds of FIers' Wall Charts we can say that those who get past the three-month hump will find their expenses leveling out at about 20 percent less than where they started—*painlessly*. These people report no feelings of deprivation, no struggling to keep to a budget, just a natural decline. Knowing that you are not getting satisfaction proportional to the expenditure of life energy in a given subcategory of spending generates an automatic, self-protective reversal of your spending habits. Over time, you actually find yourself feeling better by *not* spending; *not* buying a gazingus pin now becomes a source of fulfillment because you yourself have determined that gazingus pins don't bring you fulfillment.

Alignment and Personal Integration

There is still more to look forward to as you work with your Wall Chart. Watch that expense line go down as you ask, month in and month out, Question 2: **"Is the expenditure of life energy in this category in alignment with my values and stated life purpose?"**

This is a feedback system for integrity. Your statement of your values and life purpose reflects your highest vision, what you truly want for yourself. Thus you will *want* to act in your day-to-day life in a way consistent with your values and purpose. Unfortunately, however, it is sometimes all too easy to overlook the reality of what you're actually *doing*. It is possible to behave in ways that are not only unsupportive of but contradictory to your highest vision and intention—and to be unaware of what you're doing. Worse yet, sometimes conflicts between whims and higher purpose are resolved by swiftly silencing the voices of conscience. The data on how you spend your life energy provides a nitty-gritty, tangible measure of that integrity, which is an invaluable support in keeping your material life in line with your ideals and goals. When your spending and your goals are in alignment, you have an experience of wholeness and integrity; you feel good about yourself. When they are not aligned—when the answer to the question "Does this expenditure support my values and life purpose?" is a resounding *No!*—then the experience is more likely to be one of disappointment or self-criticism.

The subtle but effective process of reinforcement (spend money on X = feel good, spend money on Y = feel bad) actually works; it serves to break robotic spending patterns. The simple recognition that you're not experiencing alignment from a given spending category acts to realign your responses to the stimuli in that category. You will automatically begin to spend less on those things that don't support your values and life purpose, and you will feel better about yourself, knowing that increasingly you *are* putting your money where your life purpose is, integrating your material life with your inner awareness. This integration is at the heart of Financial Integrity.

As far as she could tell, **Diane Grosch** *didn't have a purpose in life. She just wanted to make it through, seeking pleasure and avoiding pain as best she could. Thinking back on her childhood, she remembered that her only* *happiness had been wandering off in the woods when her family took trips to the country.*

At the time she started the FI program, she was the only one of her siblings who had "gotten ahead." One was a recluse living on welfare, another had committed suicide and the third lived on the streets. Having a high-paying job, a sports car and a nice house made her look like a winner—to herself and to her family.

The question about aligning her spending with her values shook her complacency. Having always measured herself by externals, Diane started covertly checking out her friends and coworkers. Did they have a higher purpose? One of the people in her office was one of those "save the world" types. Intrigued by someone who didn't measure her net worth by material possessions, Diane cultivated a friendship with her. Soon both of them were attending meetings of a local peace group. The people Diane met there were all questioning how they could better live their values, and what actions they could take in the world to express their sense of purpose.

These meetings became her chief form of entertainment. Instead of expensive workshops or outings to all the latest movies, she attended lectures and participated in phone-a-thons. She found a large park near her home and spent hours on weekends wandering in the woods. And at charting time her expense line kept going down. From a monthly outlay of over $3,000, her cost of living dropped to a steady $600 to $800 per month. Looking for her purpose in life turned out to be a key component in the change she was undergoing.

WHAT ABOUT "UNUSUAL MONTHS"?

Yes, there will be "unusual" months, months when your expenses line takes an alarming leap upward. The insurance payment is due. You have an unexpected repair expense. April comes and goes, with the annual bloodletting known as taxes. How do you handle these?

For one thing, you may recognize that every month is an unusual month. You learn to take "unusual" expenses in stride and to pay for them with cash instead of hiding them under a blanket of plastic. One month's tax payment is another month's insurance payment is another month's doctor bill. Over time, these "unusual expenses" usually balance out.

Another strategy would be to prorate annual expenses over the whole twelve months. For example, if your auto insurance bill is $500 per year, you might (in addition to questioning whether a car is worth it) choose to divide that by twelve and make it a monthly expense. Ditto with health insurance, income tax payments, property taxes and so on.

There is no right way to do the accounting. You need to choose the way that gives *you* the information you need so that as you glance at your Wall Chart you know where you are and where you're going.

GETTING YOUR FINANCES OUT IN THE OPEN

There's another key to successfully working with your chart. Hang it where you can see it every day. To do you the most good, the chart must be visible so that it can inspire you—often—to stay on track. You will need to hang it up—but where?

Some people start out with their chart "in the closet"—literally. They hang their chart on the inside of their closet door. It keeps their financial affairs private while still providing a reminder every day as they dress for work that they want to be conscious in their handling of money. For those opting for Financial Independence it reinforces the awareness that work is no longer about "another day, another dollar," but rather about drawing one day closer to their goal of freedom from financial fears and fiscal failures. It's a boost, as good as a cup of coffee or a hug.

***Ivy Underwood**, who never wanted to be poor, met her Prince Charming. And so, as they say in fairy tales, it came to pass that she had a successful husband, two sons, her built-to-order dream house with three decks, two patios and furniture selected by an interior designer—and no need to balance her checkbook. Then reality intervened. The fantasies on which she'd built her life weren't strong enough to maintain her marriage—or her sanity. In 1983 she said good-bye to her husband, her house, her furniture and her high-stress job, packed a few select possessions into a U-Haul and headed west with her sons.*

*Seven years later, through the FI course, she found a path to even greater freedom. She and her friend **Margaret Parsons** invited a group of twenty friends to take the course so that they could support one another in following* *the program. They met every month, sharing insights, successes and roadblocks—and the intimate details of their financial lives.*

When Ivy did her chart she challenged herself to bring it to the group—and some of her ancient fears reappeared. Her first thought was, "My parents would think I'm crazy. You don't show people how much you earn and spend. It's—it's—it's not in good taste. It's . . ." What was that reluctance? Why was she afraid of exposing her finances? The reason, she realized, was a fear that it would allow people to judge her, deciding whether she was a person of worth. They could sum her up with a few numbers and discard her if she fell short. With the same resolve that had helped her to leave her marriage, she took her chart to the group. The fear melted, and something inside her relaxed about money. What she spent was just . . . what she spent. Her income was just her income. She could tell it to someone as easily as she could tell someone the color of her living-room couch. It was no big deal!

Over time you may find that your feelings about your chart are changing as a reflection of changes in your relationship with money. The chart becomes a representation of how well you are living your values, something that reflects the care you are taking with every decision about your material world. It becomes a source of pride—not arrogance, but that kind of deep satisfaction that comes with integrity. Once this happens, many people find that they feel so good about their progress that they bring their chart out of the closet and hang it on a wall.

Stop a minute and reflect on your own feelings about your current relationship with money. How would you feel about hanging this graphic representation of your financial affairs on your living-room wall, right out where everyone who comes into your house could see it? Would you feel at ease—or uneasy? The degree of your discomfort is a measure of the degree of your financial dis-ease. Don't worry. That uneasiness will disappear as you follow the steps of this program.

FINANCIAL INDEPENDENCE AS A BY-PRODUCT OF DOING THE STEPS

People who put the steps of this program into practice report that the process of transforming their relationship with money becomes both challenging and fascinating. Recording every penny becomes an enjoyable ritual at the checkout counter—and it also sparks some interesting discussions with curious onlookers who want to know what you're up to. Monthly Tabulation time is a highlight. Asking the three questions provides a quick yet penetrating check-in with your values and life purpose. Entering income and expenses on the Wall Chart becomes a time to reflect on the truth of your consciousness around money. After a few months or a year of following these steps you will begin to notice a very satisfying by-product of the process: as you consistently earn more than you spend, you eventually get out of debt and accumulate savings.

Does some of this seem impossible, considering your particular financial situation? It's not the conditions of your life but how you interact with them that will allow you to move forward. Followers of this program include people who were deeply in debt and out of work, who didn't have a college education and had huge gaps in their résumés, who had families to support and who lived in depressed parts of the country. They didn't have "the wind at their backs." They just made skillful use of the conditions they encountered and sailed through them.

In the strictest sense, Financial Independence, as we have defined it, means having an income sufficient for your basic needs and comforts from a source other than paid employment. But there are, as we will see, other aspects of FI, such as getting out of debt and accumulating savings.

Financial Independence Is Getting Out of Debt

For many people, getting out of debt is a tremendous milestone, very much an accomplishment of Financial Independence. Often they don't even realize what a burden debt is until it disappears.

What about you? Are you in debt? Do you know how much you owe and to whom? Do you know how much it's costing you to be in debt? Or do you just make payments on your mortgage, your car(s) and your credit cards till death do you part?

We recently heard an advocate for the homeless say that most Americans are two paychecks away from homelessness. That seemed excessive, almost beyond belief. Yet when we talked with other professionals who have their fingers on the pulse of consumer debt, some have said that two paychecks is a conservative estimate. One paycheck or one major illness would be enough to send many people over the edge.

Young Americans currently spend an average of $1.20 for every $1 they make. Are you—or were you—one of them?

One young participant in a Debtors Anonymous group said she'd accumulated $30,000 of debt before she was thirty. She'd been in a fast-track career, and her income had attracted the attention of the credit card sharks. When American Express sent her a Gold Card, she figured she'd arrived. If *they* thought she was so credit-worthy, then she must be! Head held high, shoulders square, she marched to the best furniture store in town and bought everything she wanted—never realizing that she would pay interest on her purchases.

Here's some hard reality to chew on. You pay from 16 percent to over 20 percent interest on your credit card debt. That's like working a five-day week and getting paid for four. If your employer announced such a downward revision in salaries, you and your coworkers would be up in arms. People who see debt as endless and just pay down as little as possible are actually opting for that lower income. They don't see that buying a new stereo "on time" to celebrate a raise will wipe out the gain in salary—and then some. A car bought "on time" will ultimately cost two and a half times the original sticker price. A house with a thirty-year mortgage at 10 percent could cost three times the purchase price by the time the final payment is made.

Debtors Anonymous says we go into debt to avoid feelings, especially feelings of deprivation. Like other addictions, debt allows us to deny pain, sorrow, loss, anger, loneliness and despair. Is your tendency to use your credit card simply a habit, or is it an addiction?

A survey reported in *The People's Almanac* indicates that people spend 23 percent more when they buy with credit cards than when they buy with cash. Debt has become the American Way, making it hard to see that it is debt that ties us to our jobs. It's debt that keeps us with our noses to the grindstone, making a dying to pay off pleasures we've long forgotten and luxuries we scarcely have time to enjoy.

One friend, having recognized her addiction to credit cards, decided to go cold turkey. Not trusting herself just to tuck them away, she sat right down and cut each one in half. The pieces filled a large plastic bag. Our friend may not be alone. We may well see a credit card revolution in the nineties. Formerly docile middle-class people may rise up, burning their credit cards in front of malls the way long-haired college students burned their draft cards in the sixties. "Hell no, we won't go," they'll cry in response to vacation packages to Tahiti. Don't laugh. It could happen—when people wake up to the dark side of paying with plastic.

Sally Morris *used to subtitle her life "Bombs by Day—Peace by Night." She worked for money as a graphic designer for a high-tech company with major defense contracts and worked for love on a variety of church-sponsored service projects. Thanks to her $17,000 debt, there seemed to be no alternative. And because she had been told repeatedly that there was no other way, her conscience had stopped bothering her.*

The FI program provided a merciless mirror—but it freed her. On her chart she placed a small sign that said, "On my way to debt-free." Below it she put a series of Velcro patches with numbers and kept track of the exact amount she owed. "It was as if I were melting a candle or losing a hundred pounds," she told us. Without a raise and without any feeling of deprivation, she was debt-free in two years.

When she looked for what was really fulfilling in her life, she saw that her greatest joy came from short-term work trips she'd participated in, helping with construction jobs in places like Costa Rica and Kenya. Upon returning from her first trip to Kenya, she had become extremely depressed. Yes, she'd helped build an addition to a rural hospital in a remote mountain village, but now what? She was still rich, while they were poor. So she started collecting medical supplies that would otherwise be discarded and packed them off to Kenya with safari-bound tourists.

By the time she was debt-free Sally knew just what her next step would be. She had discovered that people in Kenya were dying from untreated tooth abscesses. She quit her job, rented out her town house, leased her car and left for Kenya for a year to help establish a dental clinic. With no debts and with the rent on her house and car providing all the cash she needed to live in rural Kenya, Sally was financially liberated. Being debt-free, she now had a choice—and she chose to follow her heart.

Getting out of debt, then, is one form of Financial Independence. Retiring your debt returns to you the freedom to choose. Whatever the economic climate, being able to say, "I don't owe anything to anyone" is a statement of sanity, dignity and freedom.

Once you're out of debt you have choice. You might choose, as Sally

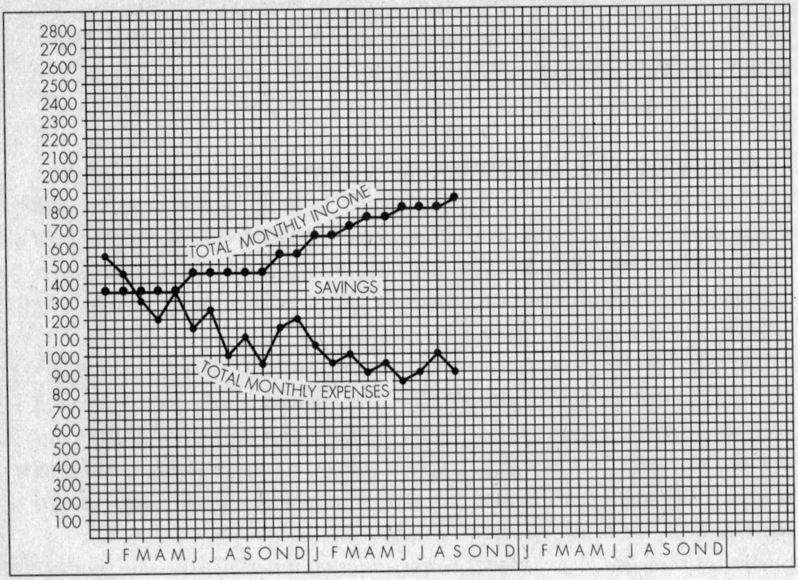

FIGURE 5-3

Wall Chart with Expenses, Income and Savings

did, to follow your heart to distant lands or different pursuits. Then again, you might continue to enjoy the process of transforming your relationship with money right where you are. As you continue to spend less than you earn (while savoring life to the fullest), an ever-larger gap will develop on your Wall Chart between your income line and your expenses line. This gap has a name, one that has fallen into disuse in recent years. It's called *savings* (see Figure 5-3). Savings are another form of Financial Independence.

Financial Independence Is Money in the Bank

How much are you saving now? What would your life be like if you had money to cover a year's worth of expenses in some form of easily accessible savings?

Since, as mentioned above, credit cards increase our spending by more than 20 percent, eliminating them would reduce your expenses by that amount. Interestingly enough, people who follow the Debtors Anonymous program also find that they spend about 20 percent less than before. Consider, too, the advice of popular financial adviser Jane Bryant Quinn. In promoting the strategy called "pay yourself first" (set aside savings *before* paying the bills and stocking your wallet), she observed that it wasn't until she herself hit a 20 percent savings rate that she even began to feel the pinch. Almost 20 percent of her money just ran through her fingers without giving her any appreciable pleasure.

The capacity for saving is truly within your grasp. It *will* happen as you follow the steps.

So what does this mean for you?

With savings, unemployment is not a tragedy. If you lose your paycheck but have savings you need not lose any of your possessions. What's more, you may see the opportunity to explore options you were too busy or too tired to consider before. You could pack up the family in a camper and travel around the country. You could strap on a backpack and tour the world. You could read. You could do every household project on your list. You could learn a new trade. You could explore your creative side, painting pictures or making music for the sheer pleasure of it. You could spend the whole year in a systematic job search for the work that suits you to a T. You could get your GED, B.A. or M.A. and qualify for a whole new level in your chosen field of work. You could volunteer full-time for a cause you care about—and maybe even be asked to stay on as paid staff. You could get reacquainted with your family.

Try this: ask yourself how you would spend your time if you could take a year off with pay. Don't be surprised if you find your mind a total blank; complete identification with your job may have temporarily suppressed your true dreams and desires. But stay with the question and discover the possibilities of what you would choose to do if you had enough savings that you didn't need paid employment for one year.

How do you feel about having savings? What are your thoughts about it—for or against? Does having savings compromise your self-image? Does it represent the passage of your youth or capitulation to your parents? Are you a spendthrift who thinks that the term "disposable income" means that it's your right to spend every last penny in your pocket? Does saving seem like an impossible dream, given your current financial status? What about your religious or political convictions about saving money? Should you be tithing your excess money to the church, giving it to the poor or donating it to a cause? The point here is not necessarily to change your savings habits but to get in touch with your predisposition about savings so that you'll be able to manage, with ease and integrity, the increase in savings that comes as a by-product of doing these steps.

Savings, then, are a form of Financial Independence. Savings can give you new courage at your job and new energy to explore the neglected parts of your life. Savings pave over the lean times in freelance or seasonal work. Savings relax any unconscious fear of becoming a street person. Savings keep you from making bad choices out of desperation.

Saving money is like building a dam on a river. The water that builds up behind the dam has an increasing amount of potential energy. Allow your life energy (money) to accumulate in a bank account, and you will be ready to power anything from painting your house to reorienting your life.

ALL THIS FROM A GRAPH?

There is nothing magical about the Wall Chart. You can enter your numbers at the beginning of the month and ignore it the rest of the month, and nothing will happen. But if you interact with it, keep it in plain sight, listen to what it's telling you and *keep going,* you will notice changes *over time.* Part of Financial Intelligence is the continuing awareness of your earning, spending and saving patterns over time.

- It is a constant *reminder* of your commitment to transform your relationship with money. It counters the "out of sight, out of mind" syndrome. It keeps you aware of your intention to change your unconscious spending habits.
- It is a *feedback system,* showing you at a glance, clearly and graphically, your current status and your progress toward your goal. You don't have to haul out your piggybank or your Monthly Tabula-

tions to see how you're doing. The two lines on your graph are either going up or going down.

- It can be an *inspiration,* an experience of satisfaction with the progress you're making that spurs you to even greater heights. When you are convinced that the process isn't working, your Wall Chart will remind you that it is.
- It can be a *motivation,* a prod to keep you on track when discouragement creeps in or your energy flags. When temptation strikes, the thought of facing your Wall Chart at the end of the month might help you make a healthier choice.
- It puts your *integrity* on the line—visibly. It is hard (or at least harder) to lie to yourself about your progress in the presence of your Wall Chart.
- It is a continuing *suggestion* that you honor your life energy. Your income represents many hours of your precious tenure on this beautiful earth, and your expenses represent ways you've chosen to use those valuable hours. The Wall Chart reminds you to steward this resource of time as well as possible.
- Finally, it enlists continuing *support.* By having it on the wall where others can see it, you're inviting interest and participation. It helps to have your friends and relatives cheering on the sidelines.

CHECKLIST OF SUPPLIES

- Graph paper—approximately 18 by 22 inches with 10 squares to the centimeter, or 24 by 36 inches with 10 squares to the inch
- Pens—black, plus two other colors

SUMMARY OF STEP 5

Make and keep up-to-date a chart of your total monthly income and your total monthly expenses.

6

THE AMERICAN DREAM—ON A SHOESTRING

It is both sad and telling that there is no word in the English language for living at the peak of the Fulfillment Curve, always having plenty but never being burdened with excess. The word would need to evoke the careful stewarding of tangible resources (time, money, material possessions) coupled with the joyful expansion of spiritual resources (creativity, intelligence, love). Unfortunately, you can't say, "I'm enoughing," or "I'm choosing a life of enoughness," to explain that mixture of affluence and thrift that comes from following the steps of this program. The word "frugality" used to serve that function, but in the latter half of the twentieth century frugality has gotten a bad reputation.

How did frugality lose favor among Americans? It is, after all, a perennial ideal and a cornerstone of the American character. Both Socrates and Plato praised the "golden mean." Both the Old Testament ("Give me neither poverty nor wealth, but only enough") and the teachings of Jesus ("Ye cannot serve both God and money") extol the value of material simplicity in enriching the life of the spirit. In American history well-known individuals (Benjamin Franklin, Henry David Thoreau, Ralph Waldo Emerson, Robert Frost) as well as groups (Amish, Quakers, Hutterites, Mennonites) have carried forward the virtue of thrift—both out of respect for the earth and out of a thirst for a touch of heaven. And the challenges of building our nation required frugality of most of our citizens. Indeed, the wealth we enjoy today is the result of centuries of frugality. As we said earlier, the "more is better" consumer culture is a Johnny-come-lately on the American scene. Our bedrock is frugality, and it's high time we made friends with the word—and the practice.

Let's explore this word "frugality" to see if we can't redeem it as the key to fulfillment in the nineties.

THE PLEASURES OF FRUGALITY

We looked up "frugal" in a 1986 Merriam-Webster dictionary and found "characterized by or reflecting economy in the expenditure of resources." That sounds about right—a serviceable, practical and fairly colorless word. None of the elegance or grace of the "enoughness" that FIers experience. But when we dig deeper, the dictionary tells us that "frugal" shares a Latin root with *frug* (meaning virtue), *frux* (meaning fruit or value) and *frui* (meaning to enjoy or have the use of). Now we're talking. Frugality is **enjoying** the **virtue** of getting good **value** for every minute of your life energy and from everything you **have the use of.**

That's very interesting. In fact, it's more than interesting. It's transforming. Frugality means we are to *enjoy* what we have. If you have ten dresses but still feel you have nothing to wear, you are probably a spendthrift. But if you have ten dresses and have enjoyed wearing all of them for years, you are frugal. Waste lies not in the number of possessions but in the failure to enjoy them. Your success at being frugal is measured not by your penny-pinching but by your degree of enjoyment of the material world.

Enjoyment of the material world? Isn't that hedonism? While both have to do with enjoying what you have, frugality and hedonism are opposite responses to the material world. Hedonism revels in the pleasures of the senses and implies excessive consumption of the material world and a continual search for more. Frugal people, however, get value from everything—a dandelion or a bouquet of roses, a single strawberry or a gourmet meal. A hedonist might consume the juice of five oranges as a prelude to a pancake breakfast. A frugal person, on the other hand, might relish eating a single orange, enjoying the color and texture of the whole fruit, the smell and the light spray that comes as you begin to peel it, the translucence of each section, the flood of flavor that pours out as a section bursts over the tongue . . . and the thrift of saving the peels for baking.

To be frugal means to have a high joy-to-stuff ratio. If you get one unit of joy for each material possession, that's frugal. But if you need ten possessions to even begin registering on the joy meter, you're missing the point of being alive.

There's a word in Spanish that encompasses all this: *aprovechar*. It means to use something wisely—be it old zippers from worn-out clothing or a sunny day at the beach. It's getting full value from life, enjoying all the good that each moment and each thing has to offer. You can "*aprovechar*" a simple meal, a flat of overripe strawberries or a cruise in the Bahamas. There's nothing miserly about *aprovechar;* it's a succulent word, full of sunlight and flavor. If only "frugal" were so sweet.

The "more is better and it's never enough" mentality in North America fails the frugality test not solely because of the excess, but because of the lack of enjoyment of what we already have. Indeed, North Americans have been called materialists, but that's a misnomer. All too often it's not material things we enjoy as much as what these things symbolize: conquest, status, success, achievement, a sense of worth and even favor in the eyes of the Creator. Once we've acquired the dream house, the status car or the perfect mate, we rarely stop to enjoy them thoroughly. Instead, we're off and running after the next coveted acquisition.

Another lesson we can derive from the dictionary definition of "frugal" is the recognition that we don't need to possess a thing to enjoy it—we merely need to *use* it. If we are enjoying an item, *whether or not we own it,* we're being frugal. For many of life's pleasures it may be far better to "use" something than to "possess" it (and pay in time and energy for the upkeep). So often we have been like feudal lords, gathering as many possessions as possible from far and wide and bringing them inside the walls of our castle. If we want something (or wanted it in the past, or imagine we might want it in the future), we think we must bring it inside the boundaries of the world called "mine." What we fail to recognize is that what is outside the walls of "mine" doesn't belong to the enemy; it belongs to "the rest of us." And if what lies outside our walls is not "them" but "us," we can afford to loosen our grip a bit on our possessions. We can gingerly open the doors of our fortress and allow goods (material and spiritual) to flow into and out of our boundaries.

Frugality, then, is also learning to share, to see the world as "ours" rather than as "theirs" and "mine." And, while not explicit in the word, being frugal and being happy with having enough mean that more will be available for others. Learning to equitably share the resources of the earth is at the top of the global agenda, and some creative frugality in North America could go a long way toward promoting that balance.

Frugality *is* balance. Frugality is the Greek notion of the golden mean. Frugality is being efficient in harvesting happiness from the world you live in. Frugality is right-use (which sounds, appropriately, like "righteous")—the wise stewarding of money, time, energy, space and possessions. Goldilocks expressed it well when she declared the porridge "not too hot, not too cold, but just right." Frugality is something like that—not too much, not too little, but just right. Nothing is wasted. Or left unused. It's a clean machine. Sleek. Perfect. Simple yet elegant. It's that magic word—enough. The peak of the Fulfillment Curve. The jumping-off point for a life of being fulfilled, learning and contributing to the welfare of the planet.

"Frugal, man." That's the cool, groovy way to say "far out" in the nineties. Surfers will talk about frugal waves. Teenage girls will talk about frugal dudes. Designers will talk about frugal fashions. Mark our words!

Keep this in mind as we explore ways to save money. We aren't talking about being cheap, making do or being a skinflint or a tightwad. We're talking about *creative* frugality, a way of life in which you get the maximum fulfillment for each unit of life energy spent.

In fact, now that you know that money is your life energy, it seems foolish to consider wasting it on stuff you don't enjoy and never use. Recalling the arithmetic we did in Chapter 2, you'll remember that if you are 40 years old, actuarial tables indicate that you have just 329,601 hours of life energy in your bank. That may seem like a lot now, but those hours will feel very precious at the *end* of your life. Spend them well now and you won't have regrets later.

In the end, this creative frugality is an expression of self-esteem. It honors the life energy you invest in your material possessions. Saving those minutes and hours of life energy through careful consuming is the ultimate in self-respect.

Step 6: Valuing Your Life Energy—Minimizing Spending

This step is about the intelligent use of your life energy (money) and the conscious lowering or eliminating of expenses. We have arranged the following hints and tips in several lists, all of them based on decades of experience with living frugally. We'll also include some of the tips that Amy and Jim Dacyczyn share so generously in their newsletter, *The Tightwad Gazette* (subtitled "Promoting Thrift as a Viable Alternative Lifestyle"), which we mentioned in Chapter 4.

Consider the lists that follow as a menu of options. Explore the ones that intrigue or inspire you and leave the rest. There's something for everyone here—but not everything will be for you. It might be instructive, though, to ask yourself why you are discarding some ideas and adopting others. You may encounter some childhood programming, some cultural myths and even some revealing information about your values. Remember, these ideas are opportunities, not should's. Frugality is about enjoyment, not penny-pinching! Happy saving—or should we say happy frugaling . . .

ONE SURE WAY TO SAVE MONEY

Stop trying to impress other people

Other people are probably so busy trying to impress you that they will, at best, not notice your efforts. At worst, they will resent you for one-upping them.

When Thorstein Veblen published *The Theory of the Leisure Class* in 1899, he didn't make a big splash, but the term he coined, "conspicuous consumption," has made it into the heart of our culture. In the foreword to Veblen's book social commentator and writer Stuart Chase summarized his thesis this way:

> People above the line of base subsistence, in this age and all earlier ages, do not use the surplus, which society has given them, primarily for useful purposes. They do not seek to expand their own lives, to live more wisely, intelligently, understandingly, but to impress other people with the fact that they have a surplus . . . spending money, time and effort quite uselessly in the pleasurable business of inflating the ego.

But just because conspicuous consumption is a cross-cultural and historic aberration of the human species doesn't mean that *you* have to fall prey to it. If you stop trying to impress other people you will save thousands, perhaps millions, of dollars. (And think how impressed people will be with how much you've saved!)

TEN SURE WAYS TO SAVE MONEY

1. Don't go shopping

If you don't go shopping, you won't spend money. Of course, if you really need something from the store, go and buy it. But don't just go shopping. According to Carolyn Wesson, author of *Women Who Shop Too Much,* "59 million persons in the U.S. are addicted to shopping or to spending." About 53 percent of groceries and 47 percent of hardware-store purchases are "spur of the moment." **When 34,300 mall shoppers across the country were asked the primary reason for their visit, only 25 percent said they had come in pursuit of a specific item.** About 70 percent of all adults visit a regional mall weekly. The number of U.S. shopping centers has grown from 2,000 in 1957 to more than 30,000 today, according to the International Council of Shopping Centers. The number of shopping malls recently surpassed the number of high schools in the United States.

Indeed, shopping is one of our favorite national pastimes. More than the simple act of acquiring needed goods and services, shopping attempts to fill (but obviously fails, since we have to shop so often) myriad needs: for socializing and time structuring, for a reward after a job well done, for an antidepressant, for esteem-boosting, self-assertion, status and nurturing. A Martian anthropologist might conclude that the mall is our place of worship, and shopping the central ritual of communion with our deity. Lewis Lapham observes, "We express our longing for the ineffable in the wolfishness of our appetite. . . . The feasts of consumption thus become rituals of communion." **Consumption seems to be our favorite high, our nationally sanctioned addiction, the all-American form of substance abuse.**

So don't go shopping. And while you're at it, stay away from advertising that whets your appetite for stuff you don't want. And for pity's sake don't tune in to the Home Shopping Network. You may be saving more than money. You may be saving your sanity, not to speak of your soul.

2. Live within your means

This notion is so outmoded that some readers might not even know what it signifies. To live within your means is to buy only what you can prudently afford, to avoid debt unless you have an assurance that you will be able to pay it promptly and always to have something put away for a rainy day. It was quite a fashionable way to live one short generation ago, before we started living beyond our means. There are two sides to the coin of living beyond your means. The shiny side is that you can have everything you want right now. The tarnished side is that you will pay for it with your life. Buying on time, from cars to houses to vacations, often results in paying three times the purchase price. Is going to Hawaii for two weeks this year worth working perhaps four additional months next year to pay it off? This doesn't mean you have to cut up all your credit cards—you just have to avoid using them.

Living within your means suggests that you wait until you have the money before you buy something. This gives you the benefit of avoiding interest charges. It also gives you a waiting period during which you may well discover that you don't want some of those things after all. He who hesitates saves money. The bright side of living within your means is that you will use and enjoy what you have and harvest a full measure of fulfillment from it, whether it's your old car, your old coat or your old house. It also means that you can weather the economic bad times when they come—which they will. Alfred Malabre, economics editor of *The Wall Street Journal,* published a book in 1987 whose title says it all: *Beyond Our Means: How America's Long Years of Debt,*

Deficits and Reckless Borrowing Now Threaten to Overwhelm Us. In it he says:

> In brief, the jig is about up and, for all the accumulated wisdom of all the eminent economists of the various schools, painless extrication from our predicament just isn't going to be possible.

Now that's a pitch for living within your means if there ever was one!

3. Take care of what you have

There is one thing we all have that we want to last a long time—our bodies. Simple attention to the proven preventive practices will save you lots of money. Brushing your teeth, for example, could save thousands in dental bills. And eating what you know agrees with your body (judging by your energy, not by your taste buds) may save you thousands in expensive procedures, not to speak of your life.

Extend this principle to all your possessions. Regular oil changes are known to extend the life of your car. Cleaning your tools extends their life. (How many hair dryers and vacuum cleaners have choked on hair balls?) Dusting your refrigerator coils saves energy and could save your refrigerator. One big difference between living beings and machines is that machines are not self-healing. If you ignore a headache it will probably go away. If you ignore a funny noise in your engine you could throw a rod, burn out a water pump or otherwise incur major (and costly) damage.

Many of us have lived with excess for so many years that it no longer occurs to us to maintain what we have. "There's always more where that came from," we tell ourselves. But more costs money. And more may not, in the long run, be available.

4. Wear it out

What's the last item you actually wore out? Americans discard 1,455 pounds of garbage every year (here is one area where we're still the world's leader), and much of that was probably still perfectly usable. Synthetic fibers are extremely durable. It's hard to actually wear out clothing these days. If it weren't for the fashion industry (and boredom) we could all enjoy the same basic wardrobe for many years. Survey your possessions. Are you simply upgrading or duplicating last year's electronic equipment, furniture, kitchenware, carpeting and linens, or are you truly wearing them out? Think how much money you would save if you simply decided to use things even 20 percent longer. If you usually replace your towels every two years, try replacing them every two and a half years. If you trade in your car every three years, try extending that to four. If you buy a new coat every other winter, see whether every third winter would do just as well. And when you're about to buy something, ask yourself, "Do I already have one of these that is in perfectly usable condition?"

Another way to save money is to ask, before trashing something, whether there might be another way to use part or all of it. Old letters become scrap paper. A chipped cup becomes a pencil holder. A broken toaster oven becomes an assortment of screws, plus an electrical cord, Nichrome wire, a small metal tray and a heat-resistant handle. Old furniture can provide the wood for your next carpentry job. The frugality experts from the 1930s (and before) always kept a pile of wood scraps and assorted junk out back and had a knack for cobbling together what was needed out of available materials. All it takes is the recognition that everything is useful and the creativity to see what those uses might be. Then instead of buying something you can ask yourself, "Do I already have this item in some other form? If so, what would it take to make it serve my current needs?"

A word of caution to the already frugal. Using something until you wear it out does not mean using it until it wears *you* out. If you must continually fiddle with a lamp to make it work and you've already tried repairing it, it may not be worth your life energy to coax it along for another year. If your car is taking you for a ride, costing more hours in tinkering (or more money in repairs) than it's giving you in service, do buy a newer one. If your knee joints are suffering from running shoes that have lost their bounce, it would be cheaper to buy a new pair (on sale) than to have knee surgery.

5. Do it yourself

Can you tune your car? Fix a plumbing leak? Do your taxes? Make your own gifts? Rewire a toaster? Change the tire on your bicycle?

Bake a cake from scratch? Build a bookshelf? Repair your roof? Clean your chimney? Sew a dress? Cut your family's hair? Form your own nonprofit corporation? It used to be that we learned basic life skills from our parents in the process of growing up. Then the Industrial Revolution put our parents in factories and, after the passing of child labor and mandatory public education laws, put us in schools. Next our grandparents were put in rest homes, removing the people who traditionally taught life skills to the children while the parents worked. Eventually home economics and shop classes had to be incorporated in the curriculum as supplements to the ever-decreasing skill-nourishment we got at home. By the 1970s it was no longer fashionable for mothers to stay at home with their children. By the 1980s many couples assumed it wasn't even possible, economically, for mothers to stay home with their children. Is it any wonder that the only way we know how to take care of ourselves in the 1990s is to be consumers of goods and services provided by others? To reverse that trend, just ask yourself, when you're about to hire an expert: "Can I do this myself? What would it take to learn how? Would it be a useful skill to know?"

Basic living and survival skills can be learned through adult education classes, extension agents, summer rural residential programs and, last but not least, books. Every breakdown can be used as an opportunity for learning and empowerment. What you can't do, or choose not to do, you can hire others to do, and tag along for the ride. Every bit of your energy invested in solving these breakdowns not only teaches you something you need to know for the next time but helps prevent mistakes and reduces the bill. One FIer tells the story of how her heating system failed one winter. Three companies sent out repair people to assess the problem and make a bid. Each one told her with absolute certainty what the problem was. Unfortunately, each told her a different story. So she cracked the books, meditated on the Rube Goldberg maze of pipes, came to an educated guess and chose the company that came closest to her analysis, thus saving herself hundreds of dollars of unnecessary and possibly destructive work. By staying with the repairman and observing his work she also was able to avert a few more expensive mistakes and to save (expensive) time by doing some of the simpler tasks. A typical working couple might have paid ten times what she did to have the job done and then felt fortunate to have two paychecks "since the cost of living in the modern world is so high."

6. Anticipate your needs

Forethought in purchasing can bring tremendous savings. With enough lead time you will inevitably see the items you need go on sale by the time you need them—at 20 to 50 percent under the usual price. Keep current on catalogs and sale flyers of national and local catalog merchandisers. Read the sale ads in the Sunday paper. Be aware of seasonal bargains such as January and August "white sales," holiday sales (such as Memorial Day and Labor Day) and year-end clearance sales.

By simply observing the poor condition of your car's left rear tire while it still has some life left, you can anticipate a need. By simply being aware of this need you will naturally notice the phenomenal tire sale that will appear in the sports section of your Sunday newspaper three weeks from now—and you'll *know* it's a phenomenal sale because you have been watching prices.

In the shorter term, shopping at the corner convenience store can be expensive. Anticipating your needs—that you'll be wanting evening snacks, that you'll run out of milk midweek or that there's some taping you want to do and you're all out of blank cassettes—can eliminate running out to the corner store to pick up these items. Instead you can purchase them during your supermarket shopping or on a run to the discount store. This can result in significant savings. Refer to the sample Daily Money Log in Step 2 (page 72) and note the price differential in blank cassettes bought at the convenience store on Friday versus those bought on Saturday at a discount store.

Anticipating your needs also eliminates one of the biggest threats to your frugality: impulse buying. If you haven't anticipated needing something when you leave your house at 3:05, chances are you don't need it at 3:10 when you're standing at the gazingus-pin counter at the corner store. We're not saying you should only buy things that are on your premeditated shopping list (although that isn't such a bad idea for compulsive shoppers); we *are* saying that you must be scrupulously honest when you're out and about. Saying, "I anticipate needing this," as you're drooling over a left-handed veeblefitzer or cashmere sweater is not the same as having *already* anticipated needing one and recognizing that this particular one is a bargain. Remember the corollary to Parkinson's Law ("The work expands to fit the time allowed for its completion"): "Needs expand to encompass whatever you want to buy on impulse."

7. Research value, quality, durability and multiple use

Research your purchases. *Consumer Reports* and other publications give excellent evaluations and comparisons of almost everything you might buy—and they can be fun just to read. Decide what features are most important to you. Don't just be a bargain junkie and automatically buy the cheapest item available. Durability might be critical for something you plan to use daily for twenty years. One obvious way of saving money is to spend less on each item you buy, but it's equally true that spending $40 on a tool that lasts ten years instead of buying a $30 one that will need to be replaced in five years will save you $20 in the long run. Multiple use is also a factor. Buying one item for $10 that will serve the purpose of four different $5 items will net you a savings of $10. One heavy-duty kitchen pot can (and perhaps should) replace half a dozen specialty appliances like a rice cooker, a popcorn popper, a Crockpot, a deep-fat fryer, a paella pan and a spaghetti cooker. So, if you really expect to be using an item, buying for durability and for multiple purposes can be a good savings technique. But if you'll be using the item only occasionally you may not want to spend the extra dollars on a high-quality product. Knowing what your needs are and knowing the whole range of what is available will allow you to choose the right item.

Besides reading consumer magazines, you can evaluate quality by developing a sharp eye and carefully examining what you are buying. Are the seams in a piece of clothing ample? Are the edges finished? Is the fabric durable? Is it washable or will you be paying dry-cleaning bills to keep it clean? Are the screws holding the appliance together sturdy enough for the job? Is the material strong or flimsy? Is the furniture nailed, stapled or screwed? Here is where you will become an expert materialist—knowing materials so well that you can read the probable longevity of an item the way a forester can read the age and history of a fallen tree. This is the opposite of crass materialism. **This**

is as much honoring the wonder of creation as standing in a redwood grove. Everything you purchase has its origin in the earth. Everything. Knowing the wear patterns of aluminum versus stainless steel is honoring the earth every bit as much as lobbying for stronger environmental protection laws.

8. Get it for less

There are numerous ways to bargain-hunt. Here are few:

1. *Mail-order discounters:* When you know exactly what you want, including make and model, you can cut out the middleman and order through discount catalogs. Discounts in film and photographic equipment, in computers and associated paraphernalia, in tapes and in stereo and video equipment are huge; see ads in photography, computer and stereo magazines. Get specialized discounters' catalogs; these are available not only for photography, computer, audio and video supplies but also for tools, automobile parts and equipment, sporting goods and much more. Besides being money-savers, catalogs are a great education in conscious consuming. Ponder those enigmatic left-handed veeblefitzers. What are they for? Why are they in the doohickey section? Were there veeblefitzers in last year's catalog or is this a technological breakthrough? Will one veeblefitzer save me the headache of replacing those @#!$@!!*%$!!! framus-pinders every year? *We* are catalog-reading addicts—everything from J. C. Penney to J. C. Whitney—and we would have to say that we have acquired more of a general education from this activity than from our years in college.

2. *Discount chain stores:* Just because you buy something at "the best store in town" doesn't mean it's of any better quality than the same item bought at a discount chain store. The discounters and warehouse stores carry many high-quality, name-brand products at a discount, but you have to know your prices. So even if you prefer to browse at a high-priced emporium because you trust their buyers to select only the best equipment, do your buying at a discount chain store. One word of warning, however: just because the stereo you want is available at Harry's Low-Cost Cash-and-Carry doesn't mean it's a bargain. Harry's price may indeed be cheaper, if he is passing on his low overhead to you, or if the item is overstocked, discontinued or being used as a loss leader (an item priced at or below cost to lure you into the store for a

buying binge). But on the other hand, it may not. *Know your prices.* How can you know when and where to buy what? See number 3 below.

3. *Comparison-shop by phone:* Where do you shop and how did you choose it? Is it where you've always shopped? At the mall closest to your home? Where your friends shop? Where advertising or status-seeking has told you is the *only* place to shop? *We* shop via the telephone. Once we know what we want, we phone around for the best price. The more educated you are about the product and the more specific you can be about the exact make or model you want, the more successful your bargain-hunting will be. You will be amazed at the range of prices quoted for the same item. If you prefer doing business with a particular store or supplier, phone-shop for the best price and then ask your favorite vendor if he or she can match it. In 1984, after much research, we decided we wanted a Toyota Tercel with four-wheel drive. We then called every dealership within 100 miles—and shaved $4,000 (33 percent) off the highest bid by purchasing a demonstrator (a deluxe model with everything but air-conditioning) that had 3,600 miles on it. Seven years and 100,000 miles later, *nothing* has gone wrong.

4. *Bargain:* You can ask for discounts for paying cash. You can ask for discounts for less-than-perfect items. You can ask for the sale price even if the sale begins tomorrow or ended yesterday. You can ask for further discounts on items already marked down. You can ask for discounts if you buy a number of items at the same time. You can ask for discounts anywhere, anytime. Nothing ventured, nothing gained. Haggling is a time-honored tradition. The list price of any consumer item is usually inflated. As soon as you hear the words, "The list price is . . ." you should say, "Yes, but what is *your* price?" According to Jim Dacyczyn you should be able to shave 24 percent off the sticker price for a car, but this strategy applies to more than houses, cars and other major purchases. You have nothing to lose by asking for a discount at any store—from your local hardware store to a clothing emporium. A case in point was our recent outing to buy new running shoes. A $60 (list price) pair was sitting on the manager's special rack with no price. They fit perfectly. We asked a salesman what they would cost. "$24.99," he replied. "Would you take $19.99?" we asked. Surveying what he had left, he said, "Eighteen dollars." We could have pointed

out that haggling etiquette suggests that his counteroffer be higher, not lower, than ours. But we were astute enough just to shut our mouths, open our wallet and take advantage of a great bargain. A reporter for *The Wall Street Journal,* researching an article on the increase in haggling precipitated by the 1990–91 recession, tried bargaining in his New York neighborhood. From hardware stores to antique boutiques to major retail department stores, the majority of retailers were willing to shave substantial amounts off the asking price. So bargain. What have you got to lose?

9. Buy it used

Reexamine your attitudes about buying used items. If you are a thrift-store or garage-sale addict, look at whether you are really saving money or whether you are buying items that you don't need just because they're "such a bargain." But if you wouldn't be caught dead in a musty Salvation Army thrift store, look around your town: thrift stores have become fashionable emporiums. Even *Newsweek* says so. In "I Can Get It for You Resale" the magazine declared that "Secondhand shopping is chic as well as thrifty. . . . The change reflects the new national Zeitgeist. . . . Quality and value are more important than flash and cash." Clothing, kitchenware, furniture, drapes—all can be found in thrift stores, and you may be surprised at the high quality of many of them. As a matter of fact, donating brand-new items to thrift stores is one way that shopaholics justify excess purchases. If you just can't bring yourself to shop at thrift stores, consider consignment shops. The prices are higher, but the quality is consistently higher as well. In our experience, thrift stores are best for clothing but garage sales are cheaper (and more reliable) for appliances, furniture and household items. If you're an early bird (arriving before the sellers have even had their morning coffee) you can often find exceptional buys. On the other hand, the later in the day you go to a garage sale, the more eager the people will be to get rid of the stuff for a song. "Swap meets" and "flea markets" are two names for the same event—weekend open-air bazaars where you'll find merchants of every stripe displaying their wares: shrewd hucksters, collectors of every kind and families hoping to unload their excess before moving across country. Just as when you shop at discounters, you have to know your prices. There are some clever nomads working the flea-market circuit who will sell you tools, imported peasant clothing, crystals and other items for *more* than you'd pay at the shopping mall.

10. Follow the nine steps of this program

The steps of this program have been successfully followed by thousands of people. These people have found that doing all the steps leads to a transformed experience of money and the material world. All the steps matter. They synergize to spur you on. If you find your pace slackening, check to see if you've skipped a step (thinking, perhaps, that it doesn't apply to you)—and if you have, go back and do it. Your speed and clarity will pick up again, guaranteed. You don't have to believe that the steps will work. It's okay to do them mechanically. But *do* them—and you will surely save more than money.

101 SURE WAYS TO SAVE MONEY

Here are more specific money-saving strategies. Again, not all may be for you, but keep an open mind and give as many as possible a fair try. You have nothing to lose but the balance on your monthly credit card bill.

Interest Payments and Financial Charges

Cutting down on how much you pay for the privilege of using borrowed money is a cardinal rule of saving money. After all, you've already done your time at the office for the privilege of having the money in your pocket. Why pay again, and drag the ball and chain of debt around too, as you hobble down the road of life?

1. Pay off your credit cards.

Credit card companies charge 16 to 20 percent interest on the unpaid balance of your bill. In 1989, the national average interest rate on credit cards was 18.66 percent. Every $100 of debt cost $18.66 a year in interest. That means that someone in the 28 percent tax bracket had to earn $25.92 before taxes to pay for the privilege of having spent that $100. Clearly, credit cards may be a convenience, but they aren't a bargain. As you begin to save money, you should look at paying off your most expensive debts first.

2. Eliminate all but one credit card for emergencies and stop paying unnecessary annual fees.

With rare exceptions, each credit card you have costs you annually anywhere from $20 to a whopping $300 for the privilege of using it —even if you *do* pay off your balance monthly.

3. Pay cash for all purchases, even major ones like your car.

Follow this simple rule and you will eliminate debt from your life. Not only that, but you will be forced to wait to make purchases until you have enough money saved up—and by then you may no longer want the latest gazingus pin.

4. Pay off your mortgage as quickly as possible.

If you have been extending your payments over the typical 30 years, you may well be spending up to three times the purchase price of your house. That means that if you buy a house for $100,000 with a 30-year mortgage at 9.5 percent you will actually have shelled out over $300,000 by the time you make the last payment. Paying off your mortgage early may be easier than you think. According to one newspaper article, an increase in payments of just 5 percent could cut almost 7 years off a 30-year mortgage. Paying an extra 10 percent would reduce the mortgage to just over 19 years.

5. If your bank account offers free checking or waives the service fee in exchange for maintaining a minimum balance, don't draw the account below the minimum.

This requires the discipline of keeping your check register up-to-date, but it's so simple to avoid these unnecessary charges. And keeping your check register up-to-date isn't such a bad practice anyway.

6. Don't bounce checks.

(See number 5.) Furthermore, rubber checks waste the life energy of a whole string of other people who then must spend some of their precious time on earth trying to collect from you. There is no better way to demonstrate to the world that you are *not* a person of integrity than to bounce a check.

Transportation Costs

7. Assess whether or not you really need that extra car (or two). You might want to eliminate it and save on gas, oil, maintenance, repairs, parking, insurance, licensing and fines.

> ***Lu Bauer** and **Steve Brandon** had inherited a car from the classic "little old lady who only drove it to church on Sunday." The body was in perfect condition (a wonder for an area that salts its roads for nearly half the year). The engine was a hummer. They didn't need the car, but they had it and decided to keep it for a spare. After a year of tracking their expenses, they recognized that just having this beauty up on blocks in their barn was costing hundreds in licensing and insurance. They realized that by selling the extra car now, they could save thousands of dollars by the time they would need a replacement for their current car. In addition, someone else in their rural community could have the pleasure of driving granny's cream puff.*
>
> ***Steve West** was in a similar position. As a home remodeler he rationalized his two extra vehicles (an old pickup truck and another beater) as useful for hauling tools and materials to his jobs. Since they weren't worth much on the open market, he'd assumed it was cheaper to keep them. Not true. Doing his Monthly Tabulations showed him the high cost of the convenience of having—and maintaining—these backup vehicles. Between paying for the new transmission, the insurance and licensing and the gallons of gas they guzzled for even short hops, Steve found that for less money he could just rent an extra truck when he needed it. He sold off the two extras—and hasn't needed to rent yet.*

8. Walk to do local errands whenever possible.

How far is too far to walk? Short hops in your car when the engine is cold are a major cause of automotive wear and tear and poor gas mileage. Take a look at the reasons you use your car for errands less than a mile from your home. Convenience? Speed? Safety? And look at what it's costing you in terms of money and exercise. Try walking instead.

9. Use public transportation.

This is usually very cost-effective, especially if parking is a problem. Remember, the cost of taking your car downtown isn't just the cost of parking. It also includes the cost of gas and wear and tear on the car. If the IRS computes mileage at 27 cents a mile, shouldn't you?

10. Keep an auto log.

FIGURE 6-1

Sample Auto Log

Date	Odometer	Gallons In	Cost	MPG	Other
7/26	48317	12.8	$14.00	26.4	
8/4	48634	13.2	14.35	24.0	Oil down ¾ qt.
8/6	48750	1 quart of Mobil 10/30 oil			
8/6	48750	Rotate tires—left rear getting bald			

Keeping a detailed automotive log is an excellent practice and provides a valuable diagnostic tool. This book is a record of everything done to the car along with the date and odometer reading when it was done. Be sure to include the amount of gas at each fill-up, how many miles per gallon you're getting at each fill-up, quantity of oil put in, tire replacement or rotation, tune-ups, repairs and replacements. (See Figure 6-1 for an example.) Such car records are used by all fleet operators and can save enormous repair bills. Not only will your mechanics appreciate knowing what has been done to your car in the past, but you will have valuable information to keep you on top of your car's health. For example, a dropoff in miles per gallon can alert you to the need for a tune-up. Parts can be replaced at regular intervals—*before* they clog, rupture or fail (the same is true with plugs, points, condenser, air and gas filters, PCV valves, oil and oil filter). Finally, people with cars that have run over 100,000 miles all agree on one simple maintenance procedure: frequent oil changes. Robert Sikorsky, author of *Drive It Forever*, recommends frequent oil changes as the best thing you can do to give your car a long life. Your *minimum* oil change interval should be the manufacturer's "severe service" recommendation, and Sikorsky even encourages people to decrease that by 10 percent in the summer and 20 percent in the winter.

11. Learn basic automotive maintenance.

Surely you've noticed the two unspoken assumptions about automotive maintenance. One is "If you are a man you naturally and intuitively know how to fix cars." The other is "If you are a woman you do not and cannot fix your own car." Both of these promote ignorance. If you think you already know something, there is no room to learn. Many men still strand themselves with an automotive problem they can't fathom, a tool kit they can't use (which probably cost them too much) and an impatient mate they can't confess their ignorance to. Likewise, if you think you don't—and furthermore, can't—know something, there is no room to discover the answer. Many women still stand around with a flat tire, waiting for a tow truck or a good Samaritan, when everything they need to do the job is right in the trunk. So find yourself a teacher—and learn. This teacher may be your brother-in-law, who does his own automotive maintenance and can teach you how to change your oil, do a tune-up and change a tire. Or you may enroll in an adult education class on automotive maintenance. Here you will learn to perform simple, safe procedures under the supervision of a professional in a shop, where mistakes can be both averted and corrected.

Here's some impressive arithmetic for the budding do-it-yourself mechanic to ponder. If a muffler job is going to cost you $65 at a repair shop, you may be able to earn yourself $32.64 per hour by doing it yourself. How? If the muffler and clamps cost $18 at a discount auto parts store, and the job takes you two hours, you are ahead by $47, or the $23.50 per hour the shop would charge you to do the work. But if you are in the 28 percent tax bracket, you would have to earn $65.28 in order to pay the 28 percent income tax and have $47 left after taxes to pay for the muffler installation. That's another $18.28 down the drain, which increases your "hourly wage" by $9.14 per hour. All told, you'd be earning $32.64 per hour by replacing your own muffler. That's pretty good money for what some of us might consider an enjoyable, educational and empowering experience. (By the way, at those wages you'd be earning $67,891 a year!)

12. Shop around for a reliable and reasonable mechanic—*before* you need one.

Sometimes adult education courses on auto maintenance are offered by local mechanics who are eager to empower their clients to become knowledgeable about their own cars, so this may also handle the challenge of finding a mechanic you can trust. Just as it is wise to select a good doctor before a medical crisis occurs, it is important to select a mechanic before a breakdown. Ask your friends where they take their cars for repairs. When evaluating candidates for the important position of Your Mechanic, there are a number of questions to ask: Is the shop clean? Do you feel you can trust him or her? What is the hourly rate? Is the mechanic certified? Is the work guaranteed? Most mechanics are undoubtedly honest, but there are some who prescribe expensive, unnecessary work that does nothing to fix or improve your car. Overcoming your own ignorance, learning to do your own basic maintenance yourself and selecting a trustworthy mechanic can make a difference of thousands of dollars.

13. Acquire needed auto parts yourself after comparing prices by phone. If needed, have a mechanic install them.

Official factory parts for your car may cost hundreds of dollars more than "after-market" parts that are equally reliable. Often you can get rebuilt parts instead of new ones, and they come with a guarantee that they will last just as long as a new part. Furthermore, padding the price of parts is one place where service stations make a little extra on each job. So do your phone-shopping at auto supply stores with the make, model and year of your car, the part name and, if possible, the part number handy. Don't forget to bargain—ask if it's on sale or if they will give you a discount. If you can't install the part yourself, see if your mechanic would be willing to install it for you and charge you only the cost of his shop time. Some will, some won't.

14. Do regular maintenance (or have it done) so that breakdowns are less likely.

Regular tune-ups and oil changes add years to your car's life. Not only will you be replacing parts before they break down, but you'll have the chance to observe the condition of the whole engine and chassis. Are the belts cracked? Are the hoses getting brittle? Are there obvious leaks anywhere? Is the muffler hanger rusting out? Are the tires wearing unevenly? Cars (like all machines) respond well to this kind of tender loving care, just as you do.

15. Carpool to work.

Some cities have a ride-share program that matches commuters from the same area. Put a notice up on your bulletin board at work or at your local grocery store. Ask your neighbors. A car with five riders costs as much to drive as a car with one rider, but at one-fifth the cost to each person. And congested cities are putting in high-occupancy vehicle lanes so that carpoolers can zip by the single-occupancy vehicles. (You get bonus points on this one for reducing pollution while reducing your expenses.)

16. Telecommute to work—that is, work at home, hooked to the office via computer, modem, fax, telephone and paycheck.

Formally or informally, many corporations are instituting telecommuting to accommodate working parents who want to be home with their children, people who want to keep their jobs when their mate is transferred and people who want their jobs structured around their lives instead of vice versa. Los Angeles County now has 700 county office staff members working at home, with measurable improvements in productivity. Not only will you save money (and time) on commuting, dry cleaning and eating lunch, but your company may gain a competitive edge by using on-line workers. Inquire at your office. They may even buy you the home-office equipment.

17. Select your home and job so that they are within walking distance of each other.

Many people have recognized that automobiles are destructive to the environment and are striving to relocate close enough to their jobs to walk to work.

18. Go to a four-day, ten-hour-per-day workweek.

This eliminates at least one day a week of commuting. It could also put you on the road before or after rush hour.

19. Bicycle when and where you can.

How far is too far to bicycle? Our hometown, rainy and hilly Seattle, has a dedicated and growing cadre of bicyclists who, with rainsuits and ten-speeds, will tackle any terrain in any weather. There is a nationwide movement to turn "rails to trail," to convert old railroad rights-of-way into bicycle trails. If your town isn't bike-friendly, perhaps you'll be the one to change that. The only fuel cost you'll have is breakfast.

20. Check out insurance rates for the new car(s) you're considering buying—some models and makes have higher rates than others and give no better service or mileage.

You'd be surprised at what is considered a sports car by insurance companies (for which they charge a higher premium).

21. Repair and keep an older car rather than buying a new one. This saves on insurance too.

Back in the fifties and sixties it made sense to trade in your car every three years or 50,000 miles. Now it doesn't. Manufacturers can afford to give seven-year warranties because they know their fuel-injected, electronic-ignition cars will perform superbly for at least that long. The older your car, the lower your insurance rates.

22. Consolidate your errands to reduce the amount you drive.

One trip to the shopping center to buy ten items uses a lot less gas than ten trips for one item each. A shopping list is a great asset in reducing transportation costs. Selecting just one day a week for errands helps focus you on assessing and projecting your needs for the whole week. Consolidating your errands also preserves another vital part of your life energy—your time.

Medical Costs

Medical costs are skyrocketing, so staying well is good for your pocketbook as well as your body. Maintaining wellness, rather than waiting to treat illness, can be a major way of eliminating expenses. Health care begins at home, and there's a great deal you can do to avoid getting sick in the first place. Here are some tips.

23. Consider getting major medical insurance with a $1,000 or more deductible.

Norman Cousins said that 85 percent of all illness is self-limiting. Your body, if given rest and good nutrition, is designed to heal itself of most illnesses. Nature, time and patience are the three great physicians. Even when you do need expert attention and must pay those expenses yourself because they are under the deductible, the overall cost is still less than if you were paying the higher premiums for full coverage. Because of consumer resistance to the high price of medical insurance, more and more companies are offering these stripped-down major medical policies. Make sure your provider has an A rating or better with A. M. Best, an organization that rates insurance companies.

24. Comparison-shop for prescription drugs, blood tests, X rays and other procedures.

Prices vary for all of these. We are often so cowed by the medical institution that we just do as we are told and never question the price. Some clinics and labs even have annual loss leaders, offering low-cost blood tests to attract new patients. Also, keep an eye out for health fairs, where you can get basic blood work and tests done free or at a minimal fee.

25. Many doctors have privileges (can see patients) at several different hospitals—find out which ones your doctor can use and comparison-shop for the lowest cost.

You'll be surprised at how much the daily rates and operating-room costs vary from one hospital to the next. One of the down sides of third-party payments (payments made by your insurance company) for health care is that the consumers themselves are not demanding affordable prices from hospitals.

26. Eat a proper diet.

Preventive maintenance, on the physical level, means listening to and taking good care of your body. Pay attention to your diet and be sure you are getting all the necessary nutrients. The essence of this is listening to what *your* body runs best on, not rigidly adhering to the latest nutritional theory.

27. Get proper exercise.

You need three kinds of exercise: aerobic, strength-building and stretching. Yoga, jogging, bicycling, swimming and fast walking provide one or more of these types of exercise. There are many books on the market to help you. A word of caution. You don't have to join a health club or buy expensive equipment to stay healthy—you may end up physically fit but fiscally depleted. Besides, isn't it ultimately more rewarding to stack your winter firewood and walk to the store than it is to ride a stationary bicycle to nowhere? A recent book, *Fitness Without Exercise*, gives many more examples of the exercise value of everyday activity. One FIer reported that he sold his riding lawn mower and returned to the old push kind, thereby eliminating his costly health club membership *and* improving his health. Another friend claims that vacuuming is good aerobic exercise, if done with a lot of energy and fancy footwork. Who needs Nautilus equipment when there's garbage to take out, leaves to rake and windows to wash? Don't think of a clogged toilet as a tragedy; think of it as an opportunity to work your pectoral muscles. Picking up children's toys provides just the kind of bending and stretching you need for warm-ups before you move into an invigorating jog from room to room preventing your preschooler from wreaking havoc with all your knick-knacks. If you're spending life energy (money) on a fitness club, perhaps that's a signal to look at spending more of your natural life energy (time) on your active chores. Cleaning your own house instead of hiring a house cleaner trims fat from more than just your expenses.

28. Maintain a proper attitude.

The physical side isn't all of it; the emotional and psychological components of good health are at least as (and possibly more) important. What is your *mental* diet like? We are learning that unhealthy attitudes, beliefs, thoughts and feelings produce stresses that play a role in causing disease. Ask yourself what benefits you get from being ill. What is your body trying to tell you by being sick? A physician friend recently told us that 75 percent of his patients had no desire to be well, while another doctor considers that a low estimate. Are you *willing* to be well? Wellness looks at the whole person and at the "dis-ease" in his or her life that is manifested as disease in the body.

29. Reduce stress.

Life isn't unduly stressful; you may, however, be unduly stressed by life. We are fortunate to live in a land with abundant instructions on how to handle stress so that it doesn't deplete our bodies. Most stress-reduction techniques teach us how to unhook stimulus from automatic response and to reinterpret "stressful" events as "opportunities for growth," "interesting adventures," or just "someone else's problem." Counting to ten is one such technique, and it often allows a lightning bolt of anger to pass through you without doing any damage. Observe how fear, anxiety, panic, apprehension and excitement course through your body. That's the mind-body connection in action. So reducing stress might mean taking it a little easier, but it also could mean reframing the events in your life so that they don't trigger those avalanches of feelings.

30. Stop smoking cigarettes.

Not only do nonsmokers have fewer health problems, but insurance companies honor that fact with lower rates. In addition, someone who starts working at age twenty with a pack-a-day habit could retire very early on what he or she spends on smoking. Consider this, from a Canadian newspaper:

> Higgins started to smoke when she was 15, paying about 50 cents a pack. She now (age 28) goes through a pack and a half a day at $1.85 Canadian a pack. She has spent about $6,800 so far. . . . [Assuming that the price of a pack of cigarettes continues to increase at the same rate, by age 70, Higgins could be paying $75 for a pack of cigarettes.] If she keeps smoking, she will spend $186,708 by then. If she quits at age 30 and puts the money into a tax shelter . . . earning 9 percent, she'll have $1,851,313.

This kind of arithmetic, by the way, can be applied to any unnecessary habit, from alcohol consumption to an addiction to candy bars. Consider this arithmetic of smoking: one man commented one day to a friend that 60 percent of the people he saw on food lines were smoking. "For the price of a package of cigarettes a day," he boasted, "I could eat very well, at least as far as nutrition is concerned. It's all a matter of making wise choices." To which his friend replied, "Show me." So he did. He decided to eat for a month on a daily budget of $1.45, the cost of a pack of cigarettes at that time. At the end of a month he was healthy, and he had $9.73 in cash plus assorted potatoes, noodles, margarine, eggs, bread and other leftovers.

31. Get proper rest.

Did you calculate lost sleep in the tally of your real hourly wage? Busy Americans may be robbing themselves of up to three hours of needed sleep a night. According to a *Reader's Digest* article, people slept nine and a half hours a night before the advent of the electric light bulb; now, if you sleep more than six and a half people think you lack drive or ambition. Sleep deprivation leads to short-term memory loss and reduced ability to make decisions and to concentrate. One in ten traffic accidents is sleep-related, and up to 20 percent of drivers fall asleep at the wheel. Depriving yourself of needed rest is hazardous to your health. And money can't buy a good night's sleep. You have to choose it for yourself.

32. If you are over the medically established healthy level for your body type, lose weight.

This also saves money on food, both the costly treats and the expensive diet programs. Now the size of your paycheck has no direct relation to the size of your waist, but it might be useful to have a column in your Monthly Tabulation labeled "Food I eat that my body doesn't need." Most doctors agree that being substantially over your medically ideal weight increases your chances of getting sick.

Living Circumstances

Housing is usually one of the most costly items on your Monthly Tabulation. The rule of thumb for housing used to be that 25 percent of your paycheck should go for rent. Now it's closer to 33 percent. People complain about mortgage bondage—being tied to a job in order to keep up payments on the house. The "more is better" mentality has us in thrall when it comes to trading up to ever-larger houses. Here are some ways to rethink your housing costs.

33. If you have a vacation home, rent it out when you aren't using it.

In our ten years of traveling to present our seminars and work on service projects, there were a number of occasions when we needed a home base for several months. We gained firsthand experience of the fact that there are between 1.1 and 1.6 (estimates vary) dwelling units for every family unit in the United States. These are second homes, abandoned homes, summer homes, homes for sale that aren't selling, homes caught up in divorce and probate battles, etc. Empty, beautiful homes. We'd find owners of the houses we were interested in through the tax assessor's office or neighbors and ask them if they would consider renting for a few months. We'd offer a large security deposit plus references from prior landlords. Without fail, the owners appreciated the extra income, the protection from vandalism and the spotless condition of their home when we left. Some even invited us back year after year—and reduced the rent to boot.

34. Rent houses that aren't for rent.

This strategy can work for long-term rentals as well. Drive around the neighborhood where you want to live, looking for telltale signs of an empty house: uncut grass, shades drawn or no curtains on the windows, untrimmed bushes, uncollected mail and leaflets. Find the owner through the tax office and inquire. Very often what's behind the empty house is a death, a divorce or a difficult experience with previous tenants. Your willingness to take good care of the property (as evidenced by an ample security deposit) can actually unburden the owner.

35. Try house-sitting.

***Jason and Nedra Weston**, whom you met in Chapter 2, became champion house-sitters on their way to FI. In the process of putting a down arrow on their rent category month after month, they opened their ears and eyes to other solutions. Soon they saw an ad asking for a couple to take care of a man who had cancer in exchange for room (their own cottage) and board. It sounded good, but the reality was even better. The man lived on a beautiful estate with a pool, a hot tub and gardens. Their only tasks were shopping, cooking the evening meal, discussing sports over dinner and cleaning up. Not only did they get the guest cottage and all their food, but he paid them $600 a month as well. They did their job so well that when the man's cancer disappeared, he invited them to stay on for the next two years. Since then, they've been in demand as house-sitters for a whole network of well-to-do people.*

There are agencies that handle house-sitting positions, but you can also find opportunities yourself through your friends, bulletin boards and the newspaper. Once you prove yourself, people will clamor for your services.

36. Rent out unused space in your home.

How many square feet does your house have? How many square feet do you actually use? Is any of that extra space private and livable?

***Penny Yunuba** had a new, lucrative job that disagreed with many of her values—and lots of good ideas about what she'd do if she didn't have to report to work every day. She found herself constantly thinking through alternatives, devising escape routes from the job that was beginning to feel like a prison. The FI course gave her a tunnel out, but it was her own ingenuity that turned on the light at the end of it. She realized that she could move into the basement of her house and rent out her own bedroom, using that rental income to handle her monthly mortgage payments. She did just that and, by implementing a few other creative strategies, managed to leave her job with enough money to live on.*

37. Explore living in an intentional community.

Share your life with people who share your values, either all under the same roof or as part of a cohousing cooperative, intentional community, land trust or planned community. While costs vary, the economy of numbers tends to lower everyone's expenses. The following resources should help you decide whether this option is for you:

- Corinne McLaughlin and Gordon Davidson, *Builders of the Dawn*
- *Intentional Communities: A Guide to Cooperative Living*
- Kathyrn McCamant and Charles Durrett, *Cohousing: A Contemporary Approach to Housing Ourselves*
- "Living Together," Issue #29, *In Context* journal, Bainbridge Island, Washington

38. Move to a less expensive area.

***Roger Ringer** has a dream. He wants us to reinhabit the heartland of this country. When he and his wife wanted to move to the country, they found that there was no place like home—the town they'd grown up in. Population: 1,000. Three-bedroom house with a basement: $30,000. Crime: none. Fun: build your own energy-efficient house, grow a garden, play with your kids, enjoy your mate, listen to great music on the stereo, rent an occasional video—just what Roger does. Roger has a vision of young men and women going to the city for five years or so, achieving Financial Independence and then returning to their rural homes with a secure cash flow and a high quality of life.*

If your job didn't keep you locked in the city, you could move somewhere where your dollars go a lot further. Here's another example, from the Home Price Comparison Index published in 1990 by *The Seattle Times:* a 2,200-square-foot home with four bedrooms, two and a half baths, family room and two-car garage would cost $916,666 in Beverly Hills, California, but only $81,666 in Corpus Christi, Texas—and, all things considered, Corpus Christi might be a nicer place to live.

Flexibility also pays for renters. A one-bedroom, one-bath unit (house or apartment) could cost as much as $980 a month in Honolulu or as little as $305 a month in Oklahoma City. Other places to avoid: New York; Boston; San Jose, California; Washington, D.C.; and San Francisco. Try instead Colorado Springs, Colorado; Austin or San Antonio, Texas; Wichita, Kansas; or even Tucson, Arizona.

39. Sell your house and live in a motor home.

Have you ever heard of "snowbirds?" They are retired people who live full-time in their motor homes. And they are having a ball. After selling a modest home, they can buy a luxury liner on wheels that has all the comforts of home—and then some. They travel with the weather, so heating and cooling are never a problem. In cities they just snuggle up to the house of a friend or family member, plug in their electricity and enjoy all the advantages of a town house. With a bit more daring, you can camp off the beaten track on Bureau of Land Management or National Forest land for next to nothing. Strap some photovoltaic panels on the roof and you even have your own electricity. If you're interested in exploring such a life-style, start by reading back issues of *Trailer Life* magazine. If there are campgrounds near your city, get out your glad hand and go strike up conversations with some "full-timers" (people who live in their motor homes full-time). They will be only too glad to show you around their rigs.

40. Buy a piece of land and put a used mobile home on it.

During one of our interviews on a radio call-in talk show a woman called to say that she and her husband had paid cash for a piece of land just forty minutes from Seattle and a used mobile home—$10,000 for both. She couldn't understand why all the other callers were complaining about paying $1,000 or more a month on their mortgage—didn't they realize there are cheaper ways to live?

41. Do your own home repairs.

If you own your home, maintenance can put a strain on your savings. With workers costing upwards of $50 an hour, a simple leaky faucet can run up quite a tab. Learning to do it yourself is not as formidable as you might think. Excellent home-repair guides are available (at the library, of course), but there's another source of education that's often overlooked: videos. Check your local building supply or hardware store, as well as the library. These videos can be borrowed free of charge, and actually watching another person tackle the job can give you lots of information that even the best-written and -illustrated book can't convey.

Sharing

Are *all* of your possessions in use *all* of the time? Of course not! So what's wrong with letting others use one of them when you aren't using it, as long as you get it back in as good shape as when you lent it? If you loosen up just a little on the mentality of "mine," life can be both cheaper and more fun. You can also barter goods and services with your neighbors instead of paying cash. The following examples are but a fraction of what's possible.

42. Start a neighborhood tool and skill swap.

Make a list of the tools and skills you have to offer. Add all the other tools and skills that you imagine others in your apartment building or on your block might have. Photocopy the list and give one to each household. Provide a space after each item where neighbors can indicate whether they have an item and what assurances they might need to be willing to loan it. No block needs more than a few pruners, one extension ladder, several lawn mowers, a couple of power saws, etc. Yet, through lack of communication, most households have one of every item sitting unused 95 percent of the time. And what about skills, or time? Is your neighbor spending her last dollars for round-the-clock aides to care for her bedridden husband while you spend three hours an afternoon watching soap operas? Might it be that the help *you* need is right next door? You may reap more benefits from such trading and sharing than just a little cash saving.

43. Trade clothes with friends who wear the same size.

What's old hat (literally) to you may provide a friend with all the newness he or she needs. Unless the two of you work at the same office, who's going to know where your new outfit really came from?

44. Or trade clothes with yourself—in the future.

Instead of rolling over your wardrobe annually and taking the castoffs to the Salvation Army, box everything that you haven't worn in the last year and put it in storage. Next time you crave something new, go to that box instead of the store. You'll be delighted at the old friends you find there.

45. Swap services—"haircuts for health care."

Within the boundaries of family we trade services all the time—cooking, cleaning, yard work, washing, dusting, vacuuming, etc. We don't charge one another for doing our chores. Try broadening your definition of "family" and swapping services with your friends. More formal barter networks are springing up around the country. The Local Economic Trading System (LETS), a computer-mediated barter system created in a community in Canada, has spread across the United States. By providing a service for another LETS member you earn a credit that you can use to pay for a service later.

46. Join a baby-sitting cooperative.

Many parents have banded together with others in their neighborhood to form a baby-sitting cooperative, giving each other free time and flexibility while saving both money and the eternal hassle of finding a reliable sitter who is available when needed.

47. Borrow books and magazines from the library instead of buying them.

The bonus is that, through interlibrary loan programs, your city or county library can get almost any book you request—even if they have to order it from a library halfway across the country.

48. Share magazine subscriptions with a friend.

Double your pleasure and halve the price. Halve the amount of paper in your local landfill as well.

49. Network. Let your friends and family know what you need.

Chances are that someone you know has just what you need gathering dust and rust in the garage or basement. That someone might be happy to loan or even give it to you. So don't be afraid of asking around. Frugality is making good use of material things, whether they're yours or someone else's. For all you know the donor could be relieved to have it out of sight; it might relieve his or her guilt over having bought yet one more gazingus pin.

***Ivy Underwood** brought her need for a simple sewing machine to her FI support group. It just so happened that Ellen had one she never used. "What do you want for it?" Ivy asked. As it turned out, what Ellen wanted most was to build a friendship with Ivy. She had just gone from an administrative job to self-employment, primarily so that she could have more time to spend with friends. So Ellen asked for four home-cooked meals at Ivy's—and they've become good friends. In the old way of doing things, Ivy would have spent $300 on a sewing machine and Ellen would have missed out on a good friendship. In the new way, everyone wins.*

Shopping—Marilynn, the "Urban Tightwad"

***Marilynn Bradley**, who reached FI after six years as a cook and caterer, gave us her strategies for making every penny count on her groceries. She does the buying for her household of six and keeps the cost per person down* *to $2 a day. While you may be shopping for only one or two, many of Marilynn's ideas are adaptable to smaller households. She claims that such careful shopping saves not only money but time. Five minutes per person per day is what her organized trips cost her household.*

50. Know your prices.

Take a day to check out all the stores in your neighborhood and record the prices for all the standard items on your grocery list. You can't recognize a bargain if you don't compare prices.

51. Make a list and stick to it.

Luckily, Marilynn isn't an impulse buyer, which is why she *does the shopping and not the housemate who doesn't know what she wants until she sees it. Marilynn has a standard list of household staples that she uses to check supplies and determine what's needed.*

52. Clip coupons.

Coupons save Marilynn up to $40 per month.

53. Do one big shopping every seven to ten days, rather than making several smaller trips.

Even if you have an iron will with regard to impulse shopping, the less exposure to temptation the better. This strategy saves time and gas as well as money.

54. Make up menus ahead of time for the seven to ten days you're shopping for, basing meals on what foods are on sale.

This saves money not only because you buy what is cheap, but also because you avoid overbuying something that doesn't get used or underbuying something so that you *absolutely must* do a midweek run to the store.

55. Comparison-shop, using newspaper ads and weekly grocery-store flyers.

Marilynn shops at three or four different grocery stores to get the best price on every item. Since they are all within a couple of miles of her home, it doesn't take much extra time to stop at all of them in one morning.

56. Buy in bulk frequently used staples such as flour, grains and spices.

Some stores have regular bins for bulk items, but these are not always less expensive. A good special on five-pound bags of store-brand flour could be a better buy.

On some items, Marilynn buys fifty-pound bags wholesale and stores the excess in sealed plastic buckets.

57. Educate yourself as to what foods are in season and therefore cheaper.

If you don't insist on having grapefruit in the summer and peaches in the winter, you can lower your grocery bill significantly. Remember the law of supply and demand. What is plentiful will be cheaper. What is scarce will be more expensive. Don't break that law and you won't end up broke.

58. Buy in larger quantity foods that are on sale—canned goods especially, but also meat if you have freezer space.

By now Marilynn knows how many cans of tuna her household wolfs down in the summer and can take advantage of good sales by buying cartons. There is no law that says you can't clear out your grocer's shelves of an item that's on super-special and roll out with 100 pounds of flour or two cases of peanut butter.

59. Be aware of where each grocery store puts out items that are reduced for quick sale.

Many foods that are still wholesome are reduced because they are a day or two past their prime. With an educated eye you can gauge which items are still fresh enough for your purposes.

60. If you have a garden to provide some of your vegetables, be frugal; grow the vegetables which give you the maximum savings for the minimum space and effort.

People garden for a variety of reasons. For example, ***Lu Bauer*** *and* ***Steve Brandon*** *garden as part of their commitment to live in balance with the earth and use its resources wisely. Everything is organic and fresh, so even if it's not much cheaper than store-bought that's OK for them. Thanks to* *a secondhand freezer they bought for $50, they have homegrown vegetables all year long.*

Many city people manage to find enough soil and sunlight to put in a few tomato plants and actually save money over buying them at the store (to say nothing of enjoying better flavor).

61. Be resourceful. If you should run low on an item before the next scheduled shopping trip, improvise with what's on hand instead of running out to the store.

As we've already mentioned, solving problems by using money often stunts your creativity. Instead of slavishly insisting on certain foods every day of the week, try feeding yourself from what you have right now. Remember that Silly Putty was just a lab error until someone recognized its true stature. Your "Tuna over Toast" might also be a winner.

62. Form a bulk-buying co-op with friends and neighbors.

Even if you don't live with a group of people, you can buy in bulk by pooling your orders with others. One FIer even saves a little extra by volunteering to pick up the orders and resack them for the group.

63. Cut out one (or more) meat meals per week and substitute a bean or pasta dish instead.

Find a few recipes you like that use inexpensive ingredients to good advantage and intersperse them with higher-cost meals on your weekly menu. This has the dual advantage of saving money *and* making healthful changes in your diet.

64. Buy from outdoor markets and local produce stands.

Such stands can save you money by cutting out several middlemen. Did you know that the average food item travels 1,300 miles from where it is grown to where it is consumed? Shipping a truckload of produce across the country costs up to $4,500. You save yourself those shipping costs when you buy locally grown produce. In addition, a dollar spent on local foods circulates in the local economy, generating $1.81 to $2.78 in other business. Furthermore, attendants at such local stands are usually more willing to bargain than are cashiers at supermarkets.

65. Know the character of your local markets and the kind of loss leaders you'll find at each one.

Some grocery stores specialize in produce, others in meats or dairy products. Others have very low-cost house brands. Some have bakeries that draw people in.

66. Bring your own shopping bags.

Many grocery stores now refund up to a nickel if you BYOB (bring your own bag). One canvas bag that you use for ten years could save you $25. If you buy it at a thrift store for $1, that's quite a saving.

67. Avoid convenience foods.

Here are some examples from our Frugal Zealots, Amy and Jim Dacyczyn:

- Their "Tightwad Hot Cocoa Mix" (⅓ cup of dry milk, 1 teaspoon cocoa, 1 teaspoon sugar) costs $.07 a serving versus $.25 a serving for Carnation cocoa mix in packets.
- Their homemade solar iced tea costs $.20 per gallon versus $1.29 per gallon for instant iced tea mix. Soda in 2-liter bottles cost $2.63, versus $4.28 for soda in six-packs, versus $7.64 for soda purchased at a fast-food chain, versus $14.98 for soda purchased at a movie theater. Water, they point out, costs nothing.
- In a careful and scientific test, Amy and Jim compared microwave popcorn to the generic pop-it-yourself kind. Microwave popcorn averaged $.125 a cup versus $.01 per cup for the generic stuff. Even better, stove-top popping is far faster than microwave popping. Amy, the stove-top popper, won the race by a mile.

Vacations

As your handling of money gets clearer and your life becomes more satisfying, you will have less of a need to "vacate." After all, if your life is fulfilling, why would you want to leave it to go sizzle your skin on a beach for a week?

68. Relax closer to home.

You might even enjoy being around the house. The amount of time you work for the privilege of owning or renting it entitles you to relax and appreciate it for a week. If you need to get away, any change of location might do—3 miles and 300 miles are both "away." And if you're going only a few miles away from home you'll eliminate the stress of packing everything you might need for a week.

Chris Northrup *came to this very conclusion and started vacationing at a beach house less than an hour from her home. Her family is more relaxed than they were on the expensive vacations they used to take to prove they were making it financially.*

69. Buy airline tickets well in advance.

If you buy your tickets at least one month before you intend to fly, you can get a better deal.

70. Take advantage of the lower prices available when you fly mid-week and stay over a weekend.

Different airlines have different policies, but generally you can fly more cheaply if you stay at your destination over a Saturday night.

71. Be your own travel agent.

Don't assume that your travel agent will get you the best possible deals. You can phone-shop for tickets like anything else, and then buy them through your travel agent, who can get his or her commission and will in turn give you good service in the future.

72. Take a camping vacation.

Think of it not as a cheap holiday but as a tour of your property. As U.S. citizens, we each "own" three acres of land—our 1/250,000,000th of the total amount of public lands (724,066,171 acres, to be exact). You'd be amazed how relaxing camping can be. You have everything you need with you, making it unnecessary to eat in restaurants and sleep in motels. You're out in the country where you don't feel compelled either to see the sights or to take advantage of the resort's eighteen-hole golf course, Olympic swimming pool, tennis courts, riding stable, shuffleboard and full-dress dinner dances. You can relax. Your beard can grow, your clothes can wrinkle and you don't have to care. Now *that's* a vacation.

73. Try a volunteer vacation that is in alignment with your values and purpose.

Through Earthwatch (680 Mount Auburn Street, Watertown, Massachusetts 02272, 617/926-8532) you can volunteer around the globe on environmental research projects. Through a variety of organizations you can travel as a citizen diplomat to countries that have strained relationships with the United States, building friendships that can ease some of the tensions. Global Exchange (2141 Mission Street #202, San Francisco, California 94110, 415/255-7296) has tour groups going to Third World nations to connect with grassroots peace and development projects. Volunteer Vacations by Bill McMillan can offer plenty of leads (see "Resources" at the end of this book).

Entertaining and Dating

The key to frugal entertaining and dating is to remember why you're doing it—to enjoy the company of other people. When you come right down to it, beyond a certain level of comfort, money doesn't make the encounter any more (or less) delightful. And the deepest levels of human connection have nothing to do with *anything* that money can buy.

74. Have potlucks rather than dinner parties.

Potlucks are the ultimate in ease and egalitarian entertaining. No one feels obligated. No one feels one-upped by the elegance of your entree. There's always something for every taste and dietary restriction. Often your guests will take back only their serving bowls, leaving the leftovers for your lunches. And you don't end up with a big dent in your food bill.

75. Invite friends to share a meal, but don't prepare anything different from your normal fare.

Rice and beans may be old hat to you, but they could be a treat for your guests. Entertaining at home doesn't have to cost any more than preparing one or two extra servings. Some of our friends have even eaten the same dish every time they've come to visit—and still love both it and us.

76. Invite friends to come for dessert and to share a videotape of a movie or documentary that's meaningful to you. Have a discussion afterward.

This is a social strategy we've often used with great success. Friends know they will meet interesting and engaging people at our gatherings, and they often stay late talking with one another. The video provides a takeoff point, the half hour of discussion usually brings some new perspective to light, and the coffee and cake provide refreshment while we talk away into the night.

77. Have a progressive dinner party.

This works well in a neighborhood or a small town but can be adapted for cities and wide open spaces as well. Start at one person's house with appetizers, go to the next person's house for soup and keep on moving from house to house for each successive course. It's like a potluck in that everyone cooks something, but no one household gets stuck with all the cleanup. We have friends who have adapted this game to house and yard work. Two or more friends agree to go to each other's homes and tackle jobs that are too difficult or boring to do alone. At house A they all clip the hedge, at house B it's floor scrubbing and at house C it's taking down the storm windows. Done as a team, these tasks become like a quilting bee. The socializing makes the time and fingers fly.

78. Go to inexpensive matinees for movies when you just can't wait for them to come out on video.

Going to the movies is often one of the first activities to get eliminated when people wake up to the amount of life energy they are pouring down the gullet of commercial establishments. But that occasional cinematic experience can be great, so find out when the bargain matinees are. For the rest, wait for it to come out on video—and then rent the video on a bargain night, if possible. Even better, invite your friends to come over and see the movie with you. Add a little freshly popped popcorn, and you will have a total cinematic happening in the comfort of your own living room. As an added bonus, you can laugh, cry and make dumb comments as freely as you want.

79. If you're a theater buff, usher at the local theater.

Call your local theaters and find out what their requirements are. This strategy works equally well for lectures, conferences, workshops and fairs. Volunteer hours can be exchanged for registration fees for almost any event you want to attend. As a volunteer you may even have a richer experience than the paying audience—like meeting the cast or driving the keynote speaker to the airport and getting stuck in traffic for forty-five minutes with a fascinating companion.

80. Borrow CD's, audiocassettes and videotapes from the library.

You will be amazed at the selection of fascinating titles available. Many people find that they only need to read (or listen to or see) something once to get what they want from it. You can listen to good music, learn a language, educate yourself on a variety of topics, enjoy a movie—all without adding to your clutter or subtracting from your pocketbook.

81. Cut back on dining out until it's a treat again.

Restaurant meals are another spending category that FIers question when they see how much of their life energy is being consumed by eating out. That doesn't mean, however, that they automatically cut out this luxury.

***Mary Yew** and her family of four live in the country outside of Paonia, Colorado. They own their home, grow their food and spend only about $300 a month. Once a week they all go to town to shop. For lunch they buy themselves a slice of pizza or a bowl of cream of broccoli soup and then kick back in the restaurant chairs while the snow melts off their boots. They plan what they are going to do the rest of the afternoon (go sledding, make chili, do artwork), tell jokes and visit with the people who come in. Pure luxury and total fulfillment— for $20 a month! No way are they going to give that ritual up.*

***Chris Northrup** concluded that her family of four gets value from dining out, not because the food is anything special but because they get uninterrupted family time. At home, at least one person (usually Chris) is constantly popping up and down to serve and clear. But this quality time doesn't have to come with a high price tag. They choose to go to inexpensive restaurants to enjoy the luxury of being together over a nourishing meal.*

***Diane Grosch**, our ex-yuppie, went on a restaurant fast for a month (during which time she learned a lot about cooking). At the end of the month she and her boyfriend took $15 and walked to the local Denny's. It was a very special treat, but Diane didn't even feel inclined to go out again for another month. ''The true value,'' she realized, ''was in what I brought to the* *experience, not how much I paid for a meal or how fancy the restaurant was."*

82. Write letters instead of making long-distance phone calls.

If your beloved (girlfriend, grandmother, ex-teacher) lives outside your local calling zone, any conversation beyond hello and good-bye will cost more than writing a letter. In addition, you may be able to say in a letter what you wouldn't dare say on the phone or in person. And your letter may well be cherished and saved for many years.

83. And remember, the nicest part of dating doesn't cost money!

Hobbies

84. Develop hobbies that are truly cost-effective in eliminating spending.

One thing that people do when they're trying to cut expenses is look for things they can make themselves rather than buy—the do-it-yourself syndrome. Many arts, crafts and do-it-yourself projects just aren't cost-effective. For example, ten hours spent making a table lamp on a wood-turning lathe might be fun and the lamp might be beautiful and functional, but the expenditure of life energy cannot be justified as "saving money." A lamp bought at a garage sale for $2 is more cost-effective than the ten hours spent making one. (This is not to imply that such an activity may not have other rewards more important to you than cost-effectiveness, such as artistic expression, satisfaction in creation, and other intangibles. That's what Lu Bauer and Steve Brandon concluded about their organic vegetable garden. They just changed the category name from Food to Hobby.)

85. Select hobbies that don't require you to travel long distances.

If your goal is to master fear, you can do that just as well at the neighborhood martial arts school as you can white-water rafting in Central Asia. If it's mountain climbing you enjoy, try conquering all the peaks within a day's drive before going to Nepal (unless, of course, you live in the Midwest, in which case you may need to drive a bit farther). Ask yourself: What are some ways to have an adventure, build my skills and challenge my courage and ingenuity that exist right where I live?

86. Select hobbies that you don't have to buy equipment to enjoy.

We all know the equipment freaks. When they take up golf, they get the best clubs made before ever getting on the green. When they take up photography, they acquire a whole suitcase of camera bodies, lenses, filters and tripods before ever taking a picture. Even the simple commitment to jogging provides the occasion for an investment of several hundred dollars in running shoes, tank tops, tights, sweatshirts, headbands, wristwatches that take your pulse and, of course, a Walkman. *We* approach hobbies the other way around. First, if we must buy expensive equipment to ante up in the game, we pass it by. For the rest, we buy only what we need for the level we are at. When our skill outgrows our equipment, we will carefully and appropriately upgrade.

87. Make a hobby out of service, or make service your hobby.

Gathering with others involved in activities that contribute to the welfare of others is itself entertaining, whether the activity is an informational or planning meeting, an envelope-stuffing session, a stint in the local food co-op or a visit to a children's home. Some people have found a way for their sport to support their values. Runners now run for everything from ending world hunger to curing cancer. Many cities stage "Give Peace a Dance" events where dancers raise money for peace work. If baking is your hobby, there are always bake sales for worthy causes. Sport shoppers are even turning their skills to finding bargains on household items for halfway houses and shelters for the homeless. If you love doing something, you'll get a special kick out of doing it for love.

88. Select or alter hobbies to eliminate membership fees for expensive clubs, spas, etc.

As we mentioned earlier, mowing the lawn with a push mower, parking your car at the far end of the parking lot, walking to your errands, bicycling to work and climbing stairs instead of using the elevator are great ways to eliminate membership fees to fitness clubs. Housework itself can be a workout.

Insurance

Why do we feel we have to insure every aspect of our lives for millions of dollars? What are we so afraid of? One male FIer concluded that many men are afraid they won't measure up as competent providers, and they paper over this insecurity with insurance policies. If I can't provide what's really needed, I can at least provide insurance so that the need can be met. Denial is expensive in more ways than one.

89. Does the current blue-book value or condition of your car warrant the comprehensive and collision insurance you are carrying?

> ***Marilynn Bradley***, *while doing famously on shopping, went on automatic when it came to her auto insurance. Two years into Financial Independence she had her car sideswiped by another driver. Except for a crumpled (but still functional) door, the car was in fine condition, but her insurance company declared it "totaled" and paid her $1,000. All well and good, but Marilynn failed to drop her comprehensive and collision insurance, which brought her annual fee above $500. She didn't even catch the irony of this action until doing her year-end accounts—two years later. When she dropped the unnecessary comprehensive and collision, her annual rate fell below $300.*
>
> Are you doing a Marilynn?

90. Are you insuring heirlooms that you would never replace even if they were stolen?

> ***Kees and Helen Kolff*** *paused in doing their Monthly Tabulations and evaluations when they got to homeowner insurance. They were paying $6 a month to insure some heirloom jewelry from Helen's grandmother. Applying FI thinking, they realized that they would never be able to replace these priceless treasures. They wouldn't even want to. What made them special was the connection with their past. So what was the $6 a month for? Consolation money? Kees, with his penchant for figuring things out, calculated how much principal would be required to yield $6 a month in interest by the time they planned to be financially independent (May 1993). The figure ($1,000) was so convincing that they dropped the insurance.*

91. If your wife has her own career, do you need as much life insurance as your father carried?

> Take some time to ponder your life-insurance situation. How much of it is reasonable protection for your family so that they can pay for your burial, pay off your debts and have enough to provide for their needs—and how much is to pave over uncomfortable feelings of fear, grief and loss of control? Are there better ways to deal with those

feelings than costly insurance policies, ways that could both deepen your relationships and boost your self-esteem?

Children

The estimated cost of raising an urban child to the age of eighteen in the United States was over $100,000 in 1986. Are kids today really black holes—bottomless pits of needs, wants and desires—or can the costs of parenting be contained? If you decide you can afford the luxury of having children, here are some tips from FIers for containing the costs:

92. Substitute creativity for money in planning for birthday parties and Halloween costumes.

__Amy and Jim Dacyczyn__, the famous tightwads from Maine, managed to save money on his income from the Navy, even with six children. Amy, claiming that ''tightwaddery without creativity is deprivation,'' has done imaginative things, like converting the inside of their barn to a pirate ship for their son's birthday using old white sheets, a tug-of-war rope, removable sides from a utility trailer and old wooden crates—all stuff they had lying around. For Halloween, another child dressed up as a spaceman with a costume made out of a cardboard carton decorated with some hardware and gauges salvaged from the dump. (He won first prize.) In her essay on creativity Amy goes on to say, ''When there is a lack of resourcefulness, inventiveness and innovation, thrift means doing without. When creativity combines with thrift you may be doing without money, but you are not doing without.''

93. Give kids an allowance and allow them to choose how they spend it.

Many FIers have reported that as soon as their kids realized they would have to spend their own money for the stuff they wanted, they got very frugal—and entrepreneurial.

94. Curb your own spending and your kids will follow suit.

It may take a while, but if your values change your children will follow along.

As soon as __Kate and Ned Norris__, a lawyer and his wife, stopped buying expensive clothes from mail-order recreational outfitters, their six-year-old daughter stopped insisting on Osh-Kosh overalls. When Kate started shopping in thrift stores, her daughter began to enjoy wearing used clothes (which she would never do before). When Laura was nine she started baby-sitting in the neighborhood. While gift money from the grandparents gets spent, all of Laura's earnings get saved in her "FI jar."

95. If the child doesn't have an allowance and asks for something, suggest that you talk about it again in a few days.

Most passing fancies are just that—they pass. If desire for an item comes up again, another strategy is to tell the child to choose one of the two or three things he or she has recently asked for. When it comes to spending, he who hesitates saves. (As a matter of fact, this is a good strategy for parents and other adults as well. A cooling-off period works wonders when you're in hot pursuit of things you don't need.)

96. Rethink a high-cost college education.

Here's a big one. Our educational system, particularly college, has become as unsustainable and overpriced as high-tech medicine. Let's consider some alternatives to paying up to $100,000 per teenager for a college education.

Kees and Helen Kolff *struggled with the issue of tuition for their two high-schoolers. Kees's parents had paid for his college eduction and medical school. Surely, he thought, he had to do the same. Then he asked all of his guests at a dinner party whether their parents had paid for their education. More than half had worked their way through school. He then asked who believed that he or she had benefited significantly from college education. The ones who had paid for it themselves were the ones who most valued their education. Stunned, he asked his best friend from college what he was going to do for his children. He was not planning to pay all of his kids' higher education costs. Weighing all the factors, Kees and Helen decided to offer each child a fixed amount for college. They could go to an Ivy League school and spend it in two and a half years or they could go to a state university for six years. The choice was theirs.*

Ted and Martha Pasternak *have thought a lot about their son's future. Even though Willie is only three, they've bought bonds to provide for everything from braces to his first car. They aren't saving for a private university, however. They achieved Financial Independence right before their son was born, and parenting Willie is a priority for both of them. "We aren't going* *back to work to pay for his education. We* are *his education. If we're doing our job right now, he won't* need *Harvard to be a success in the world. We don't want Willie to turn to us when he's eighteen and tell us he doesn't want to go to college and he sure would have liked to have had his parents around when he was growing up.'' Ted and Martha are* being *Willie's education instead of buying it.*

Perhaps when Willie gets to be eighteen he'll be like the young man in the following story:

*When **Tim Moore** graduated from high school he decided to spend some time in the ''School of Life,'' since he found he learned more in less time when he did his own projects. So instead of studying mechanical engineering he learned to be a mechanic, saving his money for several years. By day he rebuilt engines; at night and on the weekends he built a custom sports car from the chassis up. He sold the car when it was finished and had enough money to pay for two years at college. With a winning combination of passion and maturity, he's now building a prototype electric car at a university lab and plans to become an urban transportation expert. His life experience will surely enhance his educational experience to make him a skillful advocate for intelligent solutions to the urban plagues of smog and gridlock.*

Gifts

For many people giving presents is an important way to express love. You can cut back on the cost of gifts without cutting back on the love. One FIer reports that as a househusband he tends to want to give homemade gifts, while his wife, a businesswoman, likes to express her love through buying things. This is where Question 3 from Step 4 helps to reveal hidden options. If you didn't have to work for a living would you give different (and less expensive) gifts?

97. Promise children one, or at most three, toys at Christmas and have them select the ones they want. More than that is more than enough.

*This has been **Amy and Jim Dacyczyn**'s strategy ever since they observed the Fulfillment Curve at work on Christmas Day. The first one, two or three presents were greeted with squeals of ecstasy, but from then on it was down-hill. Instead of being able to play with what they had, the kids felt compelled* *to keep opening all their gifts. By the end they were tired and cranky and nothing suited them.*

98. Buy gifts at garage sales and save them for the right occasion.

Where do you think all the stuff at garage sales comes from, anyway? It's gifts people got and never used! Just keep them moving on.

99. Give services (like a massage, baby-sitting, a personal concert or hedge-clipping) instead of an object.

Wouldn't you rather have a massage or a foot rub than an electric cocktail mixer? Isn't a week off from washing dishes an ace in the hole you'll thoroughly enjoy cashing in at just the right time?

100. Make an agreement with friends and family not to exchange presents for Christmas or birthdays.

The Christmas season has become the buying season in North America, the time retailers count on for the lion's share of their annual business. There's no reason that celebrating the birth of Jesus or the birth of someone you love has to be the occasion for spending money. Part of gift-giving is social expectation. You can change that with a simple, honest conversation.

101. If you're "crafty," you can make simple and unique gifts.

One avid mountaineer considers her camera essential climbing equipment. Once she reaches the summit and has her fill of contemplating the view, she takes successive photos of all 360 degrees of grandeur. Once the pictures are developed she artfully combines them into a single long panoramic montage and gives these as gifts. Total cost: under $10. Total value: priceless.

There you are: 101 proven ways to save money. There are plenty more. In fact, one category that's missing will yield a wealth of saving—for you and for the planet: look for ways to reduce your consumption of resources. As the environmentalists say, "recycle, reduce, restore, reuse, repair." (As a matter of fact, any word that starts with *re* has a ring of frugality. Use it again, Sam. "Double your pleasure" is high-frugal thinking!)

SAVE MONEY, SAVE THE PLANET?

These hints and tips *will* help you to save your life energy—adding money to your bank account and years to your life. The next bit of good news is that this process benefits our planet as well. Ernest Callenbach, author of *Ecotopia* (a future fantasy in which Northern California, Oregon and Washington secede from the union to form an ecologically sound society), observes that your health, your pocketbook and the environment have a mutually enhancing relationship. If you do something good for one, it's almost always good for the other two. If you walk or bicycle to work to reduce your contribution to greenhouse gases you are also saving money and getting great exercise at the same time. If you compost your kitchen scraps to improve your soil (the environment) you are also improving the quality of your vegetables (your health)—and saving money on your garbage bill. Saving money may well save your life and save the earth at the same time.

It isn't just an odd coincidence that saving money and saving the planet are connected. In fact, in some sense your money *is* the planet. Here's how.

Money is a lien on earth's resources. Every time we spend money on anything, we are consuming not only the metal, plastic, wood or other material in the item itself, but also all the resources it took to extract these from the earth, transport them to the manufacturer, process them, assemble the product, ship it to the retailer and bring it from the store to your home. All of that activity and cost is somehow included in the $9.99 you spend for a new toaster. Then there are the environmental costs that *aren't* included in the price, what economists call externalities: the pollution and waste we pay for in other ways—in lung disease, cancer, respiratory problems, desertification, flooding, etc. What it boils down to is that every time we spend money we are voting on the kind of planet we want to leave to future generations.

Money is a lien on the life energy of the planet. We call this the "Pogonomics Principle"—economics from cartoon character Pogo's point of view. Pogo's contribution to Earth Day 1970, as you may remember, was the observation that "we have met the enemy and he is us." It's no mystery that the planet is polluted. *We* did it through our demand for more, better and different stuff. Think about it. Prostitution would be the world's loneliest profession without demand. The Medellín Cartel would be a 4-H club without demand. OPEC would be a solar energy and desalinization consortium without our demand.

Like facing any truth, accepting the fact that our demand is a cause of many problems can give us great power. It is empowering to know that the major driving force behind our planetary plight is not the military-industrial complex or the federal budget or defense spending —things we usually feel powerless to do anything about. Rather it is our patterns of consumption here in North America, our demand. And that is something that we *can* do something about—and benefit ourselves in the process. Creative frugality is a double win—for our wallets and for our world.

The Three Questions Revisited

As we saw in the Fulfillment Curve, fulfillment by its very definition is a function of knowing when you have enough. The three questions from Chapter 4 can be asked in a different way with the planet in mind.

The questions to ask are:

- Am I likely to get **fulfillment** from this money spent in proportion to the resources that it represents?
- Is this purchase in alignment with the **values** that we all hold in common—the desire to survive and to thrive?
- What would spending in this category look like **if I were working for the well-being of the whole world**, instead of for my individual survival?

Remember, asking these questions will not deprive you of things that really bring you fulfillment. They will simply open up new opportunities for saving money and achieving clarity in your relationship with money.

An Example of Pogonomic Thinking

Joe Dominguez *was the computer manager for a medical research study that was seeking to model how top-notch research could be done without asking for funding and with minimal cash outlay. As the statistical phase of the study began, with hundreds of print runs of statistics and graphics being* *called for, it became apparent that printer ribbons were going to be a major item. The first run alone used up one entire ribbon. Joe did some number crunching and found that, at $9.25 per ribbon, this expense would run up the costs of the project significantly. And then he remembered a small classified ad in a computer magazine for a ribbon-inking machine (whatever* that *was). He bought the machine for $60 and a pint of special ink for $18, and from a discount computer supplier he ordered 12 ribbons for $8 each, taking a chance that this investment would, over time, result in substantial savings.*

Inking machine	*$ 60.00*
1 pint ink	*18.00*
12 ribbons	*96.00*
TOTAL investment	*$174.00*

In the year after those purchases, Joe reinked each of the thirteen ribbons seven times.

13 × 7 × $8 =	*$728.00*
Reinking costs	*−174.00*
TOTAL savings in 1 year	*$554.00*
1-year return on investment:	*318%*

*This strategy saved the project hundreds of dollars—*and *had interesting implications for the earth. Think of the millions of offices that discard a printer ribbon after one use. Compute the landfill that these plastic cartridges filled with nylon ribbon require. Compute the petroleum used in the manufacture of the plastic. And, to top it all, note this fact, found in* The Wall Street Journal:

> ***Nylon Production Named as a Source of Nitrous Oxide***
> *Scientists identified nylon production plants as sources of gases believed to be depleting atmospheric ozone and contributing to global warming.*

Saving Money While You're Saving the Earth

The point of all this is not to send you off into the desert to eat berries and wear fig leaves. It is especially important to remember the mantra: No shame, no blame. We were all born into a world where consuming our way to happiness seemed both natural and benign. The kinds of changes we may all need to make to keep the environment viable will require some deliberate and courageous modifications of our current habits. But why wait for the year 2000? Avoid the millennial rush and start to live with these questions now. You will see many places where you can choose a nonpolluting pleasure and have twice the fulfillment—once for you and once for the planet. Indeed, enjoying nature and feeling your vital connection to the earth, the source of all life, is one of the greatest pleasures there is. At the cellular level there isn't much difference between you and a tree. Experiencing that kinship *without consuming it* is as much a part of an earth-friendly life-style as composting your vegetable scraps and yard waste.

If you want to find out how to save money while saving the earth, many fine books are available. The most popular one at the moment is *50 Simple Things You Can Do to Save the Earth*—but *many* books exist that can help you reevaluate your personal life-style choices in light of our current understanding about human impact on the ecosystem. If your library doesn't have the one you want, request that they buy it so that others can use it as well. That alone would be an earth-friendly act.

The key is remembering that *anything* you buy and don't use, *anything* you throw away, *anything* you consume and don't enjoy is money down the drain, wasting your life energy *and* wasting the finite resources of the planet. Any waste of your life energy means more hours lost to the rat race, "making a dying." If you have no time in your life to enjoy the fruits of your labor, perhaps what you need isn't another time management course but rather a refresher in frugality. Frugality is the user-friendly and earth-friendly life-style.

Don't stop here in your search for ultimate frugality, the most refined and advanced life-style the planet has ever seen. Read on.

1,001 SURE WAYS TO SAVE MONEY

After a year of keeping your Monthly Tabulations, you will have approximately 1,001 (more or less) single entries under your 15 to 30 spending categories. Chances are very good that you could be spending less *on every purchase*—from apples to zinnias—with no reduction in the quality of product or the quality of your life. It's the attitude of honoring your life energy that will show you the way, not following someone else's recipe for a frugal life. You will be as excited about the savings you discover as we have been about reinking printer ribbons or furnishing our home from garage sales and giveaways. The empowerment comes from *your* cleverness and *your* creativity in finding *your* strategies for frugality. That's why we call it *creative* frugality. So here's a blank slate. Write your own 1,001 tips for living on less and loving it.

1,000,001 SURE WAYS TO SAVE MONEY

Watch your thoughts. Anyone who practices meditation knows that our gray matter is like a frenetic monkey, churning out a steady stream of unrelated thoughts at the rate of at least one a second. In just 11.6 days you'll have 1,000,001 thoughts—and most of them will have something to do with desires. I want this. I don't want that. I like this. I don't like that. The Buddha said that desire is the source of all suffering. It is also the source of all shopping. By being conscious of your next 1,000,001 desires, you'll have 1,000,001 opportunities to not spend money on something that won't bring you fulfillment. Advertising doesn't make you buy stuff. Other people's expectations don't make you buy stuff. Television doesn't make you buy stuff. Your *thoughts* make you buy stuff. Watch those suckers. They're dangerous to your pocketbook—and to a lot more.

Remember, frugality isn't about being a cheapskate or a penny-pincher. It's about honoring and valuing your most precious resource—your life energy. Shopping smart, saving money, following the adage "Use it up, wear it out, make it do or do without" isn't about deprivation; it's about loving yourself and your life so much that you wouldn't think of wasting a second. It is also, as we have seen, about loving the planet so much that you want to take good care of it. And finally, it's about loving future generations so much that you want to leave this earth in better shape than you found it.

> *When we talk about preservation of the environment, it is related to many other things. Ultimately the decision must come from the human heart, so I think the key point is to have a genuine sense of universal responsibility.*
>
> *—the Dalai Lama*

CHECKLIST: THINK BEFORE YOU SPEND

1. Don't shop.
2. Live within your means.
3. Take care of what you have.
4. Wear it out.
5. Do it yourself.
6. Anticipate your needs.
7. Research value, quality, durability, and multiple use.
8. Get it for less.
9. Buy used.
10. Follow the steps of this program.

SUMMARY OF STEP 6

Lower your total monthly expenses by valuing your life energy and increasing your consciousness in spending. Learn to choose quality of life over standard of living. Be frugal; it's cool.

7

FOR LOVE OR MONEY: VALUING LIFE ENERGY— WORK AND INCOME

In Chapter 6 we talked about valuing your life energy by spending your money more consciously. In this chapter we will talk about valuing your life energy by looking at how well you spend your time. Are you getting full value for selling that most precious commodity—your life? Does work work for you?

Sometimes you have to question the obvious in order to get at the truth. The question we will be exploring in this chapter is "What is work?" The obvious answer, of course, is that work is what we do to make a living. But that definition robs us of our life. Some of us honor our jobs and neglect the rest of our lives. Others of us endure our jobs and make up for it on the evenings and weekends. In either case, we end up with half a life. In either case, we fail to value our life energy. And in either case, we often feel helpless about making changes. What we will be exploring now is whether our definition of work itself is part of the problem.

How well are you using your life energy both on and off the job? Is your job "consuming" (using up, destroying, wasting) your life? Do you love your life, using each hour—on and off the job—with care? As we said in Chapter 2, our life energy is precious because it is limited and irretrievable and because our choices about how we use it express the meaning and purpose of our time here on earth. So far you have learned to value your life energy by aligning your spending with your fulfillment and your values. Now it's time to learn about valuing your life energy by maximizing your compensation—in love or money—for the hours you invest in your work.

WHAT IS WORK?

Just as with money, our concept of work consists of a patchwork of contradictory beliefs, thoughts and feelings—notions we absorbed from our parents, our culture, the media and our life experience. The following quotations highlight the incongruity of our different definitions of work:

E. F. Schumacher says:

> the three purposes of human work [are] as follows:
> - First, to provide necessary and useful goods and services.
> - Second, to enable every one of us to use and thereby perfect our gifts like good stewards.
> - Third, to do so in service to, and in cooperation with, others, so as to liberate ourselves from our inborn egocentricity.

Economist Robert Theobald tells us:

> Work is defined as something that people do not want to do and money as the reward that compensates for the unpleasantness of work.

Studs Terkel begins his book *Working* this way:

> This book, being about work, is, by its very nature, about violence—to the spirit as well as to the body. It is about ulcers as well as accidents, about shouting matches as well as fistfights, about nervous breakdowns as well as kicking the dog around. It is, above all (or beneath all), about daily humiliations. To survive the day is triumph enough for the walking wounded among the great many of us. . . . It is about a search, too, for daily meaning

> as well as daily bread, for recognition as well as cash, for astonishment rather than torpor; in short, for a sort of life rather than a Monday through Friday sort of dying.

Kahlil Gibran, on the other hand, tells us, "Work is love made visible."

What *is* work? Is it a blessing or a curse? A trial or a triumph? Is work good for the soul or is it, as cartoonist Matt Groening suggests, "Life in Hell"? Our task will be to redefine work the same way we redefined money—by looking for what we can say about work that is consistently true. This definition will allow you to reperceive your work in ways that are more consistent with your values and your true fulfillment—as well as your bottom line.

WORK THROUGH THE AGES

Let's begin by taking a brief look at the history of "work," for it is through looking at history that we find new opportunities to shape our own personal stories. Where do our concepts about work come from? Why do we work? And what is the place of work in our lives?

Minimum Daily Requirement of Work

As human beings we all must do *some* work for basic survival—but how much? Is there a "minimum daily requirement" of work? A number of diverse sources, ranging from primitive cultures to modern history, would place this figure at about three hours a day during the adult lifetime.

Marshall Sahlins, author of *Stone Age Economics*, discovered that before Western influence changed daily life, Kung men hunted from two to two and a half days a week, with an average work week of fifteen hours. Women gathered for about the same period of time each week. In fact, one day's work supplied a woman's family with vegetables for the next three days. Throughout the year both men and women worked for a couple of days, then took a couple off to rest and play games, gossip, plan rituals and visit. . . . It would appear that the work week in the old days beats today's banker's hours by quite a bit.

Dr. Frithjof Bergmann states:

> For most of human history people only worked for two or three hours per day. As we moved from agriculture to industrialization, work hours increased, creating standards that label a person lazy if he or she doesn't work a forty-hour week. . . . The very notion that everyone should have a job only began with the Industrial Revolution.

In his study of numerous utopian communites of the nineteenth century, John Humphrey Noyes, founder of the Oneida Community, noted that:

> All these communities have demonstrated what the practical Dr. Franklin (of the 18th century) said, that if every one worked bodily three hours daily, there would be no necessity of any one's working more than three hours.

Moving on to the twentieth century, in 1934 Paramahansa Yogananda, Indian sage and visionary, spoke of self-sufficient, spiritually oriented worldwide communities in which:

> Everybody, rich or poor, must work three hours a day in order to produce only the extreme necessities of life . . . work three hours a day and live in the luxury of literary wealth and have time to [do what is meaningful to us.]

These quotations all suggest that three hours a day is all that we *must* spend working for survival. One can imagine, in preindustrial times, that this pattern would make sense. Life was more of a piece back then when "work" blended into family time, religious celebrations and play. Then came the "labor-saving" Industrial Revolution and the compartmentalization of life into "work" and "nonwork"—with "work" taking an ever-bigger bite out of the average person's day.

In the nineteenth century the "common man," with justified aversion to such long hours on the job, began to fight for a shorter work week.

Champions for the workers claimed that fewer hours on the job would decrease fatigue and increase productivity. Indeed, they said, fewer hours were the natural expression of the maturing Industrial Revolution. Fewer hours would free the workers to exercise their higher faculties, and democracy would enjoy the benefit of an educated and engaged citizenry.

But all that came to a halt during the Depression. The work week, having fallen dramatically from sixty hours at the turn of the century to thirty-five hours during the Depression, became locked in at forty hours for many and has crept up to fifty or even sixty hours a week in the last two decades. Why?

The Right to Life, Liberty and the Pursuit of a Paycheck?

During the Depression, free time became equated with unemployment. In an effort to boost the economy and reduce unemployment, the New Deal established the forty-hour week and the government as the employer of last resort. Workers were educated to consider employment, not free time, to be their right as citizens (life, liberty and the pursuit of the paycheck?). Benjamin Kline Hunnicutt, in *Work Without End,* illuminates the doctrine of "Full Employment":

> Since the Depression, few Americans have thought of work reduction as a natural, continuous, and positive result of economic growth and increased productivity. Instead, additional leisure has been seen as a drain on the economy, a liability on wages, and the abandonment of economic progress.

The myths of "growth is good" and "full employment" established themselves as key values. These dovetailed nicely with the gospel of "full consumption," which preached that leisure is a "commodity" to be consumed rather than free time to be enjoyed. For the last half century full employment has meant more consumers with more "disposable income." This means increased profits, which means business expansion, which means more jobs, which means more consumers with more disposable income. Consumption keeps the wheels of progress moving, as we saw in Chapter 1.

So we see that our concept (as a society) of leisure has changed radically. From being considered a desirable and civilizing component of day-to-day life it has become something to be feared, a reminder of unemployment during the years of the Depression. As the value of leisure has dropped, the value of work has risen. The push for full employment, along with the growth of advertising, has created a populace increasingly oriented toward work and toward earning more money in order to consume more resources.

Work Takes On New Meaning

In addition, according to Hunnicutt, during the last half century we've begun to lose the fabric of family, culture and community that gave meaning to life outside the workplace. The traditional rituals, the socializing and the simple pleasure of one another's company all provided structure for nonwork time, affording people a sense of purpose and belonging. Without this experience of being part of a people and a place, leisure leads more often to loneliness and boredom.

Because life outside the workplace has lost vitality and meaning, work has ceased being a means to an end and become an end in itself. Hunnicutt notes:

> Meaning, justification, purpose, and even salvation were now sought in work, without a necessary reference to any traditional philosophic or theological structure. Men and women were answering the old religious questions in new ways, and the answers were more and more in terms of work, career, occupation and professions.

The final piece of the puzzle snaps into place when we look at the shift in the religious attitude toward work that came with the rise of the Protestant ethic. Before that time work was profane and religion was sacred. Afterward work was seen as the arena where you worked out your salvation—and the evidence of a successful *religious* life was success in the world of business.

So here we are at the end of the twentieth century. Our paid employment has taken on myriad roles. Our jobs now serve the function that traditionally belonged to religion: they are the place where we seek answers to the perennial questions "Who am I?"and "Why am I here?" and "What's it all for?"

Our jobs are also called upon to provide the exhilaration of romance and the depths of love. It's as though we believed that there is a Job Charming out there—like the Prince Charming in fairy tales—that will fill our needs and inspire us to greatness. We've come to believe that, through this job, we would somehow have it all: status, meaning, adventure, travel, luxury, respect, power, tough challenges and fantastic rewards. All we need is to find Mr. or Ms. Right—Mr. or Ms. Right Job. Perhaps what keeps some of us stuck in the home/freeway/office loop is this very Job Charming illusion. We're like the princess who keeps kissing toads, hoping one day to find herself hugging a handsome prince. Our jobs are our toads.

Finally, we look to our jobs to provide us with a sense of identity.

Do-Be Do-Be Doooo . . . ?

We all remember the question we were asked, over and over, throughout childhood: "What do you want to be when you grow up?" Do you remember what you answered? Was it something that came from inside, or did you, with a child's intuition, say what the adults wanted to hear? Did your answer change over time? Was the hormone-ridden eighteen-year-old who selected your college major in his or her right mind? Are the dreams you had as a teenager tucked away with your high-school yearbook? Has your job history bumped and turned on byways you would never have predicted on Career Day in your high school? If you went on to be what you wanted to be when you grew up, has it met your expectations?

The very question, "What do you want to *be* when you grow up?" is actually part of the problem. It asks what you want to *be,* yet you are supposed to answer it with what you want to *do.* Is it any wonder that so many of us suffer midlife crises as we face the fact that our doing doesn't even come close to expressing our being?

We are so wedded to what we do to "make a living" that we perpetuate, without thinking, this confusion of doing with being. Indeed, in terms of sheer hours, we may be more wedded to our jobs than to our mates. The vows for better or worse, richer or poorer, in sickness and in health—and often till death do us part—may be better applied to our jobs than our wives or husbands. No wonder we introduce ourselves as nurses or contractors rather than as parents or friends.

In Chapter 5 we saw that getting out of debt and accumulating savings would allow unemployment to become a golden opportunity for discovery, learning and renewal. But what if you think that who you *are* is what you *do* to make money? No amount of savings would keep you from that loss of purpose and self-esteem. As we'll see, who you are is far greater than what you do for money, and your true work is far greater than your paid employment. Our focus on money and materialism may have robbed us of the pride we can and should feel in who we are as people and the many ways we contribute to the well-being of others. Our task now is to retrieve that birthright of knowing ourselves as human *beings* rather than as human *doings* or human *earnings*.

DID WE WIN THE INDUSTRIAL REVOLUTION?

We've come a long way since the time when our ancestors worked three hours a day and enjoyed the pleasures of socializing, rituals, celebrations and games the rest of the time. Has it been worth it?

We've certainly gained a tremendous amount by focusing our creativity and ingenuity on mastering the physical world. Science, technology, culture, art, language and music have all evolved and brought us countless blessings. Few of us would want to turn back the clock entirely, forsaking Bach or penicillin or even the internal-combustion engine. We do need to stop the clock, however, and evaluate our direction. Are we still on course? Let's look briefly at the modern workplace and job market. Where are we? And is it where we want to be?

- Some workers feel underemployed, their days filled with repetitive, menial or unchallenging tasks that call forth very little of their creativity or intelligence. Others feel overworked, especially now with corporate downsizing shifting more and more responsibilities onto the shoulders of the lucky few who retain their jobs.
- The well-publicized and documented baby-boom generation is dis-

covering that its very numbers mean that a smaller percentage will make it to the top of the corporate ladder, and many have hit career plateaus.

- The rising awareness of issues of social justice and ecology is tearing some workers in two: economically they need their jobs, but ethically they don't support the products or services their companies provide.
- Job security ain't what it used to be. In the last six months of 1990 the recession had put over one million people out of work, with many more losing their jobs in 1991.
- Retirement security is no longer secure. Even loyal employees may not be able to count on a pension, since poor company investment choices are leaving many pension funds bankrupt.
- While only half of working people claim to be satisfied with their jobs, only one-third of them would continue to work at those jobs if they didn't have to.
- A recent poll conducted by John Robinson for the Hilton Hotels Corporation found that 70 percent of those earning $30,000 a year or more would give up a day's pay each week for an extra day of free time. Even among those earning $20,000 a year or less, 48 percent would do the same.

We've had enough, it would seem, of making a dying in such a crazy world. We spend the major portion of our waking hours at our jobs, and it hardly seems worth it. We look to work to meet many of our needs, and we end up unfulfilled. Why do we give the best years of our lives to our jobs?

WHAT IS THE PURPOSE OF WORK?

Let's continue our exploration of work, this most personal and profound relationship, by reflecting on a few questions:

- Why do you do what you do to earn money?
- What motivates you to get out of bed five days a week to go somewhere and make money?

- What is the purpose, in your experience, of your paid employment? (If you are supported by a working spouse or relative, you can reflect either on why that "breadwinner" works or on some work experience from your past. If you are retired or unemployed, think about a job you once had.)

Now consider the following list of various purposes of paid employment and see which ones apply to you.

Earning money
- to provide necessities—food, clothing, shelter (survival)
- to provide amenities (comforts)
- to provide luxuries
- to provide funds for others (philanthropy)
- to leave an estate

A sense of security
- that your needs will be met
- that your value as an adult human being is recognized

Tradition
- to carry on a family tradition of following a particular profession
- to maintain a sense of continuity and connection with your past

Enjoyment
- to be in contact with interesting people
- to have stimulation, entertainment and fun

Duty
- to do your fair share in keeping society functioning smoothly

Service
- to make a contribution to others, society and the world

Learning
- to acquire new skills

Prestige and status

- to receive praise, admiration and respect from others

Power

- over people who report to you and follow your commands
- over the course of events, influencing decisions

Socializing

- to enjoy opportunities to socialize with your coworkers
- to meet the public and feel part of a larger community

Personal growth

- to be stimulated and challenged
- to expand your emotional and intellectual life

Success

- to get feedback for success
- to compare yourself with others in your field

Creativity and fulfillment

- to achieve fulfillment, that feeling of being completely used
- to be challenged, to stay sharp, to create something new

Time structuring

- to structure your time and give an orderly rhythm to your life

Just cuz

- because that's just what people do

Have you noticed that work has two different functions: the material, financial function (i.e., getting paid) and the personal function (emotional, intellectual, psychological and even spiritual)?

The original question was: What is the purpose served by *paid* employment? In reality, there is only one purpose served by paid employment: getting paid. That is the only real link between work and money. The other "purposes" of paid employment are other types of rewards, certainly desirable, but not directly related to getting paid. They are all equally available in unpaid activities.

Any stress, confusion or disappointment we might feel concerning our paid employment is rarely because of the pay itself. We have already seen that beyond a certain level of comfort, more money does not bring more satisfaction. Perhaps the trouble with our paid employment, then, is that our needs for stimulation, recognition, growth, contribution, interaction and meaning are not being met by our jobs. What if we removed most of these expectations from our paid employment and recognized that *all purposes for work other than earning money could be fulfilled by unpaid activities?*

This observation brings us to a critical point in reexamining our relationship with work. There are two sides to work. On one side is our need and desire for money. We work in order to get paid. On the other side, *and totally separate from our wages,* is the fact that we work in order to fulfill many other purposes in our lives.

REDEFINING WORK

The real problem with work, then, is not that our expectations are too high. It's that we have confused *work* with *paid employment.* Redefining "work" as simply any productive or purposeful activity, with paid employment being just one activity among many, frees us from the false assumption that what we do to put food on the table and a roof over our heads should also provide us with our sense of meaning, purpose and fulfillment. Breaking the link between work and money allows us to reclaim balance and sanity.

Our fulfillment as human beings lies not in our jobs but in the whole picture of our lives—in our inner sense of what life is about, our connectedness with others and our yearning for meaning and purpose. By *separating* work and wages we *bring together* the different parts of ourselves and remember that our real work is just to live our values as best we know how. In fact, mistaking work for wages has meant that most of our "jobs" have gotten neither the attention nor the credit they deserve—jobs like loving our mates, being a decent neighbor or developing a sustaining philosophy of life. When we are whole, we don't need to try to consume our way to happiness. Happiness is our birthright.

You may love your paid employment or you may hate it; it doesn't matter. But you do want to recognize that the purpose of your paid employment is getting paid and that your real "work" may be far bigger than this one job. By separating work and wages you can see more clearly whether you are valuing—both on and off the job—that precious commodity called life energy.

Remember our discussion about life energy in Chapter 2? If you are 40 years old, actuarial tables indicate that you have just 329,601 hours of life left in your life-energy bank account. These hours are all you've got. There is nothing in your life that is more valuable than your time, the moments you have left. You cannot put too much awareness and intention into the way you invest those moments.

By separating work from wages, you can do a better job at *all* your "jobs." When at your paid job you can value your life energy by working efficiently, diligently, intelligently and for the highest remuneration possible. When doing the rest of your work, you can value your life energy by working efficiently, diligently, intelligently and with the greatest degree of enthusiasm and love you have in you.

Breaking the link between work and wages has as much power in our lives as the recognition that money is simply "something we trade our life energy for." Money is our life energy; it takes its value not from external definitions but from what we invest in it. Similarly, paid employment takes its only *intrinsic* value from the fact that we are paid to do it. Everything else we do is an expression of who we are, not what we must do out of economic necessity. By breaking the link we regain quality, values and self-worth as our bottom line. By breaking the link we can redefine work simply as whatever we do in alignment with our purpose in life. By breaking the link we get our life back.

THE STUNNING IMPLICATIONS OF REDEFINING WORK

From this point of view it's clear why your paid employment may feel like "making a dying." Besides earning money you may be doing nothing else on the job that is in alignment with your purpose. Eight to ten hours a day. Five days a week. Fifty weeks a year. Forty or more years of your life. This opens up a host of questions. How much money do you need to be at the peak of fulfillment? Is your job providing that amount? Are you working for less than you're worth and bringing home less money than you need? Or are you earning far more than you need *for fulfillment?* What is the purpose of that extra money? If it serves no purpose, would you want to work less and have more time to do what matters to you? If it does serve a purpose, is that purpose so clear and so connected with your values that it brings an experience of joy to your hours at your paid employment? If not, what needs to change?

Let's explore together some of the implications of disconnecting work from wages, of seeing paid employment as distinct from work—work in the sense of fulfillment of purpose(s) in life.

1. Redefining Work Increases Choices

Let's say you are a natural-born teacher, but you took a job as a computer programmer because you can make more money (which you are convinced you need). In the old way of thinking, every time someone asked you what you do, you would be forced to affirm, "I am a computer programmer." What do you suppose the effect on you might be of this long-term incongruity between your inner sense of yourself and your outer presentation? You might be just mildly unhappy and not know why. You might get ill, as one friend of ours did when she gave up her dream of being a concert pianist and became a programmer instead. She developed an inexplicable illness that put her on disability for nearly a year. You might run up a credit card debt to reward yourself for doing something that doesn't suit you.

The one thing you might overlook, though, is questioning whether or not you *are* a computer programmer just because that's what you *do* to make a living. When you break the link between wages and work, however, another option opens up. When you're asked what you do, you can affirm, "I am a teacher but currently I'm writing computer programs to make money." Being able to acknowledge who you really are allows you to reevaluate how you've structured your "career." You might decide to save money and go back to school for your teaching credentials. You might decide to reduce your programming hours so that you can volunteer as a teacher. You might decide to teach computer programming. You might bring in a third love, like kayaking, and teach that on weekends while you program computers for money. Disconnecting work from wages allows the various parts of your compartmentalized life to break loose, slide around and rearrange themselves in a pattern that serves you better.

Chris Northrup *worked her way up in what used to be considered a man's world and found it didn't fit her woman's sensibilities and intuitions. As a doctor she found herself trying to promote health in an unhealthy system, a system that demanded 100-hour work weeks, not enough sleep and precious little time for anything else.*

During her residency and early years as a physician, the work was so all-consuming that she had no time to think about money, and no time to consider how she was spending it. Marrying an orthopedic surgeon only doubled the pattern of unconsciousness. Chris and her husband accumulated houses and cars and exotic investments. With lucrative practices, they didn't find it hard to adhere to their one accounting rule: spend less than you earn. The thought of keeping track of their spending was beyond comprehension. They couldn't worry about where their money went! They confused consciousness with worry—and they had enough to worry about in practicing medicine.

But Chris's days as a superdoc were numbered. She had that intensely feminine experience of bearing two children. Being a mother opened her heart and tempered her will, and she began to question the ethics and economics of the standard practice of medicine. She wanted out of the medical business *and back into her original vision of medical* service, *where she would have time to listen and administer care to her patients and also time to enjoy her family. With a mixture of trepidation and resolve she left her secure medical group with all its "benefits" and opened a clinic, staffed by women, for women, that would reflect her values.*

During this time Chris began to recognize—in herself and in her patients—deep patterns of financial passivity and dependence. Some had grown up deprived, never having their needs honored and met. Others had been given things in place of love. Many were abdicating their own power and financial responsibility in their marriages. While it seemed "natural" (or at least understandable) that women over forty-five might suffer from this unnatural ineptitude, even younger career women (even Chris!) showed signs of an unhealthy financial subservience. Being honest and courageous, Chris searched her own soul as she prescribed self-reflection for her patients. What were her *assumptions and blind spots with regard to money?*

About this time she listened to the FI tape course. In her enthusiasm she immediately went to her husband and asked him the question she was beginning to ask herself: "What would you do if you didn't have to work for money?" "What do you mean?" he replied. "I love my work." "But what if you never had to charge anyone to meet your overhead?" Unable to answer that question, he promptly went to sleep. Eventually he listened to the course, but his zeal for a new way of practicing medicine did not match Chris's. She began to work on the steps of the program but still felt out of step with her husband. How could she proceed if he wasn't with her? She finally came to the conclusion that even in a conventional marriage—or perhaps especially in a conventional marriage—a woman has to be willing to live a life of her own. Marriage doesn't eliminate the spiritual necessity of becoming a whole and autonomous person. Indeed, for a marriage to work the partners are required *to individuate. In the end she brought all the steps up-to-date herself.*

As her personal insight grew, she began to reevaluate her clinic. This was a step in the right direction but only served to show her how much further she had to go. For example, as the clinic staff's ideals met the financial realities, everyone, from the receptionist to Chris, had to look deeply into her financial belief systems. None of the staff wanted to work the long and arduous hours maintained by mainstream medical professionals, but they all had trouble adjusting to earning less money. The economics were all wrong. As Chris turned toward noninvasive procedures, her income per patient went down. Surgery is what pays the bills for most physicians. Chris preferred prevention, which meant teaching women how to be responsible for their health. She saw a way to practice medicine so that it would heal both body and soul, yet the economics of medicine kept pulling her back into the old way of working. "Either I have to do medicine differently or not do it at all."

FI for Chris is the opportunity to make new choices about the practice of medicine. She's eager to be able to experiment without needing a paycheck and to write without needing to get paid. As her Financial Independence progresses she anticipates doing more speaking and writing and performing fewer medical procedures. How this will all work out financially is still unclear, but for Chris Financial Independence is the whole process of recovery from old ways of thinking about money, work, meaning and purpose. In fact, FI is every bit as much a recovery process as recovery from alcohol or drug addiction. It is a process of healing the many ways we've given our power over to people and circumstances outside ourselves, trying to gain a sense of worth from social symbols of success while denying our inner reality. Chris is now defining how much is enough for her *to be fulfilled, and searching for the ways to guarantee herself that income while allowing herself to do the work she loves most and give the full range of her gifts to the world.*

Chris is not alone. Amy Saltzman, author of *Downshifting: Reinventing Success on a Slower Track,* found much evidence among the upwardly mobile professionals she interviewed that many people are *voluntarily* taking cuts in pay and responsibility in order to live saner, more balanced and more contributory lives.

2. Redefining Work Allows You to Work from the Inside Out

For many of us, much of life is lived from the outside in, selecting our roles and personas like dishes at a Chinese restaurant. One person might select "fireman" from the Job column, "blond hair and blue eyes" from the Wife column, "two" from the Children column, "Western wear" from the Style column, "Ford" from the Car column, "Democrat" from the Political column, and "condo" from the Housing column and figure he's got life pretty well squared away. Fitting our well-rounded selves into the square hole called Job reinforces this impression that life consists of selecting options from a fixed list. Unless you're an artist or an entrepreneur, most often your job consists of working with someone else's agenda—for which service you get paid. There's a kind of subtle yet pervasive irresponsibility in the work world, a sense that we are always doing someone else's bidding, angling to please someone else up the line a bit. In large corporations, most workers don't even have a clue as to who originated that agenda. And such corporations buy not only our work but our personalities as well, with their unspoken cultural norms about who talks with whom, what to wear, where people at various levels "do" lunch, how much overtime you have to put in to be "visible" and hundreds of other daily choices. It's clear that if we think that what we *do* to make money is who we *are*, we will end up adopting whatever pattern will allow us to survive best at our job. If you *are* a computer programmer, for example, you have probably absorbed a host of attitudes and beliefs about yourself along with the skills you acquired to do the work. But if who you are and what you do to make money are distinct, as they can be when you disconnect work from wages, you can reclaim your lost self. As you come to know yourself, your values, your beliefs, your real talents and what you care about, you will be able to work from the inside out. You will be able to do your job without giving up your self. You will be responsible and accountable, both on and off the job. You will put a priority on being able to live with yourself—and if your job won't let you do that, you may change jobs.

Margaret Parsons *is in the process of shifting from living according to others' values (living from the outside in) to discovering and living* her *values (living from the inside out). She'd already been married, had two children and gotten a divorce. As a single parent with a strong sense of duty, she wanted to earn as much as possible to support her family. That ruled out teaching, which is what she'd been trained to do. Since she was undergoing this career change in the 1980s, an obvious place to look for ample income was in financial services, and the quickest route in was to become a certified financial planner.*

So that's what Margaret did. After several years she began to feel conflict. She and her clients believed she was there to guide and protect them in the confusing world of investments. In reality, she was a salesperson working on commission—and some products were more lucrative than others. She began having stomach pains and realized she had to stop selling financial products at all costs. She stopped pursuing sales and, while her body got better, her personal financial picture got worse.

She was glad that she and ***Ivy Underwood*** *had started the Financial Independence support group of twenty people committed to working with the FI program. Their monthly meetings were islands of support and sanity where the cacophony of the consumer culture faded out and they could once again hear themselves think. As they followed the steps of the program, they found themselves ever more willing to follow the promptings of their hearts—and* *for each one of them, that looked slightly different. For example, one bright, incisive woman realized she was grossly underemployed in her civil service job. Through "honoring her life energy" she saw that she was wasting her talent in a bog of mediocrity. "They aren't paying me enough to stay here in this amount of pain." So she quit and is currently living on savings and doing research on where and how to reenter the job market. Another couple left the security of an institutional job to set up their own private practice—without going into debt to do it.*

All of these changes came out of the *process* of doing the steps of this program. Had the people in the group not gone through the requisite tracking, record-keeping and self-examination, these changes might have filled them with dread rather than hope. Had they not found their own 101 ways to reduce expenses, many wouldn't have been able to afford to take a second look. In their monthly meetings they did exercises from the workbook that accompanies the tape course so that they could reflect together on their money myths and misconceptions. Some discovered that they had no real purpose for their lives beyond their jobs and began a second monthly meeting to explore purpose. Quite a few had to find ways to make these changes in spite of costly teenagers and unsympathetic mates. It was out of doing *all* these steps that the work = wages formula split apart and they were able to discover new ways to organize their lives to match their true values and purpose.

3. Redefining Work Makes Life Whole Again

For the sake of order and convenience, we've sorted our lives into boxes. There's our work life, our home life, our community life, our inner life and our secret life. Such "systems management" allows us to track and balance our many responsibilities. But our prioritized To Do lists are *not* our lives. In theory they are there to assist us in navigating life—but more often they run *us*. Rather than perceiving life as a continuing flow of experience in the present moment, we become convinced that we have life captured in a three-ring binder with colored dividers. If we just follow the signs and connect the dots the picture of a perfect life will pop out at us. And the biggest, most compelling signs we follow are the ones that pertain to our paid employment.

If you look at work separately from wages, however, you have the opportunity to discover that you are simply performing activities, of one kind or another, from morning till night. Try an experiment for the next three days. Whenever you remember, ask yourself, "Where am I?" The most accurate answer will always be, "Here." Then ask yourself, "What am I actually doing?" No, don't just say "working" for those eight hours on your job. More likely you're writing or thinking or cleaning or speaking or walking or standing or lifting or sitting or listening or deciding or looking for something or . . . the same kinds of things you do the rest of the day. All day, every day, you're just living your life. This may make your job seem more mundane, but it will also make the rest of your life seem more vivid and whole—and make you feel more alive. Try it.

4. Redefining Work Opens Up Novel Perspectives on Unemployment

Since the Depression, full employment has been a stated goal of our government. But there are several major impediments to achieving this "ideal." The first, of course, is that with an ever-expanding population, full employment necessitates the creation of ever more jobs. To make sure there are markets for these additional goods and services we need to increase consumption, both in North America and elsewhere. Yet the limits of our resource base, the planet, make that an unlikely and perhaps foolish objective. So economic growth may not be able to supply enough jobs for this expanding work force.

In addition, as Willis Harman and John Hormann suggest in their excellent book *Creative Work,* the continuing success of the Industrial and Technological Revolution is allowing more and more human labor to be replaced by machines. We're in a cul-de-sac. Our technological success will increasingly represent our social failure as more and more people find themselves unemployed. This situation is made worse by the fact that we have regarded higher education as job training, yet college graduates are increasingly finding themselves unemployed or underemployed. It is becoming increasingly evident that any one of us could find ourselves unemployed. But if we disconnect work from wages we are able to see that no one is ever unemployed, even if they have no paid employment. At worst, they are in transition.

As we saw in Chapter 5, following the steps leads to the development of savings, which provide a cushion or safety net in case of job loss. In addition, by breaking the link between work and wages you transform unemployment to a time of learning and discovery. If you are unemployed you are not an outcast. You are not a useless person. You can still feel like a million, even though you're not earning a dime. Your worth as a person does not come from what you are paid. It comes from who you are and what you give. If you can allow this truth to grow inside you, options and opportunities for paid employment may well open up in the oddest places.

5. Redefining Work Adds Life to Your Retirement

Everyone retires someday. The only question is when. Many work themselves into an early grave and retire the day they die. Others play by the rules and retire when their company says they can or must. More recently, executives in shrinking industries have been taking "golden parachutes" or early retirement. And some people have taken the FI course (or followed a similar plan) and retired while they still had plenty of life left in them. Whenever you retire, the quality of your retirement will be enhanced if you've been able to disconnect your work from your wages. By disconnecting work from wages, you will ensure that your retirement is simply retirement from paid employment, not from life. You can continue to expand your real work after "retirement," whether you retire at forty, sixty or eighty. If you are actively engaged in a life that is meaningful to you, no one can declare that you are no longer a valuable worker. You may end your tenure at your paid employment, but you won't lose your usefulness—or your dignity. Think about your own associations with the word "retirement." If the word has any negative overtones for you, see whether redefining retirement in the way we've suggested alters those feelings. Retirement symbolizes the end of life only if you take your self-definition from your paid employment.

6. Redefining Work Honors Unpaid Activity

If you think you are working only when you are earning money, then you (and billions of other people) are very busy being unemployed a lot of the time. The everyday activities of taking care of yourself, your home and your family are all unpaid work. It's not that we don't notice these other life chores, it's that we don't always honor them. In our minds we tend to regard them as mere obstacles to surmount on the way to our "real" work, the jobs we get paid for.

What about the hours you spend being a father or mother to your children, a good neighbor, a caring friend, a loving mate and a good citizen of your city, state, country and planet? Those activities alone could fill a life with meaning, challenge, creativity and purpose. Yet, being busy with our paid work, we often try to "do" our relationship work by some imagined rule book. The busy parent provides food, clothing, shelter, assorted lessons, chauffeur service and, whenever possible, "quality time." The well-meaning but harried mate shares a bed, a house, the chores, breakfast, dinner (if no business meetings are scheduled for those times), finances and, whenever possible, "quality time." As a citizen, you vote. As a neighbor, you dig up your dandelions, chat over the fence or in the elevator and join the block watch. As a friend, you "do lunch" or talk on the phone. In our hearts we know we could do better, but life is so busy there's no time to just be with people.

Another casualty of our confusion of work with wages is our inner work—the job of self-examination, self-development and emotional and spiritual maturation. It takes time to know yourself. Time for reflection, for silence, for journal writing, for prayer and ritual, for dialogue with a caring friend to heal the wounds from our past, for developing a coherent philosophy of life and personal code of ethics and for setting personal goals and evaluating progress. Yet, instead of honoring this as important work, we squeeze what we can into evenings and weekends, devoting the majority of our waking hours to the "real work" of our jobs.

Redefining work gives us back the full experience and expression of these other activities. We can honor our household duties, our relationships and our inner work and give this unpaid employment the same creativity, respect and attention that we give to our paid employment.

7. Redefining Work Reunites Work and Play

Since we have unconsciously equated "income" (getting paid) and "work," we figure that if we are not collecting income we must not be working—we must be "merely" playing, a frivolous pastime that serves no real purpose. Sometimes play may look like work, as in an intense chess game. Sometimes work can look like and even be called play, as in professional sports. And sometimes work feels so much like play that people say (somewhat guiltily), "This job is such fun I shouldn't be paid for it." So how do we tell the difference between work and play?

Let's test some common parameters to see which ones give us an unfailing method for distinguishing work from play. Bring to mind a person doing an activity that he or she does very well and that is considered valuable by others, anything from figure skating to driving a bus on a winding mountain road to arguing a critical case in a federal court. What factor would tell you for certain that what you are observing is work?

	Work	*Play*
Competition	yes	yes
Cooperation	yes	yes
Concentration	yes	yes
Skill	yes	yes
Absorption	yes	yes
Contentment	yes	yes
Feeling of power	yes	yes
Ability to travel	yes	yes
Achievement of recognition	yes	yes
Self-expression	yes	yes
Getting paid	yes	no

Eureka! We've found the difference. If there's money involved, it's clearly work. If there isn't money involved, it's either play (which we equate with fun) or duty (necessary but not necessarily nice). You do it either because you want to or because you have to—but *not* to earn money. Isn't it true that unpaid activity, whether it's play or duty, is often seen as worth-less—worth less than paid activity? Isn't it true that there is an almost universal belief in our culture that if you are not working for money, not building a career, not employed, you are a nobody?

8. Redefining Work Allows You to Enjoy Your Leisure More

In *Downshifting,* Amy Saltzman explores the theme of "reinventing success on a slower track." As a "professional" herself, she became curious about why her generation, for all its striving, never seemed to arrive at happiness. Her book begins and ends with a meditation on empty front porches—porches that in bygone eras were a hub of activity and pleasure. She aims her book at "those of us who have dutifully played the part of career professional to the exclusion, in some cases, of almost everything else that gives life purpose and meaning." She tells the stories of professionals who changed lanes in order to enjoy a slower, more fulfilling life. What all of them reclaimed was the value of their leisure time—the "front porches" of their lives. For the Greeks, leisure was the highest good, the essence of freedom—a time for self-development and for higher pursuits. Yet here we are at the end of the second millennium unable to really relax and enjoy our leisure. Even our language betrays us by calling it "time off"—-as though leisure were just a few minutes of recuperation before we bounce back into the ring of life, punching for all we're worth. If we did not identify so strongly with what we do for money, we might honor and enjoy our leisure more. It's okay to play. It's okay to relax in the shade and listen to the birds. It's okay to take a walk to nowhere in particular. Leisure is not an identity crisis if you know you are not your job. The challenge, of course, is being able to deem your apparent idleness worthwhile. As Saltzman points out,

> Work for many of us is an easy and acceptable way to fill the hours. In our professional lives we have clear rules to follow and goals to meet. By contrast, it is completely up to us to invent the success framework for our leisure.

9. Redefining Work Sheds a New Light on "Right Livelihood"

"Right livelihood" is the ideal of finding a way for your true work or vocation to be your paid work as well. While that might seem to be what we're advocating here, there are a few pitfalls to this noble effort that the FI program neatly sidesteps.

The first pitfall is that there is no guarantee that you will find someone to pay you to do what you feel called to do. It may take many years to develop your art or your research or your social innovation or your new technology to the point where those who have money want to pay for it. Most often this has less to do with the real value of your work than it has to do with luck, chance, perseverance, connections or a host of other factors. By giving up the *expectation* that you will be paid to do the work you are passionate about, you can do both things with more integrity. You can make money to cover your expenses, and you can follow your heart without compromise.

Michael Phillips, in his book *The Seven Laws of Money,* warns of the traps and fallacies hidden in the high ideal of "right livelihood." He strongly recommends that people separate their service projects from their survival needs:

> Unfortunately, many people can't separate the two, and the net result is that their belief that the project they are working on is the most important thing they can do gets coupled with their conviction that they have to survive. The combination of these two ideas leads them to believe that *the world owes them a living.*

Other factors to consider about right livelihood:

1. Is a salary possible or even appropriate for the work we feel called to do—our informal conflict-resolution work in our church, our front-porch ministry to the neighborhood kids with nowhere to go, telephone campaigns to promote peace, being a loving friend to someone who is dying? *At the Crossroads,* a document by the Communications Era Task Force about our era, calls these "committed activities"—activities done "out of a sense of personal commitment and commitment to society":

> Committed activities are vital to the health of a society. Yet we systematically undervalue and undersupport them because they don't fit into either our market economy or the public sector. They are not supported by the market because benefits from these activities are often long-term, diffuse and difficult to define. They are not supported by government because they are not easily regulated by the bureaucracy.

***Steve Brandon**, our truck driver from Maine, had half a dozen good ways to make money. He's a registered nurse, a landscaper, a massage therapist and a farmer. "Right livelihood" for him looked like nursing, performing a real service for people and paying the bills to boot. But it didn't work that way. As a nurse he was caught in a constant flow of charting and report writing, spending more time with a pencil than with the patients. And at the end of the day he had no energy for the volunteer work he loved. If he was going to be a nurse he wanted to do it for love, not money. So he settled on driving the propane truck. He has 1,000 clients and a route that covers many miles of back roads leading to isolated farms and homesteads. In the winter he may be the only person many of these people see all week. Some are old and ill, so he stops for a chat and to see how they are doing. He might listen to their complaints and help them sort out which to worry about and which to ignore. He does a lot of education about nutrition, especially for people who have no idea what their doctors mean by a "low-fat, high-fiber" diet. Somehow, without his taking a temperature or even writing a report, they feel better when he leaves. He's a "healer without pay"—and it suits him fine. He earns his money delivering propane and gives his love for free.*

2. If you *are* being paid for the work you feel called to do, look carefully at how you are spending your time in that "right livelihood," income-producing work. Are you indeed doing the work fully and well, or are you spending an undue amount of time on financial concerns, perhaps raising money to continue your work? Many would-be saints end up as fund-raisers, and many would-be activists end up as desktop publishers, putting out newsletters for the membership to keep the flow of donations coming in. Any activity that is either publicly or privately funded is subject to someone else's whims and priorities. Any product or service that depends on a fickle consuming public might not survive in a competitive marketplace. So ask yourself, is your work secure, or are there future worries about money that may rightly concern you now?

3. Would you do this work the way you are doing it if your financial needs were handled? If not, what adjustments are you making because you need the income? Are you able to stay true to your own integrity? As long as you are receiving money for the work you do, there is the possibility, however minute and subtle, of selling out your vision, your values or your beliefs.

In *The Biology of Art*, zoologist Desmond Morris tells of an experiment in introducing the "profit motive" to apes. The first step was teaching them to be artists and to produce drawings and paintings that were decidedly lovely. Once their "art" was established he began to "pay" them, rewarding them with peanuts for their work. Under the reward system their artwork quickly deteriorated, and they began turning out hasty scrawls just to get the peanuts. "Commercialism" destroyed the apes as artists and got them scrambling for a peanut instead. This is where the need for honesty comes in. What adjustments, however subtle, are you making in your "art" (be it carpentry or archaeology or day care or anything else) to keep that flow of peanuts coming in? How much are you willing to risk in your Sunday sermons before you start thinking about the possibility of losing your job, income and parsonage, as well as your position and power in the community? Is your teaching what it would be if you weren't doing it as paid employment? Are you writing advertising copy instead of that great American novel you've been dreaming about for years? Have you sacrificed your vision of how life could be for the reality of making a dying?

Rick Paul, a former $100,000-a-year publishing executive, left his job to be a writer, but he didn't expect instant success. Instead, he took a part-time job as a ranger to keep the flow of "peanuts" coming in and intends to spend the rest of his time writing. In an article in the *Pacific* Sunday magazine, "Getting a Life" by Richard Seven, Rick said:

> Our friends ask why we [he and his wife Kathleen] would give up good jobs in Seattle to go live in the sticks. I've dreamed about two things since I can remember—living in the sticks and being a writer. I may find I'm a lousy writer, but it's better than retiring at 65 and looking back with a bunch of "what ifs."

Redefining work allows you to step back and see your dreams for what they are, and your job for what it is—and to make both work for you.

The Power of Redefining Work

Redefining work by breaking the link between work and wages has stunning implications and benefits. As Willis Harman, renowned futurist and president of the Institute of Noetic Sciences, puts it:

> Unbounded opportunities become apparent once the mind is freed by separating the functions of creative work and income distribution.

When you break the conceptual link between work and money, you give yourself the opportunity to discover what your true work is. It may turn out to be totally unrelated to what you are currently doing for money.

Whether you love your job and remain in it or move on to something new, breaking the link between work and money opens up room in your life for those parts of yourself that have been crowded out by your job. You may experience a moment of panic at the emptiness left by even this temporary suspension of your identity-as-your-job. But there are other you's: you as full-time parent, as learner, as friend, as adventurer, as community organizer, as volunteer, as artist, as dreamer and as architect of your own life's work.

A friend recently asked a colleague why he didn't seem to suffer from the stress everyone else at their overtaxed agency complained about. The colleague simply said, "My job is not the main event of my life."

Breaking the link between work and money gives you back your life. You no longer need the stamp of approval called a job to give you all the emotional, intellectual and spiritual benefits of being employed. You may even find out that it is not necessary to tie yourself to a nine-to-five grind for the rest of your life just to support yourself.

Now that we've established that the only intrinsic purpose of paid employment is getting paid (whether you love or hate your job), it makes sense to see whether you are trading your precious life energy for what it's worth. Now that you know that your *life* is bigger than your job, it makes sense to get a job that really "does the job"—i.e., pays you well. Now that you can see other options besides the "nine-to-five till you're sixty-five," making-a-dying money-go-round, it makes sense to be sure that your paid employment pays you enough to make your investment of time worth it. This leads to Step 7 of the FI program.

Step 7: Valuing Your Life Energy—Maximizing Income

Step 7 is about increasing your income by valuing the life energy you invest in your job and exchanging it for the highest pay consistent with your health and integrity.

When you pick up your paycheck, are you really getting a fair exchange for your investment of valuable life energy? The key to freedom from the "making a dying" world is valuing your life energy. We have seen that money is just something you trade your life energy for. We have also recognized that the purpose of paid employment is getting paid. Don't reason and self-respect both suggest, then, that when you are working for pay, one option is to make the most money per hour possible, consistent with your integrity and your health? While that may sound like good old-fashioned greed, follow along and you'll find yourself headed in another direction altogether.

Through following Steps 1 through 6 you have defined what is "enough" for you. Instead of defining enough as "more than I have now," thus condemning yourself to the experience of perpetual poverty, you are discovering that enough is far less than you imagined and well within your means. And remember, *your* enough will be a level of spending that evolves out of aligning your spending with your experience of fulfillment and with your life purpose and values. Enough is not the minimum amount for survival; it is the exact amount that gives you fulfillment without excess. As we pointed out in Chapter 5, this enough is usually far below your income. If you are spending less money than you earn, that means you can spend less time on the job and still have enough. It's basic. If enough is $1,000 a month and you earn $10 an hour, you *must* work 100 hours a month to meet your expenses. But if you earn $20 an hour, you *must* work only 50 hours a month at your paid employment.

Now we're moving back toward the life-style human beings enjoyed before the Industrial Revolution. You could work two or three hours a day for money and spend the rest of the time doing what you want to do for relaxation, fun, self-development, human interaction, community involvement or world service. If you chose to work more hours at your paid employment, you would do it only for good reason, since you place a high value on your life energy. You might be doing it to support someone or something else. You might be doing it to get out of debt and experience that particular aspect of financial freedom. You might be doing it to develop savings so that you can be secure no matter what the economic climate. Or you might be doing it so that you can achieve some other life goals, like going back to school or traveling around the world or even becoming financially independent. The size and intensity of your goals will determine the time and vigor you invest in the workplace. You might even be so eager to reach a financial goal that you end up working a second job—joyfully. Unlike the behavior of a workaholic, however, working extra hours is now connected with and serves your purpose.

Disconnecting work from wages for ***Rosemary Irwin*** *meant that she could move toward pursuing other goals beyond her job—goals that ranged from travel to writing to working on projects that might help the planet. While she enjoyed her job as an activities director at a retirement home, she didn't plan to devote her whole life to it. She saw clearly that the more she earned now, the sooner she could get on with her other goals. When she received a $10,000 inheritance from her grandmother, she immediately added that money to her FI nest egg. Rather than searching for a higher-paying job—with the possibility of more stress—she decided on another strategy. She got a second job working on call with a small audiotape distribution company, putting in several hours a week on evenings and weekends. The schedule was flexible, the people congenial, the stress minimal and her hourly pay was just as good as what she was getting at her full-time job. Even though she's working far more than forty hours a week, her goal keeps her energy up and her spirits high.*

Valuing your life energy and seeking the highest pay possible has nothing to do with the "more is better" mentality. You don't want more money so that you can have more material possessions. You want more money so that you can have *enough* material possessions—and more life. If money = life energy, then by increasing your income you increase the amount of life available to you. Depending on your actual hourly wage, a new car could cost a month, six months or a year of work. And you don't want more money so that you can have more status, prestige, power or security. You know that money doesn't buy those things. You want more money so that you can have more freedom to be yourself without *worrying* about the money. Likewise, you don't want more money to boost your self-esteem. You want more money as an *expression* of your self-esteem, of valuing your life energy.

NEW OPTIONS FOR PAID EMPLOYMENT

You have several creative options to explore at this point, including increasing your pay so you can work part-time, enhancing your current job or changing jobs altogether.

Higher Pay: A Matter of Attitude

Many people are passive, even fatalistic, about the size of their earnings. They act out of a victim mentality, totally at the mercy of outside forces—the boss, the wage scale, the unemployment situation, the recession, the poor local economy, the President's economic policy, Japanese competition, and on and on. The attitude is one of "I *can't* find a good job—and it's because of *Them*. *They* are keeping me in a low-paying job."

While economic realities may at times be harsh, it is also the nature of the human mind to make real the thoughts and beliefs that we hold (a fact that should encourage great care in how we think about ourselves). If you see yourself as a victim, you may well be too busy feeling sorry for yourself to notice the many opportunities to change your dismal destiny.

Think how valuing your life energy might transform *your* experience and performance on the job, as well as your ability to get another job should you want one. With such an attitude, every moment you spend at your paid employment is connected to your internally generated personal goals, purpose, vision and values. Wherever you are working, you are working for yourself. You experience yourself as valuable, as responsible for the way you distribute your life energy, as someone freely choosing to give your life energy to this particular job.

One important factor limiting your earning potential is attitude: attitudes about yourself (e.g., "I'm not good enough"), attitudes about your job or employer (e.g., "They're out to get me"), and attitudes about current circumstances (e.g., "There just aren't any jobs"). These attitudes are demeaning, debilitating and self-fulfilling. They are reflected in the quantity and quality of your work, in your interactions with employers and fellow employees and in your fearfulness about your job security.

To be successful, cultivate positive attitudes of self-respect, pride in your contribution to your workplace, dedication to your job, cooperation with your employers and coworkers, desire to do the job right, personal integrity, responsibility and accountability—and do it just because you value your life energy. You value your life energy because you value *life*. You are committed to excellence at your job because you're committed to 100 percent integrity, no matter what you're doing. You'd be surprised at the degree to which job satisfaction lies in the worker, not in the work. And it just so happens that this integrity and the increased quality and productivity of your work will easily qualify you for a pay raise. You may not even need to ask for it.

***Steve West**, the carpenter we met in Chapter 6, found that one of the gifts of the FI program was the chance to reconnect with his aspirations as a writer. He'd grown up in an Air Force family and had kept moving as an adult. He finished high school in Gulfport, Mississippi, and then moved to Austin, Texas, where he employed eight people in a remodeling business until the oil crash ripped the rug* and *floor out from under him. That and a divorce pared his possessions down to a vanload (making Step 1 very easy), and he took off. He spent a year in Massachusetts and then moved to Oregon, where he lives now. Within a year of putting the FI program into practice, Steve had enough money saved to support himself for a year, allowing him to back away from the financial edge. He decided to try writing some stories that had been with him for years, stories based on his experiences in Mississippi in the early 1970s when he built a Baptist church with some old black carpenters. To free up more time for writing, Steve started bidding his remodeling jobs a lot higher, assuming that most of those contracts wouldn't come through. What happened was a big surprise. Many people had been so impressed with his work in the past that they were willing to pay whatever he asked. He had all the work he wanted, at much higher wages. Wanting to deliver the quality they were paying for, he put even greater care into his carpentry. His reputation for* *superior craftsmanship spread, bringing in more work. His hours of paid employment went down, his income went up, his anxiety went down, his peace of mind went up and his time to write seemed boundless. He was surprised, but he wasn't going to question his good fortune—or was it his good self-esteem?*

Financial Independence as a Part-time Job

Steve West chose what we usually refer to as part-time work. However, this new way of thinking about money and work puts that term in a new light. In the world of job = identity, part-time work makes you only a part-time person who has only part-time worth. As a part-timer, this thinking concludes, you would be sacrificing many of the benefits of full-time employment. You'd lose out on health insurance and the company pension plan. You'd lose out on opportunities for advancement. You'd probably lose out on the best assignments, working instead on what's left over after the full-timers have skimmed the cream off the top. In the new way of thinking, however, you are working part-time on someone else's agenda for money so you can work as much time as possible on your own agenda. You give your employers their money's worth, but you don't define your self-worth by what you do during that small fraction of your time.

People have adopted a number of variations on this theme of part-time work. Some work three days a week, making every weekend a long one. Some work six months a year for money and do what they please with the other six months. (You'd be surprised at how many artists, writers, activists and adventurers you find among seasonal workers.) Some work four hours a day so that they can be available for their children both before and after school.

Consider for a moment the impact of an increasing number of people's choosing to work part-time. Two people could share one job, cutting down on the competition for increasingly scarce jobs. Pressure to deal with "the problem of unemployment" would be taken off the government. Pressure resulting from the "mandate for full employment" would be lifted from the environment. Job-sharing is, indeed, becoming a respected and encouraged option. With FI thinking leading to reduced expenses, one job could provide a livable wage for two people. In addition, each person might do a better job because he or she wouldn't be suffering from the burnout, boredom and "thank God it's Friday" syndrome so common among full-time workers.

But What If I Like My Job?

If you *like* your job, this new perspective (valuing your life energy) will only enhance your experience—and your earnings.

***Lu Bauer** (who is married to **Steve Brandon**, the propane-truck driver) loves her work as an accountant. She works with a vision and a mission. Calling herself a "holistic accountant," she is dedicated to empowering people to become responsible with their money. Upon doing the FI course she discovered the blind spots in her own personal finances. When she calculated her real hourly wage, she found that out of her $60-per-hour fee, she netted $5. Her husband did better delivering propane during the winter in rural Maine. Where was all that money going? Lu discovered that she had been running her practice for her clients and her employees. Very noble, but not good business.*

Because she had wanted to provide service for people who couldn't afford it, she kept her rates low and was always the one to work overtime and go the extra mile. Doing the Monthly Tabulations showed her that she wasn't making any headway economically. She had forgotten the simple lesson of valuing her own life energy.

She decided to raise her rates by 23 percent and to limit her staff to one secretary. In addition, she decided to limit both the number of clients, concentrating on those who wanted to learn to help themselves, and the number of hours she worked. After making these changes she found herself with exactly the number and type of clients she wanted, and she now works fewer hours while earning more money. Because Lu values herself and her life energy, her clients value her advice—and they learn from her to value themselves.

How to Get a High-Paying, High-Integrity Job

Sorry. This chapter isn't designed to be a job-hunting manual. As we have seen, there is no Job Charming. The people we've met in these pages have had to do a lot of soul-searching, risk-taking, experimenting and challenging of old beliefs in order to move forward into jobs with higher pay and high integrity. They've had to see that their lives are bigger than their jobs. The parts of themselves that had been suffocated by their paid employment had to be given room to breathe again. Visions from childhood of how life could be had to be excavated from under the status, seriousness and self-importance that masquerade as adulthood. They had to tell themselves the truth about whether or not their current paid employment was really doing what paid employment is supposed to do: earn money.

There are a number of excellent job-hunting guides on the market —and more coming out every day as jobs become a scarcer and more cherished commodity. The best we've seen is the classic *What Color Is Your Parachute?* by Richard Bolles. Beyond that, you're on your own. Just one word of caution. As P. T. Barnum once said, there's a sucker born every minute. There are a host of workshop leaders, agents, "head-hunters," advisers, counselors and the like who would be happy to help you find Job Charming—for a hefty fee. Some of these services are useful—but be discerning. Read the fine print on contracts. Be as sharp a shopper as you would be for a car or a refrigerator. What follows is an attitudinal checklist that might be just as helpful to you as a highly paid employment specialist.

Job-Hunting Checklist

1. **Purpose.** In order to find a high-integrity, high-paying job, you must have a clear *purpose* for having one. Since the purpose of paid employment is getting paid, high pay will certainly be part of your purpose. Another purpose could be, in part, simply the goal of leaving work you don't enjoy. But you must also clarify your larger purpose, whether it's your desire for personal growth, learning, adventure or making a contribution to others. Remember, the higher the pay, the more time you can have for other things that matter to you. It's your life energy that's for sale. Be sure to sell it to the highest bidder, consistent with your integrity and your personal health and well-being.

2. **Intention.** Intention is the will to meet your goal or achieve your purpose. Most of us know what we want to do or ought to do, but without the *intention* to do it we may procrastinate or wander off course. Weak intention, procrastination and lack of focus are often manifestations of disabling beliefs about yourself and your capacity to achieve your goal. Look inside and see whether you can identify any disem-

powering beliefs—and then open your consciousness to other, more positive, possibilities. The second source of weak intention is lack of clarity about what you really want. You can't find something if you don't know what you are looking for. The more clearly you can define the job you want, the more precise you'll be in your search and the more discerning you'll be about the offers that come to you. What is your most valuable skill—the one that commands the highest pay? What is your monetary goal (hourly wage)? What are your geographical requirements—e.g., do you need to stay where you are and, if not, where are you willing to work? What are your ethical requirements? What working conditions are essential for you? And be sure to include what you learned from Step 2 (finding out how much you are *really* trading your life energy for) as part of your criteria for job selection. A job that pays $20 an hour but has high job-related expenses and a long commute may not fit your bill anymore.

3. Willingness. Besides having strong intention, you must be willing to work for what you want. All the intention in the world won't get you a glass of water if you're not willing to go find the glass and fill it with water. To find or create a job that will meet your criteria, be active in your role as job-hunter. Get out there and *look* for a job! Educate yourself about the job-search game and play it assertively and diligently. You might need to do "cold calls," promote yourself, go to networking gatherings, consult your friends, relatives and business associates and go to the library to do research. Be willing to be assertive, creative, inventive and persistent.

4. Consciousness. You need to remain conscious during the journey. You can have all the purpose, intention and willingness in the world, but still be unresponsive to the opportunities and obstacles that present themselves. Be *conscious* of all the possibilities for jobs around you. Follow up all leads. If you determine that a course of action is a dead end, stop going up that street. Interviewing people for information on possible jobs, even when they have no job to offer you, is often an effective way of uncovering a job. Always deal directly with the person who has the power to hire you. Sometimes you can create your own job by demonstrating to a prospective employer that his or her company has a need for your skills. Plot yourself a course to that ideal job—and stay open to the unexpected. Finding a job is an active *and* interactive process. Stay conscious and you won't fall down on the job—so to speak.

You can get the right job for you if you have the purpose, intention, willingness and consciousness to find it. If you don't have the perfect job, keep running through this checklist to see where you're off course. Is your purpose clear? Do you really mean it? Are you being lazy in your search? Are you missing angles and opportunities? Keep looking.

There is power in knowing that *you* hold the reins and are in control of how many hours, days, weeks and years you need to work for money, in knowing that you can set an accurate goal for how much money you need to sustain yourself at the life-style level you choose, in knowing that once you have that amount, making money doesn't have to be the sole criterion for what you do. These insights can provide you with the motivation necessary to raise your income to new heights.

5. Recognition. Finally, you must be able to recognize when you have been successful in achieving your goal. To succeed simply means to accomplish what is intended or attempted. You steer your own success by what you choose to accomplish and you arrive when *you recognize* that you have arrived. The evidence of success is not whether or not others judge you to be successful. The only evidence is whether or not you did what you intended or attempted to do. And the only person who can determine that is you. An external symbol like a trophy or a pay hike might be a nice extra, but the real sign is your inner knowing that you did what you set out to do. Without that inner knowing, you may receive many outer rewards but have no sense of inner fulfillment—and no amount of honor will ever be "enough." With that inner knowing, you can achieve just about anything.

Ten years before striking out on the road to FI, ***Marcia Meyer*** *had left her marriage and raised four children as a single mother. She'd heard about the financial program several years before she actually took the course and had begun faithfully tracking her earnings and spending. She had no idea why that was important, but it gave her a small sense of control in an otherwise chaotic life. By the time she heard the seminar on tape, her four children were all grown and Marcia was finally free to find her own way.*

While she'd done a great deal of spiritual growing since her divorce, she still experienced herself as powerless and inept when it came to money. At this time she was living with friends, exchanging labor for room and board. Determined to become financially independent, she'd walked up the deserted stretch of road where she was living to a small coastal motel and applied for a job as a maid. She was hired on the spot and walked home on cloud nine. She was on her way to FI. But when her housemates asked her how much she would be earning, she realized she'd forgotten to ask.

Several months later Marcia moved to Seattle to look for a job that paid more than the minimum wage. What she lacked in sophistication she made up for in resolve. Within weeks of arriving she was living with a friend, had sewn herself a work wardrobe and was out on assignments from a temporary employment agency. Right away she put her Wall Chart up, and within a few months she had wiped out several thousand dollars in debt. Her progress spurred her on. For every temporary position she calculated her real hourly wage. She was ruthless in evaluating each opportunity against the real cost of the work—needing to learn a new word processing program, traveling long distances and the personalities of her coworkers were all factored into her decisions. She'd already doubled her income, from under $4 per hour to just about $8, but she didn't stop there. At each temporary job she was on the lookout for permanent positions. She made every contact and conversation count and, when a supervisor at a hospital job told her of an opening as a full-time administrative assistant to a department head, Marcia went for it. On her job interview she convinced the doctor that she was just the person he was looking for, and she landed the job. Her pay shot up above $10 per hour, and she now had benefits. While she'd never had a job like this before, she drew on her years of office skills, the kind of administrative expertise it takes to raise four children and the self-respect and integrity that come from following the FI program—and won the admiration of the whole staff.

But she didn't give up looking. She kept reading the want ads, interviewing friends in different professions and keeping her ear to the ground. By looking at her Wall Chart daily, she remained aware that the more she sold her life energy for, the quicker she'd accumulate savings—and the sooner her time would be her own again. Her next opportunity came from an unexpected direction, but she was able to seize it because she was expecting opportunities. Out of her interest in health Marcia volunteered at an annual medical conference. She just happened to be staffing the T-shirt table the first day of the meeting when the executive director of the sponsoring organization marched off the job, leaving the conference participants to fend for themselves. Marcia

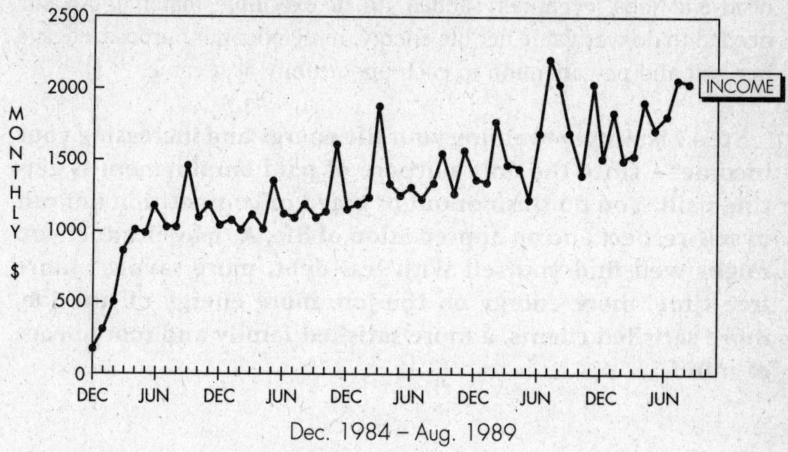

FIGURE 7-1

Marcia's Wall Chart—with Income

was part of the team of volunteers who stepped in to fill the gap. Her skills and service did not go unnoticed. When the board went looking for a new executive director, Marcia was the clear choice. So for her last two years of paid employment, Marcia served as the executive director of the organization. The board came increasingly to admire and rely on Marcia's integrity and expressed that through increasing her compensation. By the time she was done, her hourly salary was over $14 per hour, with an annual salary over $28,000, a figure that had been so unthinkable to the hotel-maid Marcia that she now had to tape extra graph paper to the top of her Wall Chart to even enter her monthly income. Her earnings had gone off the chart! (See Figure 7-1.)

Marcia's clear purpose, intention, willingness and consciousness allowed her to recognize each new opportunity for higher pay and eventually to quadruple her income. Her self-image went from "minimum-wage worker" to "executive director." She made each new experience another platform from which to reach further. Her skills and background, which she'd thought added up to a career of minor-league, dead-end jobs, eventually added up to executive material. All she needed to do was value her life energy, remember her purpose, engage her will and pay attention to each opportunity as it came.

Step 7 is simply "valuing your life energy and increasing your income"—since the only purpose of paid employment is getting paid. You do this not out of greed or competition but out of self-respect and an appreciation of life. As a by-product you might well find yourself with less debt, more savings, more free time, more energy on the job, more energy off the job, more satisfied clients, a more satisfied family and more peace of mind.

SUMMARY OF STEP 7

Increase your income by valuing the life energy you invest in your job, exchanging it for the highest pay consistent with your health and integrity.

8

THE CROSSOVER POINT: THE POT OF GOLD AT THE END OF THE WALL CHART

By doing Steps 1 through 7 you will move inexorably toward FI. You will naturally achieve Financial Intelligence, the ability to step back from your assumptions and emotions about money and observe them dispassionately. You will know how much you have, how much you spend and how much of your life energy you're investing in each aspect of your chosen life-style. Most of your old gazingus pins will no longer grab your attention, and those few that make it past the cash register will look like fool's gold very soon afterward.

By following the first seven steps you will also increase your Financial Integrity. Your handling of money will be more and more integrated with other aspects of your life. All facets of your finances will be in alignment with your values.

These changes alone may lead to a substantial increase in your Financial Independence. Your expenses may go down, your income up, your debt may disappear and your savings increase. You may even find yourself doing more sharing and repairing instead of just buying your way through life. The freedom you will experience from just these changes will feel like a miracle—a fiscal rebirth. Money will no longer be a problem in your life, and the creativity that was locked in the constant struggle with your finances will be released for making other, bigger dreams come true.

With Step 8 the possibility of complete Financial Independence opens

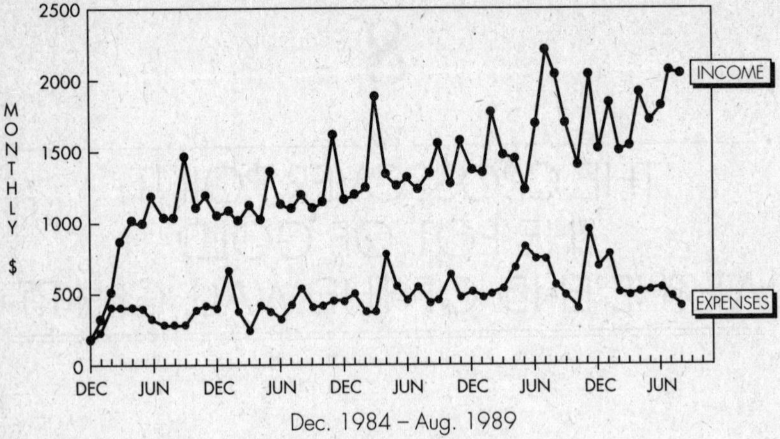

FIGURE 8-1

Marcia's Wall Chart—with Income and Expenses

up. Naturally we will all be FI sometime between now and the day we die. The only thing under debate is when. Step 8 shows you how you can cooperate with that inevitability and perhaps leave paid employment a lot sooner than you ever thought possible. We will also hear stories about other people who have reached that goal and what they chose to work on once money wasn't an issue.

In Chapter 7 we saw Marcia Meyer's Wall Chart with her income line going off the top. Let's take a look at it again, this time adding the expense line (see Figure 8-1).

Having lived on the edge of poverty for so many years, ***Marcia*** *didn't have a lot of ''big spender'' habits to contend with, so her expense line soon settled in at $450 to $550 a month. What doesn't show up on the chart is the change in her ''discretionary'' spending from ''entertainment to fill the void'' to ''activities in support of my purpose,'' and the fact that her feeling of inner peace went steadily up. Her income line, as we said in Chapter 7, went off the chart, not only from her professional work but also from some part-time piecework she did for a small local company. Marcia's chart is fairly typical*

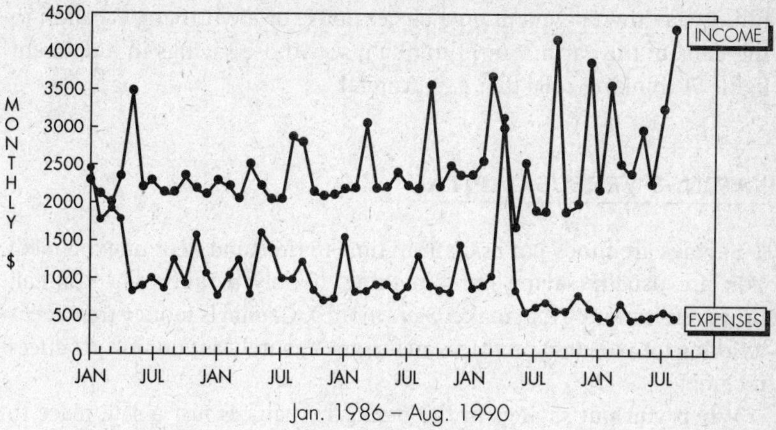

FIGURE 8-2

Diane's Wall Chart—with Expenses and Income

for a dyed-in-the-wool frugal person whose earning power goes through the ceiling.

Diane Grosch*'s chart (see Figure 8-2) is typical of a fairly steady earner and heavy spender who diligently applied the principles of this program and cut her spending in half. The first things to go were the extravagances that clearly gave her no fulfillment—disappointing travel and entertainment. The next to go were the automatic spending habits that added nothing to the quality of her life—daily restaurant meals, for example, and buying clothes out of boredom. And finally she found less expensive ways to have the things she wanted—moving to a less costly apartment, taking budget ski trips, trading in her sporty gas guzzler for a fuel-efficient car and learning to do her own auto maintenance. All of it, she affirms, added to the quality of her life and her self-esteem.*

What you see in both these charts is a growing gap between income and expenses—i.e., savings. Before FI thinking takes over, a "normal" person might regard those savings as earmarked for a splurge in the future—a down payment on a bigger house or a whizbang vacation to the ends of the earth. But FI thinking sees those savings in a different light. FI thinking calls that gap "capital."

SAVINGS VERSUS CAPITAL

Savings are funds put aside from time to time and kept unexpended. You are usually saving *for* something, if only a rainy day. Capital, however, is money that makes *more* money. Capital is money that keeps working for you, that produces an income as surely as your job produces income.

When you put savings in the bank, the bank is just a safe place to store your money until you need it. The interest you get is a nice by-product of having a bank account, but it is not the purpose of the account. When you put capital in a bank *or other interest-bearing instrument,* however, it is an investment. An investment is the conversion of capital into some form of wealth other than cash with the expectation of deriving income. There are two basic forms of investment: speculation and debt instruments (loans). Stocks, real estate, venture capital and the like are speculative investments; you hope (speculate) that the value of what you buy will increase and you will make a profit. Debt, on the other hand, is lending your capital to another and charging interest for the privilege of using your money for a specified period of time. At the end of that time your capital is returned to you intact, ready for you to loan out again. Bonds are an example of a debt instrument. In Chapter 9 we will go into detail about an FI investment program, but for now it's enough to realize that your savings are actually capital that is making money for you.

The income you receive from your capital is of a different nature than your job income. It comes in whether or not you go to work. Instead of simply lumping it with your total monthly income, you will be entering it separately on your Wall Chart according to the formula given below. This third line will be called "monthly investment income."

Step 8: Capital and the Crossover Point

Each month, apply the following formula to your total accumulated capital and record the result on your Wall Chart:

$$\frac{\textbf{capital} \times \textbf{current long-term interest rate}}{\textbf{12 months}} = \textbf{monthly investment income}$$

Your total accumulated capital is simply the money you have (usually in a savings account) that you are not planning to spend. For the "current interest rate," don't use what you get on your savings account; instead use the current yield of long-term U.S. treasury bonds. (You can find this figure in most big-city newspapers as well as in *The Wall Street Journal.*) This figure is one of the best reflections of prevailing interest rates on debt instruments. It is a conservative estimate of the return you can expect from such a long-term investment. At the time of writing this book that rate is hovering around 7.5 percent. For arithmetic simplicity we will use 6 percent, but this is a convenience for our discussion only and not a prediction or a promise about what interest rates will be when you are ready to invest. Your equation will reflect interest rates at the time when you are ready to start investing your capital.

For example, let's say you have $100 of savings. If you were to consider that $100 capital and invest it in a bond that pays 6 percent interest, the equation would look this way (remember that these figures are purely hypothetical, for illustration only):

$$\frac{\$100 \times 6\%}{12} = \$.50\text{/month}$$

For every $100 thus invested, you will get $.50 per month, each month, for the life of the bond. The original $100 remains untouched and you will eventually get it back.

So if on the first month of your chart you have $1,000 in savings and the current interest rate is 6 percent, your equation will read:

$$\frac{\$1{,}000 \times 6\%}{12} = \$5.00 \text{ monthly investment income}$$

This simply means that the $1,000 you now have in *savings* has the power to bring in $5.00 every month—if you consider it *capital* and invest it in a bond. In this example you would post $5.00 on your Wall Chart, using a pen of yet a different color. (We'll see in a moment how that looks on Marcia's Wall Chart.)

Sure it's a tiny figure compared to the towering spikes on your Wall Chart that represent your job income, but it's still $5.00 a month ($60 a year) for the life of that bond. For fun, try translating that into something tangible, some expense you consider necessary for survival. It could be 10 pounds of rice a month. Or 500 miles of gasoline for your motor scooter. Or one pound of freshly ground coffee a month. Or part of your telephone bill.

Keep applying the equation to your total accumulated savings each month. For example, if you save another $500 during the second month, add it to your previous total of $1,000 and your equation for *that* month will look like this:

$$\frac{\$1{,}500 \times 6\%}{12} = \$7.50 \text{ monthly investment income}$$

Post this figure and connect it to the previous one. After a number of months your chart will show a third line creeping up from the bottom. This line represents monthly investment income (see Figure 8-3).

Once you've saved $5,000, you can invest it according to the criteria outlined in Chapter 9. The income from that investment will become part of your monthly investment income figure, along with the figure derived from applying the formula to your further savings. The next $5,000 you accumulate will be invested in the same way, and the next and the next and the next.

Let's go back to Marcia's chart and see how that looks (see Figure 8-4).

Since she started out with some debt, Marcia's monthly investment income line didn't even show up until about a year after she took the hotel-maid job.

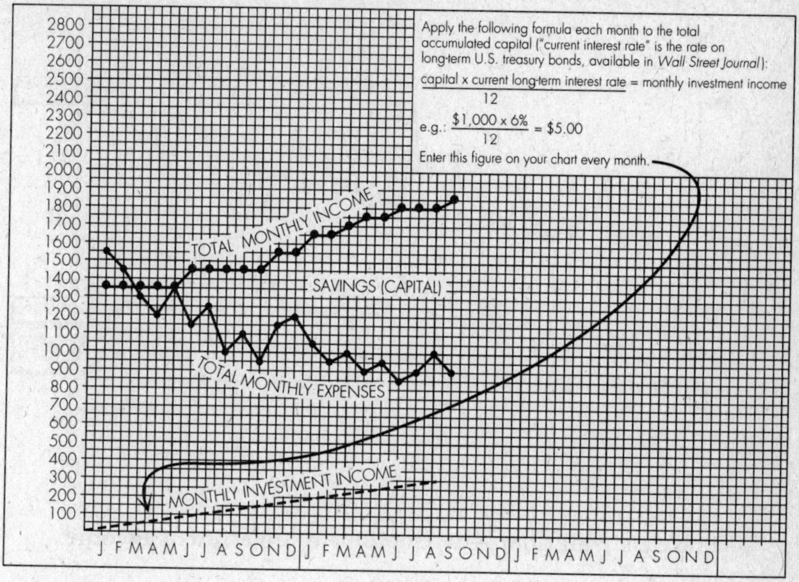

FIGURE 8-3

Applying Formula to Capital to Get Monthly Investment Income and Entering on Wall Chart

Once she started accumulating savings and converting them to capital, however, her monthly investment income kept going up. Take a look at January 1987, for example. You will notice that Marcia has a monthly investment income of $125, while her expenses are $490. By the next January her monthly investment income is $205 and her expenses are still in that $450 to $550 range. Now look at February 1989. Her monthly investment income is $315, and her expenses are still within the $450 to $550 range. What you are seeing at work here is not only Marcia's increasing salary, but also what's known as the magic of compound interest. The interest earned on her capital is being added back *to her capital; thus she is earning interest on the interest, and her capital is increased by that amount.*

What this means for you is that even if the amount added to your capital each month is a constant increment (e.g., your monthly savings

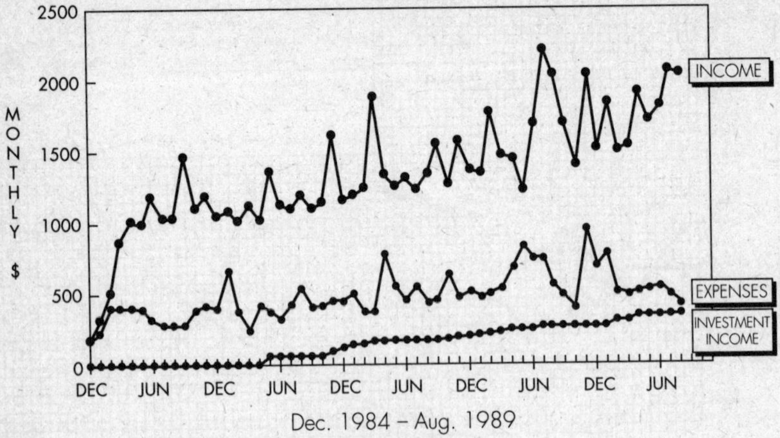

FIGURE 8-4

Marcia's Wall Chart—with Monthly Investment Income

are always $500), the compound interest would make sure that the monthly investment income line on your chart would actually curve upward, rather than remaining straight.

As you'll notice, an interesting trend is developing in Marcia's Wall Chart. That modest yet ever-increasing monthly investment income line is steadily gaining on the fairly stable monthly expenses line. We'll see the significance of this in a moment. But for now all we need to notice is that by simply doing the steps, month in and month out, Marcia's investment income is headed up. This will also happen to you.

THE CROSSOVER POINT

One day, while you're looking at your Wall Chart, you will realize that you can project your monthly investment income line into the future (see Figure 8-5).

Because you have established a fairly steady trend in your total monthly expenses, you can reasonably project that line into the future as well (see Figure 8-6). You will notice that at some foreseeable time

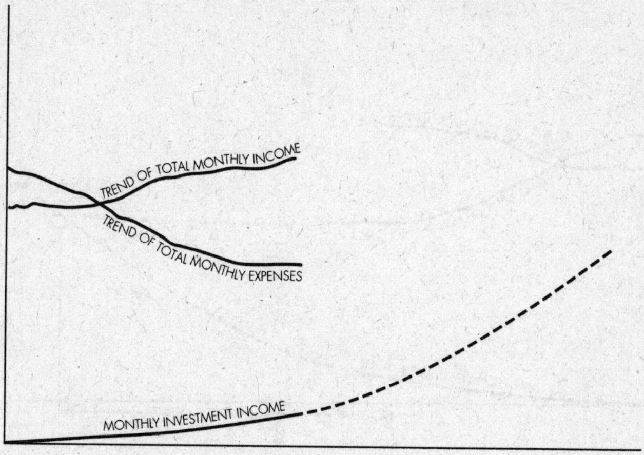

FIGURE 8-5

Projecting Your Monthly Investment Income

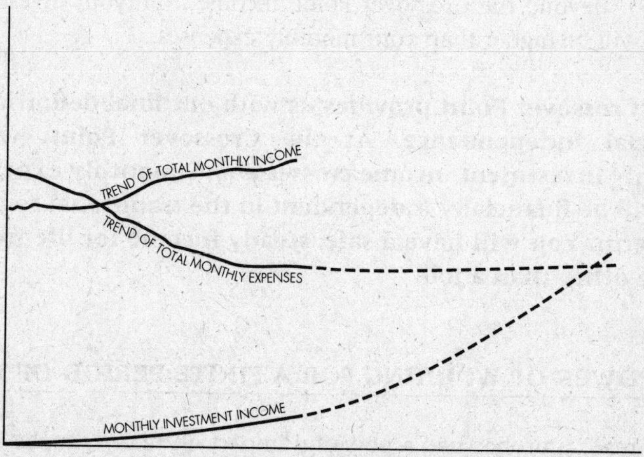

FIGURE 8-6

Projecting Your Total Monthly Expenses

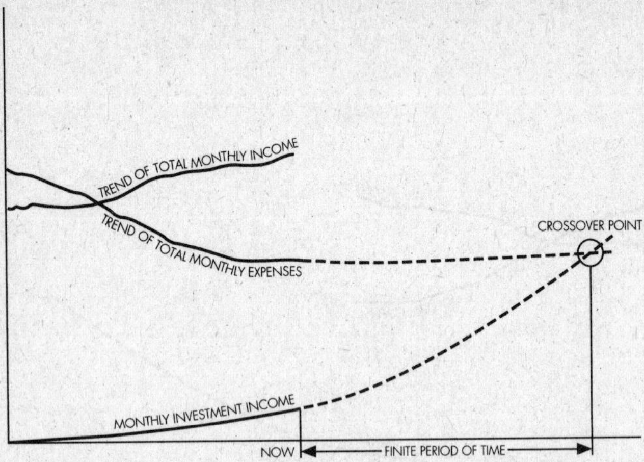

FIGURE 8-7

The Crossover Point

in the future those two lines (total monthly expenses and monthly investment income) will cross. We call that the **Crossover Point** (Figure 8-7). Beyond the Crossover Point, income from your investment capital will be higher than your monthly expenses.

The Crossover Point provides us with our final definition of Financial Independence. At the Crossover Point, where monthly investment income crosses above monthly expenses, you will be financially independent in the traditional sense of that term. You will have a safe, steady income for life from a source other than a job.

THE POWER OF WORKING FOR A FINITE PERIOD OF TIME

This realization has had a powerful impact on many people. Think about it. If you see your life as bigger than your job and can conceive of having to work for money for only a *finite and foreseeable period of time,* then you are likely to be an even more highly motivated, high-integrity worker. The qualities of self-assurance, high motivation, dedication, integrity, joyful pride of workmanship and responsibility that you adopt as you learn to value your life energy are squared when you realize that if you choose you may work for money for only a finite period of time.

Take a minute to think about what would happen if you knew that you would have to work for money for a limited, foreseeable length of time (say, five years) instead of that vague limbo of working until traditional retirement. Wouldn't you feel like putting a lot more of yourself into that job, knowing that it's only for a limited period of time? Wouldn't it make the boredom more bearable and the challenges more interesting? If you are close to retirement age, how does it feel to consider shaving off a few years in the workplace and adding them to your retirement years?

One of the cornerstones of this program, for those wishing to go all the way to Financial Independence, is concentrating on making money now so that you don't have to make money later. You are thus committing yourself to intensively earning money (without selling out your integrity or endangering your health) for a limited period of time.

Until **Steve West** *(the carpenter we met in Chapter 6) caught on to the implications of the "finite period of time," he thought the FI course was just a well-crafted presentation of principles he already knew. He'd even kept track of all of his expenses at one point in his life—but he never figured out what to do with the record, so he quit. What the tape course showed him, however, was how all the pieces could work together to create a life that was meaningful and that reflected his real self. In a letter to us he wrote, "The high point for me was realizing that I could work at my job for a* finite *amount of time. That transformed my whole attitude. As I sat listening to the tape, my heart rate quickened; my palms became sweaty, my energy level soared and I started yelling, 'Yes! Yes!' I also started laughing and crying at the same time. I realized that I could throw myself into my job with passion and a clear goal, increase my productivity and have a tangible product, a magnificent product, a long-sought-after result in about five to seven years. I can't tell you how liberating that was and is."*

In not too many years, Steve plans to be a full-time writer. He hopes to make money from his writing, but he won't have to *sell stories to cover his expenses. There will be no "starving artist" routine for Steve. He'll go from being a craftsman with wood to being a craftsman with words—with no worries about how to pay the bills.*

Penny Yunuba *had a secluded cabin in the country to which she escaped on as many weekends as possible. One weekend she and some friends were walking around a pond on the land. Everyone was captivated by the serenity and beauty of the setting and the unhurried pace of the stroll. Then Penny noticed herself computing how long it would be before she'd have to go back to the city and go to work. In that moment she committed herself to the "finite period." She said, "Financial Independence means that I don't have to extra-enjoy this minute because in the next minute it will be taken away from me. From that moment, it's like there's been no end to the size of the box my life fits into. Now, for me, the sky's the limit."*

You may remember **Roger Ringer** *from Chapter 6. He's the homesteader who wants us to reinhabit the heartland of this country. When he and his wife,* **Carrie Lynn**, *decided to try to align their personal economy with the planet's ecology, they returned to their hometown in Kansas. They bought some land from a friend, tore down an old barn for lumber and built a passive solar house with the help of sixty friends and Roger's father (a carpenter and stonemason). At the same time, Roger worked for his father hauling trash, while Carrie Lynn went to nursing school to learn a consistently marketable skill. In everything they did, they tried to embody their values—self-sufficiency, household economy, energy efficiency and eating what grew in their own garden or was locally grown. They took things slowly, being careful to pay as they went and not get in over their heads. Ideally, they hoped to eliminate over half of the standard expenses (like rent, as well as most food and utilities) and live below taxable levels. Collecting trash took only five hours a day. Roger not only enjoyed his work, but even got all his work clothes from the trash—maximum fulfillment from minimal means. Meanwhile, Carrie Lynn worked two days a week as a nurse.*

Life was sweet and they were getting ends to meet—almost. But several things happened on their way to Eden: two children, health insurance, buying the trash business from Roger's father, a car that quit and a house that just kept crying out for small improvements. Underneath the trappings of living simply, they were caught in the classic "too much month at the end of the money'' and ''where does it all go?'' syndrome. Eden, it seemed, could be as much of a trap as the suburbs.

At this point they did the FI program. When Roger saw the implications of the ''finite period of time,'' his life opened up. Garbage collecting was all well and good, but the thought of doing it for the rest of his life was not attractive. What really fired his imagination was the possibility of being financially self-sufficient and dedicating himself to developing a sustainable-yield homestead on their four acres and helping his neighbors to discover the right mix and rotation for sustainably raising cattle, wheat, feed grains and other crops in the semiarid grasslands of western Kansas.

He wants to do this not only for himself but for the larger community. He sees the small farmers disappearing. Every year the population in his part of the country goes down while the average age goes up. He wants to change that through his own example. Perhaps, he muses, young people could go to the city for five years to become financially independent, return to the heartland with their cash needs taken care of and then regenerate subsistence farming and small-town living. Perhaps his small efforts could create a good life not only for his family but for other families and rural America as well.

The ''finite period of time'' opened Roger's options from years of garbage collecting to a future filled with practical dreams. Four years after doing the FI course, Roger reached his personal Crossover Point. His investment income matched his trash income. He could stop working for money—and start working for his dreams.

What about you? Is there a "second career" inside you, waiting to come out? Do you have a talent that's never been developed? Are you "extra-enjoying" those moments of freedom away from the workplace because you've had no hope of retiring before you're sixty-five? Do you have a dream for yourself—and for your community—that you'd like to make real? What would working at your job for a "finite period of time" mean to you?

The beauty of this program is that Financial Independence is the *by-product* of following the steps. You don't need to have financial self-sufficiency as your goal in order to arrive there. You just have to devote yourself to aligning your earning and spending with your values and with what brings you true fulfillment. The concept of a "finite period of time" is a secondary rocket propelling you toward FI, not the primary thrust. For people who are highly motivated to leave paid employment in order to follow another dream, the "finite period of time" is like the lure of the stables to a horse heading home after a long ride. The homing instinct takes over and you fly toward the goal. But whether you reach Financial Independence in five years or twenty, at thirty as coauthor Joe did or at sixty-five as most Americans do, awareness that you're working for only a finite period will provide continued motivation to see your life as bigger than your job.

FINANCIAL INDEPENDENCE: HAVING ENOUGH—AND THEN SOME

At the Crossover Point, where the income from your invested capital surpasses your monthly expenses, your basic life necessities, all the components of your chosen life-style, are covered by your monthly investment income.

At the Crossover Point you have enough—and then some. Your Wall Chart provides indisputable evidence of how much it costs to maintain your optimal life-style. Every month you've asked yourself the questions about fulfillment and values, and your expenses line elegantly reflects that process of honest self-evaluation. You know with certainty that spending any more money would leave you cold. It's not that you've whittled your expenses down to bare subsistence. You've simply brought your life into harmony, and you just happen to know, to the penny, how much harmony costs. You are certain that your monthly investment income *is* enough—not out of wishful thinking, but out of hard evidence.

But what about that phrase "and then some"? If you're to feel totally comfortable relying on your monthly investment income, it's important to feel that you have some elbow room, some room for "what if's." That need for latitude is built right into the program. Remember your projections of how each spending category might look after FI? The difference between the cost of your job-associated life-style and your FI life-style is part of that "and then some." It's what gives you some elbow room in exploring your new circumstance. Some FIers have even penciled in a fourth line on the Wall Chart that tracks that post-FI expense figure, giving themselves a vivid piece of evidence for that "and then some." But the Crossover Point isn't reached until your monthly investment income line actually crosses your monthly expenses line, even though you may have determined, through experience and careful projections, that your expenses *could* be lower. In Chapter 9 you'll learn about another part of the "and then some"—the additional savings we recommend you accumulate to handle the month-to-month fluctuations in expenses as well as emergencies. Also in Chapter 9 you'll learn the nitty-gritty details of setting up a good FI investment program to guarantee you a safe, steady income for life, including how to build in or increase your "cushion" or safety net. For now, it's important simply to recognize that your Wall Chart is a powerful antidote to anxiety about the future.

At the Crossover Point you have achieved Financial Independence. You have broken the link between work and money—in your own life.

Celebrating Financial Independence

It's time to *celebrate!* You have accomplished a mighty feat. You have restructured your life around what is most fulfilling and valuable to you. You have dedicated yourself to replacing financial fictions with financial facts, challenging many old beliefs about yourself, your money and your life. You have woken up from the dream that more is better, and defined what is enough for you. You have become accountable with your life energy, tracking and evaluating the flow of money into and out of your life. You have developed an internal yardstick for fulfillment, liberating yourself from the sway of advertising and peer pressure. You have explored your values and personal purpose, and have increasingly oriented your life around what really matters to you. You have grasped ever-wider implications of your relationship with money, including what impact your spending habits might have on other people and on the planet. You have accomplished this by defining your purpose, having the intention to achieve your purpose, being willing to do whatever it took to arrive at your goal and staying conscious at every step of the process.

Now is the moment for recognition, for realizing that you have arrived at your destination. Have a party, call a friend, send out announcements to everyone on your Christmas-card list or just smile knowingly into a campfire—do whatever it takes to let yourself *know* that you have just passed over a major threshold into freedom. Breaking the link between work and money *in actual fact* will exponentially expand the possibility of discovering your true work, of reintegrating the disparate pieces of your life and of being truly whole. You will be free to work for your values and your dreams, not just for money. You will find that this freedom will affect your life in many ways. Prime among them is that the realm of choice is now expanded; you have opened the door to many new options in your life.

YOU CAN STOP WORKING FOR MONEY

This doesn't mean you *must* stop working for money. It simply means you *can* stop working for money. If your job has been robotic or stifling, robbing you of the best years of your life, you can now stop working for money and explore other pathways. You might start out with some simple pleasures, like not waking up to an alarm clock or not wearing a watch or staying in your bathrobe all day. Enjoy the delicious feeling of playing hooky for as long as it delights you. Do nothing—proudly—for as long as you are truly getting fulfillment from it. Whatever activity (or inactivity) you felt starved for while you had your nose to the grindstone, you can have now—for as long as you like. Most people find they like laziness far less than they imagined. Eventually they find themselves dusting off other dreams—and you may too. Any one you pick will draw you into a new life pattern. Or, if you enjoy your work (what you do) but dislike your job (who or what you're doing it for), you might find yourself doing the same things, only differently.

The irony of her post-FI work is not lost on **Diane Grosch**. *Since achieving Financial Independence she frequently finds herself sitting at a computer terminal doing programming. But now it's completely different. Using skills that are as natural to her as speaking, she has helped a variety of nonprofit organizations improve their bottom lines: providing service. She has worked with a self-help group of homeless people, an institute providing education* *about sustainability and a networking center for environmental activists, to name just a few. From the outside you might not be able to tell whether she's designing a form for an insurance company or helping to ensure a better future for the world—but Diane knows the difference. Her work is totally voluntary and utterly satisfying. As the saying goes, she wouldn't take money for this work if you paid her.*

While many FIers like Diane have made a choice not to accept money for anything they do after they reach FI, *this is not part of the FI program; it is a totally individual and personal choice.* As people discover the joys of volunteering, however, they become increasingly unwilling to tether themselves to a salary and the compromises that tend to go along with it. They discover, for themselves and from their own experience, a principle common to many of the world's religions. One such statement (from the New Testament) is:

> No one can serve two masters. Either he will hate the one and love the other, or he will be devoted to the one and despise the other. You cannot serve both God and Money.

Once you reach your Crossover Point this is one of the many moral choices you'll have the leisure and luxury to contemplate: "To work for money or not to work for money, that is the question."

Of course, you can as easily continue working for money, but you can approach it in a whole new way. Several years ago we came across the story of Ron Schultz, a successful tea maker from Santa Rosa, California. When he was already well established financially he and his wife traveled to the Third World to adopt two children. This direct exposure to the way people were suffering changed Ron's life. He was especially moved by the plight of Third World children, who, he learned, were dying from both disease and dehydration due to diarrhea at the rate of 15 million a year. He wanted to do something about it, but what? He wasn't a doctor or a health worker or even a fund-raiser. The only thing he knew how to do well was manufacture tea. And therein lies this tale. He went back to Santa Rosa and started manufacturing tea again—but with a twist. He had realized that he could live very well on the interest on his capital and investments, so he was able to donate all proceeds from his tea company to his new relief agency, Medicine for Children. In the first year of operation, the company raised $20,000 for refugees in northern Africa, and he was projecting $30,000 on a total revenue of $400,000. "And unlike charities, it does not rely on people being able to give but on people who like the tea. It's so simple, it's ridiculous. The catch is, there is no catch." Ron is also a great example of how obvious FI thinking is—whether or not you follow *this* particular program.

Through some restructuring of their finances, ***Ted and Martha Pasternak*** *were able to achieve Financial Independence fairly soon after doing the FI program. While they both knew that they wanted their lives to serve some purpose higher than just getting by, neither knew just what that purpose would be. Since Ted had worked in real estate, he thought of contributing to the solution of the "affordable housing" problem and joined Habitat for Humanity. Over time he realized that, while the mission was right, the form of participation was wrong for him. Then inspiration struck. What he did well was sell real estate. Why not do that for love, and donate his commissions to causes in which he and his clients believed? He now works with his clients to determine which organization they would like to support and then, when the transaction is complete, donates 50 percent of his commission to the designated nonprofit organization. A win for everyone, and an inspiring model for others. For Martha, parenting* is *her career. When their son arrived, they both chose to stay home with him as much as possible.*

Both Ted and Martha continue to explore the right mix of activities, but nothing is done out of financial necessity. "Security," Martha says, "doesn't come from outer symbols. FI feels less like steering and more like going for the ride—the blessings just keep coming. There are so many options for meaningful work. Work is now a process of discovering how to express my understanding of what life is rather than trying to make more money."

It wasn't compassion that inspired ***Wanda Fullner*** *to become financially independent. It was anger. A divorce taught her how women, by abdicating financial self-responsibility, can end up impoverished. "There is no need," she concluded, "for women to sell their souls for economic protection." She wanted to change that, starting with herself. She began to teach what she* *had learned the hard way about handling personal finances and eventually went on to become a financial counselor, achieving both financial empowerment and a good income. She had also devised her own strategy for FI. She rented out rooms in her house to students, whose rent paid her rent—and then some. In five years she had accumulated a nest egg sufficient to yield a minimal but livable income for life. This is her baseline, her assurance that she will never be dependent again. She has continued to accept pay for some work, but she is now free to choose what jobs she accepts based on her sense of mission rather than on economic need. This freedom allowed her the elbow room to explore different options until she found a perfect fit: she currently works as a writer and educator with the American Association of Retired Persons, developing materials on economic empowerment for women at midlife and beyond. She works on her own timetable, and it's just the right amount. She provides individual financial coaching for selected clients. And she can schedule a month for "re-creation" anytime she wants to and has plenty of time for other interests. For Wanda, Financial Independence has meant the freedom to allow her career and her passion to blend—on her terms. She no longer "sells her soul for economic protection"—to a mate or to the marketplace.*

What new twist might you be able to put on your job or profession if you didn't have to work for money? Might you stay on the job, but donate some or even all of your income to causes you care about? Might you try out a new profession that would offer more satisfaction but less income? For many people, earning money is one of the satisfactions that comes from working, but that income takes on a whole new meaning when it isn't needed to pay the bills.

FI IS TIME FOR YOURSELF . . .

Have you ever seen a "round tuit"? They usually hang on the refrigerators of procrastinators, reminding them of all the things they want to do when they get "around to it."

What are *your* "someday" things? As in: Someday I'll paint the house, read all of Shakespeare, have time to fish, travel around the world, spend a whole weekend alone with my wife, straighten out the attic, take a course in automotive maintenance, volunteer at the local food bank, try out all the programs that came with my computer, hike the Appalachian Trail, study about issues and write letters to my congresspeople, run a marathon . . . Take some time right now to list a few of your own "someday" plans.

After the Crossover Point, the biggest barrier to doing those things will disappear from your To Do list: your job. In Step 2 you calculated the actual hours per week you devote to your job, all things considered. If you choose to leave your job, those hours are now free time. In this sense, FI is the ultimate time management tool. Instead of gaining a minute here and there through careful planning, you can, with a simple Crossover Point, gain ten hours a day. Of course, you'll have a *new* set of time management challenges in structuring your day around the myriad things you want to do—but the kind of self-esteem and self-discipline that has gotten you to this point will help you through any difficulty you might encounter with having time on your hands.

. . . AND THE ONES YOU LOVE

Time with people—both family and friends—becomes a priority for many people who reach Financial Independence. When *Time* magazine did its cover piece on "The Simple Life," it featured Peter Lynch, whose story of leaving an outstandingly successful career to spend time with his family was a kind of fairy tale of the 1990s.

> While the 47-year-old investment superstar was busy building the Fidelity Magellan mutual fund into a $13 billion behemoth, his youngest daughter got to be seven years old, and he felt he hardly knew her. . . . With a nest egg estimated at $50 million, Lynch could well afford to quit. . . . These days, while other investment managers are scanning their market data at dawn, Lynch is making school lunches. Says he: "I loved what I was doing, but I came to a conclusion, and so did some others: What in the hell are we doing this for? I don't know anyone who wished on his deathbed that he had spent more time at the office."

Other FIers are doing much the same thing—though usually on a more modest income.

Marcia Meyer *achieved Financial Independence in May 1990, right after coordinating her second highly successful medical conference. Her expenses have remained around $500 a month—and she hasn't scrimped on anything she's really wanted to have or do. Marcia's path to Financial Independence had clarified many aspects of her life. After achieving Financial Independence, she had time to bring this clarity to her relationships with her family and heal the wounds of the past—particularly unfinished business from her difficult marriage and subsequent divorce. She took the relationships with various members of her family off maintenance status and made them a priority. Her total attention allowed a great deal of pain from the past to surface and be addressed. Her reconciliation with her children, her siblings and her mother took some work and determination, but there were as many surprises and gifts as there had been resentments and sorrows. What Marcia got from this investment of time was peace of mind—something no job, however lucrative, could have given her.*

What relationships in your life have you put on the back burner? Has friendship been replaced by strategic business relationships? Has your family survived on the scraps of time left over from an all-consuming job? And what about your relationship with yourself? Has that been taking a backseat as well? What if you had the time you needed to write in a journal or go fishing or just sit on a hillside and contemplate the inner and outer horizons? Being able to reflect on your life while you're living it (instead of in the instant before you die) is one key to fulfillment, however you go about it. When you're working full-time, though, quiet time can seem like just one more thing to do in an already overcrowded schedule.

VOLUNTARY ACTION: THE FREEDOM TO CHOOSE WHAT YOU DO AND DO WHAT YOU CHOOSE

As we said, just because you don't have to work after the Crossover Point doesn't mean you can't or won't. Even if your highest aspiration initially was not to have to get up to an alarm clock, eventually you do get up. And once you've done your "someday" things, you will still have lots of life left to fill.

Most people who achieve Financial Independence eventually go back to work—but now they work because they choose to, not because they must. They work voluntarily. And they often work, happily, more hours than they did on the job.

What would your work feel like if you were working (perhaps even at the job you now do) totally voluntarily? What aspects wouldn't change a bit? What aspects might you eliminate entirely? What decisions might you make that you aren't free to make now?

If you've been in the work force so long that working "voluntarily" seems odd to you, think about those things you do *now* that are voluntary. Why do you clean your house, go to church, serve on committees, sit on boards for nonprofit groups, play with your kids, water your lawn, go to meetings at your children's school, make love, go out for pizza with your friends and the millions of other things you do voluntarily? You do them because you choose to, because you anticipate getting value from them. Voluntary action can serve your values and your chosen purpose.

Volunteerism Redefined

Another word for voluntary action is "volunteering." In an era when everything, from child care to housework to shopping for clothes, is professionalized, volunteers are sometimes regarded as second-class citizens—less skilled, less trained and less productive than paid employees and (especially) professionals with a few letters after their name. Yet what the word "volunteer" used to point to, and could again, is a kind of activity that is more robust, self-responsible and self-expressive than the notion of volunteers as adjuncts to the real business of the world.

Robert L. Payton, director of the Indiana University Center on Philanthropy, points out that the word "philanthropy" comes from the Greek root *phil,* which means love, and *anthropos,* which means human. In this sense, all volunteers are philanthropists, expressing their love for humankind. All volunteers are "rich and powerful" in their capacity to change the world through the currency of love. And voluntary efforts are legion. In a speech at Hofstra University Payton pointed out that more than one million voluntary associations "employ" 98.4 million volunteers (people who give three or more hours a week) and 7.4 million staff members. These organizations steward $122 billion in charitable donations. Far from being marginal, the volunteer population is a powerful third sector. Perhaps philanthropy doesn't add much to the Gross National Product, since, as Payton points out, the product of volunteering is meaning. But volunteering does add to an equally essential bottom line—the vital ethical underpinnings that hold society together.

Volunteers are people who are free to act whenever, wherever and however they choose, as opposed to paid employees, who are locked into someone else's agenda. Volunteers are people who work for their values and their deepest beliefs about life. Paid employees may do that as well, but there's often as much (or more) pragmatism as principle in the job they do. Volunteers remind us about the best part of being human—precisely because they work for love, not money.

Volunteering is the epitome of self-expression—choosing what you do based on an inner prompting. Volunteering is dipping down into your internal resources—your commitment as well as your skills, your love as well as your knowledge—to accomplish something in the world that you determine is worth doing.

While some people fear that having too many volunteers would create competition for jobs with workers who need the pay to survive, the kind of creative, self-motivated volunteers we are talking about will function more like entrepreneurs than like strikebreakers. As a volunteer you may initiate projects and processes that will eventually need paid employees to administrate and carry out. Volunteers have historically pointed to social needs that eventually get funded and even become professions. Visionaries eventually need rafts of educators to teach their ideas. As a volunteer you can operate like human venture capital, increasing job opportunities for others in your community.

Taking Fulfillment through the Ceiling

Returning to the Fulfillment Curve, we can see that at the point of maximum fulfillment you have a choice. You can continue to work for your own needs and desires, to buy more possessions or experiences,

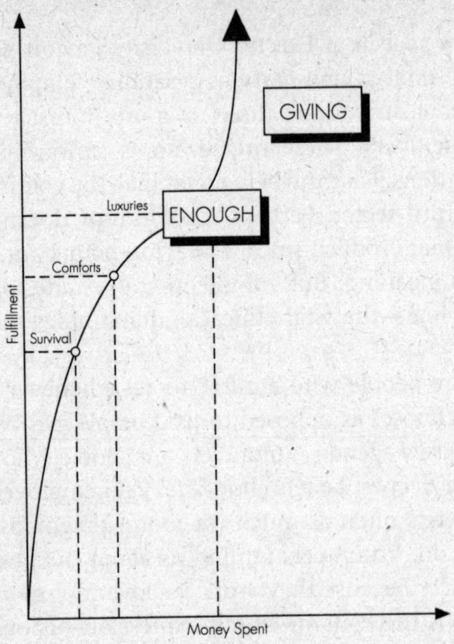

FIGURE 8-8

The Fulfillment Curve: Beyond Consumption

or you can work for something larger than yourself that gives to others and the world. You can consume or you can create. As we said earlier, once you have enough, it's the commitment to *giving* that takes that fulfillment line straight up off the top of the chart. That's what volunteering brings to your life. (See Figure 8-8 for this "new paradigm" Fulfillment Curve.)

Redefining volunteers as social and cultural entrepreneurs could well be as transforming as redefining work or money.

Volunteering and Freedom

Volunteers have an extraordinary set of freedoms. Think about these as you contemplate the possibilities in *your* future.

- As a volunteer you are free to do the type of work you choose to do, without the limitations of previous experience, previous training or availability of jobs. If you don't have the skills, you can learn them. If you don't have experience, you can start getting it now. If no organization has a slot for you, you can begin alone or offer to create the position you want. It's never too late for a volunteer. You can always start again, and again, and again.

- As a volunteer you are free of financial considerations. One FIer got the nursing job she wanted because she was able to work for free. While you are working toward Financial Independence, it makes sense to invest your time in work that pays you well. When you are working solely for your dreams and values, however, you are free to work without a paycheck.
- As a volunteer you are free to think your own thoughts. When you are working for money you get paid to think your boss's or your company's thoughts, to dedicate your intellect and creativity to solving their specific problems. Middle management of every variety—in business, government and institutions—is particularly hamstrung, implementing policies that come from above with very little latitude for originality. Volunteers, on the other hand, can be free thinkers.
- As a volunteer you are free to speak the truth. Without a job to protect, you can say what you mean and mean what you say.
- As a volunteer you are free to live according to your personal ethics, never bending your principles for the sake of security.
- As a volunteer you are free to shape your life around your sense of purpose. You no longer have to live "bombs by day and peace by night," as Sally Morris did before she cleared her debt and took off for Africa.
- As a volunteer you are free to structure your own time, set your own hours and start and stop when you choose. If you discover you are tilting toward burnout, you can stop and recover your balance (whereas a paid employee might have no choice about getting a report in by yesterday). If you are a night owl who is barely awake before noon, that's when you can start working. As a volunteer you may, in the long run, be more productive for the hours worked—because you are free to stop when your productivity goes down and free to work when you are at your best.
- As a volunteer you are free to practice your profession or move

into a new field. You are free to push yourself to grow or to coast along within your comfort zone. And you are free either to never again work on tasks you find insufferable or to break through your prejudices and self-limitations. In short, as a volunteer you have choice.

*We met **Jason and Nedra Weston** in Chapter 2 at the beginning of their journey to Financial Independence and checked in with them again in Chapter 6 to hear about their caretaking job, which provided room, board and income. In August 1990 they achieved Financial Independence, having built and managed a successful housecleaning business. Since then they've entered into an exciting career as volunteers. For the first few post-Crossover months they visited family and friends, did the reading and thinking they'd put on hold during the whirlwind of running a complex business and did research on projects they might like to assist. When they visited the Hesperian Foundation it was love at first sight. Founded by David Werner, a writer and speaker about rural and Third World health care, Hesperian's Projimo Project assists disabled children from Mexico both in getting needed surgery in the United States and in obtaining wheelchairs, braces and crutches from a Mexican workshop staffed by the disabled themselves. Jason and Nedra have had a field day in helping out. Nedra loves being with the children. After much study about population issues and much soul-searching, she had given up her desire to have children of her own—the last thing the planet needed, she figured, was more kids. So working and playing with the Mexican children, both in the San Francisco Bay Area and at the project site in Mexico, was Nedra's version of heaven. Meanwhile, Jason took on the installation of a pump to improve the Mexican project's water supply—something he'd never done but welcomed as a challenge. In addition, both Nedra and Jason have served as drivers for the Projimo van that shuttles children up to San Francisco for operations. Jason even got his father involved, and something about serving together brought out a new mutual respect and camaraderie. Besides their work with Hesperian, Jason and Nedra have helped a reforestation project in Oregon and an environmental networking project in Washington. In between projects they've enjoyed camping in their motor home. Their blend of mobility, skills and willingness to try new things makes them an invaluable volunteer team.*

THREE TYPES OF VOLUNTARY ACTION

The truth is that volunteers already do much of the world's work—they just don't make headlines as often as people who make a lot of money, like politicians, financiers and celebrities. From our own experience, and from observing many people finding their way in the world of unpaid employment, we've seen that there are three major types of voluntary action, all of them vital to the world's working as well as it currently does.

1. Helping and Caring. There are many "unofficial" and spontaneous ways to help. These include small acts of thoughtfulness, many of them unnoticed and uncredited, and social and psychological support, offered informally to friends and neighbors. Just the act of listening, without judgment, can be a tremendous help to people under stress or in pain. Common courtesy isn't that common anymore, and it can lift someone's spirits. Being cheerful is a voluntary action that is infectious and healing. And in the official volunteer sector, there are thousands of ways that people can help. Most cities have a volunteer bureau or a United Way office that can steer you to the project, institution, agency or organization that needs just the skills and love you have to offer.

A nice fringe benefit of such activity is what is known as "helper's high." Allan Luks, former executive director of the Institute for the Advancement of Health, reports that more than 70 percent of nearly 2,000 people surveyed (most of them members of a women's volunteer group) experience an identifiable physical sensation—warmth, calm, reduced depression, decreased pain, increased energy—during the actual act of helping. What's more, 80 percent of these said that the feelings returned any time they remembered the experience of helping. Such highs can also be good for your health, as reported in *American Health*:

> In a striking and controversial study at Harvard University, psychologist David McClelland showed students a film of Mother Teresa, the embodiment of altruism, working among Calcutta's sick and poor. Analyses of the students' saliva revealed an in-

crease in immunoglobulin A, an antibody that can help combat respiratory infections.

Helping, when you are financially independent, doesn't have to be a part-time job. Penny Yunuba's story illustrates helping and caring as a way of life.

***Penny Yunuba**'s post-Crossover life is as exuberant and many-faceted as she is. She works with a group in Boston called Little Brothers of the Elderly, delivering flowers and meals to an eighty-three-year-old woman who has crossed the line from client to close friend. Penny's life is so enriched by the relationship that it's no longer clear who is helping whom. Penny also volunteers one day a week with a collective that recycles white office paper. She loves and believes in the work—and she gets the added benefit of group health insurance. She also distributes leaflets for the local food co-op. Not only does she get 24 percent off her food bill, but because of a medical condition she needs to walk and leafleting gives her a good excuse. "People think I'm so virtuous," Penny says with a laugh, "but they have to drag in to work every day and I'm out here in the sun—and* they *are telling* me *I have a hard life!" And this isn't all Penny is doing. She started a local chapter of a national activist organization for busy people called 20/20 Vision. She's applied for membership in the Quaker church, a "luxury" she didn't have time for when she was working seventy hours a week. And she's also being a real friend to her friends. "I'm not distressed. I can listen to people. I'm 'free therapy' because I don't have to go to a job." Penny works both through groups and on her own; she is a full-time giver.*

2. Activism and Advocacy. This type of volunteering covers everything from protest to citizen education to party politics. Margaret Mead once said, "Never doubt that a small group of thoughtful citizens can change the world. Indeed, it is the only thing that ever has." A good deal of social and political change in the world has arisen from just such committed volunteer groups. In fact, former governor of Colorado Richard Lamm asserts that elected leaders never lead, they follow. Most projects he rubber-stamped during his tenure originated in the voluntary sector. This is particularly empowering for FIers who want to do something about the multiple stresses humanity has put on the planet. With all their time free, they can educate themselves, educate others, write policy statements, lobby, make proposals for new programs, network with like-minded activists, write letters and effect change. Their styles may vary, from high-drama showdowns to quiet, nonviolent pressure, but their impact is tremendous. Many organizations that our New Road Map Foundation has investigated for funding would much prefer a full-time, financially independent volunteer to a financial grant. "Get us people, not money," they repeatedly tell us. A full-time, focused and self-directed volunteer can transform a moderately effective group into a powerhouse.

Dwight Wilson *is a case in point. As the son of well-to-do parents and a very bright and energetic young man, he was expected to go to "all the right schools," become a lawyer and go into politics. But his idealism got in the way. A few months before he received a substantial inheritance he did the FI course, taking two days instead of the recommended one so that the information would really sink in. His inheritance became his FI capital. After some soul-searching and some hesitancy, he decided to jump into full-time volunteering. The cause that called him most strongly was bridging the misunderstandings between nations and cultures that eventually lead to war. He served as executive director of an organization of returned Peace Corps volunteers who wanted to recapture some of the heroic spirit they'd felt during their service abroad. They undertook to build a Peace Park in their sister city in what was then the Soviet Union, overcoming innumerable difficulties while creating a project that actively engaged hundreds of Americans and Soviets in a cooperative and challenging venture. The friendships established through working together, as well as the goodwill established by building a beautiful park, surely played their part in contributing to the thawing of the Cold War. Now Dwight works for another nonprofit group, organizing cooperative tree-planting projects for young people from all parts of the world. Perhaps as these young adults assume leadership in the twenty-first century, the memory of working together with others of different nations and cultures will guide them in creating a more peaceful world. Dwight's dedication to these projects has allowed him and the other staff members to focus less on fund-raising than* *on carrying out projects—and has filled the office with his unique blend of high spirits and intelligence.*

3. Innovation and Dreaming a New Dream. Martin Luther King, Jr., had a dream, and he changed the face of America. But who today can afford to be a dreamer? Most workers are as trapped in established modes of thinking as they are on the freeways during rush hour. Volunteers have the freedom to stretch the limits of the known and experiment with new road maps for life. As we've indicated, volunteers can afford to explore new territory outside what's socially or intellectually acceptable. Both the need for funding and perceived threats to the status quo often prevent business, government and other institutions from risking creative innovation. Real innovation is rarely lucrative—and innovation that is lucrative is rarely inspired. Social innovation (as Governor Lamm said of political innovation) often comes out of the volunteer sector and only later gets rubber-stamped by the financial or institutional powers that be.

Here's a story of an all-volunteer project that is challenging the status quo of medical research—and medical practice as well:

Evy McDonald, *a nurse and health administrator, liquidated all her assets in 1981. Having been diagnosed with a terminal illness, she knew she would be "retiring" within a year anyway, so she quickly applied the FI program to her finances and became a full-time volunteer. She left her stressful career and set out to live a life that expressed the love and dedication to service she'd always believed in but had never had time to practice. In the process she went through a period of deep reflection and honesty, determined to truly* live *before she died. Within months of the time when her doctor had predicted she would die her symptoms began to disappear—apparently as a by-product of her inner process. This profound personal experience, together with her insider's view of the limitations of high-tech medicine, lit a fire in her to reintroduce the mind, heart and soul into standard medical practice. She lectured and taught about her personal experience. The medical community listened politely and dismissed her story as "purely anecdotal." With no career to protect but only a gift to give, Evy collaborated with the New Road Map Foundation to come up with a strategy that would speak to the half million doctors in this country in a language they could understand—science.*

She designed a comprehensive study of the mind/body/spirit interaction in a disease that had the medical community stumped: amyotrophic lateral sclerosis (ALS), or Lou Gehrig's disease. More remarkable, she decided to ask for no funding but to do it entirely with volunteers. She had been inspired by Dr. D. Carleton Gajdusek, a Nobel laureate in medicine, who had told a group of leading researchers looking for funding to solve the riddle of ALS that money has never *been a solution to any scientific problem—that love and dedication, not grants, create medical miracles. So Evy recruited an all-volunteer staff of over fifty people, including a professional statistician, university professors, a behavioral medicine psychologist, and leading ALS doctors, based at three research and treatment centers around the United States. The team of enthusiastic data collectors spent thousands of hours and drove thousands of miles to interview 144 ALS patients nationwide every three months for a year and a half, and another team of volunteers helped collate and analyze the data. Some of the volunteers were already financially independent, but most took time off from work and other projects to participate. Professionals with other research projects reported that "somehow" this project brought them more fulfillment than the fully funded ones. Everyone who worked on the project had his or her mind and heart expanded.*

Volunteers can be watchdogs and gadflies. Volunteers can pay attention to the details of human suffering that get filtered out by layers of bureaucracy and paperwork. Remember Steve Brandon in Maine, who prefers to do his nursing as the propane-truck driver so that he doesn't have to deal with the paperwork? Precisely because they aren't paid professionals, volunteers can be experimental and intuitive. Because of their caring, because they can be activists and advocates, because of their courage to dream, volunteers have a power that paid employees don't always have. Volunteers are powerful by virtue of being free.

But What Would I Do?

If this kind of freedom seems either too far-reaching or too scary to contemplate right now, go back to Chapter 4 (page 122), where we explored purpose and values. Follow Joanna Macy's suggestions. What are some ways you can work with your passion, with projects and causes that move you and touch your heart? How might you work with your pain, helping others heal wounds you yourself have healed? What about working with what's at hand, with the small but pressing needs that surround each one of us if we would only open our eyes? If you know you want to help with a particular problem or population, but don't know where to start, your local United Way may have a data bank of volunteer jobs that are available. You can have your pick of wonderful jobs. *Volunteer USA* by Andrew Carroll is a good, comprehensive resource for people asking, "What can I do?" Marlene Wilson's book *You Can Make a Difference* is another tool for would-be volunteers, as is *How Can I Help?* by Ram Dass and Paul Gorman. Whatever you do, wherever you start, remember that your life as a volunteer will unfold organically. Author Edward Abbey is reported to have said, when asked about his career, "I don't have a career, I have a life." Once you're out of the nine-to-five straitjacket, you too will have a life. Rather than climbing a career ladder, you will be following the promptings of your heart and mind—and may find yourself on some side roads that are more interesting and enjoyable than any "job" you could have ever imagined.

Volunteering 202

Now, if you want to sink your teeth into a major challenge after you're FI, Robert Muller, former assistant secretary-general of the United Nations, has a suggestion. He reports that *The Encyclopedia of World Problems and Human Potential* contains all of the world's problems and all of the world's (as yet not implemented) solutions. The bad news is that there are over 1,000 major problems. The good news is that the solutions outnumber the problems. In Muller's optimistic and irresistible fashion he encourages us to simply pick one, any one, and get going. It may well be that courageous volunteers will accomplish what all the king's horses and all the king's men (i.e., his wealth and employees) have not been able to do—put the world back together again. It's worth a try!

Life after the Crossover Point

The essence of FI is choice. Once you've passed the Crossover Point you have choice about how you fill the hours of your day and the days of your productive life. Steve West is headed toward being a full-time writer. Roger and Carrie Lynn Ringer will make sustainable farming their vocation. Wanda Fullner enjoys the freedom of free-lancing only on projects she respects and using the extra income to finance some special projects of her own. Marcia Meyer has used her freedom to be with her family as well as to volunteer. Ted and Martha Pasternak are devoting themselves to raising their children. Diane Grosch is still at a computer keyboard but loves donating her expertise to organizations she admires. Evy McDonald is spending every ounce of her life energy in making a contribution to the scientific understanding of the mind/body connection. And, through the New Road Map Foundation, the authors are educating people on how to assume personal responsibility for their money *and* their lives—and donating all proceeds to organizations working toward a sustainable future for our world.

There is no formula for how you live after the Crossover Point. And that's the point. You are free to invent your life. You are free to explore what Buckminster Fuller meant when he said, "We are called to be architects of the future, not its victims." You have a choice.

SUMMARY OF STEP 8

Each month apply the following equation to your total accumulated capital and post the monthly investment income as a separate line on your Wall Chart:

$$\frac{\textbf{capital} \times \textbf{current long-term interest rate}}{\textbf{12 months}} = \textbf{monthly investment income}$$

When you begin investing your money according to the guidelines offered in the next chapter, start entering your *actual* interest income for your monthly investment income on your Wall Chart (while still applying the formula to your further savings). After trends become clear, project that line to the Crossover Point; you will then have an estimate of how much time you will have to work before reaching Financial Independence.

9

NOW THAT YOU'VE GOT IT, WHAT ARE YOU GOING TO DO WITH IT?

Step 9: Managing Your Finances

This step will help you become knowledgeable and sophisticated about long-term income-producing investments and manage your finances for a safe, steady and sufficient income for the rest of your life.

This chapter contains the nuts and bolts of an investment program for FI—Financial Integrity, Financial Intelligence *and* Financial Independence. This investment program will allow you to have a secure and consistent income, sufficient to cover the basic necessities of your chosen life-style, for the rest of your life. The information is based on coauthor Joe's insider's view of the Wall Street investment game, on his personal research for his own Financial Independence and on both of our post-FI experiences. The fact that more than twenty years after our FI dates we each *still* have a safe, steady income, equal to our individual needs, is proof that this investment program works. Further proof is the experience of many others who have also "survived" the excesses of the outrageous 1980s with their FI income intact and consistently sufficient.

This chapter is written for the novice, but the investment dabblers as well as the pros will also find much information worth thinking about.

EMPOWER YOURSELF

One of our primary missions in this book is empowerment—allowing *you* to take back the power that you have inadvertently given over to money. As we will see later, this includes the power you have turned over to various financial "experts," to external circumstances and to financial beliefs and concepts.

You have, throughout this program, been urged to become intimate, comfortable, and at peace in your relationship with money (life energy). Now you're ready for the final step: learning a bit about the world of investments.

No, this does not mean readopting the "more is better" mentality and learning how to "make a killing" with your capital. Having followed the steps of this program, you know how much is enough for you, and the purpose of your investment program will be to assure yourself that you will have that amount—and then some—for the rest of your life.

Nor does this mean entering the world of macroeconomics, the great debates conducted (but never concluded) by somber economists around the world. It does not mean being able to discuss the theories of supply-siders, monetarists, fiscalists, business-cyclers and their many brethren. There is an old saying, "If you get ten economists together, you will get fifteen different opinions." If these Knights of the Dismal Science can't agree among themselves, why should you confuse yourself with trying to understand their econobabble?

Becoming "knowledgeable and sophisticated" does mean learning enough so that you can free yourself from the fear and confusion (or pride and prejudice) that pervade the realm of personal investments.

The principles and financial strategies outlined in this chapter are safe, sensible and simple. They are also very inexpensive to implement and do not require extensive financial management or expertise.

A large majority of Americans have no cohesive investment plan. (According to the New York Stock Exchange, 79 percent of the population avoids even heavily marketed products like mutual funds and stocks.) For these many Americans who, through fear, prejudice or long professional experience, see Wall Street as a suburb of Las Vegas, there is a clear need for self-empowerment and development of a safe way to manage their capital that keeps to a minimum costs, complexities and risks.

Nothing in this section is to be construed as specific investment advice. The information here, like that in the rest of this book, is based on personal experience and is intended as guidelines, principles and educational data.

Don't Leave It to the Experts

So how *do* you become knowledgeable and sophisticated about long-term, income-producing investments? The strategy most newcomers to the world of investing would adopt is to go to the "experts." After all, if you go to a doctor when you're sick and a mechanic when your car breaks down, it stands to reason that when you have money to invest, you go to a financial expert. Right? Wrong.

Step 9 is about empowering *yourself* to make wise financial choices, and your first lesson involves educating yourself so as not to fall prey to unscrupulous brokers, financial planners and salespeople who want to put you into all manner of investment vehicles that pay them handsome commissions.

Securities brokers have gone by different titles over the years: customer's man, registered representative (regrep), account executive, financial consultant. They all mean the same thing: salesperson. In the majority of cases, their earnings come from commissions. To make a commission they have to sell you a product. They also make a commission when they talk you into getting rid of the product—whether or not you have made a profit. Some products generate much larger commissions than others. Some products are far more profitable to the salesperson's *employer* than others. The salesperson may be expected to generate a quota of commissions.

Being an intelligent person, you might realize that such an arrangement may not be geared to your best interests. So you search out an independent "financial planner." Then you read something like the following item from *The Wall Street Journal:*

FINANCIAL PLANNERS SQUABBLE OVER CREATING CODE OF CONDUCT

Some of the questions planners are debating:

- Should planners be required to place clients' interests ahead of their own in all circumstances?
- Should planners be required to solve clients' problems through "appropriate financial procedures," such as suggesting they pay off debt, before recommending financial products?
- Should planners be required to disclose how much compensation they will receive if clients buy products they recommend?

If this doesn't scare you away from depending on the advice of financial planners, try comparing this debate on a code of conduct with one that surely happened as purveyors of snake oil evolved into the pharmacists of today. Imagine them challenging the correctness of their established practices, like . . .

- Should snake oil salesmen be required to place the patients' needs ahead of their own in all circumstances?
- In selecting a snake oil, should we give the amount of profit less or more weight than what will be beneficial to the patient?
- In the event that bed rest is all that is needed, should snake oil salesmen be required to recommend that over the possibility of selling several bottles of worthless tonic?

In other words, why are these questions being *debated* by financial planners? Aren't they obvious ethical principles? No, we are not implying that investment intermediaries are dishonest. We are pointing out that *you* are the only person with no stake in the transaction other than your own.

Andrew Tobias, in his 1978 best-seller *The Only Investment Guide You'll Ever Need,* puts it this way: "By and large you should manage your own money. No one is going to care about it as much as you."

And, in his 1987 best-seller *The Only* **Other** *Investment Guide You'll Ever Need,* he puts it even more strongly: "Trust no one. You've got to take responsibility for your own affairs."

Herbert Ringold, author of *How to Lose Money in the Stock Market*, is equally firm:

> Repeat after me:
> A broker is a salesman.
> A broker is a salesman.
> A broker is a salesman.
> The broker is not the Delphic Oracle. He is closer to being nothing more than a high-class tout, if you really want to know the truth.

So if you shouldn't rely on the experts to guide you, does that mean you can rely totally on yourself? Probably not. The market is a game where traditionally the insiders, the pros, win and the little guys lose. You wouldn't think of getting into a professional boxing ring without knowledge of the art of boxing and the rules of the sport, as well as a manager and a trainer. You wouldn't think of engaging in a high-stakes game of poker without sufficient disposable capital, an extensive knowledge of probability theory and a good measure of apprenticeship.

So there you have the paradox: it would be wisest for you to manage your own investments, empower yourself to make decisions and use a broker *only* for the mechanics that brokers are best suited for—simply executing your buy and sell orders. *But* it's as much as your life is worth, or at least your shirt, to enter the complex world of investing alone. There are innumerable investment "vehicles," "products," "derivatives" and "instruments." The old standbys, "stocks and bonds," have evolved, multiplied, mutated and transmogrified into an assortment as varied and complex as children's sidewalk games. Their names, terms, nicknames and acronyms are legion: Nikkei puts, pork bellies, Fannie Maes, front loads, closed end, triple witching, GIC's, stripped securities, naked options, Ritzies—ad infinitum.

How can you apply Step 9, becoming "knowledgeable and sophisticated," under such contradictory conditions? Since investing our hard-earned capital is a vital part of this program (mattresses produce income for only a small part of the population) there must be some way around this quandary. There is, but you won't believe it until we discuss this obstacle to successfully completing Step 9: your belief system about investing.

Dispelling Fears

Like your assumptions about money and about work, your beliefs about investing have probably been pieced together from media hype, the opinions of coworkers, the advice you got from Uncle Harry ("Buy low, sell high, kid"), randomly generated successes and failures and sundry other unreliable sources. To pierce through these confusions and prejudices you need only recognize that most beliefs about investing rest on two primary driving forces: greed and fear.

We hope you've encountered and tamed your greed through applying the first eight steps of this program. You know, through experience, that more is not necessarily better, while "enough" is both supremely fulfilling and achievable. Indeed, the successful pros on Wall Street have discovered the same truth, which they state as "Be a bull or a bear, but never a hog!"

The Biggest Fear: Will I Have Enough Tomorrow?

Step 9 addresses the fear that so often underlies economic decisions. One of our biggest fears is fear of the unknown. The biggest unknown is the future. The biggest financial unknown in the future is: "Will I continue to have enough money over time?"

How do you whittle this fear down to size and transform it into appropriate prudence?

1. Through applying the investment criteria we will be suggesting.
2. Through establishing a reserve according to the guidelines we will be offering.
3. Through dispelling the *irrational* fear of inflation.

The social disease of the 1950s was fear of depression. Back then, frugality and thrift were still our bedrock, and "A penny saved is a penny earned" and "Waste not, want not" were still mainstays of early-childhood education. We enjoyed but didn't trust our newfound affluence. We can now look back on that era and see how that irrational fear of depression blinded us to what we currently celebrate as the "good old days." Similarly, this generation's social disease, the morbid fear of inflation, has blinded us to some basic truths and has greatly distorted our perceptions. The financial industry has been quick to capitalize on this pervasive paranoia—with the resulting proliferation of the many dubious "investment" vehicles mentioned above and the upsurge of rampant debt that has been bringing down many of our institutions and producing the highest bankruptcy rates our nation has ever seen.

INFLATION

To begin to find our way out of the investment maze, we must first shed some light on that demon "inflation," which sets the context for so much of the current investment philosophy.

Are Our Fears of Inflation Inflated?

Inflation is measured by the Bureau of Labor Statistics and presented as the Consumer Price Index, or CPI. The CPI is an index of the changes in prices of a fixed list of products and services when compared to the prices of those items during the reference base year. The prices are weighted according to consumer preferences, as shown in the base period's Consumer Expenditure Survey. (For example, if during the reference base period the consumers surveyed bought steak twice as often as chicken, steak was given a weight of 2 and chicken a weight of 1.)

In 1970 the Consumer Price Index was 38.8. In 1990 it stood at 129.9.

Here's a quiz. Given these figures, how can it be true that

1. In 1970 it cost a family of four about $15 to $20 to go to a movie, if you include the drive and the theater popcorn and soda. In 1990 the cost of a movie and trimmings can be $4.
2. In 1970 the typewriter to write a book cost $247.99. In 1990 a far more sophisticated machine cost $100 and a "word processing" machine with 16k memory cost $239.99.

3. In 1970 Joe's three-speed English touring bicycle cost $100. In 1990 an excellent ten-speed cost him $50.
4. In 1970 Joe's usual lunch cost something in the vicinity of $2. In 1990 Joe's usual lunch cost $.60—and was much more healthful.
5. In 1970 Joe spent $299.25 on gasoline. In 1990 Joe spent $177.31 on gasoline.
6. In 1970 the tape recorder Joe bought to tape music from FM radio cost $750. In 1990 Joe got much better sound from his $90 recorder.

Take a moment to reflect. These numbers are accurate. There are no misprints. How can this be? What else might have changed to offset the CPI?

Let's take a look at some more reality. The following prices are gleaned from the spring–summer 1970 Sears Roebuck catalog and from 1970 *Seattle Times* newspaper advertisements. The 1991 prices are documented sale prices found through using the careful shopping techniques discussed in Chapter 6 (items 50 to 67). Products are as comparable as we can find, considering the many technological advances that have occurred in those twenty years.

	1970	*1991*
Food		
Chicken, price/lb.	.69	.47
Ham, price/lb.	1.49	1.19
Turkey, whole/lb.	.65	.47
Eggs, price/dozen	.59	.58
Potatoes, 10 lb.	.98	.57
Tomatoes, price/lb.	.50	.39
Flour, 10 lb.	1.19	.98
Bread, 22.5-ounce loaf	.37	.33
Margarine, 1 pound	.39	.38
Household		
Mattress, twin	97.95	79.00
Electric heater	26.95	15.95
Garbage disposer, ½-hp	84.95	59.99

Smoke alarm	35.00	6.95
Garage door opener	179.95	169.95
Tools and maintenance		
Circular saw, 7-inch, 2-hp	62.49	39.99
Electric chain saw, 14-inch	139.95	59.99
Automotive		
Tires, 225/75R15, 40,000-mile warranty	62.33	31.30
Auto floor jack, 1.5-ton	120.00	43.50
Auto ramps, 2.5-ton	44.29	33.29
Entertainment and hobbies		
Sewing machine	246.00	219.00
Color TV, 18–20-inch	349.95	249.96
Basketball backboard	69.95	59.00
Miscellaneous		
BIC ballpoint pen, fine—price/dozen	2.49	.89
Adding machine with multiply function [1991 has *all* functions]	177.95	29.87
Long-distance phone call, daytime, from New York to Los Angeles	4.50	2.50

The Consumer Price Index (CPI) is *not* a "cost of living" index, no matter how often it is referred to as that. It is a list of prices for specific goods and services. It assumes that the same items are bought regularly. It does not account for the fact that you do not buy a new refrigerator every month or every year, or for the fact that today's appliance is much more energy-efficient and has many more features than its predecessor and if carefully selected can last longer. It cannot account for the fact that yesteryear's top-of-the-line model is bested in *all ways* by today's "economy" model.

The CPI does not account for changing buying habits after the base period. Prices of everyday commodities fluctuate. A freeze in Florida sends the price of orange juice skyrocketing, while simultaneously a bumper crop of apples makes the price of apple juice plummet. The rational shopper switches to apple juice. The CPI does not.

An automobile today is a marvel of technological advances. Corrosion resistance, greater durability, reduced maintenance requirements, electronic ignition 60,000-mile steel-belted radial tires, a seven-year warranty and three to four times the miles per gallon of cars of twenty years ago—how do you make a comparison?

As prices of travel and hotels soared, people discovered the joys of unhurried camping trips and simple vacations close to home (as any besieged National Park ranger can readily attest). How did the CPI handle that?

To expand on some figures we cited in Chapter 6, the 1989 price of a 4-bedroom, 2½-bath, 2,200-square-foot house had risen to $382,000 in Westchester County, New York; $418,333 in Wellesley, Massachusetts; $388,500 in Wilmette, Illinois. The same house in Corpus Christi, Texas, was $81,666; in Boise, Idaho, it was $82,667; in Fort Wayne, Indiana, it was $97,250. How does the CPI account for our very mobile society? Or for the many lovely towns with clean air all over the United States that are becoming ghost towns offering outrageous real-estate bargains simply because the yuppie ethos required migration to overpriced urban areas? In addition, look at the number of houses sitting empty—second homes, summer homes, vacation homes, abandoned homes. The *Nightly Business Report,* a daily PBS program, tells us that according to the Bureau of the Census, one of every ten houses in the United States is vacant; Vermont is highest with 22 percent vacant.

Health care and health insurance costs have increased enormously. Equally enormous has been the increase in our knowledge of how to prevent disease. We have had convincing evidence as to the ill effects on health of cigarette smoking, obesity, stress, cholesterol, saturated fats and other nutritional factors, pollution, alcohol and drug abuse, carcinogens, lack of exercise and overexposure to sunlight. While the cost of each doctor visit might be higher, we can choose to make far fewer of them thanks to the life-style choices we make. The CPI can't figure that in.

In 1970 staying trim and fit meant doing your own yard work—mowing your lawn with a human-powered mower and raking leaves. In 1990 it required a health club membership and a $300 ergonometric stationary bicycle—and these for the person who also has a 12-horsepower riding mower and a 140-decibel leaf blower.

Is Inflation a Belief or an Experience?

As the standard of living has risen, so has the *standard* for a rising standard of living. Once, we were well-to-do if we didn't have to borrow our neighbor's push mower; now we feel poor if we don't have a riding mower. (You may recall John Stuart Mill's insight that we don't want to be rich, just richer than others.) In other words, we have excelled at creating our own experience of inflation—apart from the CPI numbers.

Let's say that in the past few years you acquired your basic "durable goods"—home, car, appliances, furnishings and essential wardrobe. Let's also say that through careful research (see Chapter 6) you bought for durability, repairability, utility and flexibility. Wouldn't your overall expenses be significantly lower for the next decade than they were for the previous one? (Unless, of course, you just had to have that latest version or current fad.) Joe has sometimes been chided for buying multiple pairs of khaki pants on sale and wearing them for a decade or more, but he's in excellent company. It took consumer advocate Ralph Nader "twenty-five years to wear out the dozen pairs of Army shoes he bought at the PX for $6 a pair when he got out of the service in 1959."

Let's say that somehow you were given more time in your week. And that during that newfound time you read a couple of home repair manuals and your car's maintenance schedule (or went as far as taking an auto repair course at a local community college), and even found it enjoyable and empowering to "do it yourself." Isn't it very likely that your annual expenses would go down?

Similarly, let's say that you saw the wisdom (personal and planetary) of biking rather than driving, or of living closer to your job or of car-pooling. Again, isn't it likely that your annual expenses would go down?

Let's say that rather than going down to your local bike store and buying the latest $600 "mountain bike"—the eco-yuppie's BMW—complete with bologna tires, chrome-moly-magcitrate frame, twenty-seven forward and twelve reverse gears and hydro-turbo derailleurs, you instead looked under "Bicycles for Sale, Used" in your local *Dandy Dime, Thrifty Nickel* or *Penny Saver.* And there you saw listing after listing of yesteryear's fabulous ten-speed bikes, now out of fashion—and as little used as today's fad will be in a year or so—for $50. Wouldn't you be saving yourself a bundle, even when compared with costs twenty years ago?

Let's say that time-and-space-shifting TV movies turned out to work for you. In other words, instead of fighting the crowds to see the latest first-run movie on a big screen from a long distance away, you watched it a few months later, on a small screen but much closer up, in a much quieter setting, with lots of much cheaper popcorn. Isn't it likely that your annual entertainment budget would diminish?

Let's say that instead of hurriedly gobbling down the pastrami on rye with the side order of french fries at the crowded deli across from the office (as Joe claims he did for *all* his Wall Street years—and his cardiologist backs him up), you brown-bagged a healthful lunch to eat leisurely in the little park across from the office. Isn't it likely that your annual expenses—as well as your lifetime expenses—would go down?

Might it be that at least part of our experience of "inflation" is due to unconscious and automatic habits as well as to our chosen life-style? Having a car is a life-style choice; using it for nearby errands may be simply a habit. Buying soda from the pop machine at work, just because it's there, rather than buying it at the supermarket for a fraction of the price, may be a habit.

None of this is to say that there hasn't been real inflation, even without the distortions of the CPI. The prices of auto insurance, hospital rooms, prescription drugs, higher education and hundreds of other items have skyrocketed. Yet, despite higher prices in these areas, please notice the enormous increase in multiple-car families, documented overuse of prescription drugs and the unfounded assumption that an expensive private college provides a better overall education than a state university. These items represent choices, not necessities. On the other side of the coin, some of the higher costs are balanced by advanced technology or better service so that overall costs stay the same. An example of this might be improved outpatient and surgical techniques that reduce the number of days you need to be hospitalized.

"Inflation Hedges"?

Many brokers assert that one or another investment product has historically been a good hedge against inflation. More objective observers challenge those conclusions. Here are some facts:

Stocks and their high-cost, fancy consumer-package version, mutual funds, are often touted as one such inflation hedge. In the decade between 1964 and 1974 the CPI rose steeply and almost continuously—while the Dow-Jones Industrial Average entered 1964 at 766 and ended 1974 at 616. This means that the value of many stock-based investments, such as mutual funds, actually fell. Similarly, it has been shown that the DJIA, converted to inflation-adjusted "constant dollars," *was lower at the end of 1990 than it was at its 1929 peak.*

In *How to Lose Money in the Stock Market* Herbert Ringold points out:

> In its September 16, 1985 issue, *Forbes* magazine listed 329 mutual funds whose records it had tracked for the most recent eight and a half years—from 1976 through the first six months of 1985.
>
> The average for all the 329 funds was a gain of 14.39% over the indicated period. That works out to 1.22% a year!
>
> You would have done much better by putting your money in a bank passbook account.

And there are other ways of generating income, as the following comment from *The Wall Street Journal* suggests: "Farmers matched Wall Street and mutual funds on annual rate of return from 1960 to 1988, according to a University of Minnesota survey." (Appropriate application of *organic* manure may be more of an inflation hedge than the Wall Street variety.)

Real estate has been a central "inflation hedge" for many people—people who *lost* thousands of dollars in the depressed 1991 real estate market. From Boston to Seattle, people are lowering their asking price to unload property that they bought at inflated prices in the 1980s when everybody knew that "real estate never goes down."

The fact remains that there is no guaranteed way to stay ahead of the Consumer Price Index. One decade's financial fad will be the next decade's fiscal flop—and that can be very costly to your hard-earned capital.

In summary:

- While "inflation" may be a valid macroeconomic concept, this does not mean that it automatically rules your life.
- Your choices, attitudes, beliefs, habits, tastes, fears and desires have the ultimate effect on your bottom line.
- Consciousness is defined as the faculty of knowing what affects your mind or what goes on in your mind.
- Consciousness can grow faster than inflation.
- No investment product or program is a guaranteed hedge against inflation. Consciousness is.

Now you're beginning to see that two common assumptions about money management—that you're better off hiring an "expert" and that your first consideration should be inflation—may not be true. Now you're ready for Step 9—smart investment and Financial Independence.

THREE PILLARS OF FINANCIAL INDEPENDENCE: CAPITAL, CUSHION, AND CACHE

The basic FI investment program has three elements:

Capital: The sum that is invested in the safest possible long-term interest-bearing vehicles, ultimately producing at least as much income as indicated by the Crossover Point of Chapter 8.

Cushion: A cash reserve, in insured savings or interest-bearing checking accounts, that is enough to cover your expenses for six months. The purpose of the cushion is to handle emergencies and to smooth out cash needs to handle surges in expenses (annual health or auto insurance payment) and to cover deductibles and coinsurance liabilities in insurance.

Cache: Your continuing savings habit made manifest. (Cache may come as a surprise to many FIers.) Believe it or not, you can continue to save money after FI.

Early in your FI process, as soon as your savings have surpassed the amount you have determined to be a comfortable cushion, you can begin transferring monies into long-term investments such as those described in the following pages—thus creating your income-producing capital.

A good way to begin to become "knowledgeable and sophisticated" is by determining what type of account to use for holding your cushion as well as the money that is accumulating, waiting to be invested. Compare the advantages of federally insured savings accounts, insured interest-paying checking accounts and the "cash management accounts" that are run by the large brokerage houses. The last is a brokerage account that includes check-writing, a "debit card" (like a credit card except that it automatically draws on funds in your account rather than sending you a bill), weekly "sweeps" of your excess funds into a money market fund until you are ready to invest and monthly statements of all your transactions and investment positions. While there is an annual fee for this all-in-one account, it may be that the higher interest gained from the money market fund (as compared with a savings account or interest-bearing checking account) makes the annual charge worth it.

BASIC CRITERIA FOR INVESTING YOUR CAPITAL

Whether we are defining "Financial Independence" as being out of debt, with enough savings to withstand economic downturns, or as a full-fledged "early retirement" that makes it possible to devote yourself full-time to whatever is most meaningful to you, the following criteria apply to whatever you do with your capital:

1. Your capital must produce income.
2. Your capital must be absolutely safe.
3. Your capital must be in a totally liquid investment. You must be able to convert it into cash at a moment's notice, to handle emergencies.
4. Your capital must not be diminished at the time of investment by unnecessary commissions, "loads," "promotional" or "distribu-

tion" expenses (often called "12b-1 fees"), management fees or expense fees.

5. Your income must be absolutely safe.
6. Your income must not fluctuate. You must know exactly what your income will be next month, next year and twenty years from now.
7. Your income must be payable to you, in cash, at regular intervals; it must not be accrued, deferred, automatically reinvested, etc. You want complete control.
8. Your income must not be diminished by charges, management fees, redemption fees, etc.
9. The investment must produce this regular, fixed, known income without any further involvement or expense on your part. It must not require maintenance, management, geographic presence or attention due to "acts of God."

The reasoning behind this list of investment criteria has been made clear by the preceding chapters, especially Chapter 8. You are not using your hard-earned capital to speculate, to parlay into more capital or to try to get rich quick. You simply want it to provide you with a safe, steady income you can count on. You don't want to have to worry (at least about your own financial security) if there is a recession or a depression, if joblessness rises or if the Dow breaks above 4000 or below 1000.

As a lawyer, ***Ned Norris*** *is trained to look at all the angles and to investigate loopholes. Both the media and office chatter led him to wonder whether the pundits and prognosticators might be right when they warned that he would need twice the income in ten or twenty years to have the same buying power—even though his experience told him that his consciousness was indeed growing faster than inflation. Shouldn't he build an "inflation hedge" into his investment program? "Why just believe Joe Dominguez?" he thought. "Check it out yourself." He did some research and came up with a hot investment newsletter that had all sorts of insider information. Soon he was spending hours mentally buying and selling securities—and then following the market to see how his dream investments were doing. Every newsletter added a new twist and sent him back to the drawing board. This fascination* *lasted four to five months, absorbing most of his nonjob life energy. Then he woke up. "If these guys who write the newsletter are so smart, how come they aren't so rich that they don't have to write a newsletter for suckers like me?" he asked. "The purpose of the newsletter is to get me addicted to the newsletter, not to help me establish a safe, secure income for life." He let go of the obsession with speculation and returned to relying on his own experience and on the criteria outlined in this chapter. He got back his peace of mind.*

Safety is the key factor in any investment program designed to sustain a financially independent life-style. You do not want to trade your nine-to-five job for the round-the-clock job of worrying about how the stock market is doing, or if Zilch Corp. is cutting its dividend, or if Whoops bonds will default, or if the Inveterate Ecomyopic Movement will sabotage your windpower partnership, or if your Cosmic Oneness Interspecies Mutual Fund is a front for some cult, or if your venture capital is venturing capital to maintain someone's cocaine habit.

This list of criteria automatically eliminates most of today's popular speculations and investments. Stocks and stock mutual funds do not provide the safety of capital or the absolute safety and consistency of income that you require. Income from money market funds fluctuates dramatically according to the gyrations of short-term interest rates. Bond funds expose you to default risks in varying degrees. All of the above diminish your capital and even your income with numerous charges (failing to meet criteria 4 and 8). Bank certificates of deposit, while safe if issued by a federally insured bank, have maturities that are far too short—you would have to reinvest your capital too soon, exposing you to the risk of much lower interest rates at the time of maturity. Even a supposedly conservative investment like real estate is excluded, with the possible exception of your primary dwelling.

Only one category of investment vehicle fits the criteria perfectly: long-term U.S. treasury and U.S. government agency bonds. Note: Citizens of countries other than the United States should investigate their own nation's government bonds. While it is possible to buy U.S. treasury and government bonds almost anywhere in the world, the fluctuations in currency exchange rates would make their interest income too unstable to meet the criteria for an FI investment program.

Herein lies the solution to the paradox that we discussed at the end of the section "Empower Yourself": **You do not have to become an expert in the entire realm of speculation and investment. You can focus on one small segment that meets your criteria perfectly—U.S. treasury and agency bonds.**

Many books deal with treasury and agency bonds. We strongly suggest that you read *Treasury Securities* by Donald R. Nichols. If your library doesn't have it, try *Understanding Treasury Bills and Other U.S. Government Securities* by Arnold Corrigan and Phyllis C. Kaufman. While the information that follows can get you started, it is not intended to provide you with the kind of comprehensive education you will want in order to feel knowledgeable and sophisticated about long-term income-producing investments.

A Primer on Government Bonds

A bond is simply an IOU. The bond issuer promises to pay back to the holder of the bond the amount printed on the bond (face value) by a certain date (the maturity date). Most bonds also pay interest, at a specific percentage rate (coupon rate). This amount, though quoted as an annual percentage rate, is usually paid in two semiannual installments.

Most bonds can be bought and sold at any time (they are negotiable, or marketable) through banks and brokers. (The original issuer has nothing to do with the subsequent purchases and sales of the bond other than to send the semiannual interest check to the current holder.) Bond prices fluctuate with prevailing interest rates. Therefore, if you sell a bond before maturity, you may get more or less than you paid for it (market risk). If you hold it to maturity you will receive exactly its face value, regardless of the interest rates prevailing at that time.

U.S. treasury bonds and U.S. government agency bonds are considered by experts to be the highest-quality, safest interest-bearing investments in the world. (Note: These are *not* the same as the old familiar Series E or Series H U.S. savings bonds, which do not provide the long-term high interest that you will need to make the FI program work for you.)

U.S. treasury bonds are particularly suited to a Financial Independence investment program; following is a list of their advantages:

- Greatest safety of capital.
- Greatest safety of interest—"full faith and credit of the U.S. government" guarantee as to principal and interest.
- Exemption from state and local taxes.
- Noncallability (most can't be redeemed early by the issuer).
- Greatest negotiability, absolute liquidity, global marketability. They can be bought and sold almost instantly, with minimal handling charges and in convenient denominations (such as $1,000, $5,000 and $10,000).
- Easiest availability—directly from the federal government (Treasury Direct) and through most brokers and many banks, anywhere in the world.
- Cheapest availability—no middlemen, no commissions, no loads.
- Duration—the range of maturities available is extensive; you can buy a note or bond that will mature in a few months or one that won't come due for thirty years.
- Absolute stability of income over the long run—ideal for FI. Avoids the income fluctuations that would occur with money market funds, rental real estate, etc.

The two risks posed by treasury and agency securities are market risk and reinvestment risk. Fortunately, both of these are relatively negligible in terms of the FI investment plan. Market risk—the fluctuation in the price of the bond between the time of issuance and the time of maturity—does not concern you, since you plan to hold the bond until maturity, and your income is totally unaffected by those fluctuations. Reinvestment risk refers to the possibility that interest rates will be considerably lower at the time your bond matures, and thus you will not be able to get the same income when you reinvest the proceeds. To avoid this problem you buy the longest possible bonds (thirty years and over). In addition, if you follow the bond market over time (intelligently, not compulsively) you will see wonderful opportunities to extend the maturity of your portfolio while maintaining (or even increasing) your income level. These bond-swapping techniques are based on the fact that if prevailing interest rates drop, your yet-to-mature high-coupon bonds will increase in market price proportionally. A $10,000, 8.5 percent bond you bought at "par" (face value) might be worth $11,000 if interest rates sink to 7.75 percent. This larger amount of capital can be reinvested at lower coupon rates, with the effect of essentially maintaining the overall income level. Don't confuse this with Ned Norris's temporary obsession with investing and speculation, however. It is rare that you will need to do this sort of bond swap.

And speaking about fluctuating interest rates, we must note that, due to the profligate spending of both government and individuals, interest rates on long-term treasury and agency bonds have been at abnormally high levels. For most of this century, up until the late 1960s, interest rates were under 5 percent. Since their peak in 1981, long-term interest rates have been wending their way back down toward their historical norms. You did not need to catch the bond market at those abnormal highs in order to reach FI. Even at 5 or 6 percent, this program will work.

In 1969, when Joe reached FI, his capital was invested in bonds with interest averaging 6.85 percent and maturities extending into the 1990s. Through a few judicious bond swaps, **and with no income other than the income from the bonds,** his portfolio now has an average yield of 9.85 percent and maturities extending to the year 2007 on average. And most important, his bond income has always been more than sufficient for his needs, in spite of the supposedly huge inflation of the period.

Treasury and Agency Bonds: What They Are and How They Work

Our federal government has two basic ways to raise money: taxation and borrowing. Thus, when government spending exceeds current tax income, it has only two choices: increase taxes or borrow more. (Obviously, our government does not adhere to the principles espoused in this book of spending less than you earn.)

Treasury securities are the government's way of borrowing money. A new bond is issued every few months, with maturity dates ten, twenty, and thirty years into the future. The first thing that each new issue does is pay off the holders of old issues coming due. The remaining monies are used to make up the deficit in the federal budget. The national debt is the most senior obligation the government has—principal and interest on treasury securities must be paid when they come due, before paying for anything else. Not to do so would destroy the "credit rating" of the U.S. government in world markets, wreaking havoc with our ability to do business and greasing our slide into the status of a Third World nation.

In recent years the interest due annually on the public debt has been greater than the total deficit, so all monies borrowed by the treasury go either to paying off the principal that is coming due or to paying the interest that is coming due on the remaining debt.

Treasury bonds are sold by auction. The total amount of bonds to be issued is preset by the government's financial needs—not by the demand, or lack of demand, for the bonds. Simply stated, the interest rate on an issue is raised until a level is found at which the entire issue is bought.

The bond issue is bought by all kinds of businesses—banks, insurance companies, brokers, mutual funds, pension and retirement funds, credit unions, large and small companies—and by individuals.

Money paid for a treasury bond goes to the treasury only when that bond is originally issued. After the date of issuance, and for the rest of the life of that bond, the bond is bought and sold on the "secondary market," by individuals—the monies trading hands are never seen by the government, though it continues to pay the interest to whoever owns the bond currently. Bonds purchased through brokerage houses and banks are bought on the secondary market.

A typical 8 percent U.S. treasury bond, bought for $10,000, will pay back $34,000 over its thirty-year life—$24,000 in semiannual interest payments and $10,000 when the bond comes due.

In recent years, a dramatic change in the saving habits of Americans has affected government spending and interest rates. Savings have decreased. This lack of savings has not altered the way the government spends, but it has altered the amount, because the government needs to spend more on the higher interest rates necessary to entice savings-rich foreigners to buy bonds.

Some people believe that investing in treasury bonds implies condoning the government's spending habits. The economic facts do not support that assertion. Refusing to buy treasury bonds simply makes the problem worse by forcing the government to keep interest rates high so as to attract buyers. This causes larger deficits due to a larger outflow of interest payments. It is our taxes that finance the majority of the government's spending. In fact, the more we earn—and the more taxes we pay—the more we directly support the spending. And the more money we have invested in treasuries, the more the government *pays us*—in effect subsidizing us (a gratifying idea for some FIers involved in service to their communities).

U.S. government agency bonds are issued by other institutions of the U.S. government. While many are not "full faith and credit" obligations of the government—the highest possible warranty—most are considered to have an implied warranty. Some typical agency issuers are:

The Federal National Mortgage Association ("Fannie Mae")
The Federal Home Loan Bank ("Freddie Mac")
The Federal Farm Credit Bank
The Government National Mortgage Association ("Ginnie Mae")
The Student Loan Marketing Association ("Sallie Mae")

While *some* of the bonds from *some* of these agencies fit all our criteria, they are somewhat more difficult to deal with. The minimum amount you can purchase may be higher; availability and liquidity are nowhere near what they are for treasury issues; long maturities may not be available from some agencies; all in all, it is generally a more complex undertaking for someone venturing into Step 9.

Many of our common repositories for savings—banks, savings and loans, pension funds, money market funds, insurance companies—reinvest a portion of our funds in treasury or agency issues. The difference between our doing that directly and having these institutions do it for us is that the institutions get a large chunk of the profits. For example, banks buy government bonds earning 8 percent and pay us only 5 percent on our deposits. Cutting out the middleman by buying bonds directly is called "disintermediation."

Disintermediation (Buying for Yourself) and How to Do It

Disintermediation is the act of buying a given security, such as a treasury bond, yourself rather than investing your money in an intermediary (such as a fund, bank or other institution) that will turn around and put it into the same investments while taking a big chunk for itself.

(There is no shortage of middlemen anxious to take a piece of your pie.)

In one respected, "balanced" (i.e., it holds both stocks and bonds) mutual fund, 22 percent of the fund's dividend and interest earnings never found their way into the investors' pockets. Instead that 22 percent paid for the fund's various "expenses":

Investment advisory fee
Promotional expense ("12b-1 fees")
Transfer agent fee
Printing
Legal fees
Registration fees
Audit fees
Directors' fees
State taxes
Custodian fees
Other

A well-known "money market fund" was returning 7.11 percent on investment at a time when U.S. treasuries and agency bonds were returning between 8.3 and 9.3 percent. In good part this discrepancy was due to the fact that 13 cents of every dollar of interest earned was going into the pockets of the fund's administrators.

None of the above takes into account the huge commissions paid to brokers and financial planners on "load funds." (A load on a fund is the nonrefundable ante you pay for the privilege of buying it.) And, according to *The Wall Street Journal,* the *average* retail broker earned over $79,000 in 1990—and this was in what was considered a bad year for the industry.

So what are your choices? Treasury bonds can be bought directly from the Federal Reserve, with no commissions whatsoever, through a program called Treasury Direct. These purchases can only be made at the time a new issue is being auctioned, called the quarterly refunding, which takes place during the first weeks of February, May, August and November. The Fed will pay your semiannual interest directly to a bank or brokerage that you designate and will hold the bonds for you without charge. One disadvantage of Treasury Direct is that selling a bond before maturity requires it to be transferred to a brokerage account, incurring a fee and a delay. Full information on Treasury Direct can be obtained by contacting any Federal Reserve Bank or branch.

The other way for an individual to buy treasuries (any issue, not just the most recent one), and the most common way to buy government agency bonds, is through the secondary market. Large ("full-service") brokerage firms and commercial banks are "primary dealers" of treasury securities and as such will not charge commissions. However, there is a difference, called the "spread," between the "bid" (the price at which a dealer offers to buy the bond) and the "asked" (the price at which a dealer offers to sell it). Note that the price you pay may be slightly higher than the price quoted in the treasury bonds tables of *The Wall Street Journal* or big-city newspapers because those quotes are for large transactions (usually $1 million or more) and you (presumably) will be buying in smaller amounts.

In reading a treasury bond table you will want to understand the following terms:

"Rate" is the annual interest rate that the bond pays you, and is read as a percentage; e.g., 9⅛ means that the interest rate is 9⅛ percent of the face value of the bond.

"Maturity" or "date" is the maturity date, when the loan represented by the bond is repaid to you. It is also useful to know that interest is paid semiannually on the day and month corresponding to the maturity date and six months later—e.g., a bond maturing in May 2018 pays you interest every May and November.

"Bid" is the price at which a dealer offers to buy the bond, and "asked" is the price at which a dealer offers to sell the bond. When you buy a bond you pay the asked price, plus a premium for buying in "odd lots," under $1 million. In these tables prices are expressed on the basis of 100. To get the actual value of a $1,000 bond you must multiply the price by 10. Also, the bond prices in the table are expressed in points and 32nds of a point—e.g., a bid of 101:21 or 101-21 is actually 101-21/32 or $1016.56.

"Chg" is the change in the bid price (up or down) since the previous day.

"Yld" is the yield to maturity (expressed in percent)—current yield adjusted to take into consideration whether you bought it above or below par (the face value of the bond) and thus whether you'll have a profit or a loss when the bond is repaid.

Making the Buy

The rate and maturity date are what you use to identify the bond you want to buy (e.g., the treasury 9⅛ of May 2018) when you go to a brokerage house or bank to put in your order. In deciding with whom you place your order, remember that, unless they are in the select group of primary dealers, they will have to execute your order with a primary dealer and charge you a commission for their service. You have added middlemen.

Many investors prefer to pay the slight extra cost of buying their bonds on the secondary market, through an account at one of the large brokerage firms that serve as primary dealers, because they can choose the issue, they can buy whenever they have the money (instead of having to wait for the Fed's quarterly refunding) and they can sell it at a moment's notice before maturity.

One occasional irritant in dealing with a broker—according to numerous letters we have received over the twenty-one years that "Transforming Your Relationship with Money and Achieving Financial Independence" has been in existence—is that some may try to talk you out of your treasury or agency bond purchase. This is understandable, since the transaction would provide virtually no financial gain to the broker compared to the hundreds of dollars in commission he or she would get from the same sum put into United Veeblefitzer stock, Lynch-Majestic Fund or even Royal Junque bonds. It is also unforgivable, since the broker is there to serve you. If this should happen to you, ask to be transferred to another representative. (Treasury and agency bonds are the safest, most conservative investments in the world. There can be no legitimate objection to them.)

***Marilynn Bradley,** who cooked and catered her way to FI, grew up, like many of us, with a deep-seated belief that "mathematics and money" were areas that she just didn't understand. Following the steps of the FI program did a lot to dispel her fear and ignorance, but when she found herself with* *enough money to buy her first bond she again felt overwhelmed. "I just didn't know how to go about it," she confessed. "There was obviously a lot to learn, and I just didn't know where to start."*

The bond market seemed like a foreign country to her. She wished there were someone to tell her what to do, but she realized that Step 9 meant what it said—becoming knowledgeable and sophisticated herself *was an integral part of the program. With the determination that had gotten her this far, she decided to take on the challenge and began to educate herself. She read a simple book on bonds she'd gotten from the library—ten times at least. The first time was like reading Greek. The second time was more like German: the alphabet was familiar, but the words meant nothing. But with each successive reading it began to sink in and slowly it began to make sense to her. The next step was to read* The Wall Street Journal, *specifically the government bond tables and the section on credit markets, which explained what the bond market was doing and often explained the terms that were being used. Then she began to chart the prices of long-term treasury bonds. Her chart allowed her to see the price fluctuations, to observe the ups and downs and eventually to understand the relationship between the price and the yield. She learned how to compute current yield:*

$$\textit{current yield} = \frac{\textit{coupon rate}}{\textit{current price}}$$

She was now ready to buy her first bond. Armed with her newly acquired knowledge and her enthusiasm, she went down to the brokerage firm in person, money in hand, and opened her account. The broker she'd been assigned when she had phoned took her to his office and attempted to give guidance to this "helpless young novice."

"Let me tell you about an exciting mutual fund that I think would be just right for you," he began.

"Thanks for your advice," Marilynn replied, "but I want to buy a five-thousand-dollar U.S. treasury bond, the 9⅞ of November 2015."

"Government bonds are a pretty conservative investment for someone of your age. How about—"

But Marilynn didn't bite. She had gone in there knowing what she wanted, and she remembered that Joe had said to stick to your guns. "Thank you, but what I want is a U.S. treasury bond—five thousand dollars of the 9⅞ of November 2015.''

After a few more thrusts and parries Marilynn made her point and placed her order—and her purchase was confirmed later that day. She left feeling powerful, sure of herself and on track. Educating herself and actually buying her first bond represented a breakthrough—a victory. ''I felt wonderful, *'' she exulted. ''I did it myself! I learned to do something I would have thought impossible. If* I *can do this,'' she added, ''anyone can!''*

She passed that hurdle in 1985 and several years later she was able to leave her job as a cook and caterer to explore what her next life challenge might be. The empowerment she got from following the steps through to the impossible dream of Financial Independence (before her fortieth birthday) has served her well in her life of freedom. Whenever she's about to say ''I can't'' in response to a challenge, she thinks back to buying bonds—and she usually ends up saying ''Yes, I can!'' to the current invitation to grow beyond her perceived limits.

Now that you have an overview on treasury and agency bonds it's time to look at the elements in an FI investment program.

CUSHIONS MAKE FOR SMOOTHER LANDINGS

Whatever level your monthly expenses settle in at, you will want six times that amount readily available in a bank account or money market fund. You are not financially independent until you have a cushion to handle emergencies and handle the months between bond interest payments. Besides smoothing out the flow of money into and out of your life, however, your cushion has another important function. Like Ned Norris doubting that his own experience of consciousness was growing faster than inflation, you might find yourself doubting whether today's enough will be enough tomorrow. A cushion eases those doubts.

Rosemary Irwin *found herself getting increasingly uneasy as her projected Crossover Point approached. She was used to her job, and the thought of turning off that trusty faucet and depending on bond income alone was scary.*

Rationally she knew her bond income was ''enough and then some,'' but she still had irrational fears of not being able to reenter the job market if FI somehow didn't work. ''Maybe this is what trapeze artists feel when they are assessing when to let go of their bar so they can swing over to the other one,'' she thought. Her safety net (cushion) was in place, but it felt very far away. What she decided to do was to bring the net closer and beef it up by doubling her cushion. With those extra thousands in the bank, she found it easy to face down the inner worrywart who kept asking, ''But what if you total your car and have a major illness and your house burns down all in the same year?''

*As **Carl Merner** approached FI he, like Rosemary, found himself reluctant to turn off the flow of job income that had filled his coffers for over twelve years. He jokes that there is a tenth step to this program—remembering to quit your job. He came to realize that because he had devoted the majority of his time and intellect to being a computer programmer, he had depended on money to buy his way out of many of life's difficulties. His ''what if's'' had to do with maintaining his house and car without enough money to pay a small army of mechanics, plumbers, roofers and exterminators. He handled his fear by deciding to become knowledgeable and sophisticated about home and auto maintenance, apprenticing to some experts and reading everything the library had to offer. Turning a ''what if'' into a ''why not'' is the epitome of FI thinking.*

***Ted and Martha Pasternak** developed a different strategy for the ''what if's.'' This was especially important for them because their son, Willie, and their FI came along at about the same time. While they had no intention that Willie would be one of those $100,000 ''average American kids,'' they knew they'd have plenty of financial surprises during the eighteen years of full-time parenting. So they made what they call a Life Chart for all three of them. For each year from now until they will be eighty-five, they asked themselves, ''What needs or desires might come up?'' They included all the normal expenses of raising a healthy (but not pampered) child—things like braces, tutoring, summer camp and his first car—and determined how much each might cost. They then bought an investment vehicle called zero-coupon bonds (treasury bonds with no interest, bought at a big discount but repaid at par and especially good for future cash needs), with different bonds coming due in* *each of the years that Willie might need a big-ticket item. And if Willie doesn't need braces or want to go to summer camp, they'll just roll over the money into regular treasury bonds. They also anticipated their own reasonable needs, including housing, health care, education and travel, and calculated how the combination of their cushion and their cache could handle them with ease. They've even handled the "what if it doesn't work?" fear with the reminder that they could go back to work* for a finite period of time *to handle a completely unanticipated change in life-style. Having thought through the "what if's" and having already allocated funds to handle them, they can breathe easy in the present. Not only that, but they've projected a happy and fulfilling life for all three of them, a life in which even the normal bumps and bruises are taken in stride and are part of the adventure. They have already embraced the future and eliminated the fear and mystery that so often keep others with their noses to the grindstone.*

Your cushion will be there to handle the "what if" worries, either by proving them unfounded or by providing the cash needed to see you through. And then there's your cache, which will continue to enlarge your cushion and even increase the amount of capital you have to invest in bonds.

WHAT IS CACHE AND WHERE DOES IT COME FROM?

In pioneer days a cache was a hole in the ground where travelers buried for later use provisions that were too heavy to carry. In your FI program, your cache is a store of extra money (beyond your capital or your cushion) that builds up for future use. Funds feeding the cache account come from numerous sources:

1. In Step 4 you ask the question, **"How might this expenditure change if I didn't have to work for a living?"** Most people who choose full Financial Independence (early retirement) in order to work toward their dreams find that their expenses go down significantly when they leave paid employment. No more commuting expenses, no more dress-for-success expenses, no more restaurant-lunch expenses—and many more such reductions. So since the Crossover Point is based on your total expenses while you are engaged in paid employment, the

excess investment income will begin to pile up after you are financially independent. This is the "and then some" we referred to in the definition of FI as "having enough and then some."

2. Continuing to do the steps after FI is a natural pattern; your experience of Financial Integrity and Financial Intelligence is now so ingrained and so fulfilling that you don't *want* to stop. As a matter of fact, there may be an even higher level of zeal since, thanks to becoming FI, you *know* that these principles work. So between the ingrained patterns of consciousness, the intellectual appreciation of the obvious logic of the steps and the experiential awareness of how much more fulfilling your life is when lived at "enough," you may find that you are *still* spending less. Yet your income continues to march on at the same level—creating more cache. Here's what Wanda Fullner, an FIer who also happens to be a financial counselor, has to say:

> In my fifteen years of financial counseling—and many of my clients have incomes of under $1,000 per month—I have never seen an exception to this pattern: *with awareness of expenses and a values-oriented spending and savings plan, opportunities for capital growth proliferate beyond expectations.*

3. As time goes on, you notice the wisdom of your choices back in Step 6. Your carefully researched purchases are not breaking down. Your ability to maintain your material possessions has increased enormously, and you don't need to replace them anywhere near as often as you used to. You are also not enticed by the newest bells and whistles or the new and improved latest upgrade. Your material universe is in place. *Yet the original cost of those purchases had inflated your monthly expenses before you reached your* ***Crossover Point.*** You discover that you are spending less than your monthly income. More cache.

4. Your total monthly expenses included federal, state and local income taxes, based on a sizable income that included a very large amount going into your FI investments. After FI your total monthly income is just above your total monthly expenses. Now your tax bill has dropped considerably. More cache. Quite a few FIers have actually eliminated taxes altogether by finding they could live happily on an income that is below taxable levels. This has been gratifying both to those who have

had qualms about how their tax dollars were being used and to those who just love beating Uncle Sam.

5. Another source of cache is incidental income. This might be anything from an unexpected inheritance to notification by the IRS of an error in a two-year-old tax return that results in a refund.

6. Cache can also be supplemented by paid employment. Some FIers find that their new life directions require short-term paid employment in order to complete the mastery of new skills. Others find that putting extra income into their cache provides an added measure of security as well as giving them a little extra money to finance new dreams.

Wanda Fullner *knows that her FI income will be more than adequate once she fully moves into her next phase of life, but for now the extra income she gets from fee-only financial services is allowing her to support her daughter through college.*

Marcia Meyer *uses her income from occasional temporary jobs to build up her cache so she can travel whenever she wants to—as she did recently when a family member 2,000 miles away became ill.*

How to Get Rid of Cache

Your primary aim in moving toward FI is cache in the form of time and energy—and spending that time and energy in the ways you choose will be the greatest joy of FI. But you may well find yourself with cache in the form of money on your hands, too. To the reader who has encountered the ideas presented in this book for the first time, or who has been applying the steps for only a few months, the notion of having *extra* money may look like the height of absurdity.

The money that accumulates in your post-FI cache fund—money that *by definition* you do not need for your everyday living expenses—has an important role to play in your overall FI investment plan. Since by getting FI you have already broken the link between income and life-style choices—i.e., having money does not lead you into spending more—this cache fund is not a source of temptation.

The initial function of the cache may be psychological. It proves to you that you do have enough *and then some* over time, helping to quell any lingering "what if's."

On the outside chance that "inflation" in one or another of your spending categories gets ahead of your ever-increasing skill and consciousness in clever use of resources, your cache fund handles the shortfall.

It is from this fund that you can replace major items necessary to your chosen life-style when they finally do wear out—things like a car, a bicycle or crowns for your back teeth.

Projects and causes that you participate in may need an infusion of capital to achieve a specific objective; you can provide that capital without damaging your ability to provide that most valuable of contributions, your undivided life energy. This cache also allows you to express the spirit of generosity with your family and friends. Amy Dacyczyn, publisher of *The Tightwad Gazette*, talks about the importance of that generosity for her:

> However, I am not cheap. I will call my grandmother long distance and let her talk and talk and talk up my phone bill because I'm only going to have my grandmother for a certain period of time. We also donate money to the church . . . and we donate to other worthwhile causes. So what it's about is this: if you can engineer your resources so that you have a surplus, you can afford to be generous. And this is part of what has been lacking in our culture recently—we're all so busy pursuing the work and not having enough, in the end, of either time or money that we're not volunteering enough and we're not donating enough.

Reinvesting these funds in the same income-producing vehicles where you put your FI capital allows you to create an informal "endowed foundation." You can give the income from such investments to causes and projects that move you.

(Incidentally, the authors' personal cache funds created and maintained the New Road Map Foundation during its early years. While we had, and still have, more than enough for ourselves, our service work has called for printing, postage, and some transportation expenses—all of which originally came out of our cache.)

Your post-FI work may present interesting opportunities in other parts of the world (like Sally Morris's desire to help create a medical facility in Africa) and you will need to pay for your transportation there. Notice, however, that we haven't mentioned the obvious "splurging on a two-week vacation to Hawaii." There is nothing in the FI program that prohibits that, but for most FIers we know, post-FI life is so fulfilling that "vacating" from it seems silly—or comes around in the process of serving. That's how Evy McDonald had her dream trip to Europe, all expenses paid.

***Evy McDonald**'s plans turned around 180 degrees when her terminal illness went into remission. With a lot more life to live, she devoted herself to a number of projects, not the least of which has been finding the ways to share her discoveries about health with the medical community. Her only nostalgia for her old way of life focused on travel. When she was an up-and-coming professional she'd relished being able to hop on a plane for a weekend jaunt to visit friends or enjoy a different climate. What she'd never done, however, was travel to Europe, and she pretty much gave up her hopes for that, figuring she'd never develop enough cache for such a luxury. Not only that, but her values had changed so dramatically that she couldn't even justify the kind of whirlwind tour of the Continent she'd always dreamed of. So she let go of the fantasy and got on with the reality of her life. Several years later she received a letter from the organizer of an international medical conference. He said, in essence, that he was trying a bold and innovative approach to this meeting and felt that her story would nicely rattle the appropriate cages. Would she come to Italy to speak at the final banquet? All expenses paid, of course.*

Through connections made at that conference, Evy developed working relationships that eventually led not only to her research project on amyotrophic lateral sclerosis, but to repeated invitations to travel abroad to speak at conferences. Evy calls her service "working for God," and comments wryly, "It's not union wages, but the fringe benefits are great!"

We often hear these sorts of stories from people who've chosen to invest 100 percent of their time in projects aligned with their life purpose.

YES, BUT WHAT IF EVERYBODY DID IT?

This phrase was first used by a caveman by the name of Og, in response to his cavemate's discovery of fire.

It was also uttered when a Mesopotamian farmer told his wife that he wanted to move to something called "the city."

It seems to be the nature of the human animal that when change is proposed, the first responses that come to mind are the drawbacks, negatives, "Yes, but's" and "what if's."

Our culture and our economy have undergone many shifts in our 500-year history—shifts in fundamentals, fashions and fads. We've gone from agrarian to mercantile to industrial to technological to information to service. We've had the Westward Expansion. The Roaring Twenties and the Great Depression. The Model T, the hot rods, the muscle cars, the Volkswagen van, the Honda Civic. Short skirts, long skirts, midis, maxis and muumuus. The Love Generation, the Me Generation, the We Generation.

Whether economic changes are caused by the cyclic nature of capitalism or by purely random activity is of little importance in this book. What is important to remember is that **change will occur.** And while it is true that no trend happens all at once, we *will* see shifts in direction. Following are just a few of the possible changes.

- As more people move to a more frugal life-style, they will be retiring from the work force earlier—thus freeing up jobs. (Already many corporations are encouraging early retirement with liberal incentives.) The problem of increasing unemployment might be averted if we had such "serial employment," with jobs for bus drivers and garbage collectors and schoolteachers and salespeople and engineers continually opening up as people achieved Financial Independence. Not only that, but the stress on the planet would decrease as the demand for full employment and endless consumption eased.
- As individuals begin to develop a greater sense of purpose about their jobs (as discussed in Chapter 7), productivity will rise, integrity in the workplace will return and losses due to absenteeism,

white-collar crime and employee indifference will diminish. The result will be better and less expensive products.

- As the myth of growth loses its grip, cities will become more livable—and there will be enormous savings thanks to our no longer needing "crisis management" of everything from garbage disposal to overcrowded highways to air pollution to water shortages.
- Volunteerism—working at something you believe in, which gives you a deep sense of contribution, and which has no monetary strings attached—will continue to rise. And it may well be volunteers, not "the experts," who steer us out of the difficulties we are currently encountering as a species—the social, political and environmental challenges of the final decade of the second millennium. A tremendous amount of human energy and creativity will be needed if we are to turn the next corner of our evolution without devolving into stagnation or exploding due to massive unresolved tensions. The creative geniuses needed for this transformation can liberate themselves from "making a dying" either by working for a limited period of time to become financially independent or by exercising other prudent options to get onto solid financial ground.
- The consumer feeding frenzy that's been stoked by advertising and easy credit for a quarter of a century will slow down. As we have repeatedly pointed out in this book, our consumerism is inextricably related to the environmental, ecological, health, social and political problems facing our planet. As more people move toward more sustainable life-styles and more conscious and fulfilling uses of their life energy, the diminished impact on the earth will yield incalculable dividends.

In Conclusion: You are well on your way to taking back the power you have given over to money—and to money "experts." You are ready to become a conscientious, loving and knowledgeable steward of your life energy. Our greatest hope is that you will apply these steps to your own finances and apply your life energy to the challenges that face our species and our planet. We wish you great success.

SUMMARY OF STEP 9

Become knowledgeable and sophisticated about long-term income-producing investments and managing your finances for a safe, steady and sufficient income for the rest of your life.

EPILOGUE

NINE MAGICAL STEPS TO CREATE A NEW ROAD MAP

There are no shorter shortcuts. This whole book, with all nine steps, *is* the shortcut. The steps are summarized here for review, reference and reminders. Read the corresponding chapter for the all-important context and details.

These steps are simple, common-sense practices.

It is absolutely necessary that you do, diligently, *every* step. The steps build on each other, creating the "magic" of synergy—the whole is greater than the sum of its parts. You may not see this effect until you have been following the steps for a number of months.

Conscientiously applying all the steps automatically makes your personal finances an integrated whole; this is a whole-systems approach.

Step 1: Making Peace with the Past

A: How much have you earned in your life? Find out your total lifetime earnings—the sum total of your gross income, from the first penny you ever earned to your most recent paycheck.

HOW:

- Social Security Administration—"Request for Statement of Earnings."
- Copies of federal or state income tax returns.
- Paycheck stubs; employers' records.

WHY:

- Gives a clear picture of how powerful you are in bringing money into your life.
- Eliminates vagueness or self-delusion in this arena.
- Instills confidence, facilitates goal-setting.
- This is a very basic, fundamental practice for any business—and *you* are a business.

B: What have you got to show for it? Find out your net worth by creating a personal balance sheet of assets and liabilities—everything you own and everything you owe.

HOW:

- List and give a current market value to everything you own.
- List everything you owe.
- Deduct your liabilities from your assets to get your net worth.

WHY:

- You can never know what is enough if you don't know what you have. You might find that you have a lot of material possessions that are not bringing you fulfillment, and you might want to convert them to cash.
- This is a very basic, fundamental practice for any business—and *you* are a business.

Step 2: Being in the Present—Tracking Your Life Energy

A: How much are you trading your life energy for? Establish the actual costs in time and money required to maintain your job, and compute your *real* hourly wage.

HOW:

- Deduct from your gross weekly income the costs of commuting and job costuming; the extra cost of at-work meals; amounts spent for decompressing, recreating, escaping and vacating from work stress; job-related illness; and all other expenses associated with maintaining you on the job.

- Add to your work week the hours spent in preparing yourself for work, commuting, decompressing, recreating, escaping, vacating, shopping to make you feel better since your job feels lousy, and all other hours that are linked to maintaining your job.
- Divide the new, reduced weekly dollar figure by the new, increased weekly hour figure; **this is your real hourly wage.**
- Individuals with variable incomes can get creative—take monthly averages, a typical week, whatever works for you.

WHY:

- This is a very basic, fundamental practice for any business—and *you* are a business.
- You are in the business of selling the most precious resource in existence—your life energy. You had better know how much you are selling it for.
- The number that results from this step—your **real hourly wage**—will become a vital ingredient in transforming your relationship with money.

B: Keep track of every cent that comes into or goes out of your life.

HOW:

- Devise a record-keeping system that works for you (such as a pocket-sized memo book). Record daily expenditures accurately. Record all income.

WHY:

- This is a very basic, fundamental practice for any business—and *you* are a business.
- You are in the business of trading the most precious resource in existence—your life energy. This record book shows in detail what you are trading it for.

Step 3: Where Is It All Going? (The Monthly Tabulation)

- **Every month create a table of all income and all expenses within categories generated by your own unique spending pattern.**
- **Balance your monthly income and outgo totals.**
- **Convert "dollars" spent in each category to "hours of life energy," using your real hourly wage as computed in Step 2.**

HOW:

- Simple grade-school arithmetic. A basic hand-held calculator is needed only if you have forgotten (or are young enough never to have learned) longhand addition and subtraction. A computer home accounting program is useful only if you are already computer-literate.

WHY:

- This is a very basic, fundamental practice for any business—and *you* are a business.
- You are in the business of trading the most precious resource in existence—your life energy. This Monthly Tabulation will be an accurate portrait of how you are actually living.
- This Monthly Tabulation will provide a foundation for the rest of this program.

Step 4: Three Questions That Will Transform Your Life

On your Monthly Tabulation, ask these three questions of each of your category totals expressed as hours of life energy and record your responses:

1. **Did I receive fulfillment, satisfaction and value in proportion to life energy spent?**
2. **Is this expenditure of life energy in alignment with my values and life purpose?**
3. **How might this expenditure change if I didn't have to work for a living?**

At the bottom of each category, make one of the following marks:

– Mark a minus sign (or a down arrow) if you did not receive fulfillment proportional to the hours of life energy you spent in acquiring the goods and services in that category, or if that expenditure was not in full alignment with your values and purpose or if you could see expenses in that category diminishing after Financial Independence.

+ Mark a plus sign (or an up arrow) if you believe that upping this expenditure would increase fulfillment, would demonstrate greater personal alignment or would increase after Financial Independence.

0 Mark a 0 if that category is just fine on all counts.

HOW:

- With total honesty.

WHY:

- This is the core of the program.
- These questions will clarify and integrate your earning, your spending, your values, your purpose, your sense of fulfillment and your integrity.
- This will help you discover what is enough for you.

Step 5: Making Life Energy Visible

Create a large Wall Chart plotting the total monthly income and total monthly expenses from your Monthly Tabulation. Put it where you will see it every day.

HOW:

- Get a large sheet of graph paper, 18 by 22 inches to 24 by 36 inches with 10 squares to the centimeter or 10 squares to the inch. Choose a scale that allows plenty of room above your highest projected monthly expenses or monthly income. Use different-colored lines for monthly expenses and monthly income.

WHY:

- It will show you the trend in your financial situation and will give you a sense of progress over time, and the transformation of your relationship with money will be obvious.
- You will see your expense line go **down** as your fulfillment goes **up**—the result of "instinctive," automatic lowering of expenses in those categories you labeled with a minus.
- This Wall Chart will become the picture of your progress toward full Financial Independence, and you will use it for the rest of the program. It will provide inspiration, stimulus, support and gentle chiding.

Step 6: Valuing Your Life Energy—Minimizing Spending

Learn and practice intelligent use of your life energy (money), which will result in lowering your expenses and increasing your savings. This will create greater fulfillment, integrity and alignment in your life.

HOW:

- Ask the three questions in Step 4 every month.
- Learn to define your true needs.
- Be conscious in your spending.
- Master the techniques of wise purchasing. Research value, quality and durability.

WHY:

- You are spending your most precious commodity—your life energy. You have only a finite amount left.
- You are consuming the planet's precious resources—there is only a finite amount left.
- You cannot expect your children—or your government—to "know the value of a buck" if *you* don't demonstrate it.
- "Quality of life" often goes down as "standard of living" goes up. There is a peak to the Fulfillment Curve—spending more after you've reached the peak will bring **less** fulfillment.

Step 7: Valuing Your Life Energy—Maximizing Income

Respect the life energy you are putting into your job. Money is simply something you trade your life energy for. Trade it with purpose and integrity for increased earnings.

HOW:

- Ask yourself: Am I making a living or making a dying?
- Examine your purposes for paid employment.
- Break the link between work and wages to open up your options for increased earnings.

WHY:

- You have only X number of hours left in your life. Determine how you want to spend those remaining hours.
- Breaking the robotic link between **who you are** and **what you do for a "living"** will free you to make more fulfilling choices.

Step 8: Capital and the Crossover Point

Each month apply the following equation to your total accumulated capital, and post the monthly independence income as a separate line on your Wall Chart:

$$\frac{\textbf{capital} \times \textbf{current long-term interest rate}}{\textbf{12 months}} = \textbf{monthly investment income}$$

HOW:

- Find the long-term interest rate by looking at the interest of the thirty-year treasury bonds in the treasury bond table of *The Wall Street Journal* or a big-city newspaper. After a number of months on the program, your total monthly expense line will have established a smaller zigzag pattern at a much lower level than when you started. With a light pencil line, project the total monthly expense line into the future on your chart.

- After a number of months on the program, your monthly investment income line will have begun to move up from the lower edge of the chart. (If you have actually been investing this money as outlined in Step 9, the line will be **curving** upward—the result of the magic of compound interest.) With a light pencil line, project the monthly investment income curve into the future. At some point in the future it will cross over the total monthly expenses line. That is the **Crossover Point.**
- You will gain inspiration and momentum when you can see that you need to work for pay for only **a finite period of time.**

WHY:

- At the Crossover Point you will be financially independent. The monthly income from your invested capital will be equal to your actual monthly expenses.
- You will have enough.
- Your options are now wide open.
- **Celebrate!**

Step 9: Managing Your Finances

The final step to financial independence: become knowledgeable and sophisticated about long-term income-producing investments. Invest your capital in such a way as to provide an absolutely safe income, sufficient to meet your basic needs for the rest of your life.

HOW:

- Empower yourself to make your own investment decisions by narrowing the focus to the safest, nonspeculative, long-duration fixed-income securities, such as U.S. treasury bonds and U.S. government agency bonds. Temper the prevailing irrational fears about inflation with clear thinking and increased consciousness.
- Cut out the high expenses, fees and commissions of middlemen and popularly marketed investment "products."

- Set up your financial plan using the three pillars:

  Capital: The income-producing core of your Financial Independence.

  Cushion: Enough ready cash, earning bank interest, to cover six months of expenses.

  Cache: The surplus of funds resulting from your continued practice of the nine steps. May be used to finance your service work, reinvested to produce an endowment fund, used to replace high-cost items, used to compensate for occasional inroads of inflation, given away, etc.

WHY:

- There is more to life than nine-to-five.

RESOURCES

THE ORIGINAL FI SEMINAR

"Transforming Your Relationship with Money and Achieving Financial Independence," the original seminar on which the ideas in this book are based, is available as an audiocassette/workbook course. On these tapes, made before a live audience, you listen to Joe Dominguez as he stretches your thinking, shatters money misconceptions, skewers foibles and helps you reexamine your priorities—all with humor and compassion.

The tapes are engaging and fun—and never boring. They inspire, illuminate and occasionally even irritate. (Pearls, after all, are a product of irritation.) The audience's frequent laughter lets you know you are not the only one who has been going down a tunnel with no cheese.

The six one-hour audiocassettes are keyed to a 120-page workbook, which also includes cartoons and all of the blackboard work from the seminar. Before listening to each side you write down your answers to a few thought-provoking questions, and after listening you reflect on what you've heard by responding to review questions. Your filled-in workbook becomes a personal diary of your changes in thoughts, attitudes and beliefs—and an excellent resource when you periodically relisten to the course.

The audiocassette/workbook version of this program is *not* an "advanced" version, is *not* a "talking book" edition and is *not needed* to apply the principles and steps presented in this book. (The basic nine steps are identical to those in this book; only the presentations are significantly different.)

The audiocassette/workbook course "Transforming Your Relationship with Money and Achieving Financial Independence" is produced and distributed by the New Road Map Foundation, a nonprofit educational and charitable organization staffed entirely by volunteers. **All net proceeds go toward education in creating a humane, sustainable world and toward grants to nonprofit groups and projects working for the same goal.** (Nobody—including Joe Dominguez and Vicki Robin—receives any salaries or royalties from the New Road Map Foundation.)

Readers of this book can order the tape course by writing a check for $60 U.S. ($80 Canadian) payable to the New Road Map Foundation. (Washington residents add $4.92 sales tax.) If you want your course to include an extra workbook for your mate, send $70 (Washington residents add $5.74 sales tax). Outside of the United States and Canada add $5 for surface mail or $20 for airmail. Mail your order to:

NEW ROAD MAP FOUNDATION
Dept. PBK
P.O. Box 15981
Seattle, WA 98115

OTHER RESOURCES

Michael Argyle, *The Psychology of Happiness.* New York: Methuen & Co., Ltd., 1987.

Sue Bender, *Plain and Simple.* San Francisco: HarperSanFrancisco, 1989.

Frithjof Bergmann, *On Being Free.* London: University of Notre Dame Press, 1977.

Richard Bolles, *What Color Is Your Parachute?* Berkeley: Ten Speed Press. Frequently updated.

Ernest Callenbach, *Ecotopia.* Berkeley: Banyan Tree Books, 1975.

———, *Ecotopia Emerging.* Berkeley: Banyan Tree Books, 1981.

Andrew Carroll, *Volunteer USA.* New York: Fawcett Columbine, 1991.

Center for Creative Community, Ivan Scheier, director, P.O. Box 2427, Santa Fe, NM 87504. A center for research into and practice of volunteerism.

Arnold Corrigan and Phyllis C. Kaufman, *Understanding Treasury Bills and Other U.S. Government Securities.* Stamford, CT: Longmeadow Press, 1987.

Amy Dacyczyn, *The Tightwad Gazette.* New York: Villard Books, 1992.

Herman E. Daly and John B. Cobb, Jr., *For the Common Good.* Boston: Beacon Press, 1989.

Andy Dappen, *Cheap Tricks: 100s of Ways You Can Save 1,000s of Dollars!* Brier, WA: Brier Books, 1992.

Ram Dass and Paul Gorman, *How Can I Help?* New York: Alfred A. Knopf, 1985.

Alan Thein During, *How Much Is Enough?: The Consumer Society and the Future of the Earth.* New York: W. W. Norton and Company, 1992.

Paul Ehrlich, *The End of Affluence.* New York: Ballantine Books, 1974.

Marc Eisenson, *The Banker's Secret.* New York: Villard Books, 1991.

Duane Elgin, *Voluntary Simplicity.* New York: William Morrow, 1993.

50 Simple Things You Can Do to Save the Earth. Berkeley: Earthworks Press, 1989.

Viktor E. Frankl, *Man's Search for Meaning.* New York: Washington Square Press, 1963.

Jonathan Freedman, *Happy People.* New York: Harcourt, 1978.

Willis Harman and John Hormann, *Creative Work.* Indianapolis: Knowledge Systems, Inc., 1990.

How Earth Friendly Are You? A Lifestyle Self-Assessment Questionnaire. Seattle: New Road Map Foundation, 1990. ($3, from Quality Tape Services, P.O. Box 15352, Seattle, WA 98115.)

Benjamin Kline Hunnicutt, *Work Without End.* Philadelphia: Temple University Press, 1988.

Intentional Communities: A Guide to Cooperative Living. Evansville, IN: Fellowship for Intentional Community, and Stelle, IL: Community Publications Cooperative, 1990.

Warren Johnson, *Muddling Toward Frugality*. San Francisco: Sierra Club Books, 1978.

Frank Levering and Wanda Urbanska, *Simple Living: One Couple's Search for a Better Life*. New York: Viking, 1992.

"Living Together: Sustainable Community Development," *In Context*, issue #29. P.O. Box 11470, Bainbridge Island, WA 98110. $6 per issue.

Doris Janzen Longacre, *Living More with Less*. Scottsdale, PA: Herald Press, 1980.

Michael Lynberg, *The Path with Heart*. New York: Fawcett Columbine, 1989.

Alfred L. Malabre, Jr., *Beyond Our Means*. New York: Random House, 1987.

Kathryn McCamant and Charles Durrett, *Cohousing: A Contemporary Approach to Housing Ourselves*. Berkeley: Ten Speed/Habitat Press, 1988.

Corinne McLaughlin and Gordon Davidson, *Builders of the Dawn*. Shutesbury, MA: Sirius Publishing, 1985.

Bill McMillan, *Volunteer Vacations*. Chicago: Review Press, 1989.

Donella H. Meadows, Dennis L. Meadows, Jorgen Randers, *Beyond the Limits*. Post Mills, VT: Chelsea Green Publishing Company, 1992.

Olivia Mellan, *Ten Days to "Money Harmoney": A Workbook for Individuals and Couples*. Available from Olivia Mellan & Associates, Inc., 1841 Columbia Rd., N.W., Suite 209, Washington, D.C. 20009, (202) 483-2660.

Christopher Mogil and Anne Slepian with Peter Woodrow, *We Gave Away a Fortune*. Philadelphia: New Society Publishers, 1992.

Norman Myers, editor, *Gaia: An Atlas of Planet Management*. New York: Anchor Books, 1984.

Ralph Nader and Wesley J. Smith, *The Frugal Shopper*. Washington, DC: Center for Study of Responsive Law, 1992.

Jacob Needleman, *Money and the Meaning of Life*. New York: Doubleday, 1991.

Donald Nichols, *Treasury Securities: Making Money with Uncle Sam*. Chicago: Longman Financial Services Publishing, 1990.

Robert Ornstein and Paul Ehrlich, *New World, New Mind*. New York: Doubleday, 1989.

Amy Saltzman, *Downshifting: Reinventing Success on a Slower Track*. New York: HarperCollins, 1991.

Juliet B. Schor, *The Overworked American*. New York: Basic Books, 1991.

E. F. Schumacher, *Good Work*. New York: Harper and Row, 1979.

———, *Small Is Beautiful*. New York: Harper and Row, 1973.

Laurence Shames, *The Hunger for More*. New York: Times Books, 1989.

David Shi, *The Simple Life*. New York: Oxford University Press, 1985.

Philip Slater, *Wealth Addiction*. New York: E. P. Dutton, 1980.

Studs Terkel, *Working*. New York: Ballantine Books, 1974.

The Tightwad Gazette, RR1, Box 3570, Leeds, ME 04263-9710. 12 issues for $12.

Goldian VandenBroeck, *Less Is More: The Art of Voluntary Poverty*. Rochester, VT: Inner Traditions International, 1991.

Paul Wachtel, *The Poverty of Affluence*. Philadelphia: New Society Publishers, 1989.

"What Is Enough?: Fulfilling Lifestyles for a Small Planet," *In Context*, issue #26. P.O. Box 11470, Bainbridge Island, WA 98110. $6 per issue.

Marlene Wilson, *You Can Make a Difference*. Boulder, CO: Volunteer Management Associates, 1990.

NOTES

PROLOGUE. Why Read This Book?

xvi *since the 1950s*: "Personal Bankruptcies—the Big Leap" (graph), *Wall Street Journal*, June 18, 1991.
xvi *lower 40th percentile*: Kelley Holland, "Two Studies See Consumer Savings Rate Staying Slim," *Seattle Post-Intelligencer*, August 13, 1991.
xvi *19 percent in 1990*: U.S. Bureau of the Census, *Statistical Abstract of the United States: 1991* (111th edition), Washington, D.C., 1991, p. 462.
xvi *earn more money*: Carol Hymowitz, "Trading Fat Paychecks for Free Time," *Wall Street Journal*, August 5, 1991.
xvi *Victoria Felton-Collins*: Rebecca Teagarden, "The Last Taboo: Couples Must Learn to Talk about Money," *Seattle Post-Intelligencer*, February 17, 1990.
xvi *than in 1970*: *The World Almanac and Book of Facts 1991* (New York: Pharos Books, 1991), p. 839.
xvi *fifty-year-old is $2,300*: Merrill Lynch advertisement, *Wall Street Journal*, September 18, 1990.
xvi *free time per week*: "Are We All Working Too Hard?" *Wall Street Journal*, January 4, 1990.
xvi *of professional striving*: George Leonard, "An Avalanche of the Spirit," address at Association for Humanistic Psychology annual meeting, August 17, 1989.

CHAPTER 1. THE MONEY TRAP: THE OLD ROAD MAP FOR MONEY

5 *the ubiquitous "stress"*: Douglas LaBier, *Modern Madness* (Reading, MA: Addison-Wesley Publishing Co., 1986), as discussed in Cindy Skrzycki, "Is

There Life After Success?" *Washington Post Weekly*, July 31–August 6, 1989.

6 *five years ago*: "Shoppers Are a Dwindling Species," *Business Week*, November 26, 1990.

6 *mid-forties age range*: Opinion Research Corporation, 1984; reported in LaBier, *op. cit.*, p. 13.

6 *4.5 percent in 1990*: "Incomes Jump in U.S., But Not Enough," *Seattle Post-Intelligencer*, January 30, 1991.

6 *4.1 percent in 1988*: Mary Ganz and Carl Irving, "Americans Borrow to Consume, Japanese Pay Cash and Save," *Seattle Post-Intelligencer*, June 19, 1989.

6 *8.6 percent*: Charles Wolf, Jr., "Our Problem Isn't So Much Borrowing," *Wall Street Journal*, September 28, 1984.

6 *their disposable income*: Marcus W. Brauchli, "U.S. Tells Japanese Thrift Isn't a Virtue If Imports Are Low," *Wall Street Journal*, September 6, 1989.

6 *more than in 1980*: Rick Gladstone, "Frugality Is a Key Word for 1991," *Seattle Post-Intelligencer*, December 24, 1990.

6 *of the jobless*: "Young, Gifted and Jobless," *Newsweek*, November 5, 1990, p. 48.

8 *feelings of isolation*: Roy Kaplan's research, as reported in Kathleen Brooks, "Will a Million Let You Feel Like a Million?" *Seattle Times*, October 9, 1985.

12 *jaws of a tiger*: Robert Ornstein and Paul Ehrlich, *New World, New Mind* (New York: Doubleday, 1989).

13 *before, polls showed*: Paul Wachtel, "The Case Against Growth," *New Age Journal*, November–December 1988, p. 23.

14 *yet uncounted millions*: Herman E. Daly and John B. Cobb, Jr., *For the Common Good* (Boston: Beacon Press, 1989), pp. 143–44.

16 *momentum is remarkable*: Benjamin Kline Hunnicutt, *Work Without End* (Philadelphia: Temple University Press, 1988), p. 44.

16 *the leisure hours*: *ibid.*, pp. 45–46.

17 *ever increasing rate*: Victor Lebow in *Journal of Retailing*, quoted in Vance Packard, *The Waste Makers* (New York: David McKay, 1960), as excerpted in Alan Durning, "Asking How Much Is Enough," in Lester Brown *et al.*, *State of the World 1991* (New York: W. W. Norton & Company, 1991), p. 153.

18 *newspaper headline admonished*: "Penny Pinching by Consumers May Tarnish Economy," *Seattle Post-Intelligencer*, March 15, 1991.

19 *before 9 A.M.*: Durning, *op. cit.*, pp. 162–63.

19 *each U.S. citizen*: *ibid.*, p. 163.

19 *less developed country*: Paul Ehrlich, as reported in Dianne Dumanoski, "The People Problem," *Boston Globe*, February 5, 1990.

20 *a new reality*: from Jonas and Jonathan Salk, *World Population and Human Values: A New Reality* (New York: Harper and Row, 1981), as excerpted in the booklet *The S-Shaped Curve: Emerging Values in a New Reality* (Beyond War, 222 High Street, Palo Alto, CA 94301), pp. 38–39.

CHAPTER 2. MONEY AIN'T WHAT IT USED TO BE—AND NEVER WAS

55 *before you die*: Data taken from U.S. National Center for Health Statistics, *Vital Statistics of the United States*, annual. As printed in U.S. Bureau of the Census, *Statistical Abstract of the United States: 1991* (111th edition), Washington, D.C., 1991, p. 74.

CHAPTER 3. WHERE IS IT ALL GOING?

80 *has had enough*: Bob Schwartz, *Diets Don't Work* (Galveston, TX: Breakthru Publishing, 1982), p. 173.

84 *they've been designed*: "You and Your Shoes," *Parade* magazine, July 15, 1990, p. 6.

85 *of their bodies*: From undated photocopy of a Madrid newspaper article: "Nueve Españolas Afectadas por el 'Sindrome de la Moda,' " *El País*.

CHAPTER 4. HOW MUCH IS ENOUGH? THE NATURE OF FULFILLMENT

111 *on a shoestring*: Amy and Jim Dacyczyn publish this monthly newsletter: *The Tightwad Gazette*, RR 1, Box 3570, Leeds, ME 04263-9710.

122 *your own mission*: Joanna Macy, presentation at Seva Foundation's "Spirit of Service" conference, Vancouver, British Columbia, May 1985.

124 *other than oneself*: Viktor E. Frankl, "The Feeling of Meaninglessness: A Challenge to Psychotherapy," *American Journal of Psychoanalysis*, Vol. 32, No. 1, 1972, p. 86.

124 *in your life*: Purpose-in-Life Test; copyright held by Psychometric Affiliates, Box 807, Murfreesboro, TN 37133. Permission must be granted to use this test.

126 *with your actions*: Charles Givens, *Financial Self Defense* (New York: Simon and Schuster, 1990), p. 23.

136 *every penny count*: Robert L. Rose, "For Welfare Parents, Scrimping Is Legal, but Saving Is Out," *Wall Street Journal*, February 6, 1990.

140 *are mutually exclusive*: Buckminster Fuller, "Livingry: Artifacts for Human Success," *Forum* (J. C. Penney Co., Inc.), November 1983, p. 7.

141 *approximately 200 slaves*: Jeremy Rifkin, *Entropy* (New York: Bantam, 1981), p. 136.

141 *fashions and trends*: Janice Castro, "The Simple Life," *Time*, April 8, 1991, p. 58.

142 *important status symbol*: Ronald Henkoff, "Is Greed Dead?" *Fortune*, August 14, 1989, p. 41.

142 *heartlessness, and irresponsibility?*: Lewis Thomas, "The Iks," *Island in Space* (United Nations Association Canada, 1986), pp. 18–19.

CHAPTER 5. SEEING PROGRESS

160 *$1 they make*: Alfred L. Malabre, Jr., *Beyond Our Means* (New York: Random House, 1987), p. 27. The author states that the rate of borrowing in this country has risen sharply since World War II; consumer installment loans recently amounted to nearly 20 percent of personal income.

160 *buy with cash*: David Wallechinsky and Irving Wallace, *The People's Almanac* (New York: Doubleday, 1975), p. 341.

CHAPTER 6. THE AMERICAN DREAM—ON A SHOESTRING

171 *inflating the ego*: Thorstein Veblen, *The Theory of the Leisure Class* (New York: Modern Library, 1934), p. xiv.

171 *or to spending*: Carolyn Wesson, author of *Women Who Shop Too Much* (New York: St. Martin's Press, 1990), as quoted in Carole Beers, "Talking Shop to Those Who Can't Stop," *Seattle Times*, March 6, 1990.

171 *regional mall weekly*: "Big Spenders: As a Favored Pastime, Shopping Ranks High with Most Americans," *Wall Street Journal*, July 30, 1987.

171 *Council of Shopping Centers*: "The Pleasure Dome: Offering More than Merchandise, Malls Today Are Centers of Community Life," *Wall Street Journal*, May 13, 1988.

171 *the United States*: Durning, *op. cit.*, p. 163.

172 *rituals of communion*: Lewis H. Lapham, "An American Feast: You Are What You Buy," *Wall Street Journal*, May 13, 1988.

173 *to be possible*: Malabre, *op. cit.*, p. 145.

173 *still perfectly usable*: John E. Young, "Reducing Waste, Saving Materials," in Brown *et al.*, *op. cit.*, p. 44.

180 *the asking price*: Jeffrey A. Trachtenberg, "Let's Make a Deal," *Wall Street Journal*, February 8, 1991.

180 *flash and cash*: Nina Darnton, "I Can Get It for You Resale," *Newsweek*, June 3, 1991.

181 *spent that $100*: Georgette Jasen, "Paying Off Credit Card Debt Spells a Hefty Return," *Wall Street Journal*, November 27, 1989.

182 *privilege of using it*: David B. Hilder and Peter Pae, "Rivalry Rages Among Big Credit Cards," *Wall Street Journal*, May 3, 1991.

182 *just over 19 years*: "Paying Off Mortgage Early Doesn't Take Much," *Seattle Times*, March 19, 1991.

184 *in the winter*: Robert Sikorsky, *Drive It Forever* (New York: McGraw-Hill, 1989), p. 71.

187 *improvements in productivity*: Maryrose Wood, "Phoning It In," *Desktop*, Vol. III, No. 2, p. 46.

188 *illness is self-limiting*: Norman Cousins, speech at Unity Church of Seattle, 1989.

189 *of everyday activity*: Bryant A. Stamford and Porter Shimer, *Fitness Without Exercise* (New York: Warner Books, Inc., 1990).

191 *she'll have $1,851,313*: "Financial Security Going Up in Smoke," *Vancouver Sun*, December 2, 1985.

191 *and other leftovers*: Bob Keith, "Eating on a Pack a Day," *Living Well* (newsletter of the Northwest Health Foundation), Summer 1988, pp. 3–4.

191 *at the wheel*: Natalie Angier, "Surprising Fact about Sleep," *Reader's Digest*, June 1991 (condensed from *New York Times*, May 15, 1990), p. 33.

194 *place to live*: Home Price Comparison Index, *Seattle Times*, May 27, 1990.

194 *even Tucson, Arizona*: "Rent Variations," *Parade*, December 1, 1991, p. 16.

200 *in other business*: Daly and Cobb, *op. cit.*, p. 361.

201 *by a mile*: *Tightwad Gazette, op. cit.*. See issues No. 7, No. 2 and No. 1.

202 *to be exact*: *World Almanac and Book of Facts 1991* (New York: Pharos Books, 1991), p. 550 and p. 389.

209 *$100,000 in 1986*: "Updated Estimates on the Cost of Raising a Child," *Family Economic Review*, 1987, p. 30.

209 *not doing without*: *Tightwad Gazette, op. cit*, October 1990.

213 *mutually enhancing relationship*: Ernest Callenbach, "The Green Triangle," *In Context*, No. 26, Summer 1990, p. 13.

215 *to global warming*: "Nylon Production Named as a Source of Nitrous Oxide," *Wall Street Journal*, February 22, 1991.

218 *of universal responsibility*: *My Tibet*, text by His Holiness the Fourteenth Dalai Lama of Tibet, photos and introduction by Galen Rowell (Berkeley and Los Angeles: University of California Press, 1990), p. 55.

CHAPTER 7. FOR LOVE OR MONEY: VALUING LIFE ENERGY—WORK AND INCOME

220 *our inborn egocentricity*: E. F. Schumacher, *Good Work* (New York: Harper and Row, 1979), pp. 3–4.

220 *unpleasantness of work*: Robert Theobald, *Rapids of Change* (Indianapolis: Knowledge Systems, 1987), p. 66.

221 *sort of dying*: Studs Terkel, *Working* (New York: Ballantine Books, 1985), p. xiii.

221 *love made visible*: Kahlil Gibran, *The Prophet* (New York: Alfred A. Knopf, 1969), p. 28.

222 *quite a bit*: Marshall Sahlins, *Stone Age Economics* (Chicago: Aldine-Atherton, Inc., 1972), p. 23.

222 *the Industrial Revolution*: "From Joblessness to Liberation" (an article on Frithjof Bergmann), *Green Light News*, Vol. 1, No. 1, 1984, p. 19.

222 *than three hours*: John Humphrey Noyes, *The History of American Socialism* (Philadelphia: Lippincott, 1870).

222 *meaningful to us*: Paramahansa Yogananda, unpublished papers, 1934.

223 *during the Depression*: Hunnicutt, *op. cit.*, p. 311.

223 *of economic progress*: *ibid.*, p. 309.

224 *occupation and professions*: *ibid.*, pp. 313–14.

227 *out of work*: Rick Gladstone, *op. cit.*

227 *didn't have to*: Michael Argyle, *The Psychology of Happiness* (New York: Methuen and Co., 1987), p. 50.

227 *do the same*: Carol Hymowitz, *op. cit.*

235 *more contributory lives*: Amy Saltzman, *Downshifting* (New York: HarperCollins, 1991), p. 17.

238 *replaced by machines*: Willis Harman and John Hormann, *Creative Work* (Indianapolis: Knowledge Systems, Inc., 1990), pp. 23–24.

242 *purpose and meaning*: Amy Saltzman, *op. cit.*, p. 16.

242 *for our leisure*: *ibid.*, p. 200.

243 *them a living*: Michael Phillips, *The Seven Laws of Money* (Menlo Park: Word Wheel, 1974), p. 8.

243 *by the bureaucracy*: *At the Crossroads* (Spokane: Communications Era Task Force, 1983), p. 22.

245 *a peanut instead*: Desmond Morris, *The Biology of Art* (New York: Alfred A. Knopf, 1962), pp. 158–59.

245 *of "what ifs"*: Richard Seven, "Getting a Life," *Pacific* Sunday magazine of *Seattle Times*, August 4, 1991, p. 8.

245 *and income distribution*: Willis Harman, "Work," in Alberto Villoldo and Ken Dychtwald, eds., *Millennium: Glimpses into the 21st Century* (Los Angeles: J. P. Tarcher, Inc., 1981).

CHAPTER 8. THE CROSSOVER POINT: THE POT OF GOLD AT THE END OF THE WALL CHART

275 *God and Money*: Matthew 6:24, *The New Testament*, New International Version (Grand Rapids, MI: Zondervan Bible Publishers, 1973).

276 *is no catch*: Randi Rossman, "His Charity Is in the Bag," *Santa Rosa Press Democrat*, September 9, 1984.

278 *at the office*: Janice Castro, *op. cit.*

hold society together: Robert L. Payton, Center on Philanthropy, Indiana [illegible]rsity-Purdue University at Indianapolis, 550 West North Street, Suite

301, Indianapolis, IN 46202-3162. Also, speech delivered at Hofstra University conference, "Money—Lure, Lore and Liquidity," November 21–23, 1991.

285 *experience of helping*: Allan Luks, "Helper's High," *Psychology Today*, October 1988, p. 42.

286 *combat respiratory infections*: Eileen Rockefeller Growald and Allan Luks, "The Healing Power of . . . Doing Good," *American Health*, March 1988.

286 *that ever has*: Margaret Mead, quoted in Ivan Scheier, "Rules for Dreamers," monograph. Center for Creative Community, P.O. Box 2427, Santa Fe, NM 87504.

286 *the voluntary sector*: from a speech given at Windstar's "Choices for the Future" conference, Snowmass, Colorado, June 1986.

289 *create medical miracles*: from a speech given at an informal brainstorming meeting on "Where Is Research on Amyotrophic Lateral Sclerosis Headed?" San Francisco, July 12–13, 1986.

290 *not implemented solutions*: *Encyclopedia of World Problems and Human Potential*, 2nd ed. (New York: K. G. Saur, 1986).

291 *not its victims*: quoted in a speech given by Reverend Alfred F. Swearingen at a ceremony to dedicate one of Ivan Scheier's dreams—a Time Capsule on Volunteering to be opened in 2050.

CHAPTER 9. NOW THAT YOU'VE GOT IT, WHAT ARE YOU GOING TO DO WITH IT?

294 *mutual funds and stocks*: "51 Million Americans Own Stocks, Poll Finds," Associated Press, *Seattle Post-Intelligencer*, May 22, 1991.

295 *products they recommend*: Karen Slater and Earl C. Gottschalk, Jr., "Financial Planners Squabble over Creating Code of Conduct," *Wall Street Journal*, March 14, 1991.

295 *as much as you*: Andrew Tobias, *The Only Investment Guide You'll Ever Need* (New York: Harcourt Brace Jovanovich, 1978), p. 95.

295 *your own affairs*: Andrew Tobias, *The Only* ***Other*** *Investment Guide You'll Ever Need* (New York: Simon and Schuster, 1987), p. 13.

296 *know the truth*: Herbert Ringold, *How to Lose Money in the Stock Market* (New York: St. Martin's Press, 1986), p. 13.

301 *22 percent vacant*: heard on PBS daily television program *Nightly Business Report*, April 26, 1991.

302 *service in 1959*: Patricia McLaughlin, "Nader May Look Like an Airbag, but Fashion Doesn't Bankrupt Him," *Seattle Times*, July 24, 1991.

304 *bank passbook account*: Ringold, *op. cit.*, pp. 76–77.

304 *of Minnesota survey*: Business Bulletin, *Wall Street Journal*, April 18, 1991.
314 *for the industry*: "Brokers Averaged Pay of $79,169 in '90, Survey Says," *Wall Street Journal*, June 24, 1991.
323 *not donating enough*: Amy Dacyczyn on "What Is Enough?" produced by David Freudberg for *Marketplace*, American Public Radio, June 21, 1991.